COMMITMENT,
CONFLICT,
AND CARING

THE CENTURY PSYCHOLOGY SERIES

James J. Jenkins
Walter Mischel

Editors

PHILIP BRICKMAN

WITH

Antonia Abbey
Dan Coates
Christine Dunkel-Schetter
Ronnie Janoff-Bulman
Jurgis Karuza, Jr.
Linda S. Perloff
Vita Carulli Rabinowitz
Clive Seligman

COMMITMENT, CONFLICT, AND CARING

EDITED BY
Camille B. Wortman
Richard Sorrentino

PRENTICE-HALL, INC. *Englewood Cliffs, New Jersey 07632*

Library of Congress Cataloging-in-Publication Data

Brickman, Philip.
  Commitment, conflict, and caring.

  (Century psychology series)
  Bibliography: p.
  Includes index.
  1. Commitment (Psychology) 2. Conflict
(Psychology) 3. Love—Psychological aspects.
I. Sorrentino, Richard M. II. Wortman, Camille.
III. Title. IV. Series: Century psychology
series (Englewood Cliffs, N.J.)
BF619.B75 1987   302   86-25383
ISBN 0-13-152266-3

© 1987 by Prentice-Hall, Inc.
A division of Simon & Schuster
Englewood Cliffs, New Jersey 07632

Printed in the United States of America

10 9 8 7 6 5 4 3 2 1

ISBN 0-13-152266-3   01

Prentice-Hall International (UK) Limited, *London*
Prentice-Hall of Australia Pty. Limited, *Sydney*
Prentice-Hall Canada Inc., *Toronto*
Prentice-Hall Hispanoamericana, S.A., *Mexico*
Prentice-Hall of India Private Limited, *New Delhi*
Prentice-Hall of Japan, Inc., *Tokyo*
Prentice-Hall of Southeast Asia Pte. Ltd., *Singapore*
Editora Prentice-Hall do Brasil, Ltda., *Rio de Janeiro*

CONTENTS

FOREWORD

This book is Phil Brickman's own; it was intended to be written by him alone. Yet it is also a monument to a team—to a collaborative effort for which Phil was merely a catalyst and coordinator. Merely? Yes, that is how he often saw himself, personally ambitious though he undoubtedly was and undoubtedly deserved to be.

Phil, more than anyone else I have known, thoroughly enjoyed the collaboration of equals: brainstorm unconstrained by individual ownership of ideas, yielding collective products superior to the input of any one person. His own hunches and suggestions were as open to revision as anyone else's—undergraduates and graduate students correctly perceived that their contributions were treated seriously. The validity of the consensus, as tested in a free-for-all of suggestion and revision, was what counted—not individual components.

Phil knew that for such teams to be productive there has to be coordination, the creation of occasions, affirmation of the importance of the problems, and the feeling of collective achievement. He was sensitive to the needs of others for self-esteem and aware of how these could threaten the joys of selfless collaboration. There was a role for the "selfless servant" of the collaborative effort, and he so thoroughly enjoyed collaboration that he was happy to play that role, happy to sacrifice his own ego for the greater pleasures of selfless or unself-conscious collective activity.

That this book has been assembled from the manuscripts Phil left is a testimony to the continuing strength of the team he coordinated. It constitutes a posthumous *Festschrift*. In an important sense, considering this book to be Phil's alone runs counter to Phil's mode of operating and his ideal for the scientific process. It represents a belated concession to the institutionalized narcissism of scientific norms, in which the role of "great scientist" is to be acted out by exaggerating the originality of one's contributions. More than 80 percent of Phil's articles—90 percent of those he valued highly and all but one of the important papers on which his promotions were based—were collaborations. Perhaps his difficulty in bringing this book to completion lay in the inauthenticity, for him, of the single-author format. At the very least, his enjoyment of collaboration might explain why he so often gave this book second priority. And as here presented, it too is a collaborative product.

In addition to having this book, we—and social psychology—need a "Brickman et al." anthology of collaborative works (some of the best with as many as five authors) to be called something like *Trust, Commitment, Caring, Helping, Being Helped, Expectations, and Social Comparison Processes.* (This is a tentative title, awaiting the inspired term or neologism that captures the common core underlying these shared concerns.) It would also contain some solo works acknowledged by Phil to be inspired by the team effort. Such a book would be of equal value to the present one and would be equally expressive of Phil's special style and talents.

I may have made the title I call for a little harder to achieve by biasing my list so that the anthology might include Brickman and Campbell, "Hedonic Relativism and Planning the Good Society." This is a high moral essay, full of specific suggestions for social planners, and the first source I know of for the observation that Castro may have increased the psychic well-being of Cubans by eliminating their social comparison with wealthy American tourists. It is also profoundly pessimistic about increasing human happiness by increasing the standard of living beyond the elimination of hunger. I quote from our final section, Getting Off the Hedonic Treadmill:

> In closing, it may be well to return once again to the pessimistic theme, the theme that the relativistic nature of subjective experience means there is no true solution to the problem of happiness . . . there may be no way to permanently increase the total of one's pleasure except by getting off the hedonic treadmill entirely. This is, of course, the historic teaching of the Stoic and Epicurean philosophers, Buddha, Jesus, Thoreau, and other teachers from all ages. Unfortunately, renouncing the hedonic treadmill is a very difficult thing to do at least until, like St. Augustine, one has travelled the full path from innocence to corruption. Even in renouncing the pleasures of the flesh, however, one may experience adaptation-level phenomena in the pursuit of piety or saintliness.
>
> Truly renouncing the hedonic treadmill may mean abandoning all evaluative judgments, and even all questions about happiness, in pursuit of the notion that happiness is unself-conscious, and that when a person is happy he is unaware of it. It may be, however, that evaluative judgments, and adaptation-level and level-of-aspiration phenomena, are necessary to the restlessness and

the searching that have made human life what it is. . . . But if we are to prevent this restlessness from wreaking its most destructive consequences we
must acquire new, humane means of controlling rising adaptation levels.

Phil and I were aware of adaptation-level problems in the search for scholarly
recognition. While working on this essay, we shared reminiscences of specific
eminent psychologists whose success was soured in their old age because they failed
to receive as much acclaim as they thought they deserved. We hoped to avoid these
narcissistic traps in our own careers and hoped that our theoretical understanding
of the problem would immunize us. But who were we to be exempt from such
powerful psychological laws?

Phil's eight coauthors for this volume all started their collaboration at Northwestern University. This makes it appropriate for me to close this foreword with a
note on Phil's Northwestern years, which began in 1968, the year he completed
his Ph.D. at Michigan. Due in part to new training grants in experimental psychology
and social psychology, the Northwestern department was then expanding. The
chairman was Benton Underwood, who will forgive me (or even agree) if I characterize him as a hard-headed, scientifically conservative experimentalist. We had
some two dozen applicants for the social slot. The best two were from Ann Arbor
and looked equally good on paper. We invited Phil.

Ben Underwood firmly approved of a quaint custom in our department,
which was to invite only one candidate, and if the visit went well (and after checking
with the Dean) to offer that candidate the job as we drove him back to the airport.
So it happened with Phil. He also got another offer, from the University of Wiscon-
sin, I believe. He chose us. As it turned out, we all made the right decisions.

Early on, Phil announced that he had no talent for the lecture method of
teaching undergraduates, and he sought to invent alternatives. None of us recruited
better psychology majors or more young scholars to professional careers in
psychology. Phil had, in effect, a counter-charismatic charisma. He made students
feel their own worth, gave them confidence in their own capacity to contribute,
and provided a model for mutuality in collaboration.

It was similar for our graduate students. In an atmosphere in which no
student felt it necessary to "belong" to one and only one of the social psychology
faculty, Phil was coauthor with more graduate students than anyone else. (A number of students were coauthors with him and with others of us.) The personal interest he took in his graduate students continued long after they received their degrees. Students loved Phil for providing a sympathetic ear during their early career
years and for offering the comfort of his company at professional meetings.

Phil, most strongly of all the faculty, felt the need for infrastructure in our
social process, and he found the time to provide it. Although we were all ambitious,
and proud of a collective excellence which we felt exceeded our national reputation,
Phil seemed to us the least careerist, the one most blessed with sufficient inner
security to take the role of selfless facilitator of our collective product. Correct or

not, we let him play that role, carrying more than his share of such burdens. Too often such saints are inadequately rewarded. I am proud of Northwestern for promoting him from Assistant Professor to Full Professor in nine years. I am also proud of our graduate students for recognizing Phil's intellectual and moral talents, and for their willingness to honor his memory by bringing this book to a state of completion.

Donald T. Campbell

PREFACE

Philip Brickman always said that social psychology should be a field that deals with fundamental human concerns. This was certainly true of his own distinguished career in social psychology, which focused on such issues as justice, happiness, pain, inequality, helping, and coping. His career ended tragically on May 13, 1982, when he took his own life at the age of 38. At the time of his death, the major project Phil was working on was a book on commitment, tentatively titled *Commitment, Conflict, and Caring*. This book, and the ideas it contained, were extremely important to Phil.

Phil began thinking seriously about commitment almost 20 years ago—shortly after he accepted his first job at Northwestern University in 1968. Phil developed his ideas in collaboration with various students and colleagues and continued to refine and test these ideas over the next several years. In 1978, Phil left Northwestern to take a position at the University of Michigan. By that time, he had developed an overall organizational scheme for the book and had written drafts of the first few chapters.

The project was slowed somewhat upon his arrival at Michigan, while Phil assumed directorship of the Research Center for Group Dynamics at the Institute for Social Research. For the first few years, Phil turned his attention to the many administrative issues facing the Center. Largely through the support and encouragement of Richard Nisbett, Phil gradually was able to return to the commitment project. By the time of his death, he had taken the early chapters through several more revisions and had completed preliminary drafts of all but the final chapter, on which he was then working. He had planned to teach a graduate seminar on commitment in the spring of 1982, and his goal was to use the chapters of the book as primary readings for the course, get feedback about the strengths and weaknesses of the current draft, and then make final revisions over the summer. The first class was scheduled to meet on the day after his death.

Phil's wife BeBe and his parents, Molly and Leo Brickman, asked me to take responsibility for completing the book and making sure it was published. In some ways, I was a logical choice for this role. Phil had been my best friend and closest professional colleague for the previous 10 years. We had been on the faculty together at Northwestern and at the University of Michigan, where I joined him in 1979. However, despite our closeness, I had not been involved in the development of Phil's ideas on commitment and was concerned about bringing these ideas to completion. I spent many hours talking with those who had worked with Phil on these ideas, most notably Chris Dunkel-Schetter, Dan Coates, Antonia Abbey, and Roxane Silver.

Drawing from their suggestions and advice, I next established a core group of people to take primary responsibility to bring the project to fruition. The core group includes all the coauthors of individual chapters listed on the title page. Virtually all these people had been at Northwestern University and had worked with Phil at the time his ideas about commitment were being formulated. At the time of Phil's death these people were in their early career years at various schools throughout the country. We got together as a group to discuss such issues as who should take responsibility for which chapters and how we should handle such issues as extent of revision, style, and professional credit. At that point it became clear that the project would benefit from having a relatively senior person coedit the volume with me and provide advice and guidance to those involved in revising the chapters. Richard Sorrentino graciously agreed to serve in this role.

In the aftermath of Phil's death, we all struggled with the complex issues that the project raised for us, including intense pain at losing a close friend and collaborator and fear that we would not be able to do justice to the work he had started. For many of us, work on this project was an emotional experience at all stages. At the early stages, merely reading the manuscript was intensely painful. Especially brilliant sections of the book would cause distress when coupled with the knowledge that the person who produced them was lost to the field. More than one of us had the experience of getting very excited about the ideas and desperately wanting to discuss them with Phil. We consoled one another and shared coping strategies in an effort to keep focused on the task and get it finished.

It also seemed clear from the beginning that the project would benefit from the careful scrutiny of a more detached group of individuals. To achieve this, I decided to go ahead and teach the seminar on commitment that Phil had planned to offer, and I used Phil's manuscript as a text. Nine advanced graduate students from various disciplines at the University of Michigan—social psychology, clinical psychology, counseling, nursing, and public health—elected to take the course. The course had an intensity about it that is hard to describe and is unlike anything else

I have experienced. The students were tremendously excited by the ideas, and it was extremely rewarding to see them apply the ideas productively to their own disciplines. Many have gone on to examine the ideas empirically in dissertation work or subsequent research. Aware that the book was being revised by a group of Phil's former students, the course members eagerly provided critiques of each chapter as well as specific suggestions for revision. Their enthusiasm played a central role in keeping the project moving at a time when those of us who were closer to Phil kept being derailed by our grief.

Drawing both from these critiques and from comments provided by Dick and myself, members of the core group then revised their chapters. The revised chapters were sent out for review to some of the top scholars in the field and went through another set of revisions on the basis of the feedback received. The task of revising the chapters presented the coauthors with a number of difficult decisions. If they disagreed with Phil's analysis of a given issue, should they drop it or try to make it more convincing? Should they omit sections of the book that were confusing or out of date or try to revise them? As a group, we agreed that we would change the manuscript only when this was necessary to achieve greater clarity. In all but the first chapter, a fair number of changes were necessary. Material was frequently reworked, reordered, and reorganized. Detailed discussion of experiments was sometimes condensed when it seemed to detract from the flow of the material. We agreed that wherever possible we would try to retain Phil's unique writing style, which involves the juxtaposition of ideas from incongruous sources and intriguing asides to the main point. Phil often made a point more extremely, or in a more controversial fashion, than a coauthor would have chosen to make it. Usually, in such cases, we tried to leave in the material as Phil had written it because it represented what Phil wanted to say.

This general approach was possible in all chapters except chapter 6, "Commitment and Mental Health." The ideas in this chapter were still being formulated and developed at the time of Phil's death. In fact, Phil's draft was in such rough form that the students in the seminar uniformly recommended that the chapter be dropped from the book. It is to Dan Coates's credit that he was willing to put forth the enormous effort required to complete this chapter.

It should be noted that Phil had also intended to write a concluding chapter entitled "Commitment and Society." He had outlined such a chapter and was working on it at the time of his death. Unfortunately, the draft and outline were not detailed enough for this chapter to be completed by anyone else. Thus, the book ends with the mental health chapter by Philip Brickman and Dan Coates.

In this book, it is argued that commitment is a central psychological process. Phil introduces commitment as a unifying concept for all of psychology. The first part of the book represents a reinterpretation and integration of well-known research in social psychology in terms of commitment. As Phil himself elaborates in chapter 1, this book represents a rethinking of dissonance theory designed to make it more useful to general concerns of the social sciences. However, the book also has relevance to some of the enduring great issues in the human sciences, such as whether information processing takes place inside or outside of conscious awareness, or whether people are primarily rational or motivated by self-interest. In the second half of the book, Phil extends his analysis of commitment to these and other areas of psychology, including development and mental health. The book would be appropriate for an advanced undergraduate or graduate level course in social psychology. Students of related social sciences, such as sociology, anthropology, philosophy, and history, would benefit from exposure to this analysis. Finally, those working in the fields of mental health will find much that they can apply to such problems as how to encourage behavior change and the main tenure of desirable, adaptive behavior.

Several people deserve special acknowledgment for the role they played in bringing this volume to completion. Chris Dunkel-Schetter stayed in Ann Arbor for a week after Phil's memorial service to aid in the development of a plan to complete the book. Chris provided indispensable help with the emotionally wrenching task of sorting through Phil's notes and papers to identify those of relevance to the commitment project. Roxy Silver has served as an informal advisor to the project over the years.

Special thanks are also due to the members of the advanced seminar described above: Faye Abram, Jane Baumsteiner, Fran Board, Bruce Eaken, Kristi Ferguson, Nancy Janz, Laurel Northouse, Daniel Pesut, and Robert Piper. Their excitement about the material was contagious, and their critiques and suggestions for revision were invaluable. One of the members, Kristi Ferguson, so believed in the project that she volunteered several weeks of her time to help get references in order.

We owe a special debt of gratitude to a number of reviewers from the field, including Icek Ajzen, Daniel Batson, Ellen Berscheid, Jack Brehm, Jeff Bryson, Rebecca C. Curtis, Robert Folger, Jacqueline Goodchilds, Jerald Greenberg, Colleen M. Karuza, Ellen Langer, Richard Nisbett, Paul Rosenblatt, Richard Schulz, Abraham Tesser, and Suzanne Thompson. Each of these individuals was kind enough to read one or more chapters and to provide detailed comments about how the manuscript might be improved.

We are grateful for the sensitive editing provided by Scott Huler and wish to thank Jay Schlegel for his tireless work in searching for the missing references for this volume. Because of the circumstances under which the book was completed, it was difficult to locate all of the references and verify their accuracy. We would be pleased if readers who have any further information about the references would bring this to our attention. Finally, thanks are due to the Research Center for Group Dynamics at the Institute for Social Research, which provided financial support for project expenses.

As Dan Coates and I have written elsewhere, Phil's inexhaustible supply of creative ideas and intriguing insights made conversations with him a delight. I believe this book captures the feeling that one often had when talking with Phil, a feeling "that intellectual inquiry had no limits, that the number of new discoveries and new ideas were endless, and that discovery would be a joy."[1]

Camille B. Wortman

[1]*American Psychologist, 40*(9), 1985: 1051–1052.

COMMITMENT, CONFLICT, AND CARING

CHAPTER ONE
COMMITMENT

Philip Brickman

Words that matter to people—like *justice* or *freedom* or *power* or *love*—are hard to define. The fact that these things matter to people makes them important for psychology to study. The fact that their meaning can be endlessly debated makes them very hard to study.

Psychology grew out of philosophy in part by relaxing its concern for how words should be defined. The task of psychology is not to agree on how people should use words like *justice* or *freedom* but to study empirically how they do use them. The appropriate understanding of what something like *justice* means is a matter not of definition but of careful observation of how people behave in situations they characterize as just or unjust. I prefer to think of a definition in social psychology as a climax or culmination of our understanding of a phenomenon rather than a necessary and necessarily arbitrary or restrictive starting point. We do not need to agree on exactly what justice and freedom are before beginning to study them. Indeed, if we had to agree on exactly what they meant before beginning our inquiry, we could not begin.

People may, of course, be inconsistent in how they use these words. Just as a scientific theory is hard to get rid of if it can be stretched to cover many situations, a word in the language can be hard to get rid of—and important to people—if it can be stretched to cover many situations. So a word like *freedom* is sometimes used to mean that people have a choice among alternatives, and sometimes to mean that people can do what they want to do—even though these two meanings may conflict. (For example, I can feel free if I am doing what I want to do even if I have no alternatives.) In a famous essay on power, Robert Dahl (1957) suggested that such inconsistency might be the reason that a word like *power* is hard to define. The word actually means not one thing but many things. On the other hand, these many things probably have at least some element in common or they would not continue to be referred to by a single word. The most we can ask at the start of our investigation is to specify that common fragment of meaning. We cannot rule out variations and inconsistencies in how our concept is used. These are, in fact, the focus of study.

Here is a sampling of previous definitions of commitment from both psychology and sociology. Gerard (1965) refers to commitment as "any constraints that operate against changing behavior." Kiesler (1971) defines commitment as "the pledging or binding of the individual to behavioral acts." Abramson, Cutler, and Kantz (1958) call commitments "sequences of action with penalties and costs arranged so as to guarantee their selection." Becker (1960) describes commitment as a process by which an individual "stake(s) something of value to him, something originally unrelated to his present line of action, on being consistent in his present behavior." It is not our purpose to analyze the important but subtle differences that characterize these definitions. It is enough to call attention to that fragment of common concern that enters into all the definitions. The common concern is clearly with commitment as a force that stabilizes individual behavior under circumstances where the individual would otherwise be tempted to change that behavior. Other questions, such as whether the force that stabilizes behavior is internal or external to the individual, cannot be settled by looking at these definitions. At this point we must be comfortable with an understanding that commitment is whatever it is that makes a person engage or continue in a course of action when difficulties or positive alternatives influence the person to abandon the action.

Not visible in these definitions is an apparent inconsistency in how the word *commitment* is used. This inconsistency is so striking and so dramatic that it makes commitment appear to refer to two completely contradictory things. These two different uses of the word give us an essential clue as to what commitment is all about and why it is so important to us.

THE TWO FACES
OF COMMITMENT

Here is one example of a commitment that sustains a marriage:

Joseph and Elizabeth are deeply in love. Although they have been married for almost 20 years, they still enjoy each other's company more than any other and are eager to share their daily experiences. Their sex life is good, loving, pleasurable, and fun. Although they love their children, the two of them are looking forward to the time when the children are grown and they have more time just for each other. If they had been willing to live apart, Joseph could have held a job paying considerably more than his current job, but the couple felt that the extra money was not worth the separation. Each of them has made sacrifices for the sake of the marriage. They took turns putting each other through school, and likewise take turns tolerating each other's obnoxious relatives over the Christmas holidays. Their marriage is a tremendously positive one. *They are deeply committed to each other; indeed, this commitment is the most important thing in their lives.*

Here is another example of a commitment that sustains a marriage:

John and Susan no longer love each other or even like each other very much. They have been married for almost 20 years and are, in their good moods, utterly bored with one another. They no longer have anything to talk about, and they spend as much time apart as possible. Their sex life is nonexistent, at least within the marriage. They are staying together in part for the sake of the children, and they look forward to the time when the children are grown so they can seriously consider a divorce. Separation is unlikely, however, since it would jeopardize the standard of living, the reputation, and the social life that they both enjoy. Each of them has made sacrifices for the sake of the marriage. They took turns putting each other through school, and likewise take turns tolerating each other's neurotic relatives over the Christmas holidays. Their marriage is a tremendously negative one. *They are merely committed to each other; indeed, this commitment is the only thing holding them together.*

In the first example, *commitment* is used to mean a kind of love. In the second example, *commitment* is used to mean something that holds people together in the absence of love. If *commitment* can refer both to a state of love and to a state without love, it is obviously a term of great elasticity. This is not to say that the usage of *commitment* in these two examples is strictly incompatible. If we think hard about them, we can see that the object of commitment in the first example is not the same as the object of commitment in the second example. John and Susan are committed to being married and would actually prefer to be apart if they could only do so without losing the social and financial advantages of marriage. Joseph and Elizabeth are committed to each other, and would probably seek to stay together even if it meant (for some reason) not being able to be married. There is nothing mysterious about these examples once this is specified. However, much confusion and many lively debates arise in discussing commitment because people begin by assuming different objects of commitment and discover this only after much discussion. The fact that the same word, with a slight change in its object, can refer to such positive and such negative states makes the word fascinating. It bolsters our sense that commitment is a very central psychological process and gives us a clue that the process must involve discrepant elements.

To better understand this, let us consider in some detail two previous analyses of what we would call highly committed states. The first is a well-known paper by Howard Becker (1960), in which Becker develops the notion of commitments as side bets. This is most easily explained by an example. A man has been working for a company for many years. During this time both he and the company have made regular contributions to a pension plan for his retirement. He now receives an offer of a more attractive job, at a higher salary, from another company. If he moves, however, he loses all the money the company has invested in his pension plan. The pension plan is, in a sense, a bet the person has made that he will stay with his present job, a bet he stands to lose if he changes jobs. Becker calls this a side bet because it was not the main thing the person had in mind in taking the job. Indeed, in this case the side bet or the commitment is something the person accumulated only slowly, gradually, almost imperceptibly over the years. A side bet may have symbolic value rather than material value. For example, a person may turn down an attractive offer simply because he has given his word that he will stay with his present job. In this case the person loses not a pension but a reputation for honesty or trustworthiness if he changes jobs. The only requirements for something to be a side bet are that the person has linked this item to a course of action that was initially unrelated to it, and stands to lose the item if that course of action is not followed; that the person has chosen by prior actions to make this linkage; and that the person is aware of having made the linkage.

A person committed to a job solely because of the accumulated pension may clearly be very alienated from the job and all its associated activities. This is like John and Susan's commitment to their marriage. As in that example, it may be helpful to be precise about the object of commitment. In one sense, the person is committed not to the job at all but only to the pension fund. If he could keep the pension, he would most happily abandon the job. In fact, following a line of reasoning familiar in social psychology, one way the person knows how valuable the pension is to him is by observing how reluctant he is to give it up even for a more attractive job.

A totally different picture of commitment is given by Mihaly Csikszentmihalyi in his book *Beyond Boredom and Anxiety* (1975). Csikszentmihalyi describes the activities of such people as chess players, mountain climbers, dancers, composers, and surgeons. These are all activities in which people become passionately involved or totally absorbed. The author identifies the sensation people experience when they act with total involvement and calls it "flow." According to the description of participants, flow has the following characteristics: The activity has the person's undivided attention; all potentially intruding stimuli are kept out of attention, especially the potentially intruding feelings of self-consciousness; the person feels in control or at any rate is simply not worried by the possibility of lack of control; the experience itself contains coherent, noncontradictory demands for action and provides clear, unambiguous feedback to a person's actions; and finally the activity is autotelic, or self-motivating, appearing to need no goals or rewards external to itself. When a chess player is playing chess or a surgeon is operating, the player or the surgeon gives undivided attention to the game or the operation. They experience no conflict at all about whether to be engaged in the activity, although their skills may be taxed to the utmost by the challenge of bringing the game or the operation to a successful conclusion. The chess player ordinarily receives little money or prestige for engaging in chess. The surgeon is of course highly rewarded by society, but according to Csikszentmihalyi, the surgeon is no more likely than the chess player to refer to these rewards in explaining his or her involvement in an operation.

The word *commitment* is not used explicitly by Csikszentmihalyi. Moreover, flow as he describes it may seem too unusual or too mystical to relate to ordinary conceptions of commitment. Yet the elements of flow clearly satisfy the essential fragment of meaning we have called commitment. Giving something one's undivided attention and pursuing the activity for years, often without appreciable reward, clearly specify an important kind of commitment. This aspect is nicely captured in Csikszentmihalyi's observations of artists at work, which first crystallized his ideas.

> One thing struck me as especially intriguing. Despite the fact that almost no one can make either a reputation or a living from painting, the artists studied were almost fanatically devoted to their work; they were at it night and day, and nothing else seemed to matter so much in their lives. Yet as soon as they finished a painting or a sculpture, they seemed to lose all interest in it. Nor were they interested much in each other's paintings or in great masterpieces. Most artists did not go to museums, did not decorate their homes with art, and seemed to be generally bored or baffled by talk about the aesthetic qualities of the works they or their friends produced. What they did love to do was talk about small technical details, stylistic breakthroughs—the actions, thoughts, and feelings involved in making art. Slowly it became obvious that something in the activity of painting itself kept them going. The process of making their products was so enjoyable that they were ready to sacrifice a great deal for the chance of continuing to do so. There was something about the physical activities of stretching canvas on wooden frames, of squeezing tubes of paint or kneading clay, of splashing colors on a blank surface; the cognitive activity of choosing a problem to work on, of defining a subject, of experimenting with new combinations of form, color, light, and space; the emotional impact of recognizing one's past, present, and future concerns in the emerging work. All these aspects of the artistic process added up to a structured experience which was almost addictive in its fascination. (pp. xi–xii)

The involvement in the activity is so total that the actors are not even interested in the products of the activity itself except as the emergence of these creations marks the progress of the activity. This is reminiscent of Gully Jimson in *The Horse's Mouth* painting a mural on the wall of a building he knows is condemned and ultimately maneuvering the wrecking crane himself.

Commitment associated with the experience of flow in one's work is clearly the opposite extreme of the alienated commitment in Becker's example of the man committed to his job solely because of the pension. (In passing, let me note that Becker is a person well acquainted with the addictive joys of artistic expression. He is a jazz musician, a photographer, and a student of the sociology of art, as well as someone with whom I once cotaught a seminar on the social psychology of art.) Commitment as flow and alienated commitment are both extreme; neither is typical of the psychological state of most commitments. Yet we need the extremes fixed clearly in our minds in order to recognize elements that are common to all instances in more gentle and blurred form. We need the extremes in order to know what commitment must account for. Finally, we need the extremes in order to put to the most powerful possible test our search for common elements in a unitary commitment process. To this end, let us note that the flow experiences described by Csikszentmihalyi are not without negative elements, and indeed rather extreme negative elements: years of training and sacrifice in order to acquire the requisite skills, loss of time and taste for other activities, isolation, discomfort, and sometimes physical danger for engaging in the activity as well as disappointment and agony when the activity cannot be brought to successful fruition. The actors may bear these costs joyfully, be oblivious to them, or not consider them serious costs at all. This does not say that such costs do not exist; it says only that in the commitment involved in flow experiences, actors have a very special orientation to costs.

Before we work to reconcile the conceptions of commitment in Becker and Csikszentmihalyi, let us be clear what their dramatic differences are. People who are committed in Becker's sense do not feel free at all. People who are committed in a flow experience feel fully or ultimately free. Becker is talking about something people feel they have to do. Csikszentmihalyi is talking about something people feel they want to do. Becker's commitment involves persisting in an activity that has no intrinsic value for the person. Csikszentmihalyi's commitment involves persisting in an activity that has only intrinsic value for the person. In Becker's sense, only the rich can afford not to be committed. In Csikszentmihalyi's sense, only the rich can afford to be committed. We have one word that can refer both to acts we are required to carry out by the most coercive possible social arrangements and to acts we are motivated to carry out by the deepest and most private individual passions. As a focus of social concern and as a focus of personal concern, commitment certainly deserves to be a focus of psychological concern.

One response to the sense that commitment can mean such different things is to say that there are two different kinds of commitment. A sociologist named Michael Johnson (1973) differentiates between personal commitment and behavioral commitment. Personal commitment refers to a strong personal dedication to a decision or to carrying out a line of action, as one indicates by saying, "He is committed to spreading the Gospel." Behavioral commitment refers to prior actions by the individual that force him or her to continue a line of action, whether he or she is personally committed to it or not, as indicated in the expression "She can't back out now, she is committed." In a related manner, the famous sex therapists William Masters and Virginia Johnson (1974) draw a distinction between commitments of obligation and commitments of responsiveness. Commitments of obligation describe situations in which marital partners stay together despite the fact that they are no longer giving each other pleasure. Commitments of responsiveness describe situations in which marital partners stay together to affirm and extend the pleasure they experience with each other. These distinctions clearly capture the different spirits of commitment (or alienated commitment) as side bet and commitment as flow.

Yet there is a sense in which these distinctions miss the very heart of commitment, the thing that makes commitment such a distinctive and compelling psychological process. Commitment is not sometimes about wanting to do something and sometimes about having to do something. *Commitment is about the rela-*

tionship between "want to" and "have to." Commitment involves three elements: a positive element, a negative element, and a bond between the two. We have already seen that there are negative elements even in the most totally absorbing of commitments. Surgeons, mountain climbers, and chess players make heavy sacrifices for their skills and run risks—both material and psychological—in the exercise of these skills. Patients can die, climbers can fall, chess players can be defeated. We may even argue that the presence of these negative elements is not accidental but essential to the experience of flow. On the other hand, we have also seen that there is a positive element even in the most alienated commitment. People who stay with a job or a marriage after the life has gone out of it may no longer have the reason that initially drew them, but they still have reasons, they still have something of value that they do not wish to lose. We may even argue that it is not merely a side bet that is crucial to commitment but a process by which a side bet becomes a main bet. Thus the pension the person derives from the job, or the reputation and security from the marriage, become more valuable. What our previous analysis cannot show is that it is the connection between the positive and the negative element, and not merely their joint presence, that is critical for commitment, and further, that it is the nature of their connection or their bonding that determines the nature of the commitment. This is not merely a matter of definition but a matter for review and research that will occupy this whole book.

The three elements we have specified as essential in commitment coincide closely with the conditions that have been found necessary for the occurrence of cognitive dissonance. The theory of cognitive dissonance has probably been the dominant influence in shaping modern experimental social psychology as the field has emerged in the last two decades. Dissonance theory, as formulated by Leon Festinger (1957), had one central postulate. The occurrence of two thoughts (or cognitions) that were dissonant or inconsistent with one another would be a source of psychological tension, which the person holding these cognitions would be motivated to remove or reduce. A person's attitude is inconsistent with his behavior if he believes one thing (e.g., that smoking causes cancer) while behaving in a way that is inconsistent with this belief (e.g., smoking two packs of cigarettes per day). Dissonance can be reduced by changing one's behavior (e.g., giving up smoking), changing one's beliefs (e.g., convincing oneself that the evidence linking smoking and cancer is inconclusive), or adding new beliefs that support the behavior (e.g., believing that smoking calms one's nerves, keeps one from overeating, or leads to a more enjoyable lifestyle). Hundreds of experiments studying what people do in these situations have been reviewed by Robert Wicklund and Jack Brehm (1976).

Festinger's original formulation of dissonance theory did not specify that one of the two inconsistent elements had to be positive and one negative. Nor was Festinger precise about the exact nature of the bond that had to exist between two cognitions in order to make them dissonant. The major reformulations of dissonance theory since that time have attempted to specify these necessary elements. Elliot Aronson, in an influential 1966 statement, argued that we must know how people think about themselves before we can know when two elements will be dissonant. Deciding to buy a particular car and learning that the car is something of a lemon are dissonant only if the person believes he or she generally makes good decisions, and in particular good decisions about purchases and good decisions about cars. In our language, dissonance occurs only if the person has a self-concept that makes one of the elements negative. Other research, such as a classic study by Linder, Cooper, and Jones (1967), has indicated that choice is an essential condition for the occurrence of dissonance. Choosing voluntarily to buy a car that is a lemon will be dissonant in a way that receiving such a car as a gift will not. That a person chooses a particular outcome implies, in our language, that this outcome has some positive element. Finally, research has established that merely making a choice and receiving a negative outcome does not establish dissonance. The person must somehow feel responsible for the negative element. If the outcome could not possibly have been foreseen, no dissonance will occur. This statement must be made carefully, as Wicklund and Brehm indicate, because a negative outcome may be quite unexpected but still something the person feels he or she could have and should have foreseen. In an experiment representing the culmination of many years of research on this problem, Collins and Hoyt (1972) showed that only the combination of choosing to make a speech, knowing the speech would have consequences undesirable to the person, and feeling responsible for these consequences produced dissonance and caused people to change their minds in such a way that justified their decision to make the speech. In sum, a current formulation of dissonance theory would specify that dissonance occurs only when a person makes a choice that involves some negative consequence for which the person accepts responsibility. These elements, of course, coincide without conception of commitment as involving a positive element, a negative element, and a bond between the two.

Because of this similarity, we will be reviewing many different dissonance experiments in this book, especially in the early chapters. In one sense, this book can be thought of as a rethinking of dissonance theory designed to make it more useful to the general concerns of the social sciences. A graduate student at Northwestern, taking Donald Campbell's course in the philosophy of science, once asked Campbell if social psychology ever had a scientific paradigm in Thomas Kuhn's sense. (Kuhn, in a 1962 book that has had enormous impact on thinking about scientific progress, described a paradigm as a set of assumptions that govern the operation of normal science, assumptions that are accepted without question and often without awareness by the scientists doing research. The assumptions indicate what is worth researching and specify the appropriate procedures for conducting research. Most observers have doubted that psychology and the social sciences have ever had a consensus on these matters or have ever had a generally accepted paradigm.) Campbell remarked (after an appropriate pause) that in the field of social psychology, "dissonance theory came close." I believe dissonance theory did come close, because it dealt with the three central elements we have just described, and out of them it generated a great body of exciting and in the main coherent research.

Moreover, it fell short because it lacked a number of attributes that a general paradigm for inquiry into human behavior must possess. First, and most fundamentally, it lacked a theory of function. Little attention has been focused on the utility dissonance and dissonance reduction might have, under appropriate conditions, in enabling individuals to cope with or control their environment. It had no deep connections to the essential questions of learning and performance or the survival value of behavior. Worse yet, the research made dissonance reducation seem nothing more than an amusing bit of behavior, a minor form of prejudice by which people came to believe their own lies. It would be hard to take anything so described as a fundamental basis of human adaptation. Second, dissonance theory lacked a general theory of development. How does a capacity to experience and reduce dissonance change or develop over the life cycle? What social preconditions foster or inhibit its development? Third, dissonance theory needed an understanding of psychopathology. How can this central psychological process become disordered? What are the emotional and behavioral symptoms of its disorder? Finally, dissonance theory needed a better sense of human history than has generally characterized social psychological research (see Gergen, 1973). How has something like dissonance reduction been important to the arrangement of society in the past, and how might it be important in the future? It is the modest goal of this book to supply answers to some of these questions or at least to describe what answers to these questions might look like. If this seems like an attempt to define the universe, so be it. Theories that ask overly modest questions about human nature do not avoid error but merely commit a different kind of error than theories that ask overly grand questions. To advance, we need both kinds of error.

Commitment has been an important variable in dissonance research. The definitions cited from Gerard (1965) and Kiesler (1971) are both from researchers operating within dissonance theory's general set of concerns. However, dissonance-inspired research on commitment has been of little use to people interested in commitment to marriage and the family (Levinger, 1977) or commitment to jobs and organizations (Steers, 1977). Part of the reason is simply that dissonance theory has been interested in commitment as an independent variable, but studies of marriage or work careers have been interested in commitment as a dependent variable. Knowing that a person is committed to a particular line of action, like buying a certain car, enables dissonance theory to predict that this line of action will be bolstered rather than changed or undone if dissonance occurs. If a person is already committed to buying a certain car and a neighbor reports that the car gets poor gas mileage, the person may decide that the neighbor is a poor driver or that gas mileage does not matter very much to her after all compared to comfort or styling. If the person is not committed to buying that make of car when she hears the bad news from her neighbor, she can simply decide not to buy that car. Contrary to what is sometimes implied, commitment is not a necessary condition for dissonance to occur. It is only a necessary conaition for dissonance theorists to make interesting or nonobvious predictions. If there is no commitment, a person can resolve any dissonance that occurs simply by undoing the behavior that caused the dissonance. But people who study important life events like marriages and revolutions are interested not in commitment as an assumption, a fixed variable, but in commitment as something that grows and changes over time. They are interested in the process by which people attach value—positive and negative—to events in their lives. They are interested in what dissonance theory has traditionally taken as its dependent variable, even if it has not called this commitment.

The fact that commitment involves the bonding of a positive element and a negative element is nicely illustrated by a consideration of work and play. Our analysis calls attention to a feature of work and play that has not generally been commented on in previous writing. This is that the same activity can be either work or play and can shift quite quickly and dramatically from work to play and back. Sometimes this can happen because we are paid for something we once did for free or because we do something for free that we were once paid for. A lot of social psychological research has shown that people are more likely to call something work if they are paid for doing it than if they do it for free (Lepper & Green, 1975), though this research has not studied the effects of repeatedly switching whether people are paid or not. But consider amateur tennis players who are never paid for playing tennis or scientists who are paid a constant amount for doing research. Sometimes the tennis or the research is work, even drudgery, something in which the persons persist only because they feel they have to or because they cannot afford to quit. Sometimes the tennis or the research is play, a source of joy and excitement, something one turns to in eager anticipation of the day's activity and progress. It is not our purpose here to carry out a full analysis of why something becomes work or play. The point is merely to note that the answer lies not in the activity itself but in the orientation of the person toward that activity and that this orientation can undergo rapid change. This suggests that the person's orientation contains at all times both a positive element and a negative element. It is the way these two are structured that determines whether the activity is perceived as work or play. When the positive element dominates the field, the activity seems intrinsically motivated. When the negative element dominates the field, the activity seems like work. Many recent writers have suggested that under ideal circumstances work becomes play and play becomes work, the two indistinguishable in how productive or emotionally satisfying they are. The present analysis suggests, on the contrary, that work and play will remain distinct categorizations of human behavior because they represent distinct orientations toward that behavior.

If this analysis is correct, we should find that people experience commitment in a very special way. They should experience commitment as having two faces, but two faces that co-occur, more complementary than contradictory. This is quite different from the idea that one face of commitment will show itself only when the other face is hidden. The psychological manifestation of commitment in which the negative element is salient is *persistence*. The psychological manifestation of commitment in which the positive element is salient is *enthusiasm*. Persistence characterizes behavior that people continue to enact despite their sense that it calls for them to make sacrifices and resist temptations—they may have to work hard and resist the pleasure of quitting. Enthusiasm characterizes behavior that people enact without ambivalence about what the behavior costs, out of a sense that the behavior itself is meaningful. Persistence in commitment reflects the call of duty; enthusiasm goes beyond the call of duty. If we followed the lead of previous writers, we might distinguish between persistent commitments and enthusiastic commitments. But it is clear that this distinction does not make sense, because persistence and enthusiasm are not mutually exclusive elements. They are logically independent. One can persist in a line of action without being enthusiastic, and one can be enthusiastic in an activity without persisting. But they are not, we suspect, psychologically independent. Consider a scale designed to measure a general individual difference among people in their tendency to make or avoid commitments. In constructing such a scale, we would expect items reflecting persistence and items reflecting enthusiasm to contribute equally to a total commitment score. We have constructed such a scale, consisting of the thirty items listed in Table 1. In a college

TABLE 1-1   General Commitment Scale

Check each statement that is true of you.

1.	_____	I will do anything to keep a promise.
* 2.	_____	I am easily distracted.
3.	_____	I know what the top priority in my life is.
4.	_____	I will suffer for what I love.
5.	_____	I feel I have made much progress toward fulfilling my life's goals.
6.	_____	I do not stop until the job is done.
7.	_____	The things I am involved with often make me a different person than I was before.
8.	_____	I do not mind making sacrifices for something I believe in.
9.	_____	My life is exciting to me.
*10.	_____	It is hard for me to make up my mind.
11.	_____	I am committed to a few special things in my life.
12.	_____	I do things as a matter of principle.
13.	_____	Even when I am unhappy, I hardly ever quit until things are finished.
14.	_____	I see my life as having a definite purpose and meaning.
15.	_____	I sacrifice for what I believe.
*16.	_____	There are many things that would tempt me to abandon my current life.
17.	_____	I do my best even if the situation seems hopeless.
18.	_____	I am willing to make commitments in my life.
19.	_____	When I get going on something, I cannot quit until it is done.
*20.	_____	I find things lose their excitement over time.
21.	_____	I never get into anything halfway.
22.	_____	I will give up other things I want to do in order to do something that really matters to me.
23.	_____	I value the things I love more than I value my freedom.
*24.	_____	I often have doubts about what I am doing.
25.	_____	I give everything I have to whatever I do.
*26.	_____	I start more things than I finish.
27.	_____	I feel I have a mission in life.
28.	_____	I am committed to my work.
29.	_____	I believe in meeting deadlines.
30.	_____	I usually find a point even in activities that seem pointless.

*These items are scored for commitment if *not* chosen.

population, this general commitment scale had an internal consistency in the low .80s in both test and replication samples, reasonably satisfactory for this number of binary choice items. As can be seen, about half the items in the scale reflect persistence, and about half reflect enthusiasm.

HISTORICAL AND PERSONAL
RELEVANCE OF COMMITMENT

Socialization is the fundamental process of teaching individuals how to behave in a way that other people find appropriate. It is the fundamental process by which society is created and perpetuated. For the individual, being socialized is learning to give up certain primitive, perhaps instinctual, pleasures in order to pursue a different class of pleasures provided by society. These social pleasures include both being accepted by other people as a normal person and being admired by them as an exceptional person. The primary example of socialization used by psychologists since Freud is toilet training. Children learn to forgo the pleasure of urinating or defecating whenever they feel like it in order to win the approval of their parents. We have here an example with a positive element (adult approval), a negative element (for young children, the effort and frustration of bladder and bowel control), and a bond between the two. Thus, we have an example of commitment. Now we will have to look hard at the exact arrangement of individual capacity and societal reward and punishment that enables this to become a commitment. But bowel and bladder control is clearly a highly successful example of commitment: it is acquired by almost everyone and relinquished by people, during illness or old age, only with great emotional distress. Socialization, in short, is about commitment. In common language, it is about getting people to do voluntarily things they do not want to do. In more abstract language, the matter is nicely put by Rosabeth Kanter (1972).

> In sociological terms, commitment means the attachment of the self to the requirements of social relations that are seen as self-expressive. Commitment links self-interest to social requirements. A person is committed to a relationship or to a group to the extent that he sees it as expressing or fulfilling some fundamental part of himself; he is committed to the degree that he perceives no conflict between its requirements and his own needs; he is committed to the degree that he can no longer meet his needs elsewhere. When a person is committed, what he wants to do (through internal feeling) is the same as what he has to do (according to external demands), and thus he gives to the group what it needs to maintain itself at the same time that he gets what he needs to nourish his own sense of self. (pp. 66–67)

Societies do not ordinarily have observable points at which they begin and end. Thus it is not usually possible to tell if a certain kind of socialization or commitment practice makes a society more likely to survive. There are, however, a class of societies—utopian communes—that have specific founding dates and often specific dates on which they disbanded. Kanter (1972) studied in depth a sample of thirty American utopian communities established between 1780 and 1860 to see whether their commitment practices were related to their chances of success. Contrary to the idea that utopian communities are settings for people to do their own thing, Kanter found a general tendency for the stable and successful communes to spend more time and effort instilling commitment in their members. For example, members of successful communes were more likely to have to give up sex, to give up contacts outside the commune, to give property to the commune, and to give up distinctive or personal forms of dress. Along with these negative elements, successful communes were more likely to contain features that symbolized the positive value of the commune. For example, they appeared more likely to have songs about the community, to have a sense that commune members were morally superior to outsiders, and to believe that members had special powers outsiders did not. In talking about commitment mechanisms, Kanter distinguishes between those that involve detaching the person from things outside the commune and those that involve attaching the person to the commune. These do not exactly correspond to the negative element and the positive element of commitment, because the detachment mechanisms sometimes include a positive element (members' sense of moral superiority) and the attachment mechanisms often include negative elements (signing over of property, little opportunity for privacy, fixed daily routine, tests of faith). However Kanter's data is nicely supportive of the idea that communal commitment is experienced by members as having both a positive and negative face, as well as the idea that commitment in general is related to the stability of the social enterprise.

Commitments in traditional society were relatively predictable and stable. For instance, in most past societies everyone who could afford it married and remained married. Today the economic requirements for getting married and the economic reasons for staying married are both weaker. In most past societies parents and kin had enormous control over who married whom. In modern Western societies, people choose marital partners largely on the basis of romantic love. Likewise, in most past societies people inherited occupations from their parents rather than choosing careers on the basis of interest and education. Only in modern society is it a problem to predict whom a person will marry or what career they will follow. In traditional society, law, custom, and religion made these and other forms of social behavior relatively easy to predict. Where commitments are relatively predictable and stable, there is little need for social psychology (Zajonc, 1966). Social psychology and indeed all the social sciences are the study of how people make choices. Thus it should not be surprising that these sciences emerge only in a society where people have an expanded range of choices and where their choices cannot be predicted or explained by the traditional categories of custom, law, or religion. Society has more need than ever before to study how people make commitments, and it has invented the social sciences to do so. Commitment is thus not only what socialization is about, it is also what the study of socialization, and social behavior in general, is about.

In modern society, we worry about people's commitments, about rigid commitment, overcommitment, or lack of commitment. The deepest fear is that long-term secular change in society is making it increasingly difficult either for individuals to be healthy and happy or for society to function. The form of this worry has changed quite dramatically within the last century. Freud (1930) pessimistically thought that civilization was coming to demand too much in the way of commitment from its members, and thus increasing neuroses could be expected from increasingly excessive demands for conformity and instinctual renunciation. As we have moved from Victorian strictness to the more permissive viewpoints of the present, other authors, such as Campbell (1972), have worried that our culture has been asking too little in the way of commitment and that people have been losing the capacity to make the sacrifices necessary to surmount adversity and sustain civilization. The dominant spirit of America in the 1970s was clearly suspicious of commitments, perceiving them as things that people are manipulated into, that deny their needs, and that make them unhappy rather than happy. John Camper (1977) introduces his satiric review of the popular psychology of the 1970s as follows:

> I don't care whether you read this story. I wrote it because I wanted to. If you or my editors don't like it, I won't feel bad. I wasn't put on this Earth to fulfill anyone else's expectations.
> I love myself. I am my own best friend. I look out for Number One (me!). I respect myself. I have found the real me. My favorite songs are "I Gotta Be Me" and "I Did It My Way."
> And, though it makes no difference to me, it is clear that I am in the mainstream of American life in the '70s. This is the Me Decade, to use Tom Wolfe's term, and its slogan is, "Let's talk about me."
> Self-love is in. Social responsibility is out. Doing your own thing is in. Rigid moral codes are out. The goal is inner peace, not world peace.

Two of the best selling books of the decade have this to say about sacrifice and self-denial. Mildred Newman and Bernard Berkowitz (1974), in *How to Be Your Own Best Friend*, write, "Self-denial is one of the worst kinds of self-indulgence. It is feeding the part of you that feels worthless." Wayne Dyer (1977), in *Your Erroneous Zones*, writes, "Outlaw self-denial unless it is absolutely necessary—and it rarely is." We can pass over what Robert Ringer (1977) has to say in *Looking Out for Number One*.

I think these changes in our feelings and worries about commitment in society are cyclical rather than secular, representing a change in what is salient rather than a change in what is actually there. Just as commitments, in love and work, have two faces for individuals, they have two faces for society as well. Different decades emphasize the different faces of commitment. Decades that elicit a great deal of sacrifice for political or social causes, like the 1910s, the 1940s or the 1960s, are followed by decades in which people are less idealistic about these sacrifices and more sensitive to negative elements that cannot be transcended, like the 1920s, the 1950s, and the 1970s. As a theme, as a social and personal issue, making commitments is as good a candidate as any for the 1980s. But this change, like those that have gone before, will reflect more a change in our awareness of the forms of commitment than a change in these forms themselves. However described, the essential tension of social life is always the same. If we are talking about commitments to ourselves, the negative element is our callousness toward other people's wants and needs. If we are talking about commitments to others, the negative element is our inability to satisfy fully our own wants and needs. Both standing up for ourselves and serving other people can be sources of value. John Gardner (1964), founder of Common Cause, puts the matter so well it appears to be a platitude: "The mature person must achieve a considerable measure of independence if he is to meet the standards implicit in our ideals of individual freedom and dignity; but at the same time he must acknowledge the limitations of the self, come to terms with his membership in the society at large and give his allegiance to values more comprehensive than his own needs."

If commitments are about ambivalence, it is not surprising that we are ambivalent about commitment. For some people, it is perfectly obvious that individuals have a need for commitment in order to be fulfilled, to see value, even to be fully human. For other people, it is equally obvious that the commitments people accept do not fulfill them, do not provide value, and crush rather than display their basic humanity. The guardians of culture preach commitment. The prophets of the counterculture warn against the hypocrisy of this preaching. My own sense is that commitment does serve a fundamental human need, of which it is an almost inescapable manifestation. But, like every other human capacity, it is manipulated and distorted to serve ends quite alien to its origin. The purpose of this inquiry is not to establish commitment per se as a value—it is not—but to show that commitment is important even to people who do not value it for itself. I aim to show that commitment is harder to avoid than people may realize—and also harder to nourish or sustain than we may realize. Unlike love, freedom, or happiness, commitment is not a universal value. Indeed, insofar as personal commitment is a value, it may oppose and conflict with freedom or happiness. Yet commitment may also be a key to understanding these values and indeed the base on which they are founded. If so, commitment will also be a key to understanding what kind of creatures human beings are, where they have been, and where they are going.

COMMITMENT AS AN
INTEGRATIVE CONCEPT
FOR SOCIAL PSYCHOLOGY

I think it is possible to discern in social psychology the emergence of a coherent perspective on human nature. Other views of human nature have had a profound impact on modern thought. Economics has a distinctive set of assumptions about what "economic man" is like that has deeply affected legislation and human welfare for centuries (Heilbroner, 1953; Polanyi, 1944). Psychoanalysis has a distinctive set of assumptions about what "Freudian man" is like that have been a major force in shaping psychotherapy, social work, and twentieth-century literature. The new subdiscipline of sociobiology (Wilson, 1975) mixes a noncontroversial assumption that behavior must have survival value with a highly controversial assumption that much of human behavior is therefore genetically determined. Yet none of these other perspectives is based on as much carefully controlled observation of how people actually behave as is social psychology. Perhaps because of this, none has developed as much appreciation of the active way people process information and shape their own environment as I believe is emerging in social psychology. Today the economic view and the psychoanalytic view of human nature are considered part of what every educated person should know. Eventually, I think a social psychological perspective will also be part of our common intellectual heritage. This book is an effort to sketch the outlines of this perspective and to articulate its principal concerns.

Commitment is a compelling concept around which the integration of social psychology can be attempted. In part this is because of its relationship, as noted, to the near-paradigm of dissonance theory. In part it is because the idea of commitment is relevant to every form of behavior social psychologists study. But there is, I think, something more. If we look at social psychology textbooks today, we find them divided into a series of fascinating but apparently unrelated topics, such as altruism, attraction, attribution, achievement, and aggression. I think, without pushing too hard, these topics could be divided into two general parts. One part deals with the general theme of how people act on, cope with, and try to shape their external environment. This is the primary focus of topics like aggression and achievement. The other part deals with the general question of what determines people's thoughts and feelings, or how people structure their internal environment. This is the primary focus of topics like attitude change. attribution, and attraction. No one would claim that people's internal and external concerns are unrelated; no one would claim that an area that focuses primarily on one truly ignores the other. However, we have no area, no theory that deals specifically with the relationship between people's internal and external concerns. We have no well-developed concept that refers to the bridges people build between their internal and external concerns. Commitment is this bridging concept. Commitment refers, first of all, to the fact that people control and shape their internal environment, their thoughts and feelings, in the service of adapting to their external environment. It also refers to the fact that people struggle to twist and manipulate their external environment—persons and objects both—in the service of their inner needs. We might designate the two general themes of social psychology as the study of value (internally oriented) and the study of control (externally oriented). Commitment is then a parent process from which, I will suggest, people derive both a sense of value and a capacity for control.

Commitment is promising as an integrative concept for social psychology in another sense. It stands astride not only the topical areas just mentioned, but also a number of enduring issues about how people process information, issues that cut across all these different areas. One such issue is the question of whether such processing takes place inside or outside of conscious awareness. Before Freud, psychology under Wundt and Titchener was defined as the introspective study of the contents of consciousness. Freud transformed psychology, and a great deal else, with his demonstration of how much in the way of dreams and impulses and associations were ordinarily held out of awareness. With the advent of computer technology after World War II, psychology was provided with a powerful new model for describing information processing as a logical, self-aware process. The next decades saw the development of many different theories, all of which assumed that people try to arrange their cognitions and solve their problems in a consistent, orderly fashion (Newell, Shaw, & Simon, 1958; Abelson, et al., 1968.). Recently we have seen a renewed interest in the idea that many important cognitive processes either are nonrational or take place outside of awareness (Langer, 1978; Nisbett & Wilson, 1977). Although the connections are not crystal clear, commitment relates to the problem of awareness in at least two important ways. First, commitment is a device for automating things, simplifying them, and putting them out of awareness. One of the advantages of learning something and making up our minds about it is that we no longer have to think about it and can devote our attention to other things. Once we have decided what to wear in the morning, we can turn our attention to other, perhaps more pressing matters, like whether or not we should really go back to bed. Second, and no less important though quite the opposite, commitment is also a device for keeping things within focal awareness, for tuning out distractions and preventing our attention from wandering from the task at hand. Without this control, normal waking thought would be much more like the jumbled and chaotic flow we experience in dreams. If we could understand how commitment works, we would be much better able to understand what takes place in and out of awareness, and how this is arranged.

Closely related to the issue of awareness is the question of rationality. Do people calculate and choose what is in their own best interest—as an economic model would assume—or do they simply choose for private and often inexplicable reasons—as a psychoanalytic model would assume? This question has a nice parallel in moral philosophy. The historic debate in moral philosophy is between the utilitarians, following Jeremy Bentham and John Stuart Mill, and the nonutilitarians, from Immanuel Kant to John Rawls. Utilitarians argue that the moral choice in a society is the one that provides the greatest good (or utility) for the greatest number of people. Nonutilitarians argue that calculating utilities, or counting up opinions, is irrelevant to moral choice. Instead, there is some absolute principle that specifies certain things that must be respected no matter what the majority of people think. Philosophers have been very reluctant to accept a system of ethics that inelegantly combines both a utilitarian and a nonutilitarian principle, because neither can be derived from the other. But any philosophy that has only a utilitarian principle has no way of protecting the rights of a minority if the majority wants badly enough to trample on those rights. On the other hand, any philosophy that has only a nonutilitarian principle has no way of protecting the well-being of the majority if the principle at some point specifies that all benefits go to a minority. In short, it is hard to imagine any acceptable system of ethics that does not have both a utilitarian and a nonutilitarian principle and a rule for when to switch from one principle to the other. Likewise, in psychology it is hard to imagine any acceptable understanding of human thought that does not allow for both a rational and a nonrational component, with a rule specifying when we switch from one to the other. Typically, people choose what appears to be in their own interest. But sometimes they do not, or they distort their perceptions of this interest, or they discover a kind of interest no outside observer would have imagined. Commitment is the transition rule, the point at which people switch from rational processing to something else.

Because of what it tries to accomplish, this book will be a curious mixture of things. Psychology, like all other human thought, is a mixture of common sense and nonsense. As a science, it differs from other forms of thought only in that eventually, slowly and painfully over time, it can begin to tell which is the common sense and which is the nonsense—no small achievement. This book arrives quite early in the course of this achievement. Thus the reader from outside psychology should be prepared to encounter some concepts that seem to be common sense and others that seem like nonsense. To social psychologists, the book will sometimes seem overly elementary and sometimes overly speculative. The first half of the book is in the main a review and reinterpretation of well-known research in social psychology. These are the chapters on reason, value, and control. The second half of the book is an effort to extend these concerns to areas not normally covered by social psychology; these are the chapters on development and mental health. We will deal with both laboratory experiments and life histories, minute questions of theory and more majestic questions of application.

Any book has two grand hopes. One is to be remembered for its thesis after its details are forgotten. The other is to be read for its details after its thesis is forgotten. The second hope seems to me not only grander but a necessary condition for achieving the first.

CHAPTER TWO
REASON

Philip Brickman
Linda S. Perloff
Clive Seligman

INTRODUCTION

Why is the question of rationality important to the study of commitment? First, because there are a great many studies, some of them quite dramatic, showing that people appear to be irrational after they make commitments. This evidence is an essential clue to the nature of commitment. Until we know how to interpret it, we will not be in a position to understand what people gain and what they lose by making commitments. Second, the question of rationality is a profound one in its own right. In what sense, to what extent, are people rational? Every writer who has been to any degree hopeful about the future of the human race has founded that hope on the idea that people are rational or can become so. This includes a pessimistic thinker like Sigmund Freud, for whom human reason is just a strip of land precariously emerged from a much larger psychic sea. It includes writers like Philip Slater, who hope that people will use their intelligence to move away from technology rather than pursue it further. If the rationality is slender, the hope that people will choose the course of action that is in their own best interest is also slender. The study of commitment in turn has something to tell us about the nature of human reason, its virtues, its drawbacks, and its limits. It also leads us, I think, to the idea that there is something inherently ambiguous in the determination of rationality. These are the issues that will concern us in the present chapter.

Types of Rationality

Rationality is a topic of interest to philosophy and sociology as well as to psychology. With their different concerns, each of these fields focuses on a somewhat different aspect or kind of rationality. We call them philosophical or logical rationality, psychological rationality, and social rationality. Our concern will be with psychological rationality. Philosophical rationality is concerned with whether statements are true or not. But as the psychologist Robert Abelson (1976) points out, it may or may not be psychologically rational for a person to insist that his or her assertions be true:

> If we subject the possibility of rational habit of mind to rational analysis, we should ask, what is the typical payoff to an individual for being rational? Despite the seemingly obvious advantages in normal life adjustment of what clinical psychologists call 'reality testing,' it is not so clear what costs or punishments are incurred by individuals for being non-rational concerning remote events. If a man believes that all the bad storms last winter were deliberately caused by Chinese atom bomb tests, what corrective factors would ever disabuse him of this misapprehension? We might presume that this man would *want* to examine carefully the plausibility of a manipulated connection between bomb tests and weather, but this is merely a presumption. Why should he care? Even if he cares, how would he have the wherewithal to carry out such an examination? (p. 59)

More pressing still, if the person's friends all believed that Chinese bomb tests caused the bad weather, the person might be strongly motivated to maintain his allegiance to this belief even if he had strong evidence to the contrary (Abelson & Rosenberg, 1958).

In sociology, following Max Weber (1905-1968), rationality refers to procedures for making decisions about people in ways that can be predicted and explained. In a rational system, job applicants are sorted into a systematic set of categories, and the applicants in each category are treated the same way, whatever the rules call for. If a person has certain specified qualifications and a place is available, he or she gets the job. In a nonrational system, whether or not a person gets the job may depend on whether he or she is related to the boss, whether the boss likes him or her, or other unpredictable factors. Rationality in this sense, like rationality in the philosophical sense, is associated with affective neutrality—application of the appropriate rules in a consistent fashion no matter what one's feelings. But as with philosophical rationality, it may or may not be psychologically rational for a person to prefer participating in a social system that has these rational properties. Although we enjoy the technical efficiency of these processes, they are the very ones we complain about when we complain about bureaucracy.

Psychological rationality, in contrast, requires people to take account of their feelings rather than ignore them. In essence, if a person is psychologically rational, he or she chooses the best course of action from the alternatives available. By what criteria is something to be judged the best? By whatever criteria are important to the individual. If the most important thing for a person is to earn money, the best course of action is the one that earns the most money. If the most important thing for a person is to be liked, the best course of action is the one that makes other people like him or her the most. Very often a person cannot be sure what outcome will result from a given course of action. Then the person must guess what the likely outcomes are and, if he or she is rational, choose the course of action for which a desirable outcome seems most likely. In research on human decision making (Edwards, 1968), this is called the principle of maximizing subjectively expected utility.

THOUGHT: EFFECTS OF COMMITMENT ON RATIONAL INFORMATION PROCESSING

If a person does something and is punished for it, the person should be less likely to do more of it in the future. This is the basic idea of reinforcement theory or learning theory and also the basic idea of psychological rationality. But sometimes, when people are punished for doing something, they not only continue to do it but spend more time and money and effort to do it on a larger scale. The United States was not rewarded for its initial investment of troops in Vietnam. Yet it chose to invest more troops, not less, and repeated this choice over and over again despite repeated lack of reward for it. Eventually, this resulted in an outcome that would not have been predicted and would not have been chosen by the men who created it: a land war in Asia involving millions of American people (in direct and supporting efforts) and billions of American dollars. Eventually, that is, it resulted in an outcome that no one felt was psychologically rational.

Investing in a Losing Cause

The dynamics of this kind of commitment are brilliantly dramatized in a very simple game invented by Martin Shubik (1971). The game is called the dollar auction game. A dollar is auctioned off and players bid for it. If one player bids 10¢, and no one bids anything higher, the person bidding 10¢ gets to buy the dollar for 10¢. The only further rule is this: At the conclusion of the auction, the top *two* bidders must each pay what they have last bid. If the high bid was 80¢ and the second highest bid was 75¢, the higher bidder pays 80¢ and gets the dollar while the second highest bidder pays 75¢ and gets nothing. Once the auction narrows down to two people, both know that they must pay whatever they had last bid. At each point it usually costs only a few extra cents for the second highest bidder to get a new chance to win the dollar. The first time I played this game in a classroom, the winner purchased the dollar for $5.05, and the next highest bidder paid out $4.95.

Spending a lot of money and not getting what one wanted in return for it is certainly undesirable. But this does not in itself establish that the initial or incremental decisions to spend this money were irrational. They are certainly not irrational in the mind of the decision maker. One of my students told me the story of his having invested money in a rapidly rising stock. Soon afterwards, the stock dropped to a catastrophic low. The student then purchased a further set of shares. Now he did not make this purchase out of a desire to appear stupid, but in what he felt was the rational belief that the stock would rise again and was a good buy at its current low price. Unfortunately, this did not happen, and the net result was what the student described to me as a "super, though grossly expensive, learning experience." Similarly, our Vietnam policymakers invested more troops in Vietnam in what they felt was the rational belief that the next investment of troops would pay off, although all previous ones had not. What makes these decisions seem irrational to us is our sense that in the same situation and with the same values as the decision makers, we would not make the same choice. Someone who has previously bid 95¢ a nickel at a time to try to win a dollar may be tempted to bid one more nickel. If commitment is important, the person's willingness to make one more bid is in part due to the commitment he feels he made through all those previous bids. An observer who is simply told that 95¢ has already been bid and asked whether she wants to bid another nickel should not feel the same pressure of previous commitment. If commitment is what keeps people investing in a losing game, new personnel moved into the situation should judge these investments as less rational and should be less willing to make them.

This exact study has not been done with the dollar auction game, but a similar and very ingenious experiment using a management simulation exercise was carried out by Barry Staw (1976). In the experiment, business school students had to invest research and development funds in either the consumer products or the industrial products division of a hypothetical corporation. In one condition, subjects learned that their initial decision had not worked. Whatever their initial decision, subjects were told that sales and earnings for that division had declined while those for the other division had improved. It is neither surprising nor irrational that subjects in this condition invested a large majority of their subsequent funds in the same unprofitable division. They might have calculated, for example, that this division had all the more need for research and development funds, despite the fact that previous such funds had not helped. In another condition, however, subjects were brought in to make the second investment decision and merely told that the first decision (to invest in the division which continued to lose money) had been made by their predecessor. Under these circumstances, subjects were much less inclined to make another major investment in the losing division and instead put a majority of their funds into the profitable division.

People who are committed to a behavior may find it unnecessary to take precautions that observers would consider prudent for health and safety. A number of interesting studies that bear on this question have been reviewed by Howard Leventhal (1970). For example, Berkowitz and Cottingham (1960) compared the attitudes of drivers and nondrivers toward seat belts. Among nondrivers, a message that produced a great deal of fear about auto accidents elicited more favorable attitudes toward seat belts. Among regular drivers who were not in the habit of using seat belts, the high-fear message did not elicit any more favorable attitudes toward seat belts than the low-fear message. Leventhal and Watts (1966) compared the attitudes of smokers and nonsmokers toward taking X-rays designed to detect the early presence of lung cancer. Among smokers, a message that produced a great deal of fear about cancer was actually less effective in getting subjects to take X-rays than a message that was less fear arousing. Nonsmokers did not show this effect. People who drive or smoke are less likely to respond to information that makes this behavior seem irrational. Moreover, people may not have to do anything for very long before they become resistant to negative information about it. Kiesler (1971) had people play a simple card game in which they were asked to follow a particular strategy either once or three times. Subjects who used the strategy three times were even more likely to choose it after it had been subsequently criticized by another person, while subjects who had used it only once were less likely to choose it after subsequent criticism.

Processing New Information

There are numerous other experiments, many of them well known, showing that people are less open to new information once they have made a commitment. Brehm and Leventhal (1962) had subjects try to guess the average of a series of small weights. After lifting ten of the weights, half of the subjects were told that their next guess would be the one that counted in determining whether or not they won a prize. The other half were told their next guess would still be tentative. All subjects then encountered a new weight that was much heavier than anything they had felt previously. When the experiment was made to seem important, subjects who had made a guess that they thought counted were much less likely to revise their estimate to take into account the new evidence than subjects who had made only a tentative guess. Thibaut and Ross (1969) also looked at subjects' judgments of a series of stimuli, allegedly representing critical opinions of how talented a certain artist was. Half the subjects committed themselves to an impression of the artist on the basis of the first few items in the series. These subjects were more likely to see later items in the series as consistent with the initial stimuli or to assimilate these later items to their initial impression. Walster and Prestholdt (1966) had subjects record what they later learned was an erroneous opinion of another person. Half the subjects learned of their error only after their opinions had allegedly been mailed to the psychiatrist of the person they had misjudged. These subjects were much less willing to change their minds and revise their overly harsh or overly favorable initial judgments. In general, these are not cases in which we can label subjects' information processing after commitment as irrational by some objective criterion. Nonetheless, we can assume that observers would expect to behave in these situations like the uncommitted subjects rather than like the committed subjects. This means that observers—including ourselves—would see the committed subjects as less rational than the uncommitted ones.

The phenomenon of a commitment interfering with the processing of new information is certainly not limited to the laboratory. It may play a part in many historically important events. Both the First and the Second World Wars started from incidents that none of the parties involved intended or expected to escalate into a general conflict. In each case this involved a misreading by at least one of the parties involved of an opponent's determination not to back down or let down an ally. It is important to note that these misreadings occurred amid a growing sense on all sides that war was inevitable and an increasing investment in preparation for war. Ralph White (1966) has analyzed in detail the mind-sets of the various sides that caused them to ignore information indicating that their opponents were neither diabolical nor weak. Two important elements of each nation's pursuit of what it saw as its proper and vital interests are described by White as selective inattention and an absence of empathy. Selective inattention made the other side seem weaker or less determined than it was, while an absence of empathy made the other side seem more diabolical in its ultimate intentions than it was. In the World Wars, more of the miscalculations seemed characteristic of the Axis than the Allied powers, but in Vietnam, according to White, these miscalculations were often characteristic of both sides.

Interestingly enough, military unpreparedness and a commitment to peace can produce an opposite kind of misperception in which the aggressive intentions of the other side are underestimated rather than overestimated. Irving Janis and Leon Mann (1977) offer an interesting analysis of the American failure to anticipate the Japanese attack on Pearl Harbor. Admiral Kimmel, commander in chief of the Pacific Fleet, had in his possession by December 6, 1941, numerous indications that the Japanese were preparing to launch an attack on American territory, including the opinion of President Roosevelt, the news that Japanese missions were destroying their papers and secret codes, and the fact that American intelligence had lost track of all six Japanese aircraft carriers. In response to previous threats, Kimmel and his staff had instituted a limited alert and concluded, correctly, that a full alert would undermine the primary training mission of the Pearl Harbor base. According to Janis and Mann, their commitment to a limited alert prevented Kimmel and his staff both from correctly interpreting the seriousness of the situation and from developing intermediate degrees of alertness that would have left the base reasonably ready without interfering with training activities.

Disconfirming Beliefs

When prophecy fails.   Understandably, people prefer not to place themselves on the line; their deepest beliefs are rarely stated in a way that would allow them to be unequivocally proven wrong. Many of people's deepest beliefs concern themselves—what kind of people they are, what they love—and can be proven wrong not by external sources but only by a change in their own behavior. Others concern things like God, whose existence or nature cannot be established (according to most theologians) by the presence or absence of any particular event. Sometimes, however, people do stake their deepest personal convictions on an unequivocal prediction that must be confirmed or disconfirmed by events. The most dramatic examples are the doomsday cults who predict, on the basis of revelation, that the world will end on a particular day.

A study of what happened to such a cult on the day after the world was supposed to have ended is one of the most famous studies in social psychology. Leon Festinger, Henry Riecken, and Stanley Schachter (1956) infiltrated such a cult and observed the events that occurred. The group had predicted that on a certain day the earth would be destroyed by a flood but that they themselves would be rescued by a flying saucer from another planet. Some of them gave up their jobs and their possessions in anticipation of the event. As the day approached, they gathered at the home of their leader. Although the details of the predictions were changed a number of times, eventually it became clear that no flood and no saucer were appearing. At this point the leader had a striking new relevation: The world had been saved by the vigilance and faith of the group. Thus the members were not required to give up their belief in messengers from another planet but could perceive the predicted flood as a test of their faithfulness that they had successfully passed. Festinger, Riecken, and Schachter found it especially interesting that those believers who had waited for the end together and did not subsequently give up their belief then began an active campaign to convince the rest of the world of the group's message. They had no success, and a study of another group that had predicted the end of the world (Hardyck & Braden, 1962) found that the shattering of a messianic prediction does not always lead the group to seek new converts. Nonetheless, it is important to realize that the Second Coming of Christ was a literal and imminent prediction for early Christians. Only gradually, after repeated disappointment, was the date for the Second Coming pushed back into the indefinite future. The general success of Christianity (in secular terms) must be explained first of all by the social conditions that existed in the Roman Empire, not by the psychology of conversion. But the stubborn refusal of early Christians to relinquish their belief in the face of negative evidence and unfulfilled prophecies cannot be denied its historical importance.

Because prophecies can be reinterpreted, their failure to occur does not necessarily compel a rational believer to abandon faith in their source. Suppose, however, the evidence flatly denied the divine value of the source itself. And suppose that we knew that believers accepted this contradictory evidence as true. These are exactly the circumstances that obtained in a most ingenious experiment carried out by Daniel Batson (1975). The primary subjects were the 42 female high school members of a Presbyterian youth group who began the exercise by publicly affirming that they believed that Jesus was the Son of God. Subjects then read an article they were told had been "written anonymously and denied publication in the *The New York Times* at the request of the World Council of Churches because of the obvious crushing effect it would have on the entire Christian world." The article was datelined Geneva, Switzerland, and read in part as follows:

> It was learned today here in Geneva from a top source in the World Council of Churches offices that scholars in Jordan have conclusively proved that the major writings in what is today called the New Testament are fraudulent.

According to the information gained from the unnamed source in the head-quarters of the World Council of Churches, Professor R. R. Lowrey (author of *The Zarondike Fragments and the Dead Sea Scrolls*), assisted by other scholars, has been carefully analyzing a collection of papyrus scrolls discovered in a cave in the Jerusalem desert near where the famous Dead Sea Scrolls were found. Contained within this collection of scrolls, Lowry and his associates have found letters, apparently written between the composers of various New Testament books, bluntly stating: 'Since our great teacher, Jesus of Nazareth, was killed by the Romans, I am sure we are justified in stealing away his body and claiming that he rose from the dead. For, although his death clearly proves that he was not the Son of God as we had hoped, if we did not claim that he was, both his great teaching and our lives as his disciples would be wasted. (p. 180)

Radiocarbon dating and linguistic analysis allegedly confirmed the authenticity of the scrolls. Thirty-one of the believers doubted that the article was true; the other eleven accepted it as true. Those who doubted the article was true did not change in their belief in the divinity of Jesus and the infallibility of the Bible. Those believers who accepted the article as true, however, showed a significant *increase* in the intensity of their belief in Jesus and the Bible. Under these circumstances, it is almost impossible to argue that the response to disconfirming information represents rational information processing. As Batson indicates, it represents people simply saying: "I *still* believe in Jesus." (It should be noted, by the way, that the leaders of the youth group were fully informed of the nature of the study and wanted to use it to stimulate group discussion on the nature of religious faith.)

There is no reason to believe that intelligent people are more likely to be immune to these effects of commitment than less intelligent people. On the contrary, more intelligent people should also be better at rationalizing what they do. Among presidents of the United States, for example, historians would probably agree that Lyndon Johnson was the president with the greatest practical knowledge of the workings of government, gained from his years in Texas and in the Senate, and Woodrow Wilson was the president with the most distinguished academic career and prior scholarly accomplishments. Yet these two presidents are the outstanding examples of chief executives who ruined their careers and ultimately their health by uncompromising commitments that their contemporaries could see as unnecessary even to the ends they were pursuing. Although I know of no studies correlating intelligence with evidence of dissonance reduction, dissonance theory could easily predict that more intelligent actors would be more prone to display dissonance reduction, if only because they have a stronger expectation of making correct decisions in the first place. Individuals who expect their choices to be correct are more likely to reevaluate matters after making a decision in a way that strengthens or justifies their choice (Gerard, Blevans, & Malcolm, 1964; Malewski, 1964; Weaver & Brickman, 1974).

Adherence to scientific theories.   If there is any domain in which we should expect to find people changing their beliefs in a strictly rational fashion, it is science. This is not because scientists are especially intelligent but because science is governed by a norm of rationality. Science is an organized enterprise specifically dedicated to rationally assessing beliefs in the light of available evidence. Scientists are expected to hold beliefs that can be supported by evidence, and they are admired to the extent that they can formulate beliefs or principles that account for a wide variety of evidence. Yet Ian Mitroff (1976) learned the following in his series of extensive interviews with 42 of the most eminent scientists involved in studying the rocks brought back from the moon by the Apollo spaceflight:

> The thought arose that the passionate, and often even irrational, adherence to ideas was more the norm or distinguishing mark of the creative scientist, and that this passion might be especially the case for those scientists who were bold, imaginative, and capable enough to propose theories of origin for something so huge and complicated as a whole earth-moon system. If this adherence were indeed more the norm than the widely held and proclaimed image of the scientist as a cold, emotionally disinterested creature guided only by the dictates of impersonal logic and a rational craving for the truth, one would expect the various proponents of theories *not* to give in in the face of the first bits of negative evidence against them. In fact, such men would undoubtedly argue about what constituted "negative evidence. . . ."
>
> What was so surprising about the reactions of the scientists was not that they rejected the notion of the "disinterested scientist" as an accurate *descriptive* account of the workings of science, but that they even rejected it on the stronger grounds as a desired *prescriptive* ideal or standard. Not only was it recognized that in point of actual conduct the good scientist was often highly committed to a point of view—at the very least to his pet theories and hypotheses—but, even more interesting and important, strong reasons were evinced why this situation *ought* to be the case, that *ideally* scientists *ought not* to be without strong prior commitments. (pp. 51–53)

Mitroff's analysis of the commitment of the moon researchers to their beliefs is not unique. The historian of science Richard Westfall (1973) indicates that Isaac Newton engaged in blatant manipulation of key empirical data in developing his theory of universal gravitation. In *The Sleepwalkers*, Arthur Koestler (1963) argues that the founders of modern physics and astronomy, including Copernicus, Tycho Brahe, Kepler, and Galileo, were inspired by visions that preceded their subsequent accumulation of facts and to which they clung even when the facts appeared unsupportive. Roger Shepard (1978) has documented the impressive role mental imagery has played in a wide variety of scientific discoveries, including electromagnetism, chemical bonding, and relativity. The image of the solution apparently occurs before the scientist can put the discovery into words. Subsequent work is often a search for appropriate words and facts that will fit the image.

Donald Campbell (1960) has argued that blind variation and selective retention is the only possible basis for scientific discovery or valid knowledge. New ideas can be rationally tested but not rationally created in the first place. Since the merits of a new idea can only be known when it is subsequently tested, the idea (if it is truly new and not merely a rearrangement of current ideas) cannot be selected for its merits in the first place. One model for this process is radar. The initial process of discovery is made by a blindly or randomly varying signal. Only after a target has been located does rational decision or selection come into play to guide subsequent investigation. Genetic evolution is another example of blind variation and selective retention. If this is also the model for creative thought, there are important implications for the general role of commitment in such thought. Because the initial selection of ideas is not made on a rational basis, the selector may routinely be expected to sustain these ideas in the face of some amount of negative evidence or to immunize them from immediate rational disproof.

There may also be something nonrational about the commitment of scientists at a deeper level. So long as scientists share a common conception of what is a good hypothesis and what is a good reason for accepting or rejecting a hypothesis, science can progress by a process of debate that is relatively orderly and rational. This set of shared standards, assumptions, and values is called a paradigm by Thomas Kuhn (1962; see also chapter 1 of this volume), and work under such a paradigm is called normal science. When a paradigm is challenged, in a period of what Kuhn calls revolutionary science, there are no universally accepted grounds for judging new ideas and evidence, and questions such as which approach has greater scope or fruitfulness become important. Not only is the scope or fruitfulness of a theory a matter of subjective judgment, but scientists can disagree on how important scope or fruitfulness should be in judging a theory. The rhetoric of tradition and rebellion, ordinarily disdained in scientific dialogue, then become important. Perhaps the most famous comment on the role of nonrational factors in the history of science was offered by the brilliant physicist Max Planck. Planck felt that new ideas, like the general theory of relativity, do not win their place in science by convincing adherents of old ideas. They win their place because a new generation grows up familiar with the new ideas, comfortable with them, and the adherents of the old systems gradually die off. If this is true in science, for which rationality is the explicit and central value, how much more true might it be for artistic, political, and moral ideas?

Criteria for Rationality
(Ideal Standards)

So far we have not considered any technical criteria for rationality. We have compared the behavior of people when they are involved and when they are detached, showing that when they are involved they make choices that are apparently less sensible and certainly less sensitive to new information. But we have not specified what criteria we might expect a detached observer to employ and an involved one to discard. In some circumstances we can state precisely the form of rationality an ideal operator would follow, the procedure known to yield the best possible results for the decision maker. Three forms of such ideal rationality widely researched in the social sciences are minimax rationality, marginal utility rationality, and inferential rationality. In the concluding part of this section, I would like to consider each of these three and show that people who are committed to a goal or a relationship violate each of these technical criteria for rationality.

Minimax rationality. Minimax rationality is the principle recommending that people behave in such a way as to minimize their maximum possible loss, behaving in such a way as to be least hurt by whatever other persons in the situation do (Rapoport, 1966) or whatever the wheel of fate turns up as their lot in life (Rawls, 1971). Loving is not rational in this sense. If one's affection is not reciprocated, the person clearly suffers much more than if he or she had chosen not to love in the first place. If the affections are returned, suffering is not an issue but the person still has less power in the relationship for having chosen to love than he or she would have had by remaining detached. Thibaut and Kelley (1959) have described this as the principle of least involvement. The party who is less involved can influence the other party more while being in turn less vulnerable to influence. By this analysis, loving has some components of what has been called the trust dilemma or the Prisoner's Dilemma. Each party would be better off if they both loved each other, but when uncertain of the other, each party will minimize the risk of suffering or losing power by choosing not to love. The dilemma demonstrates that what may be psychologically rational for each individual leads to collective behavior that is not rational for the group—behavior that leaves each individual worse off than the alternative would have. Some of our assumptions in this example, such as that people are concerned only about maximizing their own outcomes, can be questioned. Nevertheless, whatever people are doing when they care deeply about something— when they love another, or a country—it is not minimizing possible loss, and it is this feature that makes love the most powerful form of commitment we know. To lose what one loves is the maximum possible loss. If the first goal is to protect against this, the rational choice is not to love.

Researchers have not paid very much attention to love as a possible trust dilemma. They have, however, thought a great deal about a number of other trust dilemmas involving the welfare of entire societies. These dilemmas can be variously described. One is called the free-load problem. It has been analyzed at length by Mancur Olson (1971) in a book called *The Logic of Collective Action*. It is to each individual's benefit to have taxes paid for certain common goods, like police protection, sewage disposal, or clean air. However, since each individual gets the benefit of these common goods regardless of whether he or she pays taxes, it is to each individual's greater benefit to have others pay but not to pay him- or herself. Contrary to previous thinking about social organization, Olson's analysis makes clear that it is not simply rational for people to organize even in pursuit of their own self-interest. All workers may want a union or all students a student government without wanting to run it or even participate actively in it themselves. If no one else is willing to run it, there is no point in participating, and if other people are willing to run it, there is no need to participate to obtain the common goods the organization provides. As one of my senior colleagues once said, generously turning over power to we newly arrived junior faculty, he would rather have our program run poorly than have to run it himself. The result of this rational calculation is that social organization often does not occur even when it is in the personal or class interests of those involved. The case is nicely summarized in the story of a French village that decided to celebrate a special day with a communal feast. The wine for the feast was to come from a common casket to which each person attending would contribute a glass. One peasant calculated that he would bring water rather than wine, for who would notice one glass of water amid all that wine? When the casket was opened, it was full of water.

Another version of the same problem has been called the tragedy of the commons (Hardin, 1968). The dilemma here is that a common resource or common good of great value is depleted or destroyed by individuals rationally pursuing their own self-interest and using it without restraint. Hardin's original example is the historic fate of common village pasturelands. If other farmers held back in their use of these lands, each individual could gain an important advantage by allowing a few more of his animals to graze on the common pasture. If other farmers were not holding back in their exploitations of these lands, the individual would certainly want to send his animals over to graze in order to get his share of the common resource before it was all used up. The result was that valuable pasturelands were overgrazed and ruined, leaving the entire countryside worse off than it would have been had some force restrained individual rationality. Air pollution is a modern example. We are collectively better off if no one pollutes than if everyone pollutes, but each individual (regardless of what others do) can run his or her factory more cheaply or get rid of his or her leaves more conveniently by ignoring their private contribution to pollution. The most serious example Hardin offers is overpopulation. In a great part of the world, each individual's personal security is far better assured by having more rather than fewer children. The world as a whole, however, is threatened with catastrophe if people continue to have more and more children.

If a society or a relationship is to work, then, it must induce people to do things they would be selfishly better off by not doing. One solution is to alter the structure of rewards and punishments. People can be forced to join unions or fined if they pollute. These measures can make it psychologically rational for the person to perform the socially desirable behavior. Yet they cannot, I think, be the whole story. We can pass laws making it illegal for people to drink or gamble or fornicate or borrow money at outrageous rates of interest, but if people want to do these things badly enough they will. And an entire underground social organization arises to serve these needs. Society can monitor only some of the people some of the time. It must be able to count on people's not engaging in important forms of antisocial behavior even when they are not being watched or it cannot count on it at all.

The general solution is commitment. Here this refers to the value people attach to the legitimacy of social rules, to obeying such rules even when obedience is not in their immediate self-interest. It also refers to loyalty, the value people attach to the society or the relationship itself. Another political economist, Albert Hirschman (1970), has addressed himself to the problem of loyalty. Hirschman notes that loyalty "is at its most functional when it looks most irrational, when loyalty means strong attachments to an organization that does not seem to warrant such attachment because it is so much like another one that is also available. Such seemingly irrational loyalties are often encountered, for example, in relation to clubs, football teams, and political parties" (p. 71). When people are committed to a society or a relationship, they are committed to doing things that they would be selfishly better off by not doing. They are committed to trusting other people not to inflict upon them the maximum possible loss they could experience, a loss their own action or restraint makes possible. When they are committed, they violate minimax rationality.

Marginal utility rationality. Marginal utility rationality is a fundamental principle of economics described at length in any introductory economics text (e.g., Samuelson, 1961). Marginal utility is in fact one of the great discoveries of modern economics. It helps explain the famous paradox of value set forth by Adam Smith ([1776] 1976) in the *The Wealth of Nations*. Smith asked, how it is that water, which is so very useful that life is impossible without it, has such a low price—while diamonds, which are quite unnecessary, have such a high price. The resolution of this paradox involves distinguishing total utility from marginal utility. The total utility of a good refers to the total value of all the units of that good a person possesses. The marginal utility of the good refers to the extra value one more unit of that good would bring the person. The total utility of water is very high, because life would be impossible without it. However, the marginal utility of water, in most parts of the world, is not very high, because most people do not feel great need for an extra unit of water. The total utility of diamonds is very low, since they are unnecessary to life. But the marginal utility of diamonds for most people is very high, since a single additional diamond in their lives would make a great difference to them. The demand for a good, and thus the price of the good, is set by its marginal utility rather than its total utility. Thus diamonds have a high price and water has a low price.

A rational consumer purchases goods according to their marginal utility. More precisely, the ideal consumer arranges purchases so that the marginal utility of the last dollar spent on any one good is exactly equal to the marginal utility of the last dollar spent on any other good. Consider a person trying to decide how much of his or her budget to spend on laundry, taxis, and movies. Suppose the marginal utility of a few dollars spent for extra laundry is greater than the marginal utility of the same number of dollars spent for another movie and still greater than the marginal utility of those dollars spent on taxis. To gain the greatest possible satisfaction, the person should clearly shift his or her spending to do more laundry and take fewer taxi rides. Only if the marginal utility of everything a person buys is equal is there nothing to be gained by shifting a certain amount of spending from one domain to another. The rational consumer maximizes the psychological value of what is purchased by not buying more of one good when spending the money on more of another good would bring greater pleasure.

When we are committed to a relationship, we violate this principle of marginal utility. There are many occasions when spending time with a stranger would bring us more in the way of stimulation or pleasure than spending the equivalent amount of time with a partner we are familiar with and committed to. But if we are committed to our partner, we choose the partner. In general, we spend time and money far beyond the point of diminishing returns on relationships to which we are committed. We do this because the relationship itself comes to have value, including the feelings of the other person on those occasions when some other activity seems more attractive to us. In being committed to society, we also violate the principle of maximizing marginal utility. This is because society requires us to specialize both economically and emotionally to a greater extent than is in our own best interest. For an accountant, spending an extra unit of time rereading tax laws may have considerably less psychological utility than spending the same unit of time gardening or writing poetry. But to get the most efficient possible accounting, farming, and poetry, it is in society's interest to have some people spend an inordinate amount of time on accounting, others on farming, and perhaps others (a few) on poetry. Individuals might be happiest if they divided their time among a variety of activities, staying with none beyond the point at which it was maximally enjoyable. For other purposes, we feel collectively better off with some people who are excellent at accounting and know nothing of poetry, or vice versa. Philip Slater (1968, 1970, 1974) has written eloquently on this issue and points out that the same process compels group members to specialize in the emotions they express and experience:

> One man learns to lose the capacity to respond to life situations with love, another man with anger, another with jealousy, another with tears, and so on. This process of emotional crippling we call personality development. Its possible side effect is the hypertrophy of other responses which permits a kind of emotional specialization within the group . . . In a culture in which a man cannot weep, his women may weep for him. If he is a group jester, there will be some dour compatriot to feel gloomy for him, and so on. (Slater, 1968, p. 80)

Thus Charles Darwin wistfully reports late in life that he has lost his taste for poetry. The fact that Darwin now has an exclusive preference for biology over poetry means that it is now psychologically rational for him never to read poetry. But we must not confuse cause and effect here, a question that will preoccupy us in the next chapter. Darwin became committed to biology before he lost his taste for poetry. The commitment to biology impelled him to choose thinking about biology even over other activities that might have struck him as more pleasurable. Only through the repeated exercise of this commitment, through what Slater might call the hypertrophy of the commitment, did Darwin find that other activities ceased to seem pleasurable. But for our accountant, whose commitment to accounting is less total or less absorbing, the marginal utility of gardening may remain permanently higher than the marginal utility of accounting.

Inferential rationality. Inferential rationality has perhaps been more widely studied by psychologists and philosophers than either of the other two. The question of how to draw valid conclusions or make valid inferences from observations is far from trivial and far from solved. Under certain circumstances, however, we can specify exactly how much evidence a person should require before making a decision. To do this, we have to know how much each bit of information costs and how much the person gains by making a correct decision or loses by making an incorrect one. We also need to know what the person's prior opinions were about the likelihood of various possible outcomes and exactly what the person learns from each possible observation. From these facts, statistical decision theory will give us a rule that a perfectly rational observer would follow in seeking evidence and arriving at a conclusion. It is easiest to satisfy these conditions in a laboratory experiment. For example, in one classic form of the experiment, subjects are told that a bag contains a mixture of red and green poker chips. Their task is to decide which chip occurs more frequently. They are told how much money they will win if they decide correctly. Subjects can see as many chips as they wish before deciding, but they know that it costs them a certain amount of money to see each chip. Usually, in this case, people have no prior opinion as to whether the red or the green chip is likely to be more frequent. Finally, what the person can learn from each observation is established by telling them exactly what proportion of the chips in the bag are the majority color. If the person knows that 99% of the chips in the bag are one color, a single observation is already a good clue as to what the majority color is. On the other hand, if the person is told that 51% of the chips in the bag are green and 49% are red, a single observation provides almost no information as to what the majority color is.

Many of the early experiments on inferential decision making were done by Ward Edward (1968) and his colleagues. Several of the experiments indicate that people tend to be somewhat cautious or conservative in revising their initial opinions on such tasks, as if they had developed some commitment to those initial guesses. More elegantly, we have a nice demonstration that people who are asked to begin by making an arbitrary guess as to which answer is correct are slower to arrive at the correct answer than people not asked to begin with such a guess and slower than a rational strategy would warrant. The experiment demonstrating this was done by Pruitt (1961). The only difference between it and the classic form of the experiment described previously is that subjects had to consider a sequence of red and green lights to decide which occurred more frequently rather than a sequence of red and green poker chips. In conditions under which subjects were asked to begin with an arbitrary guess, the correct answer was arranged to be the opposite of their guess. They could change their minds whenever they liked, but only once. Subjects who had not begun with an initial guess simply decided on either red or green when they liked, and their decisions were final. These two conditions are identical in their formal requirements for a good decision or the logic they call for from subjects. Under the circumstances of Pruitt's experiment, the optimal decision rule called for subjects in both conditions to wait for the difference between the number of times the red light and the green light had occurred to reach four and then to make a final decision for the color that had occurred more often. This was on the average how much information people required when they had not made an initial commitment. They required significantly more than this amount of information before they would change their initial guess. In short, more information is needed to change a decision than to make one. To this extent, commitment causes people to violate inferential rationality just as it causes them to violate minimax and marginal utility rationality. Furthermore, the initial commitment in this experiment was presumably not one subjects cared very much about. Consider how much stronger these effects might have been if instead of representing a preference for red or green the initial commitment represented a preference for one career or relationship over another.

Inferential rationality is closely related to problem-solving rationality in general. Probably no one would contest the fact that commitment to an incorrect or inefficient solution can make it harder for people to discover a correct or efficient solution than it would have been if they had no previous answer in mind. What is interesting is the subtle way in which this can occur, quite unnoticed by participants. Much of the research in this area has used the water jar test devised by Luchins (1942). The general goal in water jar problems is to figure out how to get a given amount of water in a particular jar. Water can be poured from one jar to another, but each jar, when used, must be filled to the top. For example, a person may be given a 10-gallon jar that is full of water and three empty jars—one 10-gallon jar, one 5-gallon jar, and one 1-gallon jar—with the goal of pouring water from jar to jar until there is exactly eight gallons of water in one of the jars. The solution is to first fill the five gallon jar and then use it to fill the gallon jar three times, each time emptying the contents back into the original 10-gallon jar. There are many variations of this problem, which is essentially a problem in basic arithmetic. Some of the variations require a long and complicated series of pours, whereas others can be solved with only one or two simple moves. If the initial problems require subjects to master a complex solution, it is then harder for them to recognize that a simple solution exists if such a solution becomes available on later problems. In a most ingenious experiment, Knight (1963) showed that this was not simply due to subjects' having learned a particular strategy but to the commitment they felt to that strategy as a function of the effort they had expended in mastering it. In the two conditions of Knight's experiment, only the first in a series of 21 problems differed, and even this problem did not differ in the formal rule (the number and sequence of moves) required to solve it. In one case, however, the arithmetic of the solution was easier than the other—the numbers could be added and subtracted in the subject's head. In the more difficult case, the addition and subtraction were less obvious and more likely to require a pencil and paper. The actual solution rule, however, was the same in both cases. Subjects who required more effort to discover the rule were less likely to abandon it in favor of a more efficient alternative solution when such a solution became available on later trials.

Commitment to a relationship or a society involves the violation of inferential rationality as well as the other forms of rationality. This violation occurs simply because the commitment entails people's accepting conclusions on trust, on faith, or on authority rather than on the basis of their own observations. People give such weight to others' opinions that their whole process of inference is distorted. There are no more dramatic experiments in social psychology than those that show the power of this effect. Many people will deny the evidence of their own senses that one line is longer than another if a group of their peers tells them that the shorter line is actually longer (Asch, 1951). People will deny the evidence of their senses telling them that they are inflicting traumatic and possibly fatal shock on another person if an experimenter tells them not to worry (Milgram, 1965). Now we all gain a great deal by accepting conclusions of a friend or a teacher rather than checking everything by our own experience; there are many things we could never experience directly, and even for those we can, our observations may be less reliable or insightful than those of others. Culture is essentially a device for transmitting to people information about events they have never experienced and may never experience themselves. But the general requirement that members of a society accept things on faith makes it inevitable that they will accept error as well as truth. Because membership in a group matters to people, members will swallow their doubts and proceed in a course of action that outsiders can clearly see is disastrous. How an intensified and misplaced sense of loyalty among presidential advisers got us involved in the Bay of Pigs and Watergate crisis is traced in detail by Irving Janis (1972) and Bert Raven (1974), respectively. To retain the perspective and the rationality of an outsider is to be an outsider. It is not what our friends, our spouses, and our country want from us.

In this section we have looked at the effects of commitment on rational information processing. We have compared the thought processes of committed actors both to those of uncommitted observers and to various ideal standards of rationality. We have not entered the larger debate over how well any rational model describes human behavior. We have aimed, instead, to establish a more limited principle. However rationality is judged, to whatever extent people are rational, they are less so following commitment. In the next section, we begin to build our understanding of what people gain from this sacrifice of rationality.

ACTION: EFFECTS OF COMMITMENT ON FUNCTIONAL BEHAVIOR

The aim of thought is action. From some perspectives, it is possible to imagine thought as a pleasure or a value in its own right. But it is not possible to imagine thinking as a capacity that would have been favored by evolution unless its exercise bestowed some behavioral advantage on individuals.

Rational Thought Versus Functional Behavior

Rational behavior, however, is not the same thing as rational thought. We may in the end wish to say that rationality is an idea that can be applied only to thought, not to behavior. Why? Because behavior that is not rational, behavior that is chosen on logically inadequate grounds or carried out with utter disregard for costs, can still be functional and effective for the actor. Indeed, it will be our contention that all behavior must to a degree be chosen on logically inadequate grounds and carried out with disregard for costs. The apparent blindness that follows commitment may be irrational and still a precondition for effective action. In understanding this, we may wish to say that a different criterion must be employed in judging behavior than in judging thought. The criterion for behavior is that it be functional—carried out successfully, with desirable consequences for the actor. The question then becomes, To what extent is rational thought the friend or the enemy of functional behavior?

The essential conflict between rational thought and functional behavior can be put very simply. Rational thought requires the consideration of all available alternatives. Effective action requires the pursuit of one alternative, not necessarily the best one, and the ignoring or suppressing of the others. Decisions must be made and actions taken even if there are arguments on both sides of the issue. Before making a decision, a person may be in a state of conflict as he or she weighs the pros and cons of the different alternatives, and indeed it may be advantageous for a person, before making the decision, to experience the conflict between alternatives as clearly and sharply as possible. With a balanced consideration of the pros and cons of each alternative, people can feel more strongly that they are making a free choice (Brehm, 1972) and be more likely to make a correct choice (Janis & Mann, 1977). Once the choice is made, however, there is little to be gained by dwelling on the advantages of the rejected alternative or the disadvantages of the chosen alternative. Action is more effective when wholehearted than halfhearted, when sustained rather than interrupted or distracted, and a cognitive process that facilitated enthusiastic action would have obvious advantages. I believe this analysis contradicts Aristotle's famous doctrine of the golden mean, if that mean is the compromise between vigorous opposing tendencies; instead, we would expect in nature a principle of the golden bimode, in which either of the opposing tendencies wholeheartedly pursued would be preferable to a weakly pursued compromise. An animal can either fight, hide, or run away, but if it tries to do more than one of these at the same time (because all of them offer some advantages), it is likely to do none of them very well and to be eaten, to its clear evolutionary detriment.

So long as the ecology of the environment favors action over inaction, it will also favor decisive action over indecisive action. It will favor acting on probabilistic information (the only kind the environment offers) as if it were deterministic information, or beliefs that are only relatively true as if they were absolutely true. Commitment to a line of action will then have value as a cybernetic mechanism that causes the individual to resist distraction while that line of action is pursued. A dissonance reduction process that enhances the value of chosen alternatives and the Zeigarnik effect—whereby attention is focused on tasks that have been started but not completed (Van Bergen, 1968)—will both serve this end. In functional terms, following Ainslie's (1975) analysis, we might even characterize the aversion to dissonance as coming from the individual's fear of regret. In this sense, dissonance reduction becomes simply one more means by which an organism seeks to overcome obstacles to the attainment of its end (cf. Asch, 1958), but in this case the obstacles are internal to the organism (a function of its own ambivalence) rather than in the external environment.

Actions under conditions of uncertainty.   Jones and Gerard (1967) have a nice analysis of action under conditions of uncertainty that makes many of these same points.

> As he stands on the threshold of action the individual cannot both act and not act; and if he decides to act, he cannot act in mutually exclusive ways. Unlike the state of affairs that sometimes obtains in a dream—when dream characters are sometimes in two places at once, when actions can be undone and great distances covered in split seconds—actions in reality must come to terms with the limiting properties of the environment. In short, whatever the nature of the conflict, indecision, or playful rumination that precedes action, the action itself is squeezed through the eye of the decisional needle and, for better or worse, its effects inexorably follow. . . .
> Many action situations involve discrete, mutually exclusive alternatives and the opportunities for compromise are absent. The boy with a nickel must choose the licorice or the jaw-breaker; he cannot have both or half of each. The voter may feel conflicted and in doubt, but must filter this conflict through an unequivocal choice in the voting booth. The high school senior must choose a college out of those that accept him and are within his budget. He cannot combine the good features of each in a new, compromise blend. And the discreteness of behavioral alternatives requires unequivocal action, which in turn sets up pressures that reach back to affect attitudes and cognitions.
> We have now arrived at the nub of the argument. It is this reaching-back process that ties attitudinal consistency to the requirements of behavior. As the individual presses toward an *unequivocal behavior orientation* (UBO), it becomes adaptive to bring his relevant cognitions and values into harmony with each other. . . . When the time comes to act, the great advantage of having a set of coherent internally consistent dispositions is that the individual is not forced to listen to the babble of competing inner voices. (pp. 179–181)

Not everyone is happy with the idea that people must achieve an unequivocal behavior orientation, even given the understanding that one's orientation at one point in time need not be the same as one's orientation at another point in time. F. Scott Fitzgerald wrote, "The test of a first rate intelligence is to hold two opposed ideas in your mind at the same time and still retain your capacity to function." Charles Hampden-Turner, who quotes Fitzgerald with approval in his "Presidential Address to the Association for Humanistic Psychology," argues that human integrity "consists of just such cross-grained laminations, wherein levels of contrary values are compressed with great potential strength." I am in sympathy with the idea that we contain within ourselves a far greater diversity and even opposition of forces than we ordinarily imagine. But I think this diversity enhances, rather than reduces, the need for a psychological mechanism to generate unconflicted action.

Others who would be unhappy with this thesis include students of human performance who contend that people can do more than one thing at the same time, even if both demand attention, provided that they do not involve incompatible responses or an undue degree of complexity. Even if this is true, it only qualifies rather than refutes our thesis, because it is still not possible to both do something (cross the street) and not do it (not cross the street) at the same time. It appears that what Ulric Neisser (1963) calls multiple processing is a larger component of human performance than many people have previously believed. For example, Neisser has demonstrated that people can learn to scan an array of symbols for any of ten different targets just as fast as they can scan it for a single target. People can not only track one voice or one visual stimulus and tune out other, secondary stimuli that are equally loud or vivid, but they can also learn over time to detect features of the secondary stimuli while still tracking the primary one (Neisser, 1976). Nonetheless, by far the majority of instances in which people do two things at once are instances in which one of the activities has been so well learned that it no longer requires much attention. For example, most people drive and talk at the same time. Both driving and talking are overlearned skills. But if the driving becomes difficult or the conversation becomes challenging—if something unexpected happens in either one—the person will find it hard to respond to that unexpectedness and still keep the other activity going even on an automatic level. Hopefully, in the case of driving and talking, the person suspends thoughtful conversation (or even automatic conversation) rather than careful driving.

Clearly, there is individual difference in people's ability to do two things at once. We are amazed that some people can type and talk at the same time whereas others, according to political legend, cannot walk and chew gum at the same time. At some level, however, the requirements of focused activity, if not focused awareness, govern us all. This can be called channel capacity and seen as a limitation on the ability of human actors to cope with their environment. Or it can be called a capacity for commitment and for focused attention and seen as a special device actors have evolved to help them deal with both their external and their internal environments. At some levels this is a very special skill that people undergo arduous physical training and spiritual exercises to acquire, as in some forms of meditation. At other levels it is built into everyone in the form of inhibitory branches of the nervous system that block out competing input or enhance the contrast between the central stimulus and peripheral stimuli once a behavior sequence has been initiated. Once a cat has begun to stalk a mouse, it no longer registers sounds that would otherwise have caught its attention (Hernandez-Peon, Scherrer, & Jouvet, 1956).

"Thinking does not endow us directly with the power to act," wrote Martin Heidegger. How then do we get from thought to action? How do we get from a process that creates doubt and multiplicity to one that requires certainty and simplicity? This event has to some extent been the missing link in our understanding of the genesis of behavior. Critics of cognitive psychology first made this point against Tolman's (1932) conception of animals calculating the expected value of different alternatives at a choice point. The question is, How do animals stop doing the mental arithmetic of balancing probabilities and get on with the action? What prevents them from remaining lost in thought at the choice point, especially if the alternatives are complex or equal in value? All general theories of behavior require both a cognitive component, to explain the individual's sensitivity to variations in the information it receives from the environment, and a motivational component, to explain why the individual bothers being sensitive in the first place. The problem has always been in linking the two systems. The answer is commitment, which takes over at a certain point and thereafter runs interference against all but the tendency the individual has decided to enact.

Simple rules and complex decisions. To arrive faster at the point of being able to act, people may pass over or short-circuit a portion of the rational thought process. In other words, people may simplify their perceptions not only to enforce or justify a decision they have made but in order to make a decision in the first place. James March and Herbert Simon (1958) elaborated this point in their influential distinction between "optimizing" and "satisficing" as two modes of decision making. Models of rational thinking assume that decision makers are out to make optimal decisions, to compare the entire set of possible alternatives and select the best one. Most human decisions, according to March and Simon, are only aimed at finding a satisfactory alternative. This is any alternative that meets certain specified criteria, even though there may be far better alternatives as yet undiscovered. "To optimize requires processes several orders of magnitude more complex than those required to satisfice. An example is the difference between searching a haystack to find the *sharpest* needle in it and searching the haystack to find a needle sharp enough to sew with" (p. 141).

The enormously exciting work on cognitive heuristics by Amos Tversky and Daniel Kahneman (1974) is largely the enumeration of specific simple rules people use to make complex decisions. One, for example, is the principle of availability. If people are asked whether more words in the English language begin with the letter *k* or end with *k*, they are apt to say that more begin with *k*. It is easier to think of examples of words that begin with *k* than examples that end with *k*. In fact, many more words end with *k* than begin with *k*. In this case, the greater availability of the beginnings of words leads to an incorrect decision; this is a particularly powerful way of demonstrating the existence of an availability heuristic. Nonetheless, the decision made by employing the availability heuristic is probably made a good deal faster than would a decision made by a laborious process of generating an unbiased sample of words and counting how many began and ended with *k*. If people rely primarily on easily available information, it must be that the speed with which this allows them to make decisions ordinarily compensates for the marginal or occasional loss of accuracy.

In a related vein, Tversky (1972) described how people can make choices following a procedure of elimination by aspects. For example, in choosing a car, prospective buyers first take their most important criterion and eliminate all makes of car that fail to meet this criterion. They then take a second criterion and eliminate those remaining cars that fail to meet this criterion. They continue in this fashion until all cars are eliminated except one. The problem with the procedure, as Tversky points out, is that the final choice of car may be determined by a relatively unimportant attribute. A car with a more favorable overall combination of attributes might be chosen if people followed a more complex and rational procedure of making comparisons on a number of dimensions simultaneously and arranging the most favorable set of trade-offs. However, elimination by aspects guarantees a choice that is satisfactory, even if it reduces the chances of one that is optimal. Once again, rationality is sacrificed for a functional procedure that makes information more manageable and a decision more easily reached.

Under some circumstances, people deliberately seek out nonrational grounds for making a decision just for the sake of having it made, even if they know that better alternatives are potentially available. This is nicely illustrated by the three-party bargaining situation studied by Hoffman, Festinger, and Lawrence (1954). A given stake, say $100, is available to any two of the three who agree to form a coalition and agree on how to divide the $100 between them. Let us suppose an initial coalition forms in which each party is to receive $50. What can the excluded third person do to break this coalition? Offer one of the parties a more generous share in a new coalition, say $60, while the formerly excluded party settles for a share of $40. What can the person who is now excluded do to break the new coalition? Offer a better deal to the party who is disadvantaged within the coalition—that is, a coalition in which that party will receive $50 instead of $40. This process can in theory continue endlessly, since there is no stable rational solution. In fact it does not, as the exchange process becomes tiring, deadlines approach, and parties find other grounds on which to make a commitment. We simulate at least some of the dynamics of pair formation in general if we imagine this situation as an N-person game in which different dyads may also have somewhat different total stakes to divide depending upon what each brings to the relationship. Even if one has found a highly attractive partner or made a favorable bargain, there will be third parties who can offer a more advantageous bargain to one partner or the other. In such a free market, commitment thus always involves the surrender of potentially more desirable possibilities. In this sense commitment itself may become the most valuable token in the exchange between partners (cf. Berscheid, Walster, & Bohrnstedt, 1973). But there is no rational basis for believing that a given partnership is the best possible one or for ending one's search with anything more selective than a flip of a coin.

Even if a decision is arrived at after careful thought and is in fact the best possible decision, there will still be arguments against the chosen alternative and in favor of some rejected possibility. These thoughts can inhibit or paralyze action, which proceeds best when there are no objections remaining to be overcome. As Henry Kissinger said, "The absence of alternatives clears the mind marvelously. Major progress is therefore likely." The essence of our argument at this point is that commitment marshals forces that destroy the plausibility of alternatives and remove their ability to inhibit action. These forces are nonrational, though their use is functional. They facilitate action but reduce the actor's sensitivity to information. Reason is what Freud called a secondary mental process. Action proceeds on the basis of primary mental processes, which are impulsive, instinctual, or emotional. The conversion of thought into action is the conversion of a weak secondary process into a strong primary one, the alliance of the forces of reason with the forces of unreason. We may choose our actions in the first place on the rational basis of their standing in our informational system, but we drive them, energize them, and justify them on the nonrational basis of our motivational commitment to them. Donald Campbell (1960) has argued that the creative process involved in finding solutions to problems is essentially one of blind variation and selective retention—considering many possible alternatives whose virtues cannot be foreseen and retaining the best. I am arguing that the behavioral process involved in enacting a solution takes exactly the opposite form: selective variation and blind retention. After solutions are selectively varied and considered, the chosen one is enacted blindly, oblivious to distracting alternatives, as if it were not only the best but the perfect one. There is no reason, of course, that periods of rational consideration and coercive enactment might not proceed in sequence. In one phase people would be aware of many alternatives, in the next phase, few or none. The important point, however, is that the two processes cannot proceed simultaneously: what takes place in one phase in part determines the content of what can occur in the next period of thought or behavior.

Commitment and Arousal

So far we have not differentiated between commitment and another, simpler notion in psychology: arousal. Arousal refers to the general level of activation or excitement experienced by an individual. As a general source of energy, arousal motivates all the individual's tendencies to respond across the board, however incompatible these might be. The stronger these tendencies are initially, however, the more they benefit from arousal. In the language of drive theory, arousal energizes dominant responses and makes them both more forceful and more likely to occur than they would have been in the absence of the arousal. For example, consider a person who has been asked to say the first thing that comes to mind after hearing the word "chair." The common, dominant response is "table." But there are many other less common responses that can be considered either bizarre or creative. People can be asked to reply either under aroused conditions, in which they feel that they are being tested, observed, and evaluated, or under relaxed conditions, in which they do not feel threatened or excited. Under aroused conditions, they are more likely to say "table" and more likely to say it without hesitation. Although other possible responses were also excited by the arousal, the net effect of exciting all the person's response tendencies was to leave the initially dominant tendency with a much greater lead over all the others. This is the principle employed by army basic training exercises that make recruits repeat over and over again a few simple actions. The idea is that the undifferentiated arousal—not to say panic—of combat will call forth these overlearned habits rather than other responses that might be more creative but would typically be less appropriate. Thus, it seems that arousal, like commitment, can facilitate action. What is the difference? What advantages, if any, does the concept of commitment have over the concept of arousal?

Commitment as a means of reducing conflict among choices.   The first, essential difference is that arousal can facilitate the enactment only of tendencies that are initially dominant. Commitment can facilitate the enactment of tendencies that are not initially dominant. While commitment and arousal may both be blind in their unfolding, commitment, unlike arousal, is selective in its choice of what to unfold. Indeed, the making dominant of a behavioral tendency that is initially non-dominant through the overcoming of resisting forces is sometimes seen as the special property of psychological commitment. Thus Kurt Lewin (1951) wrote that *"only when there is no natural need for* an action, or when there is a counter-need, *is it necessary to form an intention"* (p. 113). Deci (1980) reviews evidence that both William James and Jean Piaget used the concept of will to describe specific decisions to behave in a certain way despite thoughts that oppose this behavior. I do not wish to imply that intention, will, and commitment are all the same thing. An intention is not yet a commitment, and the concept of will may or may not be necessary to an understanding of how people make commitments. But it is clear that all three concepts are concerned with an important problem in the determination of behavior—how a tendency to action overcomes opposing forces. The fact that this central focus of commitment is also a concern of other common terms in social psychology suggests that with commitment we are dealing with a fundamental issue.

The idea of commitment as a device for enforcing choices when they are not dominant has been elaborated in greatest detail by George Ainslie (1975) in his review of research on impulsiveness and impulse control. Ainslie is especially concerned with the problem of how individuals resist making choices that are tempting in the short run but undesirable for them in the long run. There are two particularly interesting features to Ainslie's analysis. The first is that commitments are important primarily at certain times, when the immediate consequences of an action are receiving more weight than they should relative to more serious but more remote consequences. Once the point of temptation has been passed, commitment may no longer be essential for keeping the individual on the chosen course of action. The second feature is dramatic evidence that animals other than humans make commitments in the service of controlling their impulses. Pigeons can be given a choice between a small reward that is immediately available and a larger reward that requires the pigeon to wait briefly. When the pigeon has a direct choice between these rewards, it almost always chooses the smaller but immediately available reward. Rachlin and Green (1972), however, have shown that if given the choice long enough in advance, pigeons will peck a key whose only function is to keep the tempting but smaller reward from becoming available. Pecking the prior key to eliminate this alternative may be seen as a form of impulse control or as a commitment to the larger delayed reward.

In general, there is little need to speak of people committing themselves to actions that can be justified simply by how rewarding they are relative to other possible actions. People can trust themselves to perform such rewarding actions without making commitments. Commitment in Ainslie's sense is a device for supplying extra motivation for actions that cannot be justified simply by how rewarding they are. In Ainslie's analysis, the extra motivation is generally supplied through the rearrangment of external contingencies so that the person stands to lose more by not performing the action than by performing it. This allows Ainslie to relate his more general treatment to an earlier and highly influential discussion of commitment by Thomas Schelling (1960). To use one of Schelling's examples, a person can commit him- or herself to winning a game of chicken, a game in which two parties are headed for a collision (e.g., two automobiles heading toward each other down the middle of a road) that will be disastrous for both of them unless one changes course. A person can commit him- or herself to winning by tearing the steering wheel off the car, thus making it impossible to change course. The person should also wave the inoperative steering wheel at the oncoming other car to communicate this commitment to the other. In this case the person has literally bet his or her life on winning. (Black humor permits us the vision of two people tearing down the road toward each other, each waving a steering wheel.) In many societies people commit themselves to doing some difficult task by taking an oath that invokes the help of a sacred deity. If they do not then carry out the act, they expect to lose not only the good will of that sacred entity but also the good will of the rest of the community, who would also expect to suffer from the spirit's wrath at having had its name taken in vain. In general, if people want to protect against a change of mind, they act to make changing their mind even more costly than persevering in the fulfillment of an unrewarding promise.

In addition to external contingencies, the extra motivation for a costly act can also be supplied through the rearrangement of internal contingencies so that the person comes to see the act as more intrinsically valuable, the costs as less burdensome, or the alternatives as less desirable than they initially seemed. Ainslie (1975) does not in general discuss these possibilities for altered perception, thus omitting a large part of the universe of commitment devices. Furthermore, these internal mechanisms suggest a second essential difference between commitment and arousal. Only commitment can reduce the ambivalence or inhibitions associated with a response. Arousal can intensify a response, increasing its speed and vigor, but it also intensifies whatever forces oppose that response. Commitment can dissolve these opposing forces by altering the way the individual sees and experiences them. After a commitment has been made, however, the tendency anchored by that commitment will continue to operate even in quiet periods because formerly opposing tendencies have been rationalized or reduced. If we assume that action is generally more effective without ambivalence and also that there is some ambivalence associated even with dominant habits, then it follows that commitment to reduce this ambivalence will be useful even if arousal alone would be sufficient to generate the behavior. In this we differ from Kiesler (1971, p. 39), who seems to assume that there will be nothing disturbing for people in performing an act that is consonant with their beliefs. There are costs associated even with actions people have fully rehearsed and believe in, and it is the role of commitment to reduce these costs.

If a major function of commitment is to reduce potentially paralyzing conflicts between alternatives of nearly equal strength, we would expect to see the psychological effects of making or not making a commitment most dramatically at work in cases in which the initial values of the alternatives are most nearly equal.

This appears to be the case. Brehm (1959) and Watts (1966) both found that a chosen alternative comes to be seen as especially valuable following a choice in which the rejected course of action initially appeared almost as good as the chosen course. We would also expect that the absence of commitment or failure of commitment to occur would be most serious when the two action tendencies are most nearly equal in strength, and this too appears to be the case. Neurosis may be thought of as a special case of a failure of commitment to enforce an effective choice. In a famous series of experiments, Pavlov was able to produce what he called experimental neurosis in dogs by requiring the animals to choose between two stimuli (an ellipse and a circle) that were gradually made more and more similar until an effective discrimination of the right from the wrong choice was impossible. Under these circumstances, the dogs exhibited severe signs of stress and an understandable reluctance to make any choice at all. Masserman (1943, 1971) was able to produce disturbed and conflicted behavior in cats by shocking them when they ate, thus making it hard for the hungry cats to decide whether to approach or avoid food. Neurotic behavior in humans clearly embodies some form of unresolved conflict, though perhaps not precisely of the form in the Pavlov or Masserman experiments. The patient both desires and fears something, like sex, and can neither approach sufficiently to get rid of the fear nor move away sufficiently to get rid of the desire. Hamlet, whose neurotic conflict is perhaps the most famous in all literature, found that:

> Thus conscience does make cowards of us all,
> And thus the native hue of resolution
> Is sicklied o'er with the pale cast of thought,
> And enterprises of great pith and moment
> With this regard their currents turn awry
> And lose the name of action.

In a Freudian explanation of neurosis, one of the elements (either the fear or the desire) is repressed or unconscious (in Hamlet's case, some of his feelings for his mother). Thus, the patient cannot even understand why it does not seem possible to reach a satisfactory accommodation with the conscious element. The fact that the rejected alternative is repressed may be in turn what keeps dissonance reduction from working to devalue it and make it less potent. Erik Erikson (1950) considers unconflicted energy to be the basic state of psychic well-being. If commitment is essential for unconflicted energy, it is thus also essential for psychic well-being.

Not only can commitment serve to reduce a conflict that interferes with action, it can also reduce the unpleasant emotional arousal caused by having too many alternatives or alternatives that are too complex and stimulating in their variety of good and bad features and incompatible demands (Eysenck, 1955; Sales, Guydosh, & Iacono, 1974). By making a choice between two people who are each liked by the individual but who dislike each other (e.g., a girlfriend and a roommate) and devaluing the rejected alternative, the individual may balance his interpersonal relations, making it easier for him to cope with them and reducing the tension associated with them (Brickman & Horn, 1973). If the choice is made with sufficient certainty and clarity, the person can not only act on it but put the matter out of mind and proceed without giving it further thought. Amos Tversky and Daniel Kahneman have recently collected dramatic evidence (see, e.g., Kahneman & Tversky, 1979) of how much people are willing to pay to obtain such psychological certainty. For example, subjects may be told they hold a ticket with a 99% chance of winning $100 and then given an opportunity to sell that ticket in return for getting the $100 as a sure thing (i.e., having a 100% chance of winning the $100). Objectively, the additional 1% chance of winning the $100 is worth only an additional $1. In fact, subjects are willing to pay vastly more than $1 to turn their near certainty of winning into a complete certainty. Obviously, it is worth a good deal to them to get rid of even the residual uncertainty associated with holding only a 99% chance of winning. Subjects are required to think about the undesirable alternative if it has even a small probability of occurring. They are willing to pay substantially to be able to stop thinking about it entirely.

Mindlessness versus single-mindedness. This clearly shades over into the more general argument made by Ellen Langer (1978) that people prefer to enact behavior that can be performed without conscious attention, because such attention requires effort and is often either unnecessary or actually a source of interference. Langer quotes Whitehead with approval:

> By relieving the brain of all unnecessary work, a good rotation sets it free to concentrate on more advanced problems, and in effect increases the mental powers of the race. . . . It is a profoundly erroneous truism, repeated by all copy-books and by eminent people making speeches, that we should cultivate the habit of thinking of what we are doing. The precise opposite is the case. Civilization advances by extending the number of operations which we can perform without thinking about them. Operations of thought are like cavalry charges in battle—they are strictly limited in number, they require fresh horses, and must only be made at decisive moments. (p. 40)

At this point it seems necessary to draw a distinction between mindlessness (Langer's term) and single-mindedness. Both mindless and single-minded activity involve a form of commitment, and both differ from the kind of thoughtful, open, evenhanded behavior we posit as ideally rational. But the form, the location, and purpose of the commitment is quite different in the two cases. In mindless behavior, the commitment may be thought of as out of conscious awareness. Indeed, the behavioral sequence is organized, simplified, and automated precisely in order to let it unroll without making demands on focal attention. In single-minded behavior, the commitment may be thought of as dominating conscious awareness. Here the point of the commitment is to sustain awareness of the activity as the focus of attention to the exclusion of all possible irrelevant or distracting stimuli. Both forms of commitment have the advantages for action that we have been discussing, but in rather different ways. Commitments outside of consciousness proceed oblivious to distractions, provided that the distractions do not actually interrupt the sequence and force it into conscious attention. It is in fact generally held to be a property of activity that takes place outside of focal awareness that a variety of weakly organized and even inconsistent streams of thought can occur without being experienced as inconsistent or incompatible (Neisser, 1963). Intolerance of inconsistency is a characteristic of conscious awareness, not activity outside of consciousness. Thus a person can continue a mindless commitment to driving while conscious attention is elsewhere (on conversation) and other activities are taking place outside of awareness (breathing, a mulling over of something else in the back of his or her mind)—provided that nothing occurs in any of these other domains to interrupt the flow of driving. At a deeper level, a person can have an unconscious commitment to a lost loved one even while focal attention is elsewhere (on current others in the person's life), and other impulses toward that lost love quite incompatible with the first (anger or resentment) also exist outside of awareness. While their imperviousness to apparent contradiction makes mindless commitments maximally efficient, it also makes them maximally vulnerable to looking foolish or becoming a source of tension when relevant circumstances change unnoticed by the person. Moreover, being out of mind, the operation of the commitment itself is inaccessible to ordinary awareness. For example, I am committed to seeing that the house is closed up before retiring to bed at night. This is a highly routinized commitment—so routinized, in fact, that I find it impossible to remember whether I have done it or not. Unlike brushing one's teeth, this is an activity whose completion one wants to be able to remember, so it must be arranged in some special way so as to force it into consciousness. In this case, the solution is simply to do it as the last thing before going upstairs; that is, to do it at the very point at which one wants to remember having done it. If I try doing it earlier in the evening, it is hopeless. I can never be sure whether I have done it or not when it is time to go upstairs.

Single-minded commitments gain the advantages of action in a different way. They accumulate relevance rather than discard it. Everything is interpreted in the light of the focal commitment. Neisser (1976) distinguishes between a selective attention that occurs because there is active filtering or tuning out of competing stimuli and a selective attention that occurs because there is no sensitivity to or processing of the competing stimuli in the first place. The selectivity of the single-minded commitment is akin to the filtering process. The selectivity of the mindless commitment is akin to the idea of insensitivity. Making a single-minded commitment is like donning a pair of tinted glasses that allow in only light whose frequency can pass through the material of the glasses. But such glasses do not merely eliminate our attention to light of other wavelengths. They also call our attention to features of the environment that now stand out and that might otherwise have been ignored. In other words, they expand our range of awareness as well as narrowing it. If I can commit myself to writing a paper a year or so before it is due—ideally by doing a first draft or at least an outline, however crude—it is amazing to me how many things I come across in the intervening time that appear to be relevant to that paper. Too often we do not allow ourselves this lead time and instead notice how many things are relevant to our topic only after we have written and sent in our paper. This is a special case of the more commonly noted phenomenon whereby once we have our attention called to some unusual name or event, other instances of or references to that name seem to be all around us in the days that follow. Unlike mindless commitments, single-minded commitments are accessible to reflection and analysis, but have their own kinds of costs. People are not only prone to see everything as relevant to their commitment, but, as we have seen, prone to see things as favorable rather than unfavorable to it. Moreover, in the pursuit of this commitment, they are likely to ignore entirely costs and dangers in other areas of concern.

Irrational Behavior and
Social Relationships

Extreme or irrational behavior may also be functional because people reinforce us for engaging in such behavior. I do not mean here simply that people reinforce us for making commitments that they approve of, for the net effect of this would be canceled by their punishing us for making commitments that they disapprove of. I mean that people reinforce us for making commitments, in a certain fashion, whether they like or dislike what they regard as our extreme behavior. They reinforce us with their attention. To quote Goethe, "If a man gives me his opinion, let him express it positively. I have enough ambiguity within myself." Simonton (1976) has shown that the most famous figures in intellectual history are those who are associated with the consistent and extreme maintenance of a particular point of view. Those who present their case in more sensible and balanced terms are often ignored. The strategy of extremity is of course not without risks, but what is not always realized is that these are in good measure the risks of visibility and attention itself. One cannot be visible without attracting criticism as well as support, and those made too uncomfortable by criticism will prefer to remain largely invisible.

Role specialization within dyads. Role specialization within relationships, according to Slater (1977), typically involves transforming a trait that was initially possessed to some degree by both parties into one that is suppressed by one member and developed to an exaggerated degree by the other. Each party thereby gains the ability to express certain traits without ambivalence and to renounce others entirely. Moreover, both parties also gain a vicarious satisfaction from having their suppressed impulses expressed so strongly and forcefully by their partners. The cost, as with all commitment, is that people may lose sensitivity to or even awareness of alternatives and may expend considerable energy working to sustain the commitment if it does not become a natural part of themselves.

> If both husband and wife are eager and able storytellers, the most eager is likely to develop the skill to new heights, while the other permits it to atrophy. A new husband may abandon his bachelorhood culinary skills, or he may accentuate them and become the "fancy cook". . . . Gradually the traits and

abilities are sorted out and assigned . . . and eventually achieving an almost stereotypic rigidity. ("He's the smart one of the family.") . . . Widowhood and divorce often produce what appear to be startling personality changes. . . . A retiring, dependent wife becomes competent and forceful upon losing a dominant husband, while the dour spouse of a vivacious woman reveals a humorous facet when separated from her. . . .

Specialization, up to a point, reduces the amount of energy that is needed to maintain the solidarity of a relationship. The more interaction is ritualized through specialization, the more predictable it becomes, and . . . the less competition will occur. . . .

But individual human beings cannot permanently shed their overlapping characteristics . . . but instead suppress them with difficulty. And if the difficulty is too great, the energy saved in the interaction *between* the couple may be spent in maintaining *internal* balances. Furthermore, we must not assume that specialization eliminates discord since a division of labor often produces ritualized conflict: The expressive wife complains that the controlled husband is too cold while he complains that she is too temperamental. (Slater, 1977, 166, 168–169)

Conformity and group polarization. If social arrangements often call for people to commit themselves to different behaviors, they also require people to make a common commitment to the relationship or the society itself. Indeed, the specialized roles are justified and sustained in the first place by all parties' more general commitment to the collectivity. One party agrees to be dour and one vivacious because both value the relationship and see these differences as necessary to sustain it. An enormous volume of literature in social psychology has arisen to describe the mechanisms by which groups overcome their ambivalence and produce or enforce agreement among members on a desired course of action. This is, of course, the literature on conformity. Early classic work by Leon Festinger and his colleagues (Festinger, 1950) showed that the flow of communication in a discussion group would center around an opinion deviate as other members tried to convince the deviate of his error. Recent work has uncovered the especially interesting phenomenon that the opinion of group members following discussion is typically more extreme than the average opinion of group members before discussion. Members might all favor, for example, a certain candidate, but after discussion they are more strongly in favor of the candidate than they were before discussion. Because this was first demonstrated by dramatic studies showing that groups make riskier decisions than individuals (contrary to the stereotype of the conservative committee), the phenomenon was initially called the risky shift. It has subsequently been shown that groups can also shift their members' opinions in other directions, however, so it seems more appropriate to call it a general group polarization phenomenon. The history of this research is nicely reviewed by Cartwright (1974), and a catalogue of results and alternative interpretations is provided by Myers and Lamm (1976). Polarization can be both swift and subtle. Around issues concerning outsiders, polarization can be produced by the simple act of categorizing people as members of an arbitrary group (Tajfel, 1970). Much of the formal machinery of government—legislative, executive, and judicial—is implicitly designed to turn a narrow majority in favor of an action into the appearance of an overwhelming mandate for the action.

A law may be favored by only a narrow majority of people (or even by a minority, especially if the law is determined by the judiciary), but everyone is expected to obey it. A candidate elected by only a narrow majority of people (or even by a minority, as in the case of Abraham Lincoln) has the same authority of office as a candidate elected by a landslide.

The computational and political processes that exaggerate the apparent strength of majority sentiment have been criticized because they often are unrepresentative and exert coercive pressure on minority opinions (Davis, Kerr, Atkin, Holt, & Meek, 1975). From our perspective, however, they are fundamental to the problem of social action. In a famous theorem, Kenneth Arrow (1951) demonstrated that under certain reasonable conditions, it would be impossible to combine the individual preferences of members of a group in such a way that yielded an unambiguous ordering of alternatives for the group as a whole. This is clearly an unacceptable position for a group or a society to find itself in. Thus groups must routinely violate one or more of Arrow's reasonable assumptions in order to ensure an unequivocal choice. One of the easiest assumptions to relax is that there are more than two choices and that people can express a preference for more than one alternative—that is, that they can order at least three alternatives by how much they prefer each of them. Thus, as a preliminary to making binding decisions, groups typically simplify things by reducing the number of alternatives to two or by allowing members to vote only for their more preferred alternative, rather than ranking all alternatives. These simplifications are not in a strict sense violations of rationality, but they are clearly limitations of the domain in which individual choice is allowed to operate. By not allowing the full range of individuals' preferences to serve as input into a collective decision, these simplifications will often make the collective decision a less perfect or less faithful representation of members' preferences. A less than perfect group decision is preferable to a process that is cumbersome and time-consuming and might result in no decision at all. In this sense, collectivities depart from social rationality in order to make social decisions in much the same spirit as individuals departing from individual rationality in order to make personal decisions.

Leadership. No one has thought harder about the problem of turning social thought into social action than the men who first claimed that revolution was a science and who dedicated their lives to the study of its strategy and tactics. These were, of course, Lenin and Trotsky. Arthur Stinchcombe (1983) notes that both Lenin and Trotsky paid great attention to popular sentiment and indeed had "nothing but contempt for people who would try to run a revolution without the analysis of voting statistics." For support of this statement, Stinchcombe refers to several parts of Trotsky's *History of the Russian Revolution*, which he then notes makes it clear that these statistics are not to be interpreted in a bourgeois-democratic sense:

> If a referendum could have been taken on the question of insurrection, it would have given extremely contradictory and uncertain results. An inner readiness to support a revolution is far from identical with an ability to formulate the necessity of it. . . . The difference in level and mood of the differ-

ent layers of the people is overcome in action. The advance layers bring after them the wavering and isolate the opposing. The majority is not counted up, but won over. (pp. 177–178)

Clearly, the role of the advance layers of the revolution, including the revolutionary intelligentsia, is to set in motion a process that transforms sentiment into action and in turn creates further sentiment for the action. The science of revolution is knowing the conditions under which this process can be set in motion. The art or practice of revolution is knowing what to do to set it in motion. Revolution is especially interesting because it clearly involves transforming a minority impulse into a domain impulse, or transforming the status quo. In this sense, the art and science of revolution may be not unlike the art and science of knowing when and how to make resolutions that will effectively change one's personal habits.

The process of suppressing or convincing minority opinion in the service of social action creates stresses and strains in the group. Leaders, in winning support for their actions, also generate some resentment even among those who are initially or in the end moderately favorable toward the actions. A precondition for continued effective action by the group is that these ill feelings be expressed and dissipated or worked through. Understanding this led Robert Freed Bales (1958) to his influential proposition that there were two kinds of leadership, task leadership and social-emotional leadership. Bales felt that the skills required for being an effective task leader, like pushing for action and being a good talker, were to some extent contradictory to the skills required for being an effective social-emotional leader. If a group has only one leader, however, it seems clear that the leader must display both task and social-emotional leadership, polarizing and depolarizing leadership, leadership concerned with vigorous action and leadership concerned with thoughtful reflection.

In sum, when we consider both thought and action, the question of human rationality takes on a degree of ambiguity that may be overlooked when either thought or action is considered alone. Commitment may produce less rational thought and more rational behavior. This implies that there may be different standards for determining the rationality of a particular decision or a particular sequence of decisions. It would seem that deciding which standard to employ, or how much weight to give each standard, would be difficult but not impossible. In fact, I think it may be impossible, with the rationality of a sequence becoming over time inherently ambiguous or indeterminate. It is to this issue that we now turn.

THE AMBIGUITY OF RATIONALITY

Are People Rational?

Choices can and should be rational. Commitment is a process superimposed on potentially rational choice, not a process replacing it. It follows that because some choices are better or more rational than others, some commitments (those built on better choices) are better than others, and some people will know better than others how and when to make commitments. Even if commitment itself cannot be rationally justified, this does not mean that commitment to any old belief, any course of action, or any old relationship is as good as commitment to any other belief, action, or relationship (although it may be argued that even commitment to any old belief is better than no choice and no commitment). Being rational, as noted earlier, means choosing the best possible alternative. A key issue in rationality is thus whether people are aware of their alternatives and aware of their reasons for choosing one above the others. Whether or not people are actually or typically rational in this sense is a long-standing issue in psychology. The dominant assumption of the field seems to have changed at least four times in the last hundred years. The early introspectionists assumed that people were aware of their choices and their reasons and could give a direct account of them. With the coming of Freud and psychoanalysis, the dominant forces in human behavior were seen as irrational and out of awareness. Watson and the behaviorists, who took over academic psychology at this time, shared the disinterest of psychoanalysis in the contents of consciousness. The rise of computer models of decision making and theories of cognitive consistency and even cognitive behavior therapy then gave new importance to people's ability to consider and select among alternatives. Finally, too recently to be completely assessed, we have the emergence of sociobiology and a questioning of the roles of awareness in attribution theory that suggest a new emphasis on the irrational. The change in Zeitgeist is nicely illustrated by the difference between the conclusion reached by Ward Edwards (1968) in his review of the literature on decision making and that reached by Paul Slovic, Baruch Fischhoff, and Sarah Lichtenstein (1977). Writes Edwards:

> All in all, the evidence favors rationality. Men seem to be able to maximize expected utility rather well, in a too-restricted range of laboratory tasks. There are, of course, a number of well-known counterexamples to the idea that men consistently do what is best for them. More detailed analysis of such experiments (e.g., probability learning experiments) indicates that substantial deviations from rationality seldom occur unless they cost little; when a lot is at stake and the task isn't too complex for comprehension, men behave in such a way as to maximize expected utility. (p. 41)

Slovic, Fischhoff, and Lichtenstein write:

> A coherent picture emerges from research described so far. Because of limited information-processing capacity and ignorance of the rules for optimal information processing and decision making, people's judgments are subject to systematic biases. . . . (Furthermore), one could argue that laboratory studies may show subjects at their best. Use of unfamiliar substantive topics may free them from preconceived notions that could prejudice their judgments. Provision of all information necessary for an optimal decision (and little else) is, as noted by Winkler and Murphy (1973), a boon seldom offered by the real world. It may create demand characteristics forcing subjects toward optimal responses. (pp. 14–15)

This is not a debate we can settle or need to settle or even need to take a position on. All we need to do is establish that the question of rationality is at this level a meaningful one and that there is room for debate as to how rational people are. We can accept the fact that people *can be* rational when they try and when circumstances are favorable. Beyond that, my own sense is that people try and circumstances are favorable far less often than we like to think. Irving Janis and Leon Mann (1977) have written a comprehensive review and integration of the literature on human decision making with an effort to specify the conditions and stages that characterize good decisions. The five characteristic stages they suggest include appraising the challenge, surveying alternatives, weighing alternatives, deliberating about commitment, and adhering to the decision despite negative feedback. These strike students who read the chapter as too rational and not in fact characteristic of the steps they take in making decisions. Indeed, Janis and Mann themselves recognize that their stages may constitute more an account of how people should make decisions rather than how they actually do. They find that in making major life choices, like deciding on a career or deciding to quit smoking, people often do not pass through these stages or do not thoroughly consider alternatives and objections.

To help them do so, Janis and Mann have designed a form of decision counseling with two special features. The first is a balance sheet procedure in which people take a formal accounting of the positive and negative features of various alternatives. The second is a form of outcome psychodrama in which people imagine that the decision has already been made and they are experiencing its consequences. These decision counseling procedures have been shown to be helpful in a number of studies. For example, Mann (1972) found that high school seniors made different and on the whole more satisfactory choices of what college to attend when they used a balance sheet procedure than when they did not. The overriding concern of the Janis and Mann volume is with whether decisions are good or bad. In a way that contrasts with and perhaps complements this good-bad emphasis, the present analysis in the end steps around the question of rationality to concentrate instead on describing what kinds of commitments people make, how they come to make them, and what consequences or functions they have. Rather than asking whether a decision is good or bad, for example, we will be asking whether people can make a decision stick or not. It might be felt that these two questions are equivalent, in that only good decisions can be sustained. But this means deciding whether they are good or not by first observing whether people can sustain them.

The most troublesome feature of the case histories Janis and Mann present of good and bad decision making is that they are done in retrospect. Knowing how people eventually feel about a decision, looking backwards, it is easy to describe the decision, and the steps that led up to it, as good or bad. This retrospective labeling may actually tell us little about how people eventually came to feel the way they did. Worse yet, it may lead us to see an order or structure in the world of the decision maker that does not in fact exist at the time in either the world or in the decision maker's mind.

Our use of terms like hindsight or Monday morning quarterback indicates that we are aware of this bias, but this makes the bias no less irresistible. Fischhoff (1975) and Fischhoff and Beyth (1975) have shown that events that are reported to have occurred are judged as having appeared more likely and predictable than they actually did appear. Snyder and Uranowitz (1978) have demonstrated that people will misremember facts about another person's life in a way that makes that person's history seem more consistent with their subsequent image. Bem and McConnell (1970) have shown that people will misremember their own previous attitudes in a way that makes them more consistent with their subsequent behavior. A person publishes a series of papers in different areas, is rewarded for one of them, and goes on to do systematic work in that area. We see a retrospective order to his or her career and preferences that was not there at the time. We fondly remember days past in our field in which "everyone knew everyone," forgetting that who "everyone" is has only been defined in retrospect. Indeed, the very idea that events are determined may be a quality we demand in our explanations and understanding of the past—a quality we either reject or seek in vain in our efforts to predict the future. It may be quite functional to overestimate, in restrospect, how rational our choices were or how orderly the world was (and thus how rational our choices could have been if we had only paid attention and processed information properly). This may help us to stick to our choices and work to make better choices in the future. But it clearly does not help us decide what part rationality played in the initial selection. And it may make quite meaningless any effort to decide what part rationality plays in the sustaining of that initial selection.

The reactivity of choice. The essential fact that makes the rationality of commitments indeterminate is both simple and familiar. The act of choosing itself changes the parameters on which the choice was made. So do other events that follow the choice. These changes generally have the effect of making the choice look more rational or coincide more closely with the person's personal values. On the face of it, we could say that all choices are rational in retrospect. Everyone has good reasons for what they have done. When we surveyed social scientists who were hawks or doves on the Vietnam war (Brickman, Shaver, & Archibald, 1969), all saw their choice as maximizing the expected value of American policy in Southeast Asia. Ajzen and Fishbein (1974) have developed elaborate procedures for mapping out these reasons and their correlation with people's choices. But while we can demonstrate that persuasive arguments will cause people to change their minds (Burnstein & Vinokur, 1975), we cannot distinguish the end result from that explained by a very different process—that people who change their minds will find persuasive arguments for having done so. Thus we are equally free to say that all the changes that make choices look more rational over time are in fact irrational. This indeed, following dissonance theory, is the dominant perspective in social psychology. It is distortion, wishful thinking, rationalizing, or some other equally irrational process that is assumed to make people like something more when they have worked or suffered for it than when they have not (Aronson, 1973).

But let us consider a real example. A person decides to go to medical school.

Initially, perhaps, the person thinks medicine is a glamorous field and one in which there will be great opportunity to serve humanity. It then becomes clear that medicine is not so glamorous and that the opportunity to provide service to people who really need it is far less than the person had imagined. Instead of quitting, however, the person comes to feel that being a doctor will entail the exercise of skills that are deeply challenging and satisfying. Perhaps the person also comes to feel that earning money is a lot more important than he or she had previously felt, prompted to this insight by the substantial debts accumulated to pay for a medical education. A dissonance theorist would say that in these changes the person is reducing dissonance in order to rationalize or justify a continuing commitment to medicine. But this quite arbitrarily rules out the possibility that the person has indeed learned some new things about practicing medicine or about him- or herself that make the field attractive, and that these discoveries are the quite rational source of continued interest. In the simplest case, suppose a person says the following: "I know it looks foolish to you for me to be continuing in this line of action, but I have discovered that it means something to me personally, that it has value for me, that I see important things in it that I once did not see and that you, as an outsider, do not see." If the person is sincere in this statement, it is not possible, logically or empirically, to prove that the person is wrong and is rationalizing rather than reporting a rational discovery. The question of rationality has become indeterminate.

It is a matter of taste whether we consider all such commitments rational (as would the speakers) or irrational (as would dissonance theorists). In truth, I think the process that generates such statements can properly be described as neither rational nor irrational but as something nonrational or arational that needs an equally compelling label to designate its categorical status. It is perhaps interesting to consider why social psychology has simply assumed that postdecision changes are just rationalizations rather than new discoveries or genuine changes of heart. Perhaps this is an unwitting theoretical price we have paid for relying so heavily on experiments that manipulated and deceived people. Since we know that the subjects are wrong in believing that they freely chose to work on the experimental task (they were manipulated into choosing it), and wrong even in what they believed the experiment was about (that was the cover story—the experimenters' real interest was elsewhere), it becomes hard to believe that they could be right in telling us why they like or do not like something. No wonder subjects find it hard to give an account of their behavior that experimenters find credible (Nisbett & Wilson, 1977). Observers tend to explain actors' behavior by referring to the character of the actors, whereas the actors themselves explain it by referring to the nature of the situation (Jones & Nisbett, 1972). Experimenters, as observers, may have attributed rationalization, unawareness, or stupidity to subjects when the proper attribution for the appearance of such behavior was in the experimental situations and in the explanatory set they induced in researchers. Alternatively, seeing people as rationalizing rather than rational may be simply one more instance of psychology's absorption with the neurotic and pathological rather than the healthy and functional.

Because it is very hard to know, at the time, whether people's choices are rational or not, we tend to judge them in retrospect. As indicated, however, the actor in retrospect is experiencing and judging something quite different from what was experienced and judged at the time. Moreover, actors' retrospective views cannot be unambiguously classified as either rational or irrational. The upshot of all this is that certain questions about whether people really are rational or not cannot in principle be answered. But if we cannot tell in the end whether people are really rational or not, we can still study whether they think they are rational or not. There is a surprising absence of studies that have looked at the attribution of rationality. From the preceding analysis, we would hypothesize that when the attribution was made and who was making it would be critical determinants of whether a given line of action was seen as rational or not. Prior to a decision, we would expect few differences between actors' and observers' assessments of how rational different courses of action would be. At this point, the number and objective quality of the alternatives should be the major determinant of how rational each was rated. Following a decision, and especially following a sequence or history of decisions, we would expect increasing differences between actors and observers in their assessment of actors' rationality. In general, actors will tend to see subsequent changes in their opinions of objects and past events as rational while observers will see them as irrational. But observers will also be less aware of the extent to which circumstances (including the actor's inner circumstances) may be changing and will thus also be less likely to catch instances in which the actor experiences regret over apparently reasonable choices.

A Theory of Premature Decision Making

We are ready now to move toward a theory of premature decision making. With rare exceptions, life's major decisions always feel premature. In fantasy, we imagine that we will recognize Mr. Right when we see him. In reality, it is hard to tell whether someone is Mr. Right or not until we have begun to share our lives with him. After we have been to college for two or three years, we have a firm sense of how we could and should choose a college, and perhaps of how we should have chosen in the first place. But we have to choose which college to attend before we have the experience of college that would allow us to make that choice with maturity, wisdom, and certainty. If we waited until we knew that we were ready to leave home, start careers, have children, or retire, we would never do any of these things. The fullest sense of readiness is the understanding, in retrospect, that we were ready. The sense that we are truly capable of doing something and that it is right for us comes only through the doing. Now in part this may seem to be true only because we have more information about something like being married after having been married than we did before and that a greater sense of confidence comes from having more information. This, I think, is how we would explain it to ourselves, but not how it occurs. More experience and information can as easily cause people to be less certain as more certain. It is not the information but the acting on it that produces a sense of readiness, rightness, and certainty. It is not information about a place but living there that makes us feel comfortable with it and allows us to relinquish the sense that we will have to fix it up (or fix ourselves up) before we can stand it.

Our theory of premature decision making helps us to understand, and refute, an argument often made by opponents of democracy. This is the argument that people at a certain level of development are not ready to make decisions for themselves. They do not yet know enough and should defer to the wisdom of their leaders. The interesting feature of this argument is that it can be plausibly applied to people at any age, if desired. Kindergarteners do not know enough to choose how to spend their time in school, we may agree, but neither do sixth graders. College students cannot know which of their courses will be useful to them in later life, so perhaps their choices should be guided by others. Junior executives may not know enough to make decisions about company policy, but neither may senior vice-presidents. There is always more to know than the person making the decision has access to, and it is people's sense of this that leads them to relinquish control over their future to others, especially if these others have power over them. Yes, we may really be unready to make a certain decision, but we must make this judgment knowing that we will also feel unready even if we are ready. That makes it a rather fine discrimination, and we certainly need research on people's sense of readiness to make commitments at different points in their lives. We have to learn to act through or despite our sense of unreadiness because our ambivalence about doing something—including making a decision in the first place—is only dissolved through our doing it. We become good at making decisions and taking responsibility for them in the same way that we become good at anything else in life—through practice. If we are denied the practice when we are young and unskilled, we will find it hard to make the premature decisions that are called for when we are older.

Our analysis also helps us to understand how common sense appears to contain two contradictory assumptions about human rationality. One assumption, which we may call the differentiating assumption, is that some behavior and some people are rational and others are irrational. The second assumption, which we may call the empathic assumption, is that if somebody's behavior appears irrational to us, it is only because we have not understood their point of view. Psychology and the social sciences in general have played a large role in sponsoring the second assumption, and they have thereby increased our understanding of the mentally ill, children, and other cultures. However, as we have seen, psychology has also not hesitated to label certain behaviors as rational, especially those associated with active information seeking, and other behaviors as irrational, especially those that involve personal transformations or reconstructions of information. We can now see how these two equally reasonable but apparently incompatible assumptions can continue to coexist. The differentiating assumption is characteristic of judgments by outsiders and judgments of anticipated behavior. The empathic assumption is characteristic of judgments from within, or judgments by people who identify with the actor's internal perspective, and judgments of past behavior.

This analysis helps us to understand how the same behavior can alternatively and with equal validity be seen as rational and not rational. In his brilliant analysis of agrarian revolution, Jeffrey Paige (1975) explicitly assumes that:

> there is a calculus of force just as orderly and rational in its way as the principles of economics, and despite the passions which surround the use of violence, it is important to realize that men risk their lives only with the greatest reluctance; when, in Peru, Angola, or Vietnam, they do so, it is usually because their opponents have left them with no other choice. (p. xi)

By taking into account the alternative agricultural economies, Paige is able to specify when revolution (and repression) will be rational choices and to predict when and in what form agrarian social movements will take place. Yet it is equally true that revolutions are not made in the spirit of rational reflection. They are made on the basis of passionate commitment to an ideology, a cause, or a people, a commitment that forecloses tempting alternatives and endures almost unbearable hardships. The initial choice of revolution may be made because it is the best available alternative, but the fervor of the commitment derives from what it demands in the way of making sacrifices and resisting the temptation to abandon it.

If we have focused on the ambiguity of reason, or the things that cannot be accomplished by reason, it is not out of any hostility toward reason or any idealization of feeling, instinct, or passion. On the contrary, our aim is to better understand the role of reason. This will require a more orderly and ultimately more harmonious interplay between the rational and the nonrational. Curiously enough, this may represent a commitment to reason beyond what reason itself can justify. As one of my students, a freshman philosophy major, wrote, "You may find it amusing, however, that in spite of irrefutable empirical data, I find rationality all the more appealing. And it may even make you laugh knowing that I'm not sure why." The comment may be witty enough to make us laugh, but it is certainly nothing to laugh at. Reason was the faith of the ancient Greeks and is the faith of modern science. The rise of modern science is part of a complex series of developments that included the emergence of capitalism, Protestantism, and democracy. The sociologist Robert Merton (1936), however, has shown that a distinct predilection for working in the fields of science developed among the ascetic Protestant sects (despite the indifference or hostility to science of the great reformers like Luther and Calvin). Merton concludes that despite the historically visible conflict between science and religion, commitment to science may rest upon a certain kind of religious view of the world.

We are in fact ambivalent about science and ambivalent about rationality. We have seen science create problems—in war, in the environment, in politics—as well as solve them. On a deeper level, the perfectly rational individual is not necessarily the ideal even of Western culture. If through commitment something—reason—is compromised or lost, something of importance to us is also gained. This is the ability to act, but it is also a sense that accompanies the acting. In his autobiography, William Sloan Coffin, Jr., (1977) quotes our most eminent psychoanalytic theorist, Erik

Erikson, as saying, "You see, for years we psychiatrists said to people, 'This is irrational and that's irrational,' on the assumption, 'Now they will be rational.' So they are rational. You see, I'm searching for the concept, but the opposite of irrational is not rational, but something you would call 'spiritual.'" It is to these issues that we now turn.

CHAPTER THREE
MEANING AND VALUE

Philip Brickman
Ronnie Janoff-Bulman
Vita Carulli Rabinowitz

What are the sources of value and meaning in human life? How do we know that love, freedom, or money has value for us? The intrinsic value we attach to something is measured not by the positive features of our choices, but by the uncertainties and sacrifices accepted, the temptations and distractions resisted. Because these features can be known only after a choice is made and a line of action initiated, the question of value is indeterminate until after a commitment is made. This is, of course, the converse of our proposition about rationality. The question of rationality is meaningful before commitment, at which point the assessment of intrinsic value is not; the question of intrinsic value is meaningful after commitment, at which point the assessment of rationality is indeterminate.

Our thesis is that a sense of meaning and intrinsic value comes from actions. Certain preconditions are required for the creation of value through behavior—we are again faced with the familiar triad of a positive element, a negative element, and a link between the two. Intrinsic value derives from a choice (positive element), an awareness of the negative features of such a choice (negative element), and responsibility for any negative consequences that occur (link between the positive and negative elements). The positive features of a choice tell us only that we are attracted to it. It is the negative features of a choice—the concomitant uncertainties, sacrifices, and oppositional forces—that transform actions into intrinsic values.

How can we gain a better understanding of this process of value creation? Does social psychology have anything to offer us? It would be presumptuous to say that social psychology has the answer to all of our questions about the sources of meaning and value in our lives. It is not too much to say, however, that certain social psychological theories can adequately speak to these questions. Surprisingly, perhaps, the theories of cognitive dissonance (Festinger, 1957) and self-perception (Bem, 1967) are certainly relevant to the questions of meaning and value. The language of dissonance and self-perception theory differs from the language we use in discussing ultimate values and may all too readily blind us to the theories' relevance. Nevertheless, the focus of these theories on choice, responsibility, and the primacy of behavior suggests that dissonance and self-perception may provide a way to begin to understand the sources of meaning and value in our lives. We therefore begin this chapter with an exploration of these theories. We then go on to examine some ultimate human values, including romantic and parental love, and conclude by taking a closer look at the process by which goals and rewards, people and events, come to have value.

WHAT BEHAVIOR DOES TO VALUE: SOCIAL PSYCHOLOGICAL THEORIES

Dissonance Theory and Self-Perception Theory

Dissonance and self-perception have together generated the largest body of research in modern social psychology. Each has a single central postulate that can be variously stated and appears deceptively simple. The central postulate of dissonance theory, as we have discussed, is that behavior that takes place in the absence of sufficient external justification produces pressure inside the person to find that justification. More simply, and less precisely, people are motivated to explain, justify, or rationalize their behavior, preferably in a way that makes them appear in a positive light. The behavior can be a decision, a statement, or a performance. The motivational tension it sets up is called cognitive dissonance, and the act of justifying the behavior and reducing the tension is called dissonance reduction. Dissonance theory, as we discussed earlier, was first formulated by Leon Festinger in 1957, with significant restatements of the theory appearing by Jack Brehm and Arthur Cohen (1962), Elliot Aronson (1968), and a number of researchers treating the topic of personal responsibility, whose work is summarized by Robert Wicklund and Jack Brehm (1976).

The central postulate of self-perception theory is that when we observe behavior taking place in the absence of sufficient external justiciation, we assume that the person displaying the behavior has an internal or personal reason for engaging in the behavior. We learn this rule or principle in order to explain other people's behavior, but we apply it also in observing and explaining our own behavior. There is no motivational tension involved in this perspective, simply a process of perceiving and devising explanations for behavior. Self-perception theory was first formulated by Daryl Bem (1967) but has since been largely absorbed into the more general statements of attribution theory by Harold Kelley (1967, 1972) and Edward Jones and Richard Nisbett (1971). To get a sense of the phenomena that dissonance theory and self-perception theory purport to explain, we will briefly review some of the experiments generated by the two theories.

Dissonance and Self-Perception
Experiments

Most of the experiments designed to test dissonance theory have been concerned with negative or discrepant behavior. One of the first and best known of all dissonance experiments involved getting subjects to tell a lie, saying to someone else that the experiment had been quite interesting when in fact it had been very boring (Festinger & Carlsmith, 1959). In all cases, the experimenter asked the subject to do this because the confederate who was supposed to act the part had failed to show up. In one condition the experimenter offered the subject $20 to tell the lie, and in the other condition the experimenter offered the subject $1 for the lie. When subjects told the lie for only $1, they became significantly more likely to believe their own statement—to believe that the experiment had been interesting— than when they told the lie for $20. The reason, according to dissonance theory, is that $1 was not enough justification for telling a lie; subjects therefore sought an additional explanation, which they found by telling themselves that the experiment had not really been so boring after all.

Believing a lie is only one possible response to having chosen to tell it. Another possible response is to feel that lying is not so bad after all; this result would be most likely when it is impossible to redefine the lie as not really a lie. For example, if one cheated on a test, it would be difficult, although not impossible, to believe that one had not in fact cheated. Under these circumstances, dissonance theory would predict an effort to justify or explain cheating. This is exactly what Judson Mills (1958) found in an experiment with sixth-grade children. The children were tested in a situation in which it was impossible to win without cheating and in which they were given an opportunity to cheat. The next day, those children who had cheated became more lenient in their attitudes toward cheating than they had been before, whereas those children who had not cheated became harsher in their attitudes. Of course, all children who cheated did so in order to win, but winning was apparently not considered a sufficient incentive by itself to justify cheating (despite W. C. Fields's famous line, "Anything worth having is worth cheating for").

A more direct form of discrepant behavior has been studied in experiments in which subjects have been asked to insult or administer electric shocks to other people. (In fact, the other people are confederates of the experimenter and do not actually receive the shocks.) In an early study, Keith Davis and Edward Jones (1960) found that when college students were assigned to give a negative evaluation of another student's personality, they were less likely to make derogatory comments in a subsequent rating of the student than were those subjects who were given a choice of what to say but were persuaded to make negative comments by the experimenter. Being ordered to insult someone in an experiment is seen as sufficient reason for doing so; choosing to insult someone, however, even when asked to do so as part of an experiment, motivates people to seek an additional explanation, which they can find by telling themselves that the other person to some extent deserved their negative remarks. It should be noted, by the way, that this happened in the Davis and Jones study only when subjects felt they would have no opportunity to meet the other student and explain that they had not really meant their remarks; when they were told they would have this opportunity, their anticipated ability to disown their insults relieved the psychological pressure on them to stand behind their remarks.

Even when people have not been the agent directly responsible for harming someone else, they may feel implicated just through having observed and done nothing about it. People who observe suffering must choose whether or not to try to help. If they choose not to help, they come under pressure to justify their noninvolvement. Melvin Lerner has shown that derogating the victim, as subjects did in the Davis and Jones experiment, is a very widespread response in these circumstances (see Lerner & Simmons, 1966, and Lerner & Matthews, 1967, for two early experiments, and Lerner, Miller & Holmes, 1976, and Lerner, 1980, for reviews). If the victims are seen as bad or undeserving people, this provides us with a sufficient explanation for our reluctance to help.

Because inflicting pain, like cheating, is relatively difficult to deny, people will sometimes try to minimize the damage done. In a study by Timothy Brock and Arnold Buss (1962), subjects who were persuaded to administer electric shocks to male targets were more likely to say the shocks were not really painful, than were subjects who were assigned to give these shocks or subjects who agreed with a request to administer mild shocks. When the target was female, however, subjects were apparently unable to convince themselves that the shocks were not really painful. Under these conditions, they justified their behavior by enhancing their feeling that they had been obligated to give the shocks.

This brings us to the last experiment we will discuss in this connection, probably the most famous experiment in social psychology: Stanley Milgram's (1963) demonstration that ordinary people will administer shocks to another person that are not only painful but also, in the end, dangerous; that they will continue to administer them despite the fact that the other person expresses dismay and reports that he has a heart condition; and that they will continue at the urging of the experimenter, even after the other subject ceases to respond and the shock machine clearly indicates a dangerously high level of voltage.

The Milgram experiment is not usually thought of in terms of cognitive dissonance, probably for two reasons. First, Milgram did not collect any subsequent data that might have detected changes in subjects' opinions toward themselves, the victim, or the experimenter. Second, it might seem that the external pressure on subjects was sufficient for them to justify their own behavior. At the start of the experiment they were paid $4.50 for participating, and at the end of the experiment they were under the repeated urging of the experimenter to continue whenever they expressed reluctance. Nevertheless, the money the subjects were paid was clearly not enough in their own eyes to justify continuing on to the end; they did not continue blithely through but experienced mounting hestitation and reluctance. The money became less important to them, and a number of them offered to return it (as subjects did with their wages in the famous Stanford Prison experiment; see Zimbardo, Haney, & Banks, 1973). Rather, the urgings of the experimenter were sufficient– but only, we suspect, if subjects enhanced their perception of the value and authority of the experimenter beyond what it had been before the experiment or what it would have been if they had not continued to administer pain in the name of the experiment. Obedience to authority can justify a great range of other behavior, but obedience to authority must also be justified. People do this by coming to respect, admire, and depend on the authority. A source of authority obtains our loyalty in part by having us commit acts that can only be justified by attributing value to that authority and to obedience itself. This may occur in extreme form among soldiers and police, who are openly required to coerce others into doing things. But it also characterizes all citizens' involvement with government. Governments would not exist if mutually beneficial policies were obvious to all and everyone was spontaneously willing to follow them. Governments exist because collective tasks require doing and because their doing imposes burdens on sometimes reluctant or deprived groups. Our participation in enforcing these policies, or witnessing their enforcement, can be justified by the value we attach to government, obedience, and authority.

A lack of sufficient external justification can lead not only to a disturbing tendency for people to condone harming others but also, on the other hand, to an encouraging tendency for people to see themselves as personally responsible for helping others in both the present and future. Batson, Coke, Jasnoski, and Hanson (1978) conducted two experiments in which they asked subjects to participate for a small sum of money or recruited them to participate for nothing. Subjects not being paid subsequently rated themselves as relatively more helpful and cooperative; they saw themselves as internally motivated to help. Garbarino (1975) studied tutoring of first and second graders by fifth and sixth graders who were either paid or not paid for their tutoring. The tutors who were not being paid were more positive toward their tutees, less demanding and critical of them, and more successful in teaching them the task.

More interesting is that people who have helped for what they feel are internal reasons are more likely to help again. Uranowitz (1975) had a male college student ask female shoppers if they would watch his five bulky shopping bags while he went back to get something he had left in the store. In one condition he said that he had left something very important, in another that he had left something quite trivial. Subsequently, all the shoppers were given the opportunity to help still another person. Those who had initially helped for the trivial reason were more likely to help the next person than those who had helped for the important reason; the trivial reason was insufficient for shoppers to explain their initial helping, and they thus supplemented it with the perception that they were friendly and helpful.

Helping other people often means doing what they want done rather than what we would prefer to do. For children, this often means not making noise, not playing with a toy, or paying attention, when they would like to be doing the opposite. In an influential experiment, Aronson and Carlsmith (1963) asked children not to play with an attractive toy and used either a mild or a severe threat of punishment for transgressing when the experimenter left the room. Compared to those given the severe threat, the children in the mild threat condition who refrained from playing with the toy were subsequently more likely to say they did not like the toy very much and also were more likely to avoid playing with it when another tempting situation arose in the future (Freedman, 1965; Pepitone, McCauley, & Hammond, 1967). In an interesting variation of this experiment, Lepper (1973) used mild and severe threats to test children's future ability to refrain from cheating on a test in which they could obtain attractive prizes only by falsifying their scores. As predicted, children who complied with the initial request under mild threat were more likely to resist the temptation to cheat in the second session. Thus the children's initial perceptions that they followed the adult rules in part for internal reasons made them subsequently more likely to follow these rules in a different situation in the future.

It may help simply to tell children in so many words that they have been internally motivated to enact a particular prosocial behavior (e.g., Dienstbier et al., 1975). Miller, Brickman, and Bolen (1975) found this attribution treatment to be remarkably effective in teaching fifth graders not to litter and to pick up after others. An attribution group was repeatedly told that they were neat and tidy people, a persuasion group was repeatedly told that they should be neat and tidy, and a control group received no treatment. The attribution group not only showed less littering two weeks after the treatment but, with occasional reminders, continued to keep their classroom neater than it had been before for months after the experiment. The persuasion treatment was less successful apparently because while it temporarily convinced children to stop littering, it left them feeling that they were doing so for their teacher rather than for reasons of their own.

The research on inducing people to make attributions about their own behavior sheds new light on a sage recommendation by Dale Carnegie (1936) in *How to Win Friends and Influence People*. When trying to influence someone, the most difficult situations are those in which that person is suspicious or even hostile. Under these circumstances being nice or doing the other person a favor can get a person nowhere or even backfire. Carnegie recommends asking the other for a favor instead. Obviously, the favor requested must be sufficiently modest so that the other person can easily do it. But simply by asking, says Carnegie, a person has flattered the other person and indicated a willingness, at least in one time and place, to give him or her a superior position. In doing the favor, the other person may have the reasonable hope that the person asking will be appreciative and perhaps even reciprocate, if asked, at some point in the future. Yet the key is their prospective change in attitude. And the key to this, in turn, is the fact that they are not required to do the favor but are instead induced to choose to do so. To justify the choice, they must see that the person asking is not such a bad person after all.

Relative Merits of Dissonance
and Self-Perception Theory

There is an essential similarity between cognitive dissonance theory and self-perception theory which derives from the fact that self-perception was historically developed as an alternative explanation for the same events explained by dissonance theory. Thus, one is generally safe treating the predictions of one theory as the same as the predictions of the other. Greenwald (1976) has made a strong case that no crucial experiment can be performed that will establish the superiority of one approach over the other. Nonetheless, a great deal of energy has been spent in the last twenty-five years trying to find such a crucial experiment.

There have been two main points of contention between dissonance theory and self-perception theory. The first concerns actor-observer differences and is now generally considered to be moot. To test self-perception theory, Bem (1967) initially conducted an "interpersonal replication" of the Festinger and Carlsmith (1959) study. Subjects were provided with a description of the original study and were asked to predict the attitude that an imaginary subject would hold at the end of the study. Bem's (1967) demonstration that the dissonance effects obtained by actors could be duplicated in observers was taken to mean that these effects were generated merely through the perception of appropriate situational cues. Bem's critics in turn felt that showing that the dissonance effects obtained by actors could not be reproduced in observers would prove that a motivational force was operating and was experienced only by actors. Neither of these is true. The fact that observers can duplicate dissonance effects no more proves that no motivational force is operating than the fact that observers could predict which way a billiard ball will move when struck proves that no gravitational force is operating (Zajonc, 1968). On the other hand, an inability of observers to duplicate the responses of actors does not prove that a motivational force is operating on the actors but may merely indicate that actors and observers are responding to different sets of perceptual cues. It is now established that observers will often make different inferences than actors (Jones & Nisbett, 1971; Monson & Snyder, 1977) and will not necessarily report dissonance in the same way that actors experience it (Arrowood, Wood, & Ross, 1970; Piliavin, Rodin, & Piliavin, 1969).

The second and more fundamental point of difference is that according to dissonance theory, inconsistency generates a motivational force, whereas according to self-perception, it merely influences the way we perceive and explain behavior. The evidence appears to favor dissonance theory. If dissonance is a motivational drive, it should energize dominant responses and make novel responses less likely in the way that drives are known to do. A variety of studies have indicated that this is the case (see Cottrell & Wack, 1967, and Waterman, 1969, for two early studies, and Wicklund & Brehm, 1976, for a review). Especially elegant is a study by Zanna and Cooper (1974), who reasoned that if dissonance is a source of arousal, and if arousal is necessary for the attitude changes ordinarily observed, then it should be possible to eliminate these effects by giving subjects another way to explain their arousal. If agreeing to write an essay against their true opinion was a source of arousal, and if subjects were persuaded that the arousal was really due to their having been given a pill, subjects should not feel the need to justify their decision in the same way that they would in the no pill condition. This is what Zanna and Cooper found. Using arousing visual stimuli and shock rather than pills, Drachman and Worchel (1976) and Pittman (1975) found similar results. Even more dramatic is the data reported by Cooper, Zanna, and Tave (1978) indicating that amphetamines enhance dissonance-induced attitude change and tranquilizers suppress it.

Regarding this difference in proposed motivational drive, our approach is probably closer to dissonance theory than to self-perception theory. Following an ambivalent decision, some form of internal reorganization takes place. It may be a perceptual reorganization, and perhaps it should not be called dissonance reduction, but it is a reorganization with motivational force behind it, generated and sustained by the initial act.

Why the Theories Do Not Seem to Apply to Ulimate Values

Although dissonance theory and self-perception theory have played a major role in the field of social psychology, it is difficult to recognize their relevance to such ultimate values as romantic love or parental love. At first the theories seem inadequate as general explanations for the values that guide human behavior. There are two principal reasons accounting for this apparent inadequacy. The first is scope—it does not seem right to use the narrow, often supercilious language of these theories to talk about the broad range of human concerns. The second is sequence—our intuitions tell us strongly that values determine behavior and commitment, not vice versa. There is an element of truth in both of these reasons, the consideration of which may help to clarify our general analysis.

A major objection on behalf of scope is that the processes considered by dissonance and self-perception apply only to minor inferences or superficial feelings. It should be noted, however, that the consensus of laboratory evidence, as reviewed, for example, by Collins and Hoyt (1972), is that dissonance effects occur not in the most trivial situations but only in situations in which people are carrying out an action that they feel has important consequences. Deutsch, Krauss, and Rosenau (1962), for instance, found that subjects enhanced the values of a chosen food only when they were told their choice had important implications for their personality and not when they felt it was essentially irrelevant. Gerard, Blevans, and Malcolm (1964) found that subjects enhanced the value of a painting they had chosen only when they were told they could take their choice home as a gift and not when they felt it was merely a temporary expression of preference. More important, as will hopefully become evident in our discussion of ultimate values, the basic elements or preconditions of dissonance and self-perception are the same as those required for commitment to our ultimate human values. At any rate, practitioners working to change people's lives in the most fundamental way have applied the basic principles of dissonance and self-perception theory, though of course not in that language.

As is discussed in more detail below, the most important of these principles is that people have a sense that they are choosing freely (i.e., there is insufficient external justification for) the consequences that follow. For example, few groups in history have been more dedicated in the pursuit of their purposes than the Jesuit Order of the Catholic church. Here is St. Ignatius, founder of the Jesuits, on how the individual supplicant is to be brought to see the light (quoted in McClelland, 1965):

> The director of the Exercizes ought not to urge the exercitant more to poverty or any promise than to the contrary, not to one state of life or way of living more than another . . . (while it is proper to urge people outside the Exercizes) the director of the Exercizes . . . without leaning to one side or the other, should permit the Creator to deal directly with the creature, and the creature directly with his Creator and Lord. (p. 329)

The forces released by choice can be expected to operate only if they are not counteracted, so the director is enjoined to forbear from heavy-handed attempts at influence with exercitants. With people outside the order he may preach and push as he may.

What appears to be a problem of scope is largely a problem of language or perspective. Reducing dissonance is seen as irrational, foolish, and self-deceptive, and is considered so not simply once in a while, like all behavior, but in essence. With its present pejorative language, dissonance theory seems suited to account for distorted or unimportant commitments, ones we can laugh about, but not for the important ones, like faith in God or a parent's love for a baby. Our purpose is to link our understanding of the processes first mapped out by dissonance theory with an understanding of the phenomenology of meaning and commitment. The change we seek in our perspective of dissonance theory will not make the theory obvious but will at least free it from having to carry on its back the additional and unnecessary burden of a narrow-minded view of human nature. The problem with self-perception is also narrowness, but of a different sort. If dissonance theory portrays people as too foolish and irrational, self-perception theory portrays them as too cold-blooded and rational. We need a third alternative that incorporates the idea of inner movement, like dissonance theory, but that has some understanding both of the functions of this movement and of values as people experience them.

The relevance of dissonance and self-perception to ultimate values also raises objections related to sequence. It is maintained that however our attitudes are affected by our behavior, we have some reasons for choosing that behavior in the first place, and these reasons represent the prior influence of values on behavior. First, we should note that behavior is not nearly as well predicted by attitudes as common sense might suppose or as social scientists might like (see Wicker, 1969, and Fishbein & Ajzen, 1978, for reviews of this literature). If attitudes are more a residue of past actions than a primal cause of future ones, we would naturally expect relatively modest attitude-behavior correlations. We would be especially cautious in using attitudes to try to predict behavior in situations that a person has not yet experienced (Songer-Nochs, 1976; Regan & Fazio, 1977; Fazio & Zanna, 1978). A second problem with postulating attitudes as the simple cause of behavior is that even if prior and sometimes intrinsic values govern our choices, they are not sufficient to deal with the ongoing problem of ambivalence. In a normal sequence, a modest initial feeling might initiate a tentative line of action that in turn shapes a stronger, less conflicted emotional state that in its turn institutes a more decisive, persistent, and enthusiastic line of behavior. This is, of course, an elaborated version of the James-Lange hypothesis (Lange & James, 1922) that behaviors cause emotions rather than vice versa (i.e., "we are afraid because we run"; see also Leventhal, 1974; Schachter & Singer, 1962; Zillman, 1978).

Finally, and most important, the values that guide the initial selection of behavior can themselves be understood as the residue of years of prior behavior. The difficulty people have in accepting behavior as a cause of value, rather than vice versa, occurs largely because the focus of common sense is on the short run rather than the long run. In the short run, it may appear that our values cause behavior or at least cause its initiation, but in the long run these values are themselves caused by the cumulative effects of behaving in one way or another. We think it will turn out to be true surprisingly often in social psychology that in the short run the cause-and-effect relationship between two variables is the opposite of the causal relationship that predominates over a longer period of time. In the short run, for example, high self-esteem probably causes high performance, attraction to an object causes exposure to it, and cohesiveness in a group causes conformity to it. In the long run, however, high self-esteem is built out of high performance, exposure to an object causes attraction to it, and conformity generates cohesiveness.

Our science is not helped by our lack of good machinery for distinguishing short-run from long-run causal effects. For the question of value and behavior, commitments should be thought of not as creating intrinsic value from scratch each time a decision is made but as incrementally adding to or subtracting from an existing degree of intrinsic value with each decision. Choices are thus affected by intrinsic values that have been created by prior choices. The influence of such prior choices—and of attitude change (Cook & Flay, 1978) and, by implication, attitudes in general—only holds if they are anchored in behavior and commitment.

Preconditions for Dissonance and Self-Perception Effects

Our thesis is that a sense of meaning and intrinsic value comes from actions; behavior creates value, rather than vice versa. The primacy of behavior is also evident in dissonance and self-perception effects, and an awareness of the preconditions for these effects can provide us with an answer to a central question for an understanding of commitment: Under what circumstances will people come to see themselves, or someone else, as intrinsically motivated to do something? Curiously enough, despite the obvious centrality of this issue, it is not so easy to find a succint and comprehensive discussion of the matter in otherwise excellent accounts of recent research. Nonetheless, although there may be no standard formulation to which everyone refers, and researchers may use somewhat different terms, we believe there is a general, implicit agreement on the two preconditions for dissonance and self-perception.

The first is usually called choice and has been generally recognized since the seminal work by Brehm and Cohen (1962) and Linder, Cooper, and Jones (1967). The second has been harder to distinguish because it is so close to choice, often produced by the same manipulation that makes people aware of having a choice. This is responsibility for the consequences of the choice, in particular the negative consequences of the choice. Joel Cooper (Cooper, 1971; Cooper & Worchel, 1970) and Barry Collins (Hoyt, Henley, & Collins, 1972; Collins & Hoyt, 1972) have done the work most crucial to establishing responsibility for negative consequences as a separable and necessary precondition for dissonance reduction.

For intrinsic motivation to be felt, people must choose and must accept responsibility for the negative consequences of their choices. These two key elements can be called *freedom* and *responsibility*. People free to choose will do something that has some positive feature for them. People who are responsible recognize that they cannot break the connection between their action and any negative consequences that action may have. A positive element, a negative element, and a bond between the two are of course the components of commitment we specified earlier. Recognizing these preconditions as freedom and responsibility allows us to relate our study to the concerns and the language of the ordinary person on the street, which is no small benefit. People know that freedom is important to them, but they also know that they do not want freedom studied by itself or in isolation. They want freedom studied in connection with responsibility, in the same way that they want freedom in the world to be exercised in connection with responsibility. Of course, this is exactly what the heart of social psychology has been doing, albeit with only dim recognition of the fact.

ULTIMATE VALUES

No one would disagree that our highest values and deepest feelings reflect what people take to be the strongest possible intrinsic motivation. However, can we accept the idea that this intrinsic motivation comes from the same combination of circumstances we have been looking at so far—uncertainty, an ambivalent choice, and a shift that removes this ambivalence? Are freedom and responsibility important to faith in God or romantic love in the same way that they are to the attitudes that have typically been studied in laboratory experiments? Some authors have already suggested as much, though not using the language of experimental social psychology. In his book *Zen and the Art of Motorcycle Maintenance*, Pirsig (1974) writes:

> You are never dedicated to something you have complete confidence in. No one is fanatically shouting that the sun is going to rise tomorrow. They *know* it's going to rise tomorrow. When people are fanatically dedicated to political or religious faiths or any other kinds of dogmas or goals, it's always because these dogmas or goals are in doubt. The militancy of the Jesuits . . . is a case in point. Historically their zeal stems not from the strength of the Catholic Church but from its weakness in the face of the Reformation. (p. 146)

It is easy to think of examples in which a fervent kind of loyalty or a deep sense of value is attached to an ambivalent concern. Sudeten Germans and Americans living in the Panama Canal Zone display a more emotional patriotism than their peers at home who can take their national identification for granted. Indeed, the strident nationalism of the whole German people in modern times is traced by Erikson (1950) to the Germans' historic difficulty in uniting as people and their insecurity about their late national identity. Erikson also suggests that the virulent anti-Semitism in Germany derives in part from the Germans' envy of the ability of the Jews to maintain a sense of national identity despite their global dispersion, just as anti-Semitism peaked in other European countries (e.g., England, France, Spain, Poland) at times when these countries were forging their national identities. For another example, handguns and rifles now play a less important role in procuring food or security, for either individuals or nations, than they have at any point since their invention. It is at just this point that defense of the right to bear arms by the National Rifle Association has become most fervid and ideological, perhaps the most feared lobby in Washington. For a final example, alumni fund raisers know full well that people are far more likely to donate to their undergraduate school than to their graduate school. Yet it is graduate school that students attend with the clearer sense of purpose and from which they receive the more obvious professional payoffs. Undergraduate years are more typically a time of turmoil (breaking away from home) and confusion (what to do for a career), for which college offers no obvious answers but provides instead a setting in which school spirit and warm memories apparently grow.

There are languages other than dissonance theory in which these observations can be couched. Psychoanalytic theory, for example, has long treated any fervent avowal or denial of feeling as prima facie evidence that the opposite impulse is also present and has been denied or repressed. More recently, something called catastrophe theory has emerged from mathematics as a potentially useful way of representing situations in which behavior can jump suddenly from one extreme to another (Zeeman, 1976; Flay, 1978). These representations can become quite complex as they involve at least three dimensions and numerous parameters, but the essential idea for situations of interest to us can be stated quite simply. Consider a behavior that can be controlled by two independent forces, an instigating force and an inhibitory force. When the inhibitory force is absent or zero, behavior is essentially a linear function of the strength of the instigating force. For example, in the absence of any good reason for resisting a persuasive communication, a person's final state will be a simple function of the persuasiveness of the communication. Each additional persuasive element in the message will make the person's final attitude toward the object of the message a little more favorable. When the inhibitory force is strong, however, behavior is postulated to be a discontinuous function of the strength of the instigating force, jumping sharply at a certain point from one extreme level to the opposite extreme. In our persuasive communication example, if a person has good reason for resisting the communication, for a long time additional persuasive elements will make no difference in the person's final attitude, which remains the same. Finally, however, when the message becomes extremely persuasive, the person changes his or her mind suddenly and completely. When the inhibitory forces are strong, in a catastrophe theory representation, there is no neutral or middle ground. There will either be no response, if the instigating force is weak, or a very strong response, if the instigating force is powerful. Clearly, this may be a very useful way of thinking about the phenomena of interest to dissonance and self-perception theory.

Are there strong inhibitory forces, or strong sources of dissonance, operating around each of what we might consider to be people's ultimate values? Can we argue that the sense of ultimate value comes from people's willingness to act in spite of overwhelming oppositional forces? We can examine this question only by looking in turn at a number of the deepest and most powerful feelings people experience, reflecting things for which they are willing to die, or to kill. Let us consider romantic love first.

Romantic Love

Love, one of the most profound human emotions, has great power to shape and reshape people's lives. Common sense already holds that love, especially romantic love, is hard to explain and hard for the lover to justify. The idea that we benefit from our relationship with another person, whether the benefit is sex or money or power or social ease, does not fully fit with the idea that we love this person. The sense that we sacrifice for the person, on the other hand, is fully compatible with the belief that we love him or her. In other spheres of life we are happy to announce a bargain, but we would hesitate to say of a loved one that "he or she is a bargain." We would not, however, hesitate to say that he or she is "worth it," implying sacrifice rather than profit. There is, surprisingly enough, a certain amount of research documenting the tension between love and several of the extrinsic values with which we would ordinarily justify behavior, including, for example, sex or money.

Fisher and Byrne (1978) have demonstrated that people see a sexual encounter as more intensely sexual when it takes place for its own sake, outside of a love relationship, than when it takes place within such a relationship. In a most elegant and careful longitudinal study of dating couples, Letitia Anne Peplau, Zick Rubin, and Charles Hill (1977) have demonstrated the converse, that a relationship is experienced as more intensely loving when it takes place, at least for a while, without sex rather than with sex. Men and women in couples having intercourse later in their relationship were more likely to report that they were in love, that they felt close to one another, that they knew one another well, and that they were likely to get married. Further, the women in couples who had had sex early were more likely to report that intercourse was satisfying and to rate themselves as career oriented, creative, intelligent, self-confident, and desirable as a date. Some of these attributes too can serve as bases for a relationship, but in their presence, the inference of love appears less likely.

The tension between sex and love does not, incidentally, disappear with marriage. Marriage counselors deal constantly with complaints from women that their husbands are interested in them only when they want sex. If love is to be preserved, as William Masters and Virginia Johnson (1976) point out, it remains necessary for both parties to periodically enact symbolic renunciations of other interests in a way that dramatizes the importance of their relationship. Simply being together for the sheer pleasure of being together means sometimes forgoing the additional pleasure of sex, especially, at least in the past, for males.

Love also takes a back seat when a relationship promises to bring tangible rewards in the form of wealth, status, or prestige. Women traditionally have had more at stake in their choice of a marriage partner than men because their future wealth and status has been more likely to be determined by their choice of partner. Contrary to stereotype, women turn out to have a more pragmatic and less romantic orientation to marriage than men (Rubin, 1973). In past times, getting married and especially having children was much more important to the wealth, status, and security of both males and females than it is in the present. Marriages were often the occasion for the formation of economically important alliances between kin groups, and the daily labor of both husband and wife were often critical to their joint economic survival.

As we might expect under these circumstances, romantic love was a less important element in marriage in the past. Romantic love may indeed be thought of as a functional substitute for these economic bases of marriage, more likely when there are many alternative relationships and there is more ambivalence about the necessity for marriage. Paul Rosenblatt and his colleagues have carried out a series of studies demonstrating the relationship between romantic love and the circumstances that work for or against marriage in different cultures. Coppinger and Rosenblatt (1968) have shown that romantic love is less important in societies where the husband and wife are highly dependent on one another for subsistence. Rosenblatt, Fugita, and McDowell (1969) have shown that the opportunity for sexual and personal involvement during betrothal is less in societies where the marriage is an occasion for an economically important transfer of wealth between kin groups. Rosenblatt (1967) demonstrated that romantic love is considered more important in societies where the newlyweds reside near their kin, who are likely to put pressures on the couple that make their relationship more difficult and less obvious to maintain. (Newlyweds need not reside near their kin in Western societies, but other pressures make the marriage relationship difficult to maintain.) Cozby and Rosenblatt (1972) have discovered that both romantic love and greater evidence of male-female antagonism in courtship (insulting, teasing, playing pranks)—a clear indication of ambivalence—occur in societies where marriages are not arranged by parents but where spouses can be freely, even arbitrarily, chosen.

In a very ingenious experiment, Clive Seligman, Russell Fazio, and Mark Zanna (1978) have shown that merely making the extrinsic reasons for going out with someone else salient can reduce people's perceptions of how much they like or love that person. Subjects who were asked to rank the importance of seven extrinsic reasons for going out with their partner (e.g., the partner "is the type of person my parents would approve of," "is wealthy and allows us to go to expensive places together," "knows a lot of important people") reported that they liked or loved their partners less than subjects who ordered the importance of seven "intrinsic" reasons (e.g., "we share the same interests and concerns," "we always have a good time together," "she/he is interesting and intellectually stimulating"). The latter subjects, in turn, reported loving or liking their partners less than subjects in a control group who did not rank order any reasons for going out with their partner (i.e., no reasons were made salient). Interestingly enough, Seligman, Fazio, and Zanna were not especially comfortable with this result, but it fits nicely with the present analysis. Even the reasons these authors call intrinsic can serve as an alternative to love as the basis for justifying a relationship. Thus it is not surprising that a condition in which no reasons at all were made salient is the one in which couples reported strongest feelings of love and intimacy.

The ambiguity and tension of the relationship between love and money is nicely captured in the following joke, in which a woman at once both affirms and denies it. A world-class poker player has just been busted out of the World Series of Poker, losing his stake of $10,000.

> Roberts, a noted ladies' man, then stood up and said to his latest girlfriend, "Well, honey, I got broke. You still love me?"
> "Sure do, sugar," the girl said. "And I'm gonna miss you." (Stainback, 1978, p. 66)

There is also some fascinating evidence that having power over someone else, or simply being concerned with having power over someone else, may make it harder for people to see themselves as loving the other person or committed to and satisfied with the relationship. Kipnis, Castell, Gergen, and Mauch (1976) found that respondents who said that they had the final say when disagreements arose in their marriage devalued the worth of their spouses and were less happy with their marriages. Stewart and Rubin (1974) found that the more males in a dating relationship were concerned with power, as assessed by a projective measure, the less satisfied the couple was, the more likely they were to anticipate problems, and the more likely they were to have broken up two years later. It is easier to infer that someone trusts someone else when that person has risked his or her future well-being by putting it in the other's hands than when he or she retains control over what happens. Indeed, research on conflict situations has shown that it may be possible to establish trust if and only if people have an unambiguous opportunity to signal their trust in this way (Deutsch, 1958; Swinth, 1967). Correspondingly, it is easier to infer one's own trust and love for another person in a situation in which one has given power to the other person than in a situation in which one has retained power. The fact that males have traditionally had more power within marriage may have made them less romantic after marriage, even though they are more romantic than females before marriage.

Consistent with our analysis, philosophers from Ovid to Bertrand Russell have agreed that romantic love occurs only in the face of some obstacles to its consummation. By this they have meant that romantic passion is a by-product or transformation of sexual frustration. Also, as Sigmund Freud (1922) wrote, "Some obstacle is necessary to swell the tide of libido to its height; and at all periods of history whenever natural barriers in the way of satisfaction have not sufficed, mankind has erected conventional ones in order to enjoy love" (p. 213). By our analysis, love is associated not with sexual frustration per se but with any opposing force that induces people to experience their pursuit of another as a commitment. As we have seen, these can include obstacles or sacrifices in domains that have to do not with sex but with wealth or power. This helps us to understand how outside interference in ongoing relationships, either by rivals or by parents, can intensify rather than dampen the ardor of love. Rivals kindle an especially painful emotion called jealousy, often considered an unworthy feeling but still one that partners throughout history have looked for as a sign that love is still alive. Parents have the advantage over rivals in kindling love in that their interference can be experienced as something negative by both parties rather than by only one. As we have seen, Rosenblatt (1967) found romantic love more likely in cultures in which parental interference with newlyweds was also more likely. In a survey of dating and married couples, Driscoll, Davis and Lipetz (1972) found that for the unmarried couples, the perception of parental interference was positively correlated with the intensity of their feelings of romantic love. Moreover, increases in parental interference over time were correlated with increases in feelings of love. Not surprisingly, Driscoll, Davis, and Lipetz called this the Romeo and Juliet effect.

Our thesis that love for an object is associated with profound ambivalence toward that object should be distinguished from the related analysis put forth by Ellen Berscheid and Elaine Walster (1974) that love is the result of a particular labeling, or mislabeling, of general arousal. This arousal can be either positive or negative (see, e.g., Dutton & Aron, 1974; Stephan, Berscheid, & Walster, 1971). This misattribution argument is that subjects misattribute the general arousal generated by an irrelevant stimulus (e.g., previous erotic stimuli, anticipated electric shock) to the other person present and label it as excitement this individual has caused them to feel. Our analysis does not deal with arousal in general but rather with a specific form of arousal that may be generated by the apprehension of negative features associated with the love object. We are concerned not with misattribution (i.e., mislabeling) but with correct attribution.

Although love may involve some sacrifice of sex or money or power or ease, none of these surrenders seems essential to the phenomenon. It is certainly possible to think of examples of love that do not require sacrifice of any of these. Now for our general thesis we need only establish that love involves some element of sacrifice, not that the sacrifice must involve any particular dimension, such as sex or money. Nonetheless, there is a dimension of sacrifice that is common to all examples of love. This is the willingness of the lover to accept or endure negativity and dependency, raw forms of emotional expression and their associated demands, from the loved one. If family members or intimate friends brought into the laboratory to work on a group problem are compared to groups of strangers working on the same problem, one of the characteristic features of the family groups is a much higher level of hostile and critical comments in the discussion. When sufficiently exasperated by some bit of rudeness on the part of the children, the father of one of the coauthors (PB) used to say, "Treat me like a stranger. Just give me the ordinary politeness you would give a stranger on the street." Laboratory research has demonstrated that people are more likely to communicate negative information to others they trust (O'Reilly & Roberts, 1974; Read, 1962). Communicators value very highly recipients' ability to accept and absorb their confused, contradictory, or hurtful comments. It is this that allows you to "dare to be yourself," as C. Raymond Beran notes in a statement called "What Is a Friend?" that is sometimes turned to for uplift and reassurance:

> You do not have to be on your guard. You can say what you think, so long as it is genuinely you. He understands those contradictions in your nature that lead others to misjudge you. With him you can breathe freely. You can avow your little vanities and envies and hates and vicious sparks, your meannesses and absurdities and, in opening them up to him, they are lost, dissolved on the white ocean of his loyalty. He understands. You do not have to be careful. You can abuse him, neglect him, tolerate him. Best of all, you can keep still with him. It makes no matter.

The ability to absorb negativity is clearly important to an intimate relationship, because upon it rests not only the commitment of the partners but also their ability to communicate with one another. There is some evidence that couples that can express aggression more freely, in an appropriate context, are happier and better adjusted (Young, Korner, Gill, & Beier, 1977). Nonetheless, the task of absorbing negativity places major demands on an intimate relationship. It is always a source of strain, and the strain can become insurmountable. This is especially likely if one of the parties becomes severely depressed and begins injecting large and continuing amounts of negative affect into the relationship. Dan Coates and Camille Wortman (1980) have recently shown how the reactions of friends and family to this negativity can inadvertently make things worse for the depressed person. First, out of consideration for the person's suffering, intimates will not only express sympathy and absorb the negativity but suspend their own expressions of hostile or critical feeling in order to avoid upsetting the depressed person further. Recognizing this, however, depressed people come to feel that they cannot trust what their friends say, since their words are seen as reassurance rather than truth. Then, frustrated and frightened by their inability to help the depressed person, intimates may blow up at the person or avoid the person altogether. Because these attacks or avoidances are not contingent on any particular behavior by the depressed, they only confuse the person further and confirm their sense of badness or helplessness. Finally, guilty over their inability to absorb the negative affect of their loved one, intimates return to their first reaction of suppressing criticism and set in motion the same unhelpful cycle all over again.

Many of the processes that characterize intimate relationships, including gifts, joking, and sexuality, may be seen as efforts designed to deal with the problem of accepting and managing negativity. Erikson (1950) has written about orgasm as an event in which the accumulated tensions of a relationship are discharged in a highly satisfying climactic turmoil. Joking and gift giving have a remarkably similar structure in that they both involve tension that is accumulated through a period of anticipation and discharged when the surprise (the punch line or the gift) is revealed. In healthy relationships, jokes, gifts, and sexuality may be places people can put the tension that has been generated elsewhere. By transforming their ambivalence into the process of playing or taking a joke, giving or accepting a gift, people can both discharge the tension and demonstrate their commitment to the relationship.

If our thesis is correct, it would be unlikely for popular wisdom in folklore and fairy tale not to already acknowledge it, and sure enough, it does. Consider the beautiful princess whose hand is to be offered to the most worthy suitor. How is the princess, or her father, to know that a suitor is not just interested in the royal treasury? The answer to the princess's attributional dilemma has been to impose a series of tasks that must be completed in order to win her hand and the kingdom, tasks so difficult that a suitor has no reasonable hope of accomplishing them. Rational considerations alone, like an interest in the royal treasury, would discourage rather than encourage the informed suitor from embarking on the quest. The suitor's commitment is revealed by his embarking and continuing on a venture in spite of rather than because of what he can expect. Of course, commitment alone is not sufficient for winning the princess's hand in these stories. The contestant must also be young, handsome, and favored by a secret ring, a magic cloak, or a mysterious potion.

Handsome princes, like princesses, face the attributional dilemma that because every maiden in the kingdom should be happy to give their proposal most serious consideration, they do not know whether the acceptance springs from love or ambition. Sex role conventions in these stories prevent princes from imposing similar obstacles or impossible quests to test or establish the commitment of their would-be brides. Instead, a more devious and passive form of testing is provided by having the prince appear in disguise, preferably in rags on a cold and snowy night, perhaps even having temporarily forgotten his true identity. He may even appear as a frog. If the maiden can overcome her doubts and love him under these circumstances, she must surely care for something other than the exterior trappings of his body or his position.

If there are no naturally occurring obstacles to the attainment of the love object, then, as Freud noted, either the target may introduce them as a test or the lover may seek them out as a demonstration and intensification of love. If the target has no drawbacks and no difficulties, then the idea of love may be impossible, or at least, as Gilbert and Sullivan (1881) indicate, without virtue:

Grosvenor. What's the matter?
Patience. Why you are perfection! A source of ecstasy to all who know you!
Grosvenor. I know I am. Well?
Patience. Then, bless my heart, there can be nothing unselfish in loving *you*!
Grosvenor. Merciful powers! I never thought of that!
Patience. To monopolize those features on which all women love to linger! It would be unpardonable!
Grosvenor. Why, so it would! Oh, fatal perfection, again you interpose between me and my happiness!
Patience. Oh, if you were but a thought less beautiful than you are!
Grosvenor. Would that I were; but candor compels me to admit that I'm not!
Patience. Our duty is clear; we must part, and for ever!
Grosvenor. Oh, misery! And yet I cannot question the propriety of your decision. Farewell, Patience!
Patience. Farewell, Archibald! But stay!
Grosvenor. Yes, Patience?
Patience. Although I may not love *you*—for you are perfection—there is nothing to prevent your loving *me*. I am plain, homely, unattractive!
Grosvenor. Why, that's true!
Patience. The love of such a man as you for such a girl as I must be unselfish!
Grosvenor. Unselfishness itself! (pp. 170–171)

Grosvenor's poetic perfection may not exist in real life, nor is it easy in real life for people to adopt the fairy tale solution of disguising their assets and talents in order to establish a lover's purpose. Love may be a luxury, but it is one that even the rich cannot buy. One wealthy person even goes so far as to say, "If you are rich you can pretty well give up the idea of being loved for yourself. People look at you as a resource, something to be exploited" (Reilly, 1975).

This testing of commitment is thus the reason that the moment in romantic love when one or the other party reveals any hidden secrets or inner weaknesses is so crucial. One may have many good feelings about another because the other is worthy but can love the other only in spite of his or her unworthiness. One form of pathology in love relationships derives from the fact that one or both parties cannot get adequate reassurance from the other that their worst points are understood and accepted, and therefore feels compelled to continue revealing and emphasizing these worst points in order to continue receiving the ambivalent message of acceptance. Judith Viorst (1975) differentiates between love and less ambivalent feelings of admiration as follows:

Question: What is the difference between infatuation and love?
Answer: Infatuation is when you think that he's as sexy as Robert Redford, as smart as Henry Kissinger, as noble as Ralph Nader, as funny as Woody

Allen, and as athletic as Jimmy Connors. Love is when you realize that he's as sexy as Woody Allen, as smart as Jimmy Connors, as funny as Ralph Nader, as athletic as Henry Kissinger, and nothing like Robert Redford in any category—but you'll take him anyway.

If the above describes the process for some females, the following may be more characteristic of some males:

Love is what makes a person who is philosophically opposed to monogamous sexual relationships on the grounds that jealousy and possessiveness between women and men are not intrinsic to human nature but simply the outmoded byproducts of a decadent capitalistic system take it all back.

Curiously enough, the harshest tests and the greatest sacrifices may be imposed on themselves by people who are most cynical about love, most controlling, manipulative, or even exploitive in their ordinary relations with people. They may not be exempt from the need to love, the need to see something in their lives given value by love, but the forces opposing this commitment are so great that it can be established only by the most extreme forms of behavior. This describes the relationship between Charles Manson and many of his female followers. In the end Manson demanded extreme and brutal proofs of loyalty from them. Manson understood that his aloofness and demandingness were not accidental to his followers' fanatical love. Asked at one point why they would be willing to follow him anywhere, even to the gas chamber at San Quentin, Manson replied: "Because I tell them the truth. Other guys bullshit them and say 'I love you and only you' and all that baloney. I'm honest with them. I tell them I'm the most selfish guy in the world. And I am" (Bugliosi, 1975, p. 545).

For most of us, who are not especially rich or famous or attractive, the pressure of trying to figure out whether other people are doing things because they care about us or because they expect to get something out of us is intermittent and remote. The problem is to a degree solved by role relationships. If we bring our car to a mechanic, we expect the mechanic to be interested in the car, not in us, and to be interested only until the bill is paid. If a friend joins us in working on the car, we expect the friend to be interested in us, in conversation, and in seeing what happens, not just in the car and a payoff. (We probably expect less competence in the second case, but we may not expect so much in the first case, either.) Not knowing whether we are dealing with someone who is interested in us personally or professionally is a real source of strain, especially if we mistake professional interest for personal interest. It may be noted, incidentally, that life is made more difficult by attributional dilemmas for disadvantaged as well as advantaged persons. In a white society, blacks must continually decide whether the color of their skin is a factor in causing other people to accept or reject them, but whites can in general assume that skin color is not a factor. Thus even if blacks and whites are treated the same, different attributions may cause the quality of their experiences to be quite different.

At this point it would be well to allay a possible source of confusion arising from the difference between objective (generally agreed upon) value and subjective (uniquely experienced) value. Whereas objective value may be inimical to the inference of love, subjective value is essential to it. If a woman is very beautiful in the world's eyes, it may be harder for her or for anyone else to know whether she is loved for her own sake. However, if a woman is not beautiful in the eyes of her lover, it is harder to believe that she is loved. Seeing someone as beautiful in consequence of love is different from seeing the person as beautiful prior to or in the absence of love. We would expect lovers to rate the people they love as possessing many desirable features not apparent to other observers. Because we see desirable features in many people with whom we are not in love, it seems reasonable to assume that when we are in love the desirable features are not perceived as the cause of love. Further, we might expect that people who are intimate with one another and expect their relationship to continue will see their relationship as more fair and equitable than people whose love was less committed (Walster, Walster, & Traupmann, 1978), since equity too is a desirable feature—even though, as we have seen, the experience of love in the first place might be kindled by commitment in the face of objective inequity.

The causal relationship between ambivalence and love is also a point of potential confusion. Our thesis—that love grows out of the resolution of ambivalence—should be distinguished from an older argument that love generates ambivalence. As Berscheid and Walster (1974) note, the more benefits the loved one provides, the more afraid the lover may be that the love will end. Feelings of love for someone else, Thibaut and Kelley (1959) point out, give that person extraordinary power over the loved one, who may in turn fear being overwhelmed. The primal love of infants for their caretakers occurs in a context of enormous dependence. Thus such psychoanalysts as Reik (1943) and Klein and Riviere (1953) associate love with anxiety about dependency and fear of dependency. Love does make people dependent, dependency is a source of ambivalence, and it is quite congenial to our analysis that people's handling of their negative feelings about dependence should be a critical determinant of their capacity to love. We can accept the idea that there is an eventual interplay between love and ambivalence, however, without believing that the love and ambivalence come into being simultaneously or that the love comes first. If this were true, it would argue that the experience of love is unambivalent at first but gradually becomes more ambivalent as the dependency is experienced more fully. Our analysis, on the contrary, would suggest that the ambivalence and the keenness of love is greatest at first and that love gradually becomes less passionate and less conflictful as this ambivalence (of which dependency is only one source) is more definitely resolved. Furthermore, if love were the cause of ambivalence, we would expect people who had the fullest experience of love to be most ambivalent. If ambivalence were primary, we would expect people who have experienced the greatest frustration and uncertainty in close relationships to be most concerned with love and affection.

We are now in a position to provide some insight into a number of the enduring mysteries about love. The first is whether one can love and hate someone at the same time, or whether love is closer to hatred than it is to simple liking or indifference. If passionate love is created out of intense ambivalence by a commitment to the positive side, it is easy to see that under certain circumstances a relatively small change could push people over to the negative side, after which tension and ambivalence are generated by all the previously positive feelings. Hatred is the emotion generated by attacking or withdrawing from someone toward whom the actor also has intensely positive feelings. To recall our catastrophe theory representation, the speed of a change is less but the intensity of it is greater when it occurs in the presence of inhibitory forces. Without ambivalence, change is simply an increase or a decrease in liking for someone else. With ambivalence, change is a transformation from love to hate or vice versa.

Love is in a sense seeing something as ideal that is not ideal. The primal dissonance that accompanies romantic passion is therefore the pursuit of an impossibility, the placing upon a partner of hopes and dreams and fantasies that cannot possibly be fulfilled. The partner that would be required to fulfill them would have to be ideal and unchanging, and real partners are not only not ideal, they do not like being idealized. Furthermore, they change, they grow old, and ultimately they die. The objects of love are not permanent, but romantic passion commits itself to permanence. Poets since the time of the Greeks have agonized over the pain of loving things that do not and cannot last and therefore must disappoint. If there is a difference in the maturity of love, it probably lies in whether love proceeds by denying the imperfections of the loved one or recognizing them, accepting them, and loving anyhow. But disappointments are only alleviated, not removed, by their being expected and accepted. Moreover, this mature form of love is probably less intense and less passionate than the form in which everything is idealized. It is not only jealousy but passionate love itself that is regarded as a sickness and aberration by Greek and Roman philosophers who value rationality above all. From this, the counsel of reason and also the counsel of free spirits has been to withdraw. A modern version of this sentiment is provided by Zonker Harris, a carefree, Snoopy-like character in Garry Trudeau's *Doonesbury*, when Mike Doonesbury, a more serious, worried, Charlie Brown sort, asks him why he hasn't ever fallen in love. "What can I say, man? Maybe it's because in the past, I've seen nothing but good people like yourself betrayed by a promise that was always more gorgeous than its realization. . . . If that's being in love—and I submit to you that it is—then I would rather spend my days underwater, watching bubbles rise out of my beard, leaving the hurting to others."

There are profound rewards in loving, perhaps the most profound we know. But they are rewards that come from the loving itself, and the experiencing of the world it makes possible, rather than rewards in the more conventional sense of things, pleasures, or services received from another person. The latter are profits from being loved, not from loving. In this sense it may be rational to encourage love from someone without making the strategic error of falling in love oneself. But what about giving in order to get, falling in love in order to be loved in return? This describes a process of exchange rather than a process of love. The idea of loving for what one will get in return not only does not describe how people experience love but, as our evidence has shown, is inimical to this experience. Moreover, it is poor strategy. Just as it is not rewards from other people that causes us to fall in love, it is not the reward of our loving that causes others to love us in return. Eventually, a relationship may require an interplay of love on the part of each partner, but this does not mean that either love created the other. The rational basis of exchange is liking, which we can elicit in other people, not loving, which is produced deep inside the other person.

Finally, we have an understanding of why love is so hard to define or explain to other people. This is something psychotherapists have used to argue that love is a result of unconscious needs, which by definition people cannot be aware of. The tone of writers commenting on the apparent inarticulateness of love is often scornful. For example, Moreno (1977) writes:

> There are essentially two ways of explaining why we have the special feelings we call love. The first one is by asserting that those whom we claim to love are objectively deserving of special consideration: "If you knew her as well as I do, you would realize how wonderful she really is." The problem with this type of explanation is that the special qualities we see in those we say we love are seldom, and never to the same degree, seen by anyone else not equally in love with the person in question. So sooner or later we resort to the other type of explanation: "I love her because I love her." We abandon the pretension that our loved ones are really special or we try to make ourselves believe that others are unable to see their true qualities, and we explain how, regardless of whether or not they are endowed with special qualities, and regardless of whether other people can detect these qualities, they are special to us by the mere fact that we feel deeply about them. This second explanation, which is the more common one and which is always put forward when the first is challenged, is of course no explanation at all. (pp. 36–37)

Yet the inarticulateness of love is not its flaw, but its essence; not its lack of insight, but its insight. If we could ascribe our feelings to the attractiveness or the virtue of the loved one, our love would be attached to this attractiveness or that virtue rather than to the love object itself. Love is precisely the sense that we are acting far beyond the call of any particular external qualities, that we are creating or generating value from deep within ourselves. Carson McCullers (1951) writes:

> There are the lover and the beloved, but these two come from different countries. Often the beloved is only a stimulus of all the stored-up love which has lain quiet within the lover for a long time hitherto. And somehow every lover knows this. He feels in his soul that his love is a solitary thing. He comes to know a new, strange loneliness and it is this knowledge which makes him suffer. So there is only one thing for the lover to do. He must house his love within himself as best he can; he must create for himself a whole new inward world—a world intense and strange, complete in himself. (p. 26)

We may not share this image of love as something lying fallow within the lover, or the fateful sense that the beloved cannot also be a lover, but we do share the image of love as a very personal, even lonely, creation of the lover, whose personal nature is paradoxically expressed in its inability to be communicated. We may count the ways we love someone, but not the reasons. Robert Browning did after all write "How do I love thee?" not "Why do I love thee?" The same inarticulateness attaches to any offer of life's deepest passions. Here is auto racer Johnny Rutherford experiencing precisely this as he reflects on his dedication to a near-suicidal sport (Singerman, 1978):

> I looked over at Rutherford reclining on the bed, at his hands covered with a network of scar tissue from burns, at the accident-damaged right arm he can no longer fully extend, and marvel at the sheer force of will that propels him to continue. In July, 1974, he broke his left leg auto racing. Why does he do it? I wonder. "It's an unfortunate truth about life," he says, "that those things that mean the most to you are often unexplainable. I can't tell you why."

It is a necessary paradox that a creature so deeply concerned with justifying its actions has ultimate values that cannot be justified.

Parental Love

We have treated romantic love first and at length partly because there is research available on it and partly because it can serve as a paradigm for other things people experience as ultimate values in their lives. A closely related example is parental love, an emotion that can attain a peak of ferocity that has become proverbial. The costs, the sacrifices, and the inconveniences of having children, especially for mothers, must be clearly recognized by potential parents in the modern West, for so many of them are choosing not to have children or to have many fewer than they might. Nonetheless, to list a few we can mention sleepless nights, drastically reduced parental flexibility and freedom in both career choices and social life, the financial burdens of care, feeding, and education, and the general and continuing costs of trying to socialize an often unwilling recruit to civilization. The joys of being loved are great, but they do not by themselves sustain sacrifices of this magnitude. In fact, there is mounting evidence that those parents most needy for love from their children are most likely to become frustrated and abusive of their children, who cannot possibly supply such needs (Helfer & Kempe, 1968).

Nor can parents consider children to be what they would consider adequately grateful for their parental investment. The sociobiologist Robert Trivers (1974) has recently pointed out that there is probably a biological basis for this King Lear effect. For parents, children are their biological stake in the future, and it is to the parents' deepest biological interest (not necessarily the same as their psychological interest) to see that their children survive. For children, parents are not their biological stake in the future, and once they are old enough to be of use to themselves or others, it will be more to their evolutionary advantage to look after themselves and their own offspring than their parents. Parents will be equally well served by the survival of any of their children and will be motivated to spread their care around in such a way as to ensure that as many as possible survive. Children, however, will be better served by their own survival than by that of a sibling and can therefore be expected to seek an extra share of parental resources and at best settle only reluctantly for what parents regard as their fair share. Parenting, in short, is supported by loving and other forms of commitment, not by being loved and other forms of rewards, however pleasant—and important—these might be as well.

Before resting our case, we should note that throughout human history children have typically been a more important source of wealth and power than they are today. There are two general points to be made about this. First, wealth and status from children come primarily only after they are at least partially grown—only after long years of care, sacrifice, and nurturance on their behalf. The rhetorical question "What use is a baby?" (put to people who seem bent on insisting that everything in life must have some immediately recognizable use) is relevant even in societies where everyone knows the utilitarian value of a ten-year-old. Humans are not notorious for their ability to endure great short-term costs in the interest of long-term gains simply on the basis of an appropriate rational calculation. On the contrary, as an impressive series of studies on social decision making have shown (Platt, 1973), people are fatally tempted to choose acts that are profitable in the short run (overgrazing their herds, smoking) but ruinous in the long run. Perhaps, as one of our colleagues helpfully noted, lack of foresight has played a greater role in the continuing saga of human reproduction than we like to give it credit for. But we still need to account for the care given to a child once it has arrived, and for this we need our analysis of commitment.

Second, as we would predict, parents in eras when children had greater material value had correspondingly more instrumental or pragmatic orientations to their children. In tribal societies, injuries or disputes between kin groups could often be settled by the sending of a child from one group to the other in compensation (Paige & Paige, 1978). The historians Philippe Aries (1962) and Edward Shorter (1975) have argued not only that any romantic conception of childhood or motherhood is a completely modern idea, a recent invention, but that traditional European family structure lacked almost anything we would recognize as sentiment or affection between its members. Their account of traditional family life is so grim, in fact, that it makes parental bonding among humans seem less concerned and affectionate than that among animals. They have probably overstated their case, but it may also be true that in the course of cultural evolution humans did indeed pass through a period in which they were less kind to their children than their ancestors had been or, we can only hope, their descendents will be. While the biological advantage to having offspring is the same for humans and other animals (as the only means of passing on one's genes), humans alone, through the existence of cultural and social organization, gain important symbolic and material rewards from grown offspring. It is possible that this added incentive made parents more pragmatic and less affectionate in their orientations toward children through at least a period of human history. Other historians and sociologists have argued that capitalism and the industrial revolution have dehumanized our relationships with other people by leading us to take a profit or market orientation toward them all. At least in the realm of parent-child relationships, however, the effect has probably been the opposite. By reducing the economic value of children, we have allowed for the creation or perhaps the restoration of their symbolic and affectional value. Historical changes, it should be noted, need not be permanent. If inflation continues and the proportion of elderly and retired persons in the population increases, working children may once again become important to the economic security of one's old age.

Faith in God

Are there forces opposing faith in God? First of all, how would one feel about believing firmly in something for which there is not only no known evidence but no possibility of there ever being any rational evidence? This is the case for belief in God. Every serious theologian has agreed that particular events, including those that appear to be miracles, are logically irrelevant to the question of whether or not God exists. If a person prays for rain in the midst of a drought and it rains the next day, this does not constitute rational grounds for belief that God exists. Conversely, if one prays for rain and it does not rain, this does not prove that God does not exist. One believes either that God sends everything or God sends nothing, and it is presumptuous to believe that God sends only the things we think are good for us. It would seem that there could be no stronger dissonance than that associated with a belief that cannot possibly be proven. Yet there is more in the doubts that challenge the faithful.

The most difficult obstacle to faith is the agonizing problem of earthly pain and suffering, the slaughter of innocents, and evil triumphant. McReady and Greeley (1976) have recently carried out the first national opinion survey designed to assess people's beliefs about the fundamental question of good and evil in the universe. Based on people's responses to five possibly tragic events, such as their discovery that they had a terminal illness or that their child was born retarded, the authors found that their respondents could best be characterized as either optimistic, pessimistic, or hopeful (characterized by such items as "There is no denying the evil of what is happening, but the last word has not been said yet"). How people view evil and tragedy is clearly a benchmark of their belief in God, since the presence of evil and tragedy makes it harder to believe in God. Indeed, examination of the history of pestilence, famine, and cruelty on earth may seem not only to test faith but to suggest that God either does not exist, is not all-powerful, or has somewhat peculiar tastes. To believe in spite of this evidence requires a most powerful faith. The problem of evil and unfairness is perhaps most pressing for those who have personally suffered the most (see Kushner, 1981). Thus, it is interesting to note that religion appears especially important to the handicapped (Cameron, Titus, Kostin, & Kostin, 1973) and to inmates of concentration camps (Frankl, 1959). No wonder Tertullian said "Credo quia absurdum" ("I believe because it is absurd") or that it is a tenet of fundamentalist faith that belief cannot be explained in advance or to nonbelievers: "Once one believes, he will know why he believes."

For the religious person, the question of whether there are forces opposing faith in God has a religious answer that corresponds quite well with the present analysis. There are powerful forces opposing faith, the forces of the Devil and of man's own sinful nature. William James (1902) traced the fundamental nature of all religious experience to the problem of the divided self, with faith the act that integrates and unifies these ambivalent, conflicting impulses:

> There is a certain uniform deliverance in which religions all appear to meet. It consists of two parts:
>
> 1. An uneasiness; and
> 2. Its solution.
>
> The uneasiness, reduced to its simplest terms, is a sense that there is *something wrong about us* as we naturally stand.
> The solution is a sense that *we are saved from the wrongness* by making proper connection with the higher powers. . . .
> The individual, so far as he suffers from his wrongness and criticises it, is to that extent consciously beyond it, and in at least possible touch with something higher, if anything higher exists. Along with the wrong part there is thus a better part of him, even though it may be but a most helpless germ. With which part he should identify his real being is by no means obvious at this stage; but when stage 2 (the stage of solution or salvation) arrives, the man identifies his real being with the germinal higher part of himself. (p. 383)

James's description of religious exprience is similar to our description of commitment: a positive element, a negative element, and a bond between the two. The initial weakness of the higher part and the powerful attractions of the lower part obviously make it very difficult for people to arrive at a religious identification. Furthermore, as we would expect, the more acute the inner tension between a dominant impulse toward secular pleasure and a latent impulse to renounce these pleasures, the more likely that the person's discovery of religion will take the form of a dramatic and sudden conversion. From their observations of a West Coast millenarian cult, Lofland and Stark (1965) concluded that converts must encounter the cult during a turning point in their life, after having experienced a powerful and enduring set of inner conflicts.

Two objections can be raised to this view of religious faith, both arguing that we have made faith seem more difficult and less rational than it is or than it appears to ordinary people. Once again, we must keep in mind our understanding that acts will appear more rational in retrospect or to those involved than they do in prospect or to outside observers. The first objection is essentially Pascal's wager. If an eternity in heaven is the reward for belief, and an eternity in hell the punishment for disbelief, it is certainly better to believe. These stakes are so high, the philosopher Balise Pascal pointed out, that it is a good bet to believe in God even if we think there is only the minutest chance that God actually exists. Psychologically, however, the fact that it might be good for us to believe something is not sufficient grounds for people to believe it but only to wish that they could believe it. Logically, as Bertrand Russell has pointed out, Pascal's wager is flawed. Perhaps heaven is God's reward only for those people wise and strong enough *not* to believe in Him on the basis of insufficient earthly evidence. Perhaps heaven is God's reward for people who enjoy earthly pleasures to the fullest, rather than those who renounce sex, alcohol, or material wealth. In a somewhat related spirit, William James offers the idea of God as a hypothesis which, if accepted, may make us feel better about our earthly existence. Though his analysis of the religious experience is profound, James's recommendation of a tentative belief in God, tested to see whether it makes us happier, is unacceptable to religious writers. Two other philosophers, Michael Polanyi and Harry Prosch (1975), comment:

> The truth of the matter is that we may not feel better, or be "better off," if we embrace a religion. We may instead reap suffering, struggle, and sacrifice. Anyway, we do not accept a religion because it offers us certain rewards. The only thing that a religion can offer us is to be just what it, in itself, *is*: a greater meaning in ourselves, in our lives, and in our grasp of the nature of all things. James' conditionally undertaken belief cannot be a genuine belief, since we entertain it with our fingers crossed. In reality, as we have seen, a religion exists for us only if, like a piece of poetry, it carries us away. (p. 180)

The second objection to this view of religion is that it is a poor description of the conventional motivation that underlies the behavior of many people who go to religious services and say they believe in God. Perhaps they go because their parents and their friends go, because they enjoy dressing up and seeing familiar people, because they are praised for going and criticized for not going. These are people who may never have thought or felt seriously about God, or who believe that a rational proof of God exists. There is no reason to doubt that they are committed to religion as an institution or religious practice as social behavior—and no reason to believe that they are committed to the idea that God exists. It is passionate belief in God, not conventional religious behavior, that we connect to the agonizing experience of doubt. Whatever the reasons people tend to believe in God, it is the sacrifices they make for their belief that determine how strongly religious they are.

Nationalism

In modern times, the concept people have been most willing to fight and die for is nationalism. We have learned so well the costs of nationalism and the ruinous wars and hideous barbarism it has sustained that it is almost superfluous to mention them. (On the other hand, we have not learned them so well as to rule out the possibility of even more ruinous wars in the future.) To support a war is to support an action in which one's job, home, family, and life might well be lost; what greater sacrifices could be possible as testimony to the ultimate value attached to national feeling? The feeling affects civilians as well as soldiers, but it is especially interesting to observe how it operates on those going into battle. The historian John Keegan (1978) has recently assembled evidence that men have been far more reluctant to go into battle, and that far more drastic measures have traditionally been employed to get them there, than our standard textbook accounts would have us believe. Keegan addresses the problem of motivation for combat as follows:

> "A rational army," wrote Montesquieu, "would run away." By this he meant that some of the most important events of public life—as much as of private life—are not the fruits of rational reflection. The observation is also true as a particular statement: To take part in a battle is to subdue every rational as well as instinctual concern for personal safety, particularly in the short run. And since, as in John Maynard Keynes' memorable rejoinder, in the long run we are all dead, the short run may be the best time scale in which to make calculations about running or fighting. What is it then—honor, courage, cruelty, greed, coercion—that prompts men to stay and fight, as they usually do, rather than run away on the battlefield? (p. 30)

First of all, though soliders may usually stay, they do not necessarily fight. In a famous study of World War II combat units, S. L. A. Marshall (1947) found that a majority of soldiers were more likely to stand around than to take a very active role in the fighting, and that the outcome of a battle was often determined by a surprisingly small number of troops. Ordinary soldiers recognize the Catch-22 in Joseph Heller's (1955) great novel. You have to be crazy for the army to ground you from combat missions. All you have to do to be grounded is ask. Yet as soon as you ask, you demonstrate that you are not crazy and therefore have to fly more missions. "Orr would be crazy to fly more missions and sane if he didn't, but if he was sane he had to fly them. If he flew them he was crazy and didn't have to; but if he didn't want to he was sane and had to" (Heller, 1955, p. 47). Having gone into battle, however, having risked one's life or at least sacrificed one's comfort for one's country and having survived into the honorable status of veteran, brings men to a quite different view of the matter. Historically veterans' organizations have been unsurpassed in their patriotic fervor.

There has been a historical shift in the motivational basis for warfare. War now demands more in the way of commitment and mobilization, and hence attaches intrinsic value to these activities, than it did in the past. Booty and liquor, two traditional sources of military motivation, no longer have their honored place in army manuals of field procedure, though profit taking and drugs were in ample evidence in Vietnam. Keegan writes:

> Factors that before Waterloo had helped to reduce or overlay human fear on the battlefield began to disappear. The first was the prospect of loot. In medieval warfare loot usually meant ransomable prisoners; later it was personal possessions of intrinsic value, taken at the sack of towns or from captured baggage trains or purloined from prisoners or the dead. But with the increase in the size of armies in the 19th century, the stricter policing of soldiers' behavior, and the development of military banks in which soldiers could deposit their pay, the chance of loot decreased and with it the power of avarice to offset panic. Drink, which commanders had used to anesthetize their soldiers' reactions from the earliest times, was also found more sparingly on battlefields as soon as developments in the complexity of modern weapons began to impose the requirement for soberness in their operators. (p. 36)

These changes coincided with the much more profound change we have been discussing, the growth of nationalism. Nationalism has meant, first and foremost, the ever-increasing involvement of civilian populations in warfare, both as conscripts in mass armies, as producers of the goods and services needed by these mass armies, and as victims of these same armies. Neither drink, hope of booty, nor desire for personal glory can motivate or explain massive civilian involvement in warfare. The motivation, and the explanation, is nationalism. That fighting for one's country and people is to a degree incompatible with fighting for booty or personal glory has accelerated the decline of the latter as dominant or even acceptable forms of military motivation. Armies that have fought for booty, from Roman times on, have been marked by the absence of national loyalties, though they have often been extremely loyal to their commanders.

Nationalism is quite compatible with obedience to authority and a sense of loyalty to one's comrades, two other important elements in military discipline (Moskos, 1969). It has only an uneasy relationship with professionalism, however, whether we speak of soldiers as a special honored caste or soldiers as technical experts. Professional pride, from the time of Frederick II through the noon of the British Empire to the Green Berets in Vietnam, is marked by a sense of coolness and detachment from civilians, even on one's own side, and often a sense of kinship with fellow professionals on the other side. Each American war of the last hundred years—the Spanish-American War, World War I, World War II, the Korean War, and Vietnam War—has been fought with less patriotic fervor and more professionalism than the last. In part this is no doubt due to the increasing technical complexity of modern warfare. In part it may also be due to the fact that, fortunately for the United States, the more recent wars have been fought further from home. But the change in attitudes appears to have characterized the civilian as well as the military population, and it is possible that the peak of national fervor was attained in the Western world in the earlier part of this century.

Pursuit of Pleasure

Since there are ordinarily few forces inhibiting people's pursuit of external rewards, we do not ordinarily see people as intrinsically motivated to pursue these external rewards. Commitment is ordinarily not needed to explain or justify people's interest in power or money or sex. However—and this is a very important point—people can become committed to the pursuit of a particular external reward, can indeed come to treat that reward as the ultimate value in their lives. Misunderstanding of this point has led to some confusion in attribution theory, as recently pointed out by Kruglanski (1975) and Calder (1977). It has also led to frustration on the part of students of organizational behavior who have attempted to classify work goals or work outcomes as intrinsic or extrinsic (see Blau, 1964; Dyer & Parker, 1975). In the depression of the 1930s, some people jumped out of windows when they lost all their money. Others accepted their loss and picked up their lives, sometimes going on to recoup another fortune in the next period of prosperity. It is clear that for the people who killed themselves when they were wiped out, money had come to have more than instrumental or extrinsic value. Similarly, money in the form of salaries has come to have intrinsic value for the women's movement in its struggle to win recognition for women as equal contributors to national well-being. As Joanie Caucus in *Doonesbury* says during her first day on the job as a day care worker: "I must say, this isn't a whole lot different than just being a hassled mother. It's the same struggle to get through the day. Taking care of crying infants, feeding them lunch, supervising their play, picking up after their messes, stopping their fights, making them take naps . . . BUT I'M GETTING PAID FOR IT!"

Luxuries, extravagant living, and conspicuous consumption can be seen to acquire meaning in themselves when we observe people pursuing them or demonstrating them even when they are inconvenient or uncomfortable. The pattern of conspicuous consumption described by Thorstein Veblen sounds more like work than play. Hoarding is a superficially quite different pattern, but also one in which ultimate value has been ascribed to material goods. Periodically the newspapers will carry a story about some elderly person or couple (the Collier brothers in New York were a famous example) who are discovered, perhaps on their death, to have accumulated such mountains of junk in their house that the rooms are virtually impassable. Not a scrap has been thrown out for years and a multitude of garbage trucks are needed to haul everything away. This bizarre state does not come about all at once. For some reason, perhaps illness or an unwillingness to venture out of the house, people begin saving things instead of throwing them out. Gradually, unless the cycle is broken, they incur more and more sacrifices in the service of their saving. An increasing inability to have people over may enhance their sense of being attached to their special way of life. Gradually, they come to see themselves as more and more committed to their hoarding.

People can be committed to the pursuit of pleasure to the extent that they sacrifice other things—money, health, careers, relationships—to their interest in pleasure. Interestingly, people have the capacity to find pleasure in and attach value to the most amazing variety of superficially unpromising—and even bizarre—objects. "We have only to imagine a dog having to touch an old bone before getting an erection, a squirrel who must be beaten up before being sexually aroused, a chicken who gets sexually excited by looking at representations of chickens copulating, or a bull trying to pass himself for a cow, to have an idea of how peculiar our sexual behavior can actually be" (Moreno, 1977, p. 65). Without wishing to exaggerate the difference between humans and other animals, the capacity to attach value in this apparently bizarre fashion is probably an essential component of human beings' unique capacity for symbolizing. Ironically, while the ability to symbolize is in turn a critical feature of human language and communication—from which it derives—it also serves to work against the possibility of communication or to establish limits on what can be communicated. This is because we can agree on extrinsic value but not intrinsic value. Intrinsic value, created by our ability to attach a symbolic significance to things, is hard to explain and hard to justify to those who do not share the value (Brickman, 1978). Anything can be given intrinsic value by someone or some action, and—our crucial proposition—*something is given intrinsic value by every action*. If a task is done for no money, it is the task that is given intrinsic value. If the task is done for money, it is the money. Our object in the remainder of this chapter is to come to terms with this inescapable feature of human behavior, the creation of value through action.

VALUE CREATION

We once saw values as absolute or existing outside ourselves, whether in a Platonic or a Christian sense. Kant attempted to save their absolute status, while still locating them in behavior, by postulating that there were certain moral acts, categorical imperatives, that no rational being could avoid willing without self-contradiction. Kant's influence remains the most important opposition in philosophy to the idea that values reflect utilities, but it has not been sufficient to anchor any set of absolute values. With Kierkegaard, Nietzsche, and the death of God, we have come to a much more personal—and perhaps more terrifying—conception of value associated with existentialism (Barrett, 1958). With the death of God, people become as gods, and this in its most important sense means become the source of value. Efforts to grade objects or activities as more or less intrinsically rewarding (Blau, 1964; Dyer & Parker, 1975) are doomed to failure unless it is understood that the nature of value originates in human behavior.

Our thesis is not only that a sense of meaning and intrinsic value comes from actions, but that actions are the only place it can come from. Where else could value come from, besides action? There are only two other serious candidates for the answer to this question. One is that values come from what we are told, taught, or given reinforcement for. The other is that values come from our perception of the actual intrinsic worth of things, a perception that is presumably self-evident to every enlightened thinker. The second of these alternatives, philosophers have reluctantly concluded after two thousand years of trying to prove otherwise, is false. The first of these is not false, but incomplete. By itself, what we are taught and receive reinforcement for establishes extrinsic value, establishes our sense of what other people value. These things take on intrinsic value for a person only if they are transformed by the person's own investments, sacrifices, and actions.

Transforming Effort

The assignment of value is not simply a passive inference made from the observation of behavior in the absence of extrinsic reward. It is an active process of transforming the effort involved in that behavior. In this it differs from self-perception, which suggests a recording of something that is already there. Dissonance reduction is also an active process, but not one in which people are typically seen as creating value.

To be transformed, the effort must be seen in relation to at least a germinal goal. It is transformed, in short, through its bonding with an element with a positive valence. The bonding itself consumes energy, but the composite so created has a positive valence more intense than that of the initial positive element. In a widely cited experiment, Aronson and Mills (1959) showed that subjects valued their membership in a group more highly if they had to undergo a severe or embarrassing initiation in order to join. These negative events, however, must be seen as relevant to the group in order to create this value. If they are not, the value of the group will not be enhanced (Gerard & Mathewson, 1966). In many situations, there are positive elements readily available to which negative events can be attached almost effortlessly. In psychological experiments, for example, the value of contributing to science and the value of learning about oneself are generally available as free-floating positive elements. In two experiments, Houston, Bloom, Burish, and Cummings (1978) compared subjects who expected to receive a series of electric shocks with those who did not. The groups under stress rated the experience as more worthwhile. They could believe the stress had a purpose, even if the experimenter had not explained to them directly what that purpose was.

If a negative event is perceived as purely arbitrary, it cannot be transformed. What it produces then is the simple experience of frustration, and perhaps an attack on either the source of the frustration or the nearest safe target (Dollard, Doob, Miller, Mowrer, & Sears, 1939). Arbitrary frustrations are especially likely to lead to aggression (Pastore, 1952). Under these circumstances, the negative event makes the situation less attractive rather than more attractive. The cumulative effect of arbitrary frustrations is burnout, a loss of caring typically experienced by overwhelmed helping agents for the very populations they are supposed to be trying to help (Maslach, 1976). The fact that prisons are seen by offenders as arbitrary and meaningless punishment is perhaps the major single reason that prisons have failed utterly in their efforts to rehabilitate offenders and win from them a new allegiance to social norms (Brickman, 1977). Some critics favor accepting this defeat and abandoning any hope of reintegrating offenders (Wilson, 1975). If sentences can be established that involve offenders in making what they (and others) feel is meaningful restitution for their crimes, however, there is good reason for expecting this to produce results (Azrin & Wesolowski, 1974; Eglash, 1951). This also helps account for the cogency of Dreikers's (1968) recommendation that wherever possible punishment should "fit the crime" rather than be an arbitrarily arranged social consequence. The vast difference between negative consequences that can be transformed and negative consequences that cannot is perhaps alluded to by Sylvia Plath, who described one of her poems as being about two kinds of fire, "the fires of hell, which merely agonize, and the fires of heaven, which purify" (Sheppard, 1977).

The capacity to transform energy and enhance intrinsic value may be built into people biologically. When given a choice between getting free food and working for food, rats and pigeons prefer to work for the food (Carder & Berkowitz, 1970; Jensen, 1963; Neuringer, 1969; Singh, 1970). There is evidence in animals other than humans that effort enhances the value of a stimulus associated with the expenditure of effort (Lawrence & Festinger, 1962; Lewis, 1965). Behaviorists have recently given increasing attention to enormously effortful behavior, like the migration of eels or salmon, that does not appear to be generated or maintained by a history of reward. Skinner (1975, 1977) suggests that we call such behavior phylogenic behavior, calling attention to what he regards as its inherited origin and also what he feels is its affective neutrality. He thus places it outside the two categories of behavior previously considered fundamental in Skinnerian analysis, respondent (reflexes maintained by classical conditioning) and operant (behavior maintained by its reinforcing or rewarding consequences). Herrnstein (1977a, 1977b) objects to this radical change. He prefers to call such behavior self-reinforcing, maintained by the ultimately positive quality of the stimuli arising from the effort itself. By whatever name such behavior is called, it is clear that behaviorism has taken a long step toward recognizing behavior that other approaches would call intrinsically motivated.

In humans, at least, choice is the main operator of the transformation of effort. It is seeing the effort as a consequence of choice that allows it to be transformed. This is, of course, our familiar triad of a positive element (represented in the choice), a negative element (represented by the effort), and the perception of a link between the two (represented by the person's sense of responsibility). The variable of choice was studied explicitly in an experiment on people's reactions to reward by Folger, Rosenfield, and Hays (1978). Subjects given a choice about their participation developed more subsequent interest in an experimental game when they were not rewarded for working on it than when they were lavishly rewarded. Subjects not given a choice showed more subsequent interest in the game when they were rewarded for their participation than when they were not. The joint effects of choice and effort were studied by Brickman, Bradshaw, and Wasylyshyn (1978). Children were assigned (i.e., no choice) to a club in their classroom or were permitted to choose their club (i.e., high choice). The teacher manipulated effort by varying the amount of time the children spent on tedious numbering and writing tasks, the amount of free play time, and the dismissal time (early versus late) for lunch. In the high-choice condition, children liked their club just as much (actually, slightly more) in the high-effort as in the low-effort condition. In the low-choice condition, children liked their club more in the low-effort than in the high-effort condition.

When a task is interesting, effort is easy to transform; an interesting task can be thought of as one that the person would have chosen. In looking at student evaluations of courses, Frey and Flay (1978) found that a teacher who is skillful at getting the material across and who is high in warmth or rapport receives higher ratings when demanding a lot of work from students. Teachers who are not skillful instructors and not warm, whose classes are presumably less interesting, receive lower ratings when they set a high work load than when they set a low one. Several studies have demonstrated that an interesting task is not liked any better when subjects are paid for doing it, and may even be liked less. The money is not essential to the transformation of the effort involved, and it may even hinder it. On the other hand, a boring task is liked better when subjects are paid for doing it. Calder and Staw (1975) found that subjects were less likely to enjoy assembling jigsaw puzzles with interesting pictures when they were paid for doing it but more likely to enjoy assembling blank jigsaw puzzles when they were paid for doing it. Hamner and Foster (1975) found that contingent pay enhanced subjects' interest in coding relatively dull math instruction surveys but not in coding more interesting sex attitude surveys. Kim and Schuler (1978) found that employees of a public utility with stimulating jobs were equally likely to be satisfied with a high and low degree of feedback from their supervisors and co-workers, but employees with nonstimulating jobs were more satisfied with their work when they received high rather than low feedback.

The present perspective is compatible with two apparently different explanations that have been offered for the finding that children given extrinsic rewards for engaging in an activity are less likely to pursue that activity in a subsequent period of free choice (Lepper & Greene, 1975; Lepper, Greene, & Nisbett, 1973). The first is that extrinsic reward undermines intrinsic motivation. The second, proposed by Reiss and Sushinsky (1975), is that the anticipated reward is a distraction and that curiosity in a novel play situation can be undermined by the presentation of a distraction. Smith and Pittman (1978) distinguished between distraction potentially associated with the promise of pay and distraction associated with an extraneous source. In their experiment, they produced external distraction by playing a taped lecture while subjects attempted to complete a skill game. Distraction over a few trials disrupted subjects' interest in the game during a subsequent free-choice period, but distraction over many trials, during which subjects presumably had a chance to get used to it and discount or work through its effects, did not. Reward over either few or many trials disrupted subjects' subsequent interest in the game. Thus it appears that both reward and distraction have effects, though the effects of distraction do not explain the effects of reward.

In our view, distraction and reward, though different, produce their effects through a common operation. They both interfere with the process by which the subject expends energy and thereby transforms the value of the activity being pursued. Distraction makes it harder to expand the energy in concentrated and unconflicted form; reward makes it harder to see the energy expended as attached to the activity itself rather than to the reward. Sexy illustrations in advertisements make it more difficult for subjects to recall the brand names of the products advertised (Steadman, 1969). This can occur both because subjects are less likely to spend time viewing the product itself and because they are less likely to perceive the energy they do spend as motivated by interest in the product rather than interest in sex. There is less energy to transform, and less likelihood that it will be transformed in a way that enhances the value of the product.

People may desire the transformation of effort, especially when they are expending enormous effort in one domain and their lives contain no other sources of meaning or meaningful investments. We think this explains in part why alcohol and drugs are perceived as having such enormous power by people who devote their lives to their pursuit and consumption. The costs involved in regularly consuming large amounts of alcohol or drugs are so great as to leave very little else in a person's life intact. The effort involved in simply getting, maintaining, and protecting a supply of these items is quite substantial in itself, especially in the case of drugs, but also in the case of alcohol after addiction has proceeded for a while. As a number of observers have pointed out, users evolve out of the activities of procuring, using, and suffering for their habit an entire life-style, complete with a set of supportive and adversarial social relationships that confirm the user's interpretation of events. This is what Berne (1964) meant by calling alcoholism a game people play. Purely physical attempts at a cure, like antabuse for alcohol or methadone for heroin, are doomed to fail because they provide no alternative set of meanings and addicts reject them (Preble & Casey, 1972). Curiously, at the same time users are making such enormous sacrifices for their habits and experiencing what they feel is the overwhelming, irresistable power of the alcohol or the drug, they maintain fiercely that their goal is controlled usage and that they can quit whenever they want. They must maintain some sense of choice in order to be able to transform their sacrifices into the feeling that they are pursuing something of great value.

When all else fails, when every other redeeming feature is lost, there is always one transformation remaining that can attach meaning and value to suffering and even despair. The transformation of last resort is the idea of being a lesson to others, of bearing witness. An 80-year-old man writes to Ann Landers (1977) to describe his lifetime of hell married to an alcoholic and to recommend that no one else put up with the same. He says, in conclusion, "I hope you feel this letter is good enough for your column. If just one person takes my advice, I will feel I have done some good in this world." Or after the catastrophes in the Book of Job and *Moby Dick*, the lone survivors justify both their agony and their survival with the words, "And I only am escaped alone to tell thee." Their message is delivered presumably to avert the repetition of their suffering by others. Similar feelings are conveyed by survivors of concentration camps (Frankl, 1959), with their passionate conviction that the world must remember what was done. Cancer patients find meaning in their cancer through a commitment to making the adaptation of other cancer patients less traumatic (Wortman & Dunkel-Schetter, 1979). Survivors of a man-made disaster (the collapse of a dam made vulnerable by negligence) at Buffalo Creek appear to have been unable to find a message in the wreckage of their homes, which would probably have to take the form of rage at corporate greed and indifference. Instead, write Lifton and Olson (1976, p. 8), "They remain locked in their death anxiety, survivor guilt, numbing, and impaired human relationships, bound to the disaster itself and to its destructive psychological consequences" (see Janoff-Bulman & Frieze, 1983; Silver, Boon, & Stones, 1983). Erik Erikson (1950) wrote that people could endure almost any frustration, provided they saw it as having meaning. What would make them neurotic, or worse, was frustration that seemed to have no meaning.

Attaching Significance to Reward

Rewards are not significant in themselves. They acquire significance through their association with effort. Dissonance theory experiments, such as the severity of initiation study by Aronson and Mills (1959), support this conclusion. Shaffer and Hendrick (1971) have shown that subjects rate a difficult task as more interest-ing and enjoyable than an easy one when they merely anticipate working on it as well as when they actually work on it. Research on achievement motivation, mean-while, has regularly found that people see success on a hard task as more valuable and more worthwhile than success on an easy task (Atkinson & Feather, 1966; Weiner, 1974), and indeed, success on hard tasks has been found to have greater benefits for future performance than success on easy tasks (Linsenmeier & Brick-man, 1978). The literature on achievement motivation has suggested that success on difficult tasks has greater incentive value because people can take more pride in their achievement and their sense of personal mastery when the task is hard rather than easy. Our analysis suggests a different perspective. Difficult tasks require more effort for a reward, success, that is less certain. There is clearly more ambivalence to be overcome in undertaking a difficult task than an easy one. Under ordinary circumstances, therefore, people undertake difficult tasks only when they see them-selves as prepared to expend considerable effort and thus only when they see them-selves as highly committed to success. The fact that people take more pride in success on difficult tasks comes from their greater willingness to see a hard success as the result of praiseworthy ability and effort. But their willingness to make such an attri-bution can itself be understood as something that symbolizes and sustains the more difficult commitment they are making. If they must undertake or continue the task but cannot anticipate success, we would no longer expect them to enhance the incentive value of success but to instead find some other basis for their commit-ment, such as "It's not whether you win or lose, but how you play the game."

This helps explain why a relationship or a project cannot be salvaged merely by taking steps to reduce the work or effort of those involved. Sometimes, in an attempt to keep a spouse in a relationship that is not deeply satisfying, the partner will give the spouse complete freedom. In other words, the spouse can have the rela-tionship and all the rewards he or she wants outside of the relationship too. Yet in the few cases we have observed, the spouse leaves anyway. In reducing their costs to zero, their partners have also reduced to zero their ability to attach significance to any of the rewards in the relationship. A task can never be made easy enough for those who feel they have had no choice in the matter or can find no personal mean-ing in the activity. The effort in such instances is much more disagreeable than the vastly greater effort the person could be making in another domain in which that effort is fused with the available rewards in a way that makes both seem significant. This has, of course, been amply recognized by people and institutions zealous to cultivate loyalty. Though armies may permit members greater earthly rewards than religions—insisting on less in the way of poverty and chastity—military discipline is as much a byword as religious discipline. This is even the path to the most signifi-cant reward of the contemplative Eastern religions. "Descriptions abound of the harsh discipline to which the Zen novice submits. His enlightenment is associated with the effort and the suffering of this discipline, which detaches his life from the flow of normal experience and opens to him access to ecstatic meditation far re-moved from the humdrum interests of life" (Polanyi & Prosch, 1975, p. 30).

A number of the major contributors to the study of intrinsic motivation have attempted to distinguish between a type of reward that is significant in itself and a type that is not (see, e.g., Deci, 1975; Lepper & Defoe, 1979; Ross, 1976). The idea in all cases is that rewards people perceive as informative about or determined by their competence at a task will increase their intrinsic motivation for that task, while rewards that people feel are not informative about their competence or are determined primarily by someone else's desire to control them will decrease their intrinsic motivation. Our perspective is somewhat different. Rather than rewards that have informational value building up commitment to an activity, it is a person's commitment to an activity that gives rewards their informational value.

For success to have meaning, a person must be able to say, in effect, "I would not have done so well unless I really cared." Premature or arbitrary rewards are demoralizing rather than satisfying, as Camus found his Nobel Prize, and can lead to a sense of depression rather than a sense of fulfillment (Seligman, 1975). This is especially true for rewards that signal the end of working before the person is ready to end working. If people short-circuit effort by cheating, they totally undermine the informational value of the reward for themselves, though it may still appear to have value to other people. They likewise undermine the informational value of a reward if they explicitly ask for it to be given, as reassurance, rather than earning it. People do this when they are anxious or depressed, and this helps account for why the reassurances they receive under these circumstances have so little value for them (Coates & Wortman, 1978)—sometimes to the bafflement and irritation of those giving the reassurances. Ingratiation, if too easy, can also pay this price. Other people's liking is not valued or trusted if too easily obtained.

All of this implies that Cooley's (1902) conception of the looking-glass self is too passive an image to capture fully the process of self-knowledge. Other people are indeed a kind of mirror who reflect back to us who we are, which we learn from the way they treat us. But what this image means to us is itself determined by the energy we have spent in interacting with them, by the quality and quantity of our own caring. As we discussed the confusions and satisfactions of cross-cultural contact, a Jamaican woman said to one of us, "You must reach out to others in order to know yourself." The quality of the knowing is determined by the quality of the reaching out.

If we do try our hardest, if we feel we have lived up to our potential or given the task our best shot, defeat is in good measure deprived of its sting. Stretching ourselves to the limit creates its own value as well as attaching value to winning (Csikszentmihalyi, 1978). This is really a proposition that needs no empirical research, but there is ample evidence for it in the testimony of one group that thinks and cares a great deal about such things—athletes. Here is the reflection of one all-state high school basketball player who played well in college but failed to make a professional team: "The situation wasn't right. I wasn't in the right place at the right time. But I felt I gave it my best shot. So I wasn't disappointed. I had to think about doing something else" (Bell, 1978, p. 22). Here is Jerry Sloan, who did play professional basketball and was in fact known for the intensity with which he played, but whose team never won a championship: "What stands out most in my mind is that we played probably as close to our potential as we could. We had the right chemistry, or whatever, and I like to think we went as far as we could, even though we were basically losers in the public's eye" (Hillyer, 1978, p. 34). Here is Mike Marshall, a baseball relief pitcher with fierce concentration: "Nothing matters to me but the competition against the hitters. By comparison, whether the game is won or lost is absolutely unimportant. Losing doesn't bother me if I've done the best I can" (Jauss, 1978, p. 6). Fans also appreciate intensity at this level. It is one of the things that made Arnold Palmer king of golf and kept him there years after he ceased to be the dominant player. "When he won, he rattled everyone's teeth. When he lost, he had gone for broke. No one could say he hadn't tried. Sometimes he'd tried too hard" (Husar, 1978, p. 1).

The Structure of Costs
and Rewards

In talking about transforming effort and attaching significance to reward, we are back to the idea of commitment as a positive element, a negative element, and a bond between the two. The bond is the key. Without it, costs are merely painful and rewards are of no significance. With it, value should be positively associated not only with the rewards of the activity but also with its costs. We may illustrate this point with some data Allen Blocker and one of the coauthors (PB) collected on people's feelings about their church and religion. Eighty college students who had some church affiliation completed a questionnaire on their church activities. It was found that their happiness with their church was positively correlated and about equally correlated with the benefits they perceived themselves as receiving from church (e.g., entertainment enjoyed through the church, power gained because of inner strength, resources received in times of need, excitement experienced in church services) and the things they perceived themselves as giving up for church (e.g., activities such as drinking or sex that the church would not approve of, resources donated to charity, time that would have been spent on more interesting activities, friends who did things the person could not approve of).

Masters and Johnson (1974) make a very similar point about people's commitment in love, sex, and marriage. They place a great deal of emphasis on sexual pleasure, on what they call the seal of commitment. But they also look for evidence that each partner will temper his or her own search for pleasure, both within the relationship and outside of it, in the interests of securing the other partner's pleasure and the relationship itself. The pleasure bond, as they call their book, derives its value from both of these elements.

It is hardly surprising that most behavior has both costs and rewards. What is surprising, perhaps, is that an identical sequence of costs and rewards can be structured in ways that lead to totally different perceptions of that sequence. In one, the intrinsic value of the sequence predominates. In the other, the sequence appears to have only extrinsic value. One example is the difference between a sequence of mutual gifts and a sequence of exchanges or trades. In each case the essential condition is the same: a principle of fairness or reciprocity that ensures that each party to the transactions receives goods and services that balance the goods and services they contribute (Blau, 1964; Gouldner, 1960). The difference is only the rather subtle one that in the cases of gifts there can be no bargaining about what the return will be, no coercion of the return, and indeed no insistence that a return be made promptly (Malinowski, 1922; Mauss, 1954). Prompt repayment is the height of good form in economic exchange but the height of bad form in returning a gift. Put bluntly, a sequence of mutual gifts is only a slower, less precise, more cumbersome form of exchange.

What, then, do participants gain that makes gifts so important in society, and what is the source of that gain? They gain the sense that each is committed to the other person rather than to the goods and services in transit, the sense that they have intrinsic value for each other rather than only extrinsic value. The entire protocol of gift giving aims to support this sense by forbidding either donors or recipients to attend too obviously to the material value of the gift (Blau, 1964). Donors must downplay the importance of substantial gifts ("It's nothing"), while recipients must express appreciation even for awkward or minor gifts ("It's the thought that counts"). The basic characteristic of the process that makes the perception of intrinsic motivation possible, however, is its very slowness, imprecision, and cumbersome nature. One gives with only a vague understanding of what one will get in return or when one will get it, and perhaps with only a vague memory of what one has received in the past. The isolation of giving from past and future receiving makes very salient the perception of initiative in the giver, which is to say both intrinsic motivation to give and commitment to the relationship in which the giving takes place. The actual balance of items exchanged as sales or contracts may be identical to the balance exchanged as gifts, but the difference in the timing of the two processes allows extrinsic value to dominate the former while intrinsic value dominates the latter.

The difference between the orientations underlying contracts and gifts is fundamental to the most basic split in the history of Western civilization according to Kaplan and Kaplan (1979). They draw on the religious philosophy of Lev Shestov (1966), who explores the conflict between Aristotelianism (from Athens), with its epistemology of objective reason, and Abrahamism (Jerusalem), with its epistemology of subjective revelation. They write:

> This, for Shestov, is the contrast between Abraham and Socrates. One who emulates Socrates "looks before he leaps" while one who emulates Abraham "leaps before he looks." This, to us, is the essence of the distinction between *contract* and *covenant*. Abraham agrees to accept the *covenent* with God *without* preconditions other than mutual fidelity (the destination of his journey is not specified in advance), allowing the terms of the covenant to slowly reveal themselves to the two participants. Indeed the Hebrew Bible can be seen from this perspective as the outworking of the Arahamic covenant. Much Greek (and Western) thought after Plato, in contrast, seems to emphasize the ideas of contract, of the mutual obligations spelled out *in advance* between state and citizen. (p. 101)

And, as Kaplan and Kaplan (1979) write, this difference is reflected in the child-sacrifice legends of the Hebrew and Hellenic civilizations. Agamemnon sacrifices his daughter Iphegenea in return for good winds to sail his fleet; this is a contract. Abraham, on the other hand, offers to sacrifice his child Isaac, *"what he is and can be* in return for *absolutely nothing*. This is what we mean by the essence of covenant" (p. 102).

Sequences can involve an exchange of hostilities as well as an exchange of gifts. In this case, however, people are much more likely to see themselves in a quid pro quo exchange governed by the other person's acts than to see themselves as engaged in the unsolicited expression of their own feelings. This means, of course, that the two parties to an exchange of hostilities perceive the exchange in quite different ways (Watzlawick, Beavin, & Jackson, 1967), each seeing the other as the initiator—in contrast to the exchange of gifts, in which both see themselves as the initiator. There are three possible explanations for this difference. First, exchanges of gifts tend to be slow and widely spaced; exchanges of hostility tend to be intense and concentrated. Spaced exchanges probably support participants' perception of themselves as intrinsically motivated, while in faster exchanges participants probably see themselves as motivated by events. Second, it is less socially desirable to admit that one is motivated by hatred or negative feelings than by love or positive feelings, especially if one continues rather than terminates the relationship. People minimize the extent of their responsibility for negative sequences in order to escape blame for them. But they can be committed to such sequences; marital therapists know this and typically try to get people to understand it. Finally, the greater salience of intrinsic sources in positive sequences and extrinsic sources in negative sequences may be not a difference in social desirability but an effect of the sequences themselves. Experiencing behavior as intrinsically motivated may be associated with experiencing the exchange as positive, while experiencing behavior as extrinsically motivated may be associated with feeling the exchange is hostile.

When we look at the immediate cause of an event in a person's life, it may seem to be unequivocally internal or external to the person. As we trace back a sequence of causes, however, we find that internal causes are in turn produced by prior external causes and vice versa (Brickman, Ryan, & Wortman, 1975). This gives an ultimate chicken-and-egg ambiguity to the question of whether a particular event was chosen by or imposed on the person. Which the person feels depends upon whether the person highlights the internal or external events in the sequence. The fact that both are in the sequence, however, accounts for the fact that a person's perception can reverse with startling suddenness, as in divorce, in which the value attributed to the spouse and the marriage undergoes a dramatic, if temporary, disappearance. It also accounts for the fact that a person's perception of a situation or a relationship can oscillate with dismaying frequency, as in many marriages in which partners alternate between periods of dominance and impulse expression and periods of penance and inhibition. An extreme but lucid example is a marriage in which the husband is an alcoholic. He beats and abuses his wife when he is drunk, and she criticizes and shames him during periods when he is sober. By understanding the value both attach to their periods of suffering, which they see as penance, and the value they also attach to their periods of expressive dominance, which they see as richly earned, we can understand how such marriages are much more stable than observers would expect (Berne, 1964). At the same time, we can understand how the partners' feelings about the relationship fluctuate wildly, depending upon whether they are in a period in which the costs of the relationship dominate their perceptual field or a period in which the costs are transformed and intrinsic value is dominant.

At times we are acutely aware of the ambiguity of the motivational field, either in agony or in amusement. In agony, Holden Caulfield, in J. D. Salinger's (1964) *The Catcher in the Rye* wonders how he could ever trust his motivation to be something such as a lawyer:

> Even if you *did* go around saving guys' lives and all, how would you know if you did it because you really *wanted* to save guys' lives, or because you did it because what you *really* wanted to do was be a terrific lawyer, with everybody slapping you on the back and congratulating you in court when the goddam trial was over, the reporters and everybody, the way it is in the dirty movies? How would you know you weren't being a phony? The trouble is, you *wouldn't*. (p. 172)

In a different mood, author Eric Ambler recalls the advice he was given by Noel Coward on this same point of ambiguity: "Noel Coward used to say, 'You must write for yourself, dear boy. But if enough people don't like what you write for yourself, you must find another profession'" (Ginna, 1977, p. 94). It is reported that Puritan divines deliberated at length the case of a man who had ice skated to church on Sunday. Skating, like all forms of recreation, was forbidden on Sunday. The man's defense was that the roads were impassable and that skating on the frozen river was the only way he could get to church. The divines' rejoinder was a question: Had he enjoyed the skating? It would not be a sin if he had not enjoyed it.

Ordinarily, however, we do not experience an oscillation between intrinsic and extrinsic value in an activity, because our perception of that activity is structured in a stable way that makes one dominant. Sometimes we will not see the other at all, such as when a person in love claims that the costs involved in helping a loved one are not costs at all, or when a person alienated from a job can find no rewarding feature at all in the drudgery. More usually, one will dominate the field without totally obscuring the other, so that people will claim that their involvement in an activity is primarily intrinsic or extrinsic but that elements of the other are also present. This stability, however, is like the stable image in a reversible figure. It may be hard to see the alternative organization, but it is there. Actually, the analogy of intrinsic value as an embedded figure or a hidden Gestalt is slightly more precise than the simple image of intrinsic and extrinsic value as reversible figure and ground. They are reversible, but they are not equally likely perceptual outcomes. Extrinsic value is initially and ordinarily dominant. The sense of intrinsic value comes from an act akin to perceptual integration. It may become stable, but its stability rests upon a continuing expenditure of effort by the perceiver. If this expenditure ceases, the field will eventually collapse into a simpler one in which only extrinsic value appears to be present.

The present analysis helps us to understand the enduring puzzle of altruism and egotism in human motivation. The long debate (see Wispé, 1972) has concerned whether humans can be truly altruistic or whether even in acts that appear unselfish people are actually serving their long term self-interest or satisfying subtle forms of a need for appreciation or a need for competence. By our analysis, altruism in the truest sense is a special kind of intrinsic motivation that can indeed grow out of and guide a person's behavior. But it exists embedded within a context of self-interested behavior and extrinsic value that is always available for observers to call attention to. There are biological limits on how altruistic an organism can be and still survive. Beyond that, however, the question of altruism versus egotism is structured in a way that makes a stable answer impossible, since the answer depends upon what elements dominate the observer's perception of behavior.

Individual Versus Shared Meaning

Although we have been talking about how people create value for themselves, how the value so created relates to other people's or society's values is overwhelmingly important. This is important first in determining how the individual is accepted by other people. Becker (1968) provides an illuminating discussion of the rationalizations people offer for crimes, placing these rationalizations along a continuum from highly deviant to quite conventional. A conventional justification (e.g., extreme poverty), if one can be found, makes life much easier for the criminal, for "only the possibility that others might recognize the justification as reasonable allows the actor to expiate his behavior" (Becker, 1968, p. 322). Although dissonance theory has focused heavily on the study of single isolated individuals, the dramatic early investigation of a doomsday cult (Festinger, Riecken, & Schachter, 1956) clearly indicated the importance of social support for individual belief systems. Members who were in the presence of others with similar beliefs at the time the prophecy failed maintained their belief in the prophet and accepted her reinterpretation of events, while members who were alone and isolated did not.

How well individual and collective values fit together is also of obvious importance to the welfare of society. In fact, as Campbell (1975), among others, has argued, the primary purpose of socialization is to instill in individuals at least enough prosocial or altruistic motivation to sustain a sense of collective purpose and allow society to function. Rituals are designed to generate this sense of shared meaning. Polanyi and Prosch (1975) note that their formality and artificiality is not accidental but vital to this purpose:

> We have a special difficulty in our day in truly dwelling in formal rituals and customs. Our modern temper balks at all such things. Since they are essentially unoriginal, we tend to deem them incapable of expressing genuine feelings and to reject them as shallow pretense. But this, of course, totally misses

their point. It is the very artificiality of traditional forms that enables them to act as a framework, detaching the events to which they apply and thus endowing them with a forceful and lasting quality through the work of our own luminous imaginative powers. The destruction of formal occasion in the name of authenticity has the effect of diffusing our existence into scattered details, deprived of memorable meaning. Only through our surrender to such occasions do we find ourselves affiliated to a comprehensive, lasting framework which gives meaning to our life and death and to the myriads of separable events in between. Otherwise we do not see the universality that we share with others. Occasions, such as our birth and death, and those of others whose lives we share, can be seen as essential to a lasting whole of things when marked by appropriate ceremonies or rites. But without such ceremonies they become no more significant than the stone we stumbled over in the path or the coin we lost in the subway. Each of the numberless events in our lives is then adventitious, and the whole is inchoate and merely "a tale told by an idiot, full of sound and fury, signifying nothing." (p. 119)

Opposing society's need to sustain a sense of collective purpose are individuals' rational, and perhaps genetic, tendencies to pursue their own self-interest, regardless of consequences for others. It may be, however, that Campbell and similar critics overemphasize the enduring importance of establishing collective values in the face of individual selfishness. Certainly there have been long periods in history where the greater danger has come from collective demands and heroic efforts have been necessary to preserve even small areas of individual freedom. What may distinguish our treatment of value creation from previous discussions of the same idea is our understanding that the process of creating values has a range of definite, nonarbitrary functions for both the individual and for society, though the functions are not the same for the individual and for society. Indeed, the primary stake of both in the value creation process may be creating values that limit the demands that can be placed on each by the other.

Collective values can be created by novel collective actions just as individual values are created by individual actions. Community organizer Saul Alinsky (1972) analyzes a historical example, the transformation of the almost spontaneous sit-down strikes of the United Automobile Workers in their 1937 drive to organize General Motors to a new ideology.

The seizure of private property caused an uproar in the nation. With rare exception every labor leader ran for cover—this was too revolutionary for them. The sit-down strikers began to worry about the illegality of their action and the why and wherefore, and it was then that the chief of all C.I.O. organizers, (John L.) Lewis, gave them their rationale. He thundered, "The right to a man's job transcends the right of private property! The C.I.O. stands squarely behind these sit-downs!"

The sit-down strikers at G.M. cheered. *Now* they knew *why* they had done what they did, and *why* they would stay to the end. The lesson here is that a major job of the organizer is to instantly develop the rationale for actions which have taken place by accident or impulsive anger. Lacking the rationale, the action becomes inexplicable to its participants and rapidly disintegrates into defeat. Possessing a rationale gives action a meaning and purpose. (pp. 163–164)

More commonly, collective values are traditional and individuals are simply taught collective values. These collective values, however, do not automatically become personal values. In fact, no amount of mere instruction can make them compelling or real to individuals (Brickman, 1978). Collective values become personal values only through the same process of work, effort, and sacrifice that, under the right circumstances, makes anything a personal value. We may make a mistake in trying to teach people to appreciate the heritage of the past without allowing them to experience something of the effort that went into creating that heritage. It is a testable hypothesis that children appreciate exposure to great art more after they have first tried their own hand at different forms of art and attached value to their own efforts. It is certainly our hypothesis that graduate students appreciate exposure to statistics more after they have first tried their own hand at working with data they have collected. Likewise, for people to appreciate their political institutions, they must have some sense of the effort and struggle that went into their creation and indeed some sense of having contributed themselves to this effort and creation. Both Mao Tse-tung and Thomas Jefferson believed this, each of them advocating a revolution approximately every 20 years so that the political order of society would be renewed and revitalized by each generation.

The paradox is that things that society labels as having intrinsic value have, by definition, extrinsic pressure on them. Because people are under pressure to attain these values, it is harder for people to see their attainment as the result of personal choice. This is especially threatening to adolescents who have not yet established their own identity. For adolescents, writes Douvan (1974), "When compliance and inner drive are served by one act, the task becomes more subtle and difficult. One must perform the act yet find some other way to express its inner spring and establish clearly that it is not compelled. When this becomes too difficult adolescents may be seduced by their autonomy needs and negativism into doing what they really do not care to do or into failing to do what they truly want" (p. 25). One pathway out of the paradox comes from the realization that social roles are much more poorly defined, much more open to improvisation, and much more demanding of individual skill for their successful enactment than adolescents suspect:

Almost without exception roles are only roughly prescriptive—they are like an architect's rough drawings that become converted to detailed blueprints only as they are filled in by particular role occupants. And somewhere along the line most adolescents will discover that a relationship that started as a role relationship can become a full personal friendship—with an admired teacher, club leader, or minister—that the role does not contradict the special qualities and capacities of the person who fills it. (Douvan, 1974, p. 33)

This is the pathway followed by most people in their jobs, a theme that comes through repeatedly in the interviews in Studs Terkel's (1974) panorama of America, *Working*. Workers in all walks of life see more intrinsic value and less extrinsic value in their occupation than others imagine. There is more skill and more satisfaction involved in their lines of work than other people realize, but they are not as well paid as other people think. The result of this combination of perceptions is a considerable degree of intrinsic motivation sustaining the performance of a socially prescribed role.

CONCLUSION

The process of value creation, like the process of thought, takes place outside of awareness. It is the values created, like the products of thought, that people recognize, even when they cannot correctly identify what factors produced these outcomes (Nisbett & Wilson, 1977). We have already noted how the components of intrinsic value may be hard to put into words. The very effort to specify them or bring them into awareness may disrupt them (see Csikszentmihalyi, 1978), as the organization of a figure is disrupted when we attend separately to its parts. The process of value creation is not easily changed just because we know about it. This is in part the case because the process takes place outside of awareness. More generally this is true because awareness of the forces operating on us is not in itself sufficient to change these forces. We still get wet even if we know why it rains, we still get hurt even if we know why we are rejected, we still wonder whether a situation is an emergency or whether we should help even if we have heard of Kitty Genovese. Our behavior will still have consequences for us even after we understand the changes it sets in motion.

On the other hand, a general understanding of the process of value creation is an important human achievement. By now it should be clear that the idea that behavior creates value is an expression, not a limitation, of human power. To have the capacity to create value for ourselves is to be as gods. Admittedly, the domain of these godheads is limited, because it extends only to ourselves, and even there it falls short of the omnipotence we have traditionally ascribed to gods. Over its limited domain, however, this creative power involves all the opportunity, and responsibility, we can handle.

Sex is a good example. For people who are fortunate, the physical pleasure of sex is enormous. The meaning or the value of sex, however, is determined by the conditions under which people experience it. If people can choose these conditions, they can choose exactly what meaning and value this primal source of pleasure will have for them. We may feel that other people or people of other times have attached too much value to sex or made sex too important, in which case the correction is to be more casual about when we engage in sex. We may feel that other people or people at other times have attached too little value to sex or made it too routine, in which case the correction is to reserve sexual behavior for special circumstances. The meaning of sexuality, however, comes not from what we say but from what we do, and from that it comes unavoidably. Understanding the power that we have in committing ourselves to a line of behavior may make us more confident that we will be happy in what we choose, and more aware of the importance of choosing wholeheartedly. At the same time, it may make us more cautious about choosing in the first place. Should we allow ourselves to become happy in a relationship or a career when we are not sure that this is the best we can do? Eventually, we may look to a new form of therapy that can help people better understand and better use their own power to create value.

Values are not arbitrary, nor are they all equally good. On the contrary, they bear an orderly relationship to human behavior, and they—like the behavior—may be more or less functional for the individual and more or less functional for society. All things, however, can acquire value, and good things do not automatically acquire value. That is the responsibility we bear for our behavior.

CHAPTER FOUR
CONTROL OR COMMITMENT?

Philip Brickman
Jurgis Karuza, Jr.

Research on control in the last decade has primarily been devoted to a series of vivid demonstrations of the importance of a sense of control. Individuals who believe that they have control, or will have control, over their environment are better able to withstand a series of shocks or stresses that the environment imposes (Glass & Singer, 1972). In this chapter we shall look more closely at what is involved in both the exercise of control and the belief that control can be exercised. With this in mind, it seems appropriate to begin by describing explicitly and formally what we see as the relationship between commitment and control. We shall then review some of the extensive control literature, arguing that the commitment process is vital to the effective exercise of control and that many of the benefits heretofore attributed to the prospect of control are in fact derived from the commitment process. Continuing, we will examine situations in which control and commitment coexist and will argue that effective control rests on a structure of commitment in which the commitment process gives behavior the momentum necessary for a person to achieve control and reach success. Finally, we will examine the limits of control and the virtues of commitment by considering cases in which either control without commitment or commitment without control is possible. We end by highlighting commitment's ability to sustain action and purpose in the harshest of circumstances, and its promise for growth.

A MODEL OF COMMITMENT
AND CONTROL

The notion that individuals seek control is, on one level, as much a truism as the idea that individuals seek pleasure and avoid pain. By control we mean, initially, nothing different than the ability to influence the environment. This control may be *imperfect*. A fisherman's net, for example, affects only a small part of the river, but the fisherman only needs the net to occasionally affect a few fish at a few spots in the river. Control may also be *indirect*. Relatives of the person doing the fishing may gain fish not by their influence over the fish but by their influence over the fisherman. Indeed, they may prefer to rely on someone else's control of the larger environment than to try to directly control this environment themselves. When people exercise this preference, it is because they are more secure in their belief that they can influence another person who will succeed than in their own belief that they can directly control the environment. Control may, in some instances, require *minimal effort*. Fishing by placing a net in the river is a passive form of control, as is gathering fruit that has fallen from a tree. Nonetheless, even in these instances, the individual is still required to recognize the availability of a reward and to control it by generating an appropriate response—even if the response is merely reaching out to take the reward or opening one's mouth to ask for it.

Nonetheless, focusing on the question of control has two conceptual advantages for psychology over focusing on the question of reinforcement. The first is that the question of control naturally calls attention to individuals' relationship to their environment. Control, or lack of control, specifies a particular kind of relationship individuals have with this environment. A reinforcement, on the other hand, is an object in the environment. True, this reinforcement, such as food, may acquire its reinforcing value from a drive state within the individual, such as hunger. As Kurt Lewin long ago and repeatedly told us, psychology should study behavior as a function of both the individual and the environment. We can do this by continually reminding ourselves to study both drives and reinforcements, both traits and situations. Studying control, however, makes this easier by giving our topic of inquiry a label that refers directly to the relationship between the individual and the environment. Having defined control, we now turn to our model.

Any behavior or action of an individual can have potential consequences for both the external environment and the individual's internal states. In the language of our book, control involves the external correspondence of an act, the idea that one's behavior corresponds with important consequences (Brickman, 1978). People who believe that they have control, in Rotter's (1966), Seligman's (1975), Bandura's (1977), or our sense, believe that the reinforcements they receive are contingent on the responses they make. In contrast, an act's internal correspondence involves its meaning for the individual, the value generated by and attached to the behavior itself (Brickman, 1978). Although the categories of meaning may be learned, the process by which they are attached to responses is direct and immediate, without a period of reflection or comparison.

Action thus has two possible consequences. The first is control, which, if successful, results in reinforcement, which in turn operates to sustain action. Behavioral psychologists have focused their research on this cycle for the last 50 years—though not always with explicit attention to the idea of control. The second is commitment, in which the internal sense of meaning and value, if attained, strengthens commitment which, in turn, operates to sustain action. Our general model that depicts the flow of events through these commitment and control cycles is shown in Figure 4-1. Action, the event that links these two cycles, is sustained by either cycle or, ideally, both.

The basic distinction we make is between a process that sustains behavior by reinforcements and a process that sustains behavior through commitment. The reinforcing consequences of a behavior may either be produced by the individual or provided by someone else. It may be either something that occurs inside the individual or something that the individual observes occurring in the environment. In any case, reinforcement is a consequence of behavior that can be distinguished from the behavior. The meaning of a behavior, on the other hand, is something a person experiences directly from the successful organization of behavior. Clearly, our major departure from previous understanding is this distinction between meaning and reinforcement. All actions mean different things depending on their intentions and circumstances. But behavior that generates a sense of meaning is necessarily intrinsically motivated or characterized by a sense of intrinsic value. This, as discussed in chapter 3, "Meaning and Value," entails the transformation of the effort involved in the behavior, which in turn requires the bonding of positive features of a behavior with its negative features, such as the costs, uncertainties, and sacrifices it involves. All actions that are fully meaningful have something in common, however: they are experienced as the best possible—and in this sense, perhaps the only possible—actions given the circumstances and given one's capacities. Such actions leave the person free of regret. This implies a certain indifference to outcome, a sense that any outcomes that ensue are also the best or only possible ones. Throughout history, an appreciation of meaning on this level has been symbolized by a variety of different beliefs. The Romans knew it as *amor fati* (love of fate). Christians

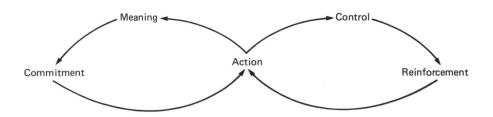

FIGURE 4-1   The Control and Commitment Cycles of Action

call it God's will. In a Hindu or Buddhist tradition, people speak of one's karma. In a more carefree vein, one says *qué sera, sera.*

Recently, psychologists have expanded the notion of control beyond the ability to change the environment, to now include the ability to derive meaning from events (see, e.g., Rothbaum, Weisz, & Snyder, 1982; Thompson, 1981). At this point it may be useful to consider the parallels between our general model and some of these formulations of control. Rothbaum, Weisz, and Snyder (1982), for example, distinguish control that is directed toward changing the outside environment—that is, primary control—from control that is directed inwards—that is, secondary control—changing the self so that it fits better with the external world. They hold that the inward and passive reactions associated with failure can be motivated and persistant, reflecting the exercise of secondary control.

For us, the issue here is not the directness or passivity of the control or whether the control is exercised internally or externally. The issue is distinguishing between behavior sustained by the consequences it produces, such as avoiding pain and maximizing rewards, and behavior sustained by the meaning and commitment it generates. One can control things in the internal environment, such as one's cognitions, as well as things in the external world. Control aimed inward, which changes or reinterprets beliefs about events and individual's abilities, can yield such reinforcements as reduced anxiety as surely as control over external events (see, Miller, 1980). Conversely, notions such as "secondary control," "cognitive control," or "reinterpretive control" (Thompson, 1981) can also imply changes in organization of meaning and value for the individual. The extent to which *control*, however it is defined, is aimed at gaining reinforcements is the extent to which we see it as part of the control cycle. The extent to which control attempts to generate a sense of meaning (in our sense of the term) is the extent to which we see it as part of the commitment cycle.

For action to be sustained, at least one of the two cycles must be in operation. The key point, however, is that *action can be sustained by the operation of one of these cycles in the absence of the other.* In the face of illness and death, loss of control and loss of reinforcement, people can keep going if their actions continue to engage meaning and commitment. For a misfortune to be meaningful, it has to be connected to some past, present or future positive element. For example, people can commit themselves to the experience of an illness if they see the illness as a challenge, with their coping as having positive value for themselves or others, or if they see it as a price they should be willing to pay for a pleasurable or privileged life. They cannot commit themselves to bearing the illness if they see it simply as the result of carelessness with no particular virtue attached to its pain. Conversely, people can keep going if their actions engage control and reinforcement even though they fail to generate a sense of meaning or value. Not only are the commitment and control cycles alternative bases of action, but, as the reader may suspect, they are in many circumstances mutually exclusive. As we have seen, a sense of meaning and value often arises in conjunction with the decision to relinquish control. In the extreme, the headlong pursuit of control may result in the sacrifice of all other values and can be justified, if at all, only by the pursuit of control itself in its various forms, such as money, power, or sex.

The four possible combinations of commitment and control cycles are shown in Table 4-1. They will serve as the basis for our discussion in the remaining sections of this chapter and also for our treatment of the development of commitment and pathologies of commitment in the chapters to come.

The case in which both the commitment and the control cycles are operative represents what people would like to think of as normal, healthy, reasonably fortunate behavior. Individuals feel both committed to and effective in their actions. We will explore the nature of commitment and control operating in tandem later in this chapter, in the section on turning means into ends. The case in which neither commitment nor control cycles are engaged represents a breakdown in functioning. Individuals do not feel that their actions are meaningful in themselves or that their actions are effective in controlling the environment in a desirable manner, hence they do not feel that they have a basis for action. This is our understanding of what it means to be depressed (see Seligman, 1975) or, in an organizational context, to be "burned out" (Maslach, 1978). We will speak at more length on this topic in the chapter on commitment and mental health.

The cases in which one of the cycles is operative are more difficult to characterize unambiguously because the state they elicit depends not only on the cycle experienced but also on one's orientation to the inoperative cycle. When the commitment cycle alone is operative, individuals can experience their actions as meaningful but cannot exert any effective control over the environment. If they can accept their lack of control and draw on the strength of the commitment cycle, they can be not only serene but can find their situation rich in opportunities for learning and growth. If they are primarily oriented to retaining or reinstating control, their state will be one of extreme frustration. We will return to this topic later in this chapter in our section on life and growth. When the control cycle alone is engaged, individuals can influence their environment but do not feel that their actions are meaningful, and such individuals feel alienated. If they accept this alienation and draw their satisfaction from the control cycle, their life-styles will be

TABLE 4-1 Combinations of Control and Commitment Cycles

	CONTROL	
	Yes	No
COMMITMENT Yes		
No		

defined by habit or routine. If they continue to seek commitment and meaning, their lives are likely to be marked by a series of abrupt changes, often just when others see them as having become successful in an area (see Kenniston, 1960). We will discuss these issues further both in our section on the dangers of pure control and in the chapter on commitment and mental health.

But first, we need to spend a little more time exploring what the exercise of control entails. Our exploration will take us through a variety of situations and environments, ranging from diets to laboratory studies on stress. What we hope to show is that the possibilities of control and commitment can exist parallel to each other and that in many cases the benefits assumed to accrue from control may actually reflect the power of commitment. In fact, it may be that of the two, commitment is more important in sustaining desired behavior than control.

CONTROL AND COMMITMENT

Importance of Choice

To start, it may be helpful to our case to consider that studies that have demonstrated the importance of control have simultaneously manipulated the internal reorganization of an action's meaning for individuals and so the possibilities of commitment. Individuals who perceive that they have control over the environment know, by definition, that external events are contingent on their behavior, at least eventually (Seligman, 1975). If events are not to their liking, they believe that they only have to keep trying, or perhaps try harder, to produce the desired outcomes (Dweck, 1975; Janoff-Bulman & Brickman, 1981; Weiner, 1974). This, however, gives them a choice, the choice of how to influence events and how much to invest in influencing them. In making this choice, as we have seen, individuals must deal with their own ambivalence and commit themselves. The process of commitment enhances an individual's ability to initiate and sustain action in two ways. First, it mobilizes responsiveness, creating an unconflicted state of internal readiness. Second, it imbues the ensuing action with a sense of meaning and value.

These two internal effects may, separately or collectively, make people who have control over whether to expose themselves to an aversive stimulus better able to bear the resultant stress. In the well-known study by Glass, Singer, and Friedman (1969), for example, subjects were exposed to unpredictable blasts of noise. Half of the subjects believed that they could terminate the noise, if they wished, by pressing a button the experimenter had given them. The other half believed that they had no control over the noise. Even though people in the condition with control did not use the button to escape from the noise, they appeared to suffer less from its effects. They showed somewhat less physiological reaction to it and, afterwards, less disruption in trying to solve a difficult (actually, insoluble) problem. The decision not to use the escape button was clearly a major psychological commitment made in the face of considerable ambivalence, and it could thus be expected to produce both of the effects we have just specified. Under some circumstances, such a decision will cause people to rate the stimulation itself as less aversive. Corah and Boffa (1970) gave subjects a series of noise bursts that they could sometimes escape, sometimes not. Half the subjects received instructions that they should escape or not escape on certain trials. The other half of the subjects were always given a choice. They were encouraged to escape on "escape trials," but allowed not to if the sound was comfortable. They were encouraged not to escape on the "no escape trials," but were allowed to if the sound was too uncomfortable. Subjects who felt that they had chosen to endure the sound in the "escape trials" rated it as less aversive than the equivalent sound they heard in the "no escape" trials, and rated the sound as less uncomfortable than did subjects who were told to simply endure the sound (also see Bandler, Madaras, & Bem, 1968; Houston, Bloom, Burish & Cummings, 1978).

Perhaps the most persuasive evidence for the importance of choice in performance comes from the study of achievement motivation (Atkinson & Raynor, 1974)—even though this research has not explicitly addressed the functional value of choice or control. According to the theory of achievement motivation, the tendency to approach success motivates people to work on a task while the tendency to avoid failure inhibits them from working on or motivates them to avoid the tasks. According to the theory, everyone has both tendencies. However, people high in achievement motivation are people for whom the tendency to approach success is greater than the tendency to avoid failure, while people low in achievement motivation are people for whom the tendency to avoid failure is greater than the tendency to approach success. People high in achievement motivation choose achievement oriented tasks themselves and people low in achievement motivation often have to be motivated to undertake achievement challenges by extrinsic pressures, such as a desire to please the experimenter. Our commitment analysis suggests an element of difference between people of high and low achievement motivation not noted in the achievement motivation theory. Although people who have high achievement motivation are predominantly positively motivated in choosing to undertake a challenging task, their activity further reduces any ambivalence or negative feelings they may have. On the other hand, the extrinsic pressures that typically force people low in achievement motivation to work on a challenging task do nothing more than support their initial ambivalence. This is similar to the analysis of Diener and Dweck (1978), who found in their study that when subjects who are ambivalent about a task are frustrated or fail at it their attention quickly wanders to distracting or self-preoccupied thought, but when subjects who are unconflicted about the task are frustrated, their attention zeroes in on the task itself.

If choice and commitment are components of situations in which people feel they have control, it should not be surprising that a sense of control often also exists together with a sense that one's behavior is meaningful. This can be readily seen in the work place. Organ and Green (1974) found that senior scientists and engineers felt more in control of their work situations and attributed more purpose and meaning to their jobs. Kobasa (1979a) found that executives who remained healthy despite intense stress felt that they could control the events in their lives and had a strong sense of commitment toward themselves, vigorous activity, and novel experiences. Further, if people believe that their behavior is itself meaningful, they should be more likely to engage in this behavior even in the absence of an external reward or incentive supplied by someone else. Exactly this was found by Dollinger and Taub (1971). Children who believed that their reinforcements were, in general, under their internal control worked equally well on a coding task when the experimenter did not provide them with an explicit rationale for doing a task as when the experimenter did. Children whose belief in their ability to control reinforcements was low worked less well when given no rationale for the task.

Timing of Events

Sometimes people cannot control whether an unpleasant event will occur but can control when it will occur. Even in these cases, commitment is still possible. From a commitment perspective, since they are not choosing the event at first, individuals cannot be expected to attach any special significance to the event. But in choosing when it will occur, they can be expected to attach significance to the timing of the event. From the fact that they choose to experience it at a certain point in time, individuals can infer that they will be ready at that point and can indeed prepare an appropriate state of readiness. Staub, Tursky, and Schwartz (1971) found that subjects who could control how much electric shock they would receive and exactly when they would receive these shocks rated them as less uncomfortable than another group of subjects who received exactly the same shocks but did not know how strong each would be or when each would occur. Similarly, DeGood (1975) showed that subjects in a shock experiment allowed to determine when their rest periods would occur had lower blood pressure than a group for whom the experimenter chose when the rest periods would occur. It may not matter whether subjects believe that the exact timing is important. Stotland and Blumenthal (1964) explicitly told people who were to take two tests that the order in which they took the tests would have no influence on their scores. They then allowed half the subjects to choose which order of the tests they preferred. Those who were allowed to control their test order showed less palmar sweating than those who did not expect to control their test order.

Commitments in Health Settings:
The Importance of Meaning

Individuals can obtain benefits stemming from internal mobilization by knowing exactly what the event will be like when it occurs, even if the event and its timing are both beyond the individual's control. This can perhaps be most dramatically seen in medical settings where patients have little control over their symptoms or choice in how or when to be treated. Following surgery, patients typically experience considerable pain, both at the site of the incision and where the internal functioning of their body has been affected. Unless they are told to expect these sensations, patients may be surprised by them and think that something serious has gone wrong. Janis (1958) found that patients who had not been informed of these sensations were much more upset by them and, subsequently, more likely to regret their operation and be angry at the medical staff. Johnson (1973) found that subjects rated the distress of having a tourniquet applied to their arm for a period of time as less if they had been given an accurate description of what sensations to expect. At this point, however, we are beginning to step outside the realm of control entirely and move further into the realm of meaning, value, and commitment. Preparatory information does not give people control over either the occurrence of the event or its timing in any simple sense. What it does allow people to do is to interpret these events more clearly and to see their responses to them as meaningful.

Informed surgery patients can understand their postoperative pains as caused by essential components of the operation, not by some unknown malfunction, and as such can attach to the pain some of the same value they attach to the surgery. This sense of meaning could help people mobilize their internal readiness for the pain, but it might also benefit them even if they were unable to exert much effective control over their initial response to it. Sometimes people can be instructed directly to reinterpret their pain. Holmes and Houston (1974) demonstrated that subjects who were told to think of electric shocks as interesting new physiological sensations (vibrations) experienced less anxiety and sweating and lower pulse rates than subjects not given such instructions. In an interesting experiment, Langer, Janis, and Wolfer (1975) compared the effects of helping surgery patients find meaning and value in their experience, through what the authors called a "coping strategy," with the effects of simply giving them preparatory information about what symptoms to expect. Subjects who reinterpreted their experience rated themselves as less anxious and better able to cope. A significantly smaller percentage of them required analgesics and sedatives. Merely telling people about the symptoms, in the absence of instructions on coping, tended to make them more anxious. In their discussion of the coping instructions, the authors indicate that they regard these instructions as a pain controlling device. The instructions are quite remarkable, however, and clearly go beyond the issue of controlling pain in any narrow sense. They are worth quoting at length:

> They were told that nothing is either all positive or all negative and that it is the wise person who finds alternative views of threatening situations and therefore prevents oneself from becoming stressed. Illustrative examples from everyday life of alternate ways of viewing seemingly negative events (e.g., losing one's job) were provided. Patients were then asked to generate examples from their own lives and present positive alternative views of events. The communication then went on to relate the coping device to the hospital experience. If there are indeed at least two ways of interpreting every experience, then there must be a positive non-stress-provoking view of being in the hospital. Attention was called to the positive or compensatory aspects of undergoing surgery in a good hospital, focusing on the improvement in health, the extra care and attention the patient would receive, the probable weight loss (if appropriate), and the rare opportunity to relax, to take stock of oneself, to have a vacation from outside pressures and the like. The suggestion was

made that the patient rehearse these realistic positive aspects whenever he starts to feel upset about the unpleasant aspects of the surgical experience. He was assured that this approach was not equivalent to lying to oneself. The coping device did not encourage denial but rather encouraged maintaining an overall optimistic view by taking account of the favorable consequences and reinterpreting the unfavorable ones. (Langer, Janis, & Wolfer, 1975, pp. 158-159)

Information about what to expect is unlikely to help unless it also alters the interpretation of the event. Girls who are unprepared for menstruation often experience their first bleeding as quite traumatic. But Shainess (1961) found that even among the girls who had been prepared for menstruation, 75% approached it with anxiety, fear, and dread. The problem is that menstruation is viewed in virtually all cultures, including our own, as unclean, shameful, or taboo (Bardwick, 1971). This can make reinterpretation of the event difficult and unlikely to occur. On the other hand, in a study of paralyzed accident victims, Bulman and Wortman (1977) found that those who saw their accidents as the unavoidable result of a meaningful activity were rated, by a nurse and a social worker familiar with their case, as coping better. Feeling that the accident could have been avoided and that it was someone else's responsibility was associated with poor coping. Thus people who were injured skydiving or playing football—activities they had chosen with a conscious awareness of the risks involved—coped better than people who were injured in automobile accidents or shootings, which typically resulted from an action to which a person had given no particular thought (e.g., accepting a ride home from someone) and which carried little significance. Since these events had occurred in the past, people's beliefs about them could not be said to have enhanced their ability to predict the paralysis or control its progress or anything else in the present life. Nonetheless, their feelings about these past events had an important impact on current adjustment.

Similarly, a commitment analysis offers an alternative explanation for the observation that children often reenact in their play previous traumatic experiences. The traditional interpretation of this phenomena is that the child attempts to establish a sense of mastery over events that were initially out of his or her control (Erikson, 1950). By acting out the events involved in a traumatic experience, such as going to the hospital, children presumably experience some measure of control over these events and make their memories of an actual stay in the hospital less frightening. Clearly, children gain no real control over going to the hospital by this playing, and it may be questioned whether gaining a sense of such control is the primary purpose of the play. The special virtue of this type of play is that it creates a situation in which children can freely express their feelings or in which behavior can become internally correspondent to important feelings (Brickman, 1978). In this sense, the reenactment of trauma in play is designed to associate a sense of meaning with activities that were initially experienced involuntarily. Elizabeth Douvan (1974) writes:

When the small child replays his tonsillectomy over and over, he does actively to the doll (or his dog or little sister) what he has previously experienced only as a passive recipient. Mastery comes with the shift in control, but it also comes from the derivation of meaning from events. As a passive receiver, with little inner reserve or distance from sometimes frightening events, he cannot order or understand them. By reruns paced and controlled internally, he places the events and makes them his own in a cognitive framework of his own design. (p. 23)

Likewise, an initial resistance to accepting events imposed on a person by others—reactance (Brehm, 1972; Wortman & Brehm, 1975)—may be based on the fear of losing a sense of meaning as well as the fear of losing a sense of control.

Commitment and social supports.   Our analysis of the generation of meaning in the commitment process opens the way to a reinterpretation of two famous studies of control among elderly people living in institutions, a reinterpretation that may help reconcile their apparently conflicting results. Langer and Rodin (1976) compared the effects of a communication from a nursing home administrator on the elderly residents from two floors of a nursing home. On one floor, the administrator's communication emphasized the residents' responsibilities for themselves. In addition, the residents were asked if they would like to take a plant and care for it and what night they would like to see a movie. On the second floor, the administrator's communication emphasized the staff's responsibility for the well-being of the residents. The residents were also told that the staff would take care of plants given to them and would take the residents to a movie on a particular night. In subsequent weeks, residents who heard the self-responsibility communication showed an increase in self-reported happiness and were rated by nurses as being more active and healthy in contrast to the comparison residents on the other floor.

Schulz (1976) compared the effects of visitation on nursing home residents. Undergraduates visited elderly nursing home residents under one of three conditions. In the first case, residents were given control of how long visits would be and of their frequency. Visitors indicated that they would leave when the resident wanted and would come back any time the resident liked. Residents receiving visits in the next two conditions were yoked to residents who controlled their visits so that people in all conditions received visits of the same length and frequency. In the second condition, the visitors told the residents how long they could stay and when they could come again, which allowed residents to predict but not control these visits. In the third condition, visitors dropped in unannounced and stayed for the assigned time, without telling the residents either how long they would stay or when they would come again. A fourth group received no visits. The visitations occurred for a two-month period. At the end of the period, residents who received visits they could either control or predict scored higher in zest for life, activity, happiness, and general health status, which was defined by medication need and observation by the activities director of the home.

The contradiction between the two studies comes in their follow-up data, collected 18 months later by Rodin and Langer (1977) and at 24, 30, and 42 months by Schulz and Hanusa (1978). Rodin and Langer found that the gains of the residents who were given responsibility were sustained 18 months later. Schulz and

Hanusa found that there were no positive long-term effects for the residents who had been able to predict or control the student visits. In fact, the health and zest for life of these residents showed a sharp decline after the visits were terminated.

From our perspective, the Langer and Rodin experiment manipulated not so much the individuals' perceptions that they could control their environment—which, it should be noted, parenthetically, were not influenced even in the right direction by the manipulations—but their commitment to certain actions, which thereby acquired significance and meaning for them. By choosing to accept the plant and personally tend it, the residents could not avoid establishing a sense that the plant was something about which they cared. More significantly, people in the responsibility condition were encouraged to choose to spend more time visiting other patients and talking to the staff, and they did so, thereby fostering the sense that they cared about other patients and cared about talking to staff. In an environment that may initially have been quite barren of things the residents could care about, these simple actions may have resulted in a substantial increment in the extent to which people felt that their existence in the home was meaningful.

In the Schulz study, on the other hand, the manipulations seemed better designed to establish the perceptions that the visitors cared about the residents rather than the residents cared about other people. In a sense, the evidence of caring provided by the student visitors makes these treatments more like those of the comparison group in the Langer and Rodin study, in which the staff seemingly displayed that extra degree of caring for the residents by tending a plant for them and taking them to a movie. In one condition of the Schulz experiment, the residents could choose how often and how long they wanted the visits to be and could thereby establish a sense that they cared about these visits. Even this was a dubious benefit, however, since they were not given the same choice about when they wanted these visits terminated; the visits simply stopped when the experiment stopped. Harris, Tessler, and Potter (1977) provide suggestive evidence that allowing a person some choice over whether to seek help and no choice over when to terminate it (simply telling people to try the task without help now versus asking them to try it without help when they feel they are ready) is the worst possible combination of fostering their perceptions of self-reliance. The initial presence of choice builds up people's sense that they need or value the helping relationship, while the absence of choice in the end fails to counteract this with a belief that they no longer need or value the relationship.

This in no way demeans the importance of caring for others. In a nursing home where residents were keenly aware of the absence of supportive relationships they had known earlier in life, the student visitors in Schulz's study may have substantially increased the residents' perception that someone else cared about them—except when the unpredictability of the visits may have undermined the perception that the visitors cared about the residents. Cohen and Syme (1985) review an impressive amount of evidence that supportive interactions protect people from the undesirable consequences of many life stresses. For example, pregnant women who had recently experienced a great amount of change in their lives and who did not have much social support were much more likely to undergo complications in their pregnancy than comparable women who had not experienced such life changes (Sosa, Kennel, & Klaus, 1980). Women who experienced a large amount of change and had social support were no more likely to undergo complications in pregnancy than women who had not experienced the stress of life changes. Brown, Bhrolchain, and Harris (1975) found that women who suffered severe life crises and lacked a person they could confide in were approximately 10 times more likely to be depressed than those who had suffered the event with a confidant or those without a confidant and who had not suffered such a crisis (see also Lowenthal & Haven, 1968). The difference between a sense of personal responsibility and a sense of social support is not that one is more valuable than the other, it is that they have very different effects when the conditions that produced these two things were removed. The commitments a person has made can continue even when the promptings by others who first elicited these commitments are discontinued. Social support, however, disappears when those who have offered that support go away. When that happens, individuals who have benefited from a great deal of loving care may suffer even more by contrast, than those who never had the pleasure of such support. In his famous study of depression and death among infants left in institutions, Spitz (1945) observed that babies who had previously known warm nurturance seemed to suffer more severely than babies who had never known such care. Close social supports may contain the cruel irony of causing greater pain for individuals when the relationship is terminated because of their adaptation to the inherent comforts of the support (see Brickman, Coates, & Bulman, 1978).

Although a sense that a person is making the important decisions in his or her own life and a sense that other people are making important contributions to that life can be antagonistic, the two are by no means mutually exclusive. Indeed, the very treatments by which patients are given the opportunity to make choices and attach new meaning to their actions can often be provided only by people who care a great deal about these patients. Egbert, Battit, Welch, and Bartlett (1964) found that patients who were told what pain to expect after abdominal surgery and how to move comfortably needed half the narcotics and several days less of hospital care than a comparison group of patients. Along with this information, it should be noted, they had the support and encouragement of their anesthetists who visited them at least once a day until they no longer required narcotics. Jasnau (1967) found that patients who were simply counseled en masse suffered an increased mortality rate after institutional relocation, while patients who were counseled individually had a lower than expected mortality rate. Individualized counseling conveys messages of caring and support as well as offering an opportunity for establishing a commitment to the relocation.

Why Diets Fail and How
to Make Them Work

Recently, there has been a decided emphasis on prevention of disease as a valuable alternative to the traditional medical model. Yet, a multitude of studies remark on the notorious difficulty in getting people to stick to diets or to maintain other good health and safety habits, like fastening seat belts. According to our analysis, these behaviors are so difficult to get people to practice because they are typically motivated solely by extrinsic concerns or interests in control, and the reinforcements available are not sufficient to sustain these good habits. These cases illustrate the power of commitment and, as we shall see, suggest—in cases in which one must sustain difficult behaviors, like diets—the value of fostering commitment to behavior rather than maintaining control of it.

Even when people do embark on a diet or exercise program, it is almost impossible to get them to maintain it. Every diet works in the short run (hence the ease with which new diet books become best sellers), and no diet seems to work in the long run (hence the continued market for new diet books). Thus, Drenick (1973) found that 90% of a sample of 105 patients who had lost weight successfully on a fasting treatment program had returned to their pretreatment weight after two years. One review of the literature (Glennon, 1966) could not find a single successful long-term weight reduction study, even when dietary restrictions were supplemented by drugs, exercise or psychotherapy. If a diet is unsuccessful, people tend to become discouraged and quit. If a diet is successful, they tend to feel that they have reached their goal and thus go off the diet. This is a diet's Catch-22, very much like the story of the Arkansas traveler who noticed that his host's roof was leaking and asked him why he didn't fix it. "Can't fix it now," said the farmer. "It's raining." "Then why don't you fix it when it's not raining?" inquired the traveler. The farmer replied, "Roof don't leak when it don't rain."

The underlying problem is that human appetites evolved over a long period of time when people were physically active and food was often scarce. In an affluent and sedentary society, these appetites can naturally lead to overweight. Weight control under these circumstances calls for a permanent change in life habits. As the nutritionist Jean Mayer notes, people must be willing to either exercise regularly and vigorously throughout their lives or go through life a little bit hungry, or both. Most people see changes in their eating or exercise habits as undesirable means to the desirable end of weight control, a point of view that is just not sufficient to sustain a rigorous diet or exercise regimen. This is true even though weight control has behind it such important incentives as increasing one's physical attractiveness. To be continued permanently—something most dieters never even contemplate—a diet and exercise program must be seen as having meaning and value in its own right. In view of this, how surprising would it be to learn that people have an intrinsic motivation not just to eat, but to overeat, to be fat? Being fat involves sacrifices. If people see themselves as willing to incur the costs of not fitting into clothes, being the butt of jokes, and being awkward and unattractive rather than change their eating habits, it should not be surprising that they attach considerable value to those overeating habits. It should not be surprising if they, and the people they live with, come to see being fat as having definite advantages, such as being excused from certain social obligations, or being seen as good humored. Interviewing a dozen men and women who had each lost at least 100 pounds, Haber (1978) found that they were happy but also anxious, confused, and uncertain about how to deal with the many opportunities now available to them. Dieting for strictly extrinsic reasons is all the more hopeless if people are overeating for intrinsic reasons. One of the authors (P.B.) along with Peter Herman, Janet Polivy, and Roxane Silver developed a set of scales designed to measure intrinsic and extrinsic motivation for dieting and eating. People are seen as extrinsically motivated to diet when they report feeling pressured by others to diet, dieting to reach specific goals, having to watch themselves closely to stick to their diets, and having no enthusiasm for dieting itself. In a sample of 104 high school, college, and adult night-school students, Roxane Silver and Deborah Horberg found a significant negative relationship ($r = -.25$) between extrinsic motivation to diet and how successful people felt they had been in dieting during the previous year.

Diet clinics and fat farms take advantage of this to get repeat business year after year. They encourage the perception that all weight loss, at the clinic, is due to the clinic's successful program, while all weight gain, away from the clinic, is due to the patient's intrinsic incurable motivation to eat and to grow fat. The net effect is likely to be a person who is less able to maintain a sensible diet and exercise program than someone who never took the treatment in the first place. All of this also suggests a great deal of caution in considering organized approaches to dieting that feature public praise or embarrassment for weight change each week, or periodic competition and prizes for greatest weight loss and improvement in charm and beauty. Groups such as Overeaters Anonymous, who see dieting itself as a valuable and central part of a whole new way of life, may have a better chance to generate in individuals a sense of commitment to their new habits. Empirical support for this can be found in another study of college students done by Roxane Silver. She found the more overweight the students, the less they had an intrinsic motivation to diet.

The effectiveness of self-improvement pursuits requires the subject to attach value to the symptoms of the wanted behavior, such as attaching value to the hunger in dieting or to the feeling of putting on seat belts. We are talking, of course, about the transformation of effort of the behavior that is part of the commitment process. Feeling hungry at some point during the day can be bonded to a sense of vigor, zest, and health; putting on seat belts can be bonded to a feeling of being a professional driver. To the extent that our bodies adjust to a reduced level of food intake or that buckling seat belts becomes second nature, these activities require less effort. We may also become less conscious of their value. Between the initial state in which these behaviors are motivated by external incentives and the state in which they are automatic, there is a long interim period in which behaviors must be sustained by a sense of their own meaning and value.

Getting started: How control can be counterproductive. We have given examples of avoidance behaviors, such as the avoidance of fattening foods. We know that once such behaviors have been launched, they can be continued almost indefinitely in the absence of any further reinforcement. There is an old joke in which a man on a train tears up a newspaper. "Why?" he is asked. "To keep the elephants away," he replies. "But there isn't an elephant within two thousand miles of here." To which the man says, "See how well it works?" There are no elephants on the train—and there is no occasion to find out that tearing up newspapers has no value for keeping them away. Our analysis suggests that repeated enactment of avoidance has given it a positive value of its own so that it might be preferred even if individuals were assured that it was objectively unnecessary or that the alternative was perfectly safe. What we need to understand better is how much behavior can be launched without initial trauma.

One thing is clear. If the techniques we use to control our behavior undermine our commitment to that behavior, they will be self-defeating. If we reward ourselves for sticking to a diet, such as by treating ourselves to new clothes, we cannot convince ourselves that our new diet habits are of value in themselves. On the contrary, the message is that the diet habits are so unattractive that we cannot follow them without the incentive of external reward. If we pay other people for making us stick to a diet, such as by checking ourselves into a clinic that rigidly controls food intake, we undermine the possibility of acquiring meaningful new dietary habits in a different way. Since we have no choice over what to eat in such a situation, we cannot generate a sense of commitment to new diet habits. If sticking to a diet was difficult but attractive in itself, we would not reward ourselves for having done it, but give thanks for having done it. A traditional Jewish custom is expressing joy and appreciation for a stroke of good fortune or a success in life by contributing to charity. It is giving, not seeking reward for sticking to a diet, that could convince the dieter that new behaviors have a value in themselves.

What the behavior modification literature on self-reinforcement ignores is that people are affected not only as recipients of rewards but as dispensers of them as well. Behaviorism has often been criticized for having a one-sided view of human nature as reactive and passive, easily controlled by external rewards. This one-sidedness is dramatically illustrated by behaviorism overlooking the contradiction between the self as recipient versus the self as agent of reinforcement. If external rewards, or external controls, are not readily and continually available, the role of self as agent appears more important than the role of self as recipient. In quitting smoking, for example, one behavior modification strategy that concentrates on the person as consumer of reinforcements emphasizes not having cigarettes available. Not having them around helps control smoking by making it more difficult to smoke. The effort of keeping cigarettes out of the house does not make smoking less desirable, but may actually have the opposite effect as people see what elaborate steps they apparently have to take in order to keep themselves from smoking. Other people have quit smoking following quite a different strategy. They kept cigarettes around, in one specific place, and claimed that it was important for them to know that cigarettes were available if they really needed them. Not drawing on the cigarettes under these conditions made it clear to them that they did not really need the cigarettes. It is not always possible to arrange the situation so that the tempting alternative is there, but not so salient or so tempting that the person cannot avoid it. On the other hand, it is even less likely that an environment can be arranged so that the tempting alternative—cigarettes, alcohol, or attractive extramarital partner— are not available at all.

Overcommitments. One must be careful, however, to keep dieting from having the same degree of importance sleep or sex has for a person who has been continually deprived of these things. They become enormously valuable not simply for themselves but as imagined keys to success and happiness in all phases of their life. Adolescents may feel that sex is important in itself, indeed the most important thing is life, but in fact adolescent sex is likely to be only a means to status for boys and affection for girls. An insomniac may feel that sleep is important in itself, as it may seem to have become the focus of the insomniac's existence, but in fact sleep is likely to have acquired its exaggerated importance as a perceived means to avoid worries, reduce irritability, and solve the many other problems that arise during the day. Simply counting how many hours one has slept, or how many people one has slept with, or how many pounds one has shed is a sign that a person is involved in the goal, rather than the process of the activity. To return to dieting, Mahoney and Mahoney (1976) argue that a diet designed to keep weight off permanently will discount pounds lost in any given period but will focus entirely on building up new dietary habits.

Though it may be difficult, there is no doubt that people can develop a dangerous intrinsic motivation to diet. Anorexia nervosa is an eating disorder suffered primarily by adolescent girls, who become so committed to dieting that they literally starve themselves to death. They enjoy the feeling of hunger and see themselves as just becoming attractive long after they have become skin and bones in the eyes of the rest of the world. Polivy (1978) administered our measures of commitment to eating and dieting to a sample of anorexic patients. Anorexics were significantly more committed to dieting than a comparable group of normal college women. Further, anorexics report that they eat much more for extrinsic reasons and much less for intrinsic reasons. They feel pressed to eat, eat to reach specific goals, and have no enthusiasm for eating itself. Thus eating, for anorexics, has become only a means to an end, adopted reluctantly and under great duress, just as dieting for most obese and normal people is only a means to an end. Clearly, treatment based on forcing anorexics to eat has little hope of effecting a permanent change, because they already feel forced to eat. Just as clearly, people can commit themselves to many different kinds of behavior—some adaptive, others less so.

COMMITMENT IN THE SERVICE OF CONTROL: TURNING MEANS INTO ENDS

Having reviewed the control literature and finding that the possibilities of control and commitment can exist together and that some of the benefits ascribed to control can be seen as stemming from commitment, we will continue by examining situations in which the control and commitment cycles operate in tandem. As we first saw in considering the question of rationality, commitment supplies behavior with the momentum that the actor needs to achieve control. When behavior has momentum, it appears to have a life of its own, to be proceeding irresistibly toward its goal. This goal may be one that the actors were aware of all along, like victory in a basketball game (momentum is very important in sports), or it may be one that the actor has no intention of pursuing until swept along by the behavior, like writing a book. Psychologist Edwin Megargee (1972) describes how an ever-expanding chapter on the California Psychological Inventory turned into a book when he discovered that stopping and condensing what he had written

> seemed to be about as easy as suggesting to a woman in hard labor that perhaps she ought to think twice about having a baby. Although I was not consciously aware of it, my decision had apparently been made a long time before I started writing and I was just now learning about it. (p. xii)

Momentum of this sort appears to have two components. The first is a sense of the behavior being *automatic*. This does not have to mean it is easy, only that it proceeds in a coherent fashion wthout continual attention to the details of execution. The second is the sense that the person is *intrinsically motivated* to pursue the behavior, perhaps even to the exclusion of all other interests. Again, attention is focused on the behavior, not on the details of its execution. This is a conjunction of what we have previously discussed as mindless and single-minded behavior. The experience of irresistible momentum in an activity (e.g., flow) is produced by a combination of a mindless and a single-minded involvement with it.

Achieving momentum involves slightly different issues, depending upon whether we are talking about initiating behavior, sustaining an ongoing behavior, or bringing a particular behavior sequence to a conclusion. With an eye toward understanding the function of commitments in activities, we may find it useful to start by examining the impact of the commitment processes at each of these three points in a behavior sequence.

Start-up

There are almost no activities that do not require participants to go through a period of warm-up before they are optimally effective. This is as true for rhythmic activities in which one can eventually let one's mind wander (like distance swimming) as it is for activities whose demands are constantly changing and so require a constant pitch of attention (like writing). The initial stage is awkward, no matter how well learned the activity or how high the stakes. The awkwardness remains until the activity's rhythm, both mental and physical, has been established. Until this occurs, people need to pay attention to what they are doing. Sometimes people may experience an initial resistance to the activity, such as the well-known writer's block. A common characteristic of warm-up activities is that they are done in the same order and at the same pace every time. This permits a gradual exclusion of other interests and stimulation. People who sleep well are blessed with what are called, significantly enough, good sleeping habits. This essentially means approaching bedtime in the same way every night. The exact content of these prebed activities, such as bathing, brushing teeth, or reading, is less important than that they are familiar and comfortable. They cannot be started too early, or the mood they create will vanish before bedtime. Neither can they be started too late, or the proper mood will not be created.

Whether a runner is doing stretching exercises or a pianist is doing finger exercises, the warm-up exercise has a direct physical relationship to the subsequent activity. Parallel to this activity are those elements in the warm-up that have no obvious relationship to the activity that follows—that is, the elements of ritual or superstition that surround the activity. Sportswriters are fond of endlessly pointing out how much ritual and superstition pervade sports (Womack, 1978). We all know a particular baseball player who can be counted on to tug at his cap or tap the plate with the bat that special way each time he comes up. We have all heard of the player in the middle of a hot hitting streak who is rumored to eat the same breakfast, drive to the park along the same route, and put on his socks in exactly the same way before each game because of the belief that failure to do any of these things will bring bad luck. From our perspective, the purpose of this ritual and superstition is clear. It progressively involves the player in the rhythm of his or her activity, which helps work through any ambivalence about facing another round of competition. The fact that these so-called rituals have no obvious payoff or point, the fact that they are seen by others as quite arbitrary, is not incidental but essential to their function. These rituals are designed to involve people in the meaning of their activity. This purpose is uniquely well served by a warm-up activity that is clearly done for its own sake rather than one that has some obvious mundane purpose. It should not be thought for a moment that such ritual or superstition is a property only of physical activity or competitive sports. At Northwestern University, Howard Becker once ran a graduate seminar on writing, in which participants talked about what they actually did when they wrote. Ritual apparently is less notable in writing than in sports only because writing is ordinarily a private behavior. Still, every seminar participant confessed to setting irrational conditions they had to meet before they could write. Some could only write with a certain kind of pen, pencil, or paper. Others could only write in a certain light, in a particular place, or at a certain time of day. Many could write only after giving themselves certain reassurances, such as that they would tear up the first page they wrote or that what they wrote would clearly be understood to be a first draft. Everyone had his or her own special way of assembling and arranging their materials. Such is the stuff of great beginnings.

Sustaining Behavior

Once an activity is underway, commitment plays a vital role in sustaining it. In the absence of external difficulties, the sequence of behaviors can unroll automatically and will do so most easily if a sense of commitment and meaning has removed any residual ambivalence an individual has toward the activity. When external difficulties arise, it will be helpful for people to give their behavior their undivided attention, which will again be easiest if they are committed to the activity and see it as meaningful. As we found in our own laboratory, when people see themselves as intrisically motivated to pursue an activity, they can better endure the stress of that activity. Some evidence can be found in Darlene Binns and Les Kocher's study of 40 high school cross-country runners, 36 of them male. The coaches' ratings of how well the runners coped with 15 different potentially stressful events were positively related to the runners' self-ratings of how much pleasure they got from the sheer physical and mental activity of their sport ($r = .29$), and with how much pleasure they got from participating in the sport ($r = .33$). Interestingly, the coaches' coping ratings were uncorrelated with the runners' reports of how much pleasure they got from winning or from the anticipation of earning some or all of their future living from such a sport, both extrinsic factors to the act of running itself.

A variety of studies have shown that people are more successful on tasks when they feel the tasks are difficult and when they personally set hard goals for themselves. This is true whether the tasks are solving anagrams (Locke, 1968) or raising money for United Way campaigns (Zander & Newcomb, 1967). In the work place, Berlew and Hall (1966) found that the initial job assignments of recruits in two AT&T operating companies were unrelated to the recruits' personal characteristics but were positively related to their future performance and salary levels. The recruits who started in the more challenging positions did better. The superior performance of individuals who undertake what they feel are difficult tasks may be due to the fact that in mobilizing for these tasks, they come to see themselves as intrinsically motivated to pursue the tasks and thus committed to the task activity and its goal. Significantly enough, as demonstrated by Stedry (1960), difficult goals elicit superior performance only if individuals accept them as their own and not if they are simply assigned by someone after individuals have set goals by themselves. If accepting a challenging task indeed tends to elicit intrinsic motivation, greater meaning, and commitment, then the consequences of long-term involvement with such a task might extend far beyond the task itself.

Concluding a Task

Concluding a task is a salient event, so it is perhaps not surprising that the relationship between commitment and concluding a behavior has been the most studied of all. For one thing, it encompasses one of the classic phenomena in social psychology, the Zeigarnik effect. The effect refers to the tendency of people to have keen memories of tasks they have not yet completed but to soon forget the details of tasks they have finished. This first came to the attention of Kurt Lewin and his students, including Zeigarnik, who noticed that waiters in a busy German restaurant did not write down customers' orders but kept track in their heads exactly what everyone was to be served. When questioned at the end of the day, however, the waiters were quite unable to recall what different people had been served. What happened was that they remembered each order until the bill was paid, then they promptly forgot the order (Atkinson, 1964). When people are interrupted in a task, they are more likely to remember it, although there is some evidence that people tend to forget tasks on which they feel they have failed (Van Bergen, 1968).

The Zeigarnik effect refers to a tension that is set up by the launching of a behavior and is only discharged when that behavior is brought to a successful conclusion. Moreover, the force of this tension is greater when the behavior has been carried out for a while and the goal is close than when the behavior has just been initiated and the goal is distant. People are frustrated and upset if their behavior is interrupted when it is about to be completed (Haner & Brown, 1955) or when they feel things have been improving (Davies, 1962).

Zeigarnik effects also have practical value and can be used by people as a creative device to lock themselves into continuing a behavior they find desirable. According to Hemingway, a writer should never stop writing for the day at the end of a scene but always in the middle of one. The lack of closure will make it easy for the writer to keep his or her thoughts on the scene and perhaps also generate some creative associations to the scene in the meanwhile. Turning away from an unresolved line of thought has also been recommended by Bertrand Russell in solving mathematical problems. A second advantage of interrupting one's writing (or reading) in the middle of a passage is that it makes it easier to resume one's engagement with the material the next day, perhaps with less warm-up. Here we have come full circle, making commitment in the service of concluding a behavior work also to help initiate a subsequent round of the same behavior.

Another feature of concluding a task is that if people feel that the point at which they can or must conclude a task is farther off in the future, they are likely to work at a more leisurely pace and take more time to complete the task (Aronson & Landy, 1967). This is, of course, one of Parkinson's laws: Work expands to fill the time available. Conversely, as people feel that the end of their work is near, they are more likely to allow themselves to experience fatigue and other forms of release associated with the end of their commitment to their task. Walster and Aronson (1967), for example, found that subjects who believed that they had three rounds of a set of boring mechanical and perceptual tasks to carry out started reporting that they were tired on the third round, while subjects who believed that they had five rounds to carry out did not.

Let the Means Become the Ends

It is possible that the form of commitment necessary to initiate a behavior sequence is different from the form of commitment necessary to sustain it or the kind necessary to conclude it. Some people may have no trouble starting an activity but have a hard time sustaining it or a hard time finishing it. Still others may have no trouble sustaining or finishing an activity but a hard time starting. If commitment functions in characteristically different ways to control behavior at these three points in time, it may also malfunction in characteristically different ways at these three points. This is a question we will have to return to in our discussion of pathology. At this point, we would like to concentrate on the role of commitment in sustaining behavior rather than starting or stopping it.

Since beginnings and endings are usually quite visible, it is not surprising that they are in some ways easier to think about. We have, as usual, contradictory proverbs about their importance. One says, "Well begun is half done." Another says, "When a job is 90 percent done it is half over." Moreover, starting is often relatively easy, while the question of finishing does not even arise unless the problem of remaining persistent and enthusiastic over time has been solved. Still, in life's most important activities—like careers and marriages—the stretch from after the start to just before completion is vastly greater than the more visible periods of initiation and conclusion.

The key to using commitments to sustain action is what might seem a curious proposition: Let the means become the ends. To be committed to an ongoing activity, the person must cathect the action, not the goal or reward. Quite simply, the more distant the goal, the more the behavior must be sustained by the commitment cycle rather than the control cycle. To some extent, to be sure, behavior oriented to distant goals can be sustained by the attainment of intermediate goals that serve as reinforcements. But even intermediate goals often take some time to achieve. Passing an exam may help sustain a person's motivation to do well in a required course needed to get into medical school, but the exam itself requires prolonged studying. Furthermore, the intermediate goal, passing the exam, often has no value other than the symbolic value it derives from the person's commitment to the activity that encompasses it.

The idea that means become ends has been clearly stated many times in the past. It is Gordon Allport's (1937a) principle of functional autonomy, that an activity becomes its own source of motivation, its own goal, even if it was originally engaged in for some other reason. There appear to be three reasons, however, why the principle of turning means into ends has not usually been given the force of a recommendation but has rather been viewed as a troublesome, even dangerous, development. First of all, that people attach value to a particular means, or a particular way of doing things, often becomes visible only when that means ceases to be effective. As Robert Merton (1949) first noted, we see bureaucrats as attached to their rules above all because we see them adhering to these rules even in cases that obviously cry for exception. We tend to overlook the fact that in adhering to these rules bureaucrats are able to make a vast number of decisions reliably, quickly and correctly—which, as Weber (1968) points out, was exactly why rules and bureaucracies were instituted in the first place. When we support the rule and sanctity of law as our surest long-term safeguard against injustice, we are attaching value to a means. We have an entire literature that struggles with the fact that upholding the rule of law in general means that in particular cases an innocent person suffers or a guilty ones goes free.

A second, more serious objection to removing the distinction between means and ends is not inefficiency or lack of creativity but evil. The phrase "the ends justify the means" has been the last excuse for cruelty and horror throughout history. Letting the ends justify the means, however, is quite different from letting the means become the ends. The first principle can support any means, however evil, provided they are believed to lead to a sufficiently good end. Our principle requires the means to justify themselves, to be seen as a good in themselves.

The third reason for overlooking the significance of the feelings people attach to means is simply that the basis and the function of these feelings have not been clearly established. The importance of commitment to the process has not been theoretically elaborated in the same way as, for example, the importance of making internal attributions for success and external attributions for failure (Weiner, 1974).

The evidence is clear. We have already looked at studies indicating that people cope better with stress when they are intrinsically motivated in their behavior; this intrinsic motivation enables them to attach greater meaning to their activity and so strengthens their commitment to the activity. To this can be added evidence that people perform better when they attend to the process of the performance rather than the goal of performing. People who are anxious about taking tests do worse, in part, because they think too much about whether they will succeed or fail and not enough about the test items themselves (Wine, 1971). Mastery-oriented children do better than helpless children following failure not by thinking about the failure but by visibly involving themselves further in the task, instructing themselves to pay closer attention, and making positive statements about their involvement in the task (Diener & Dweck, 1978). A nice bit of evidence for the importance of commitment to the process of carrying out a task is the discovery that practice in concentrating on the task can be just as valuable as practice in actually doing the task. The mental practice is unaccompanied and undiluted by any external rewards. Basketball players have been found to improve their ability to shoot foul shots as much by mentally rehearsing the process of shooting as by actually shooting (Clark, 1960), though some previous experience with the skill may be necessary for the mental practice to be fully effective (Corbin, 1967).

In an elegant set of experiments, Wildfogel (1979) has demonstrated that simply instructing people to pay attention to carrying out an activity improves their performance in critical situations, while instructing them to pay attention to the goal or purpose of the activity does not. Wildfogel was interested in "choking" phenomena—that is, the tendency of some individuals in challenging situations to perform less well than they normally do. On the first day of an experiment involving tossing bean bags at a target, all subjects choked in that their tosses were closer to the center when aiming for a large target rather than a more challenging small one. Subjects instructed to attend to the goal of the toss and subjects given no instructions continued to choke on the second day, but subjects instructed to attend to the process of tossing made tosses at the small target that were significantly closer to the center than those at the large target. In a second experiment, choking was defined as doing worse on trials when it was critical to beat an opponent's score than on trials when it was not. Subjects who choked were instructed to mentally rehearse the feel of a good toss and to let their body follow the rehearsed patterns. These subjects improved their tosses on critical trials more than those choking subjects who were given no instructions or were simply told to breath deeply.

Rigid means and flexible goals.   We are imbued with the idea of being flexible in pursuit of our aims, by which is generally meant being resourceful. For example, Pruitt and Lewis (1975) argue that people will achieve the most favorable outcomes in a complex bargaining task if they approach the task with high and somewhat inflexible goals for themselves but complete flexibility about means to those goals. Our analysis illuminates an important sense in which the converse is true, where the optimal combination is one of flexible goals and rigid means. Arguably, this may characterize the stance of enduring institutions, like the Roman Catholic Church, or enduring peoples, like the Jews. The Church has pursued very different goals, at least different secular goals, in fascist Spain and the democratic United States, Bavaria and Africa, medieval Europe and contemporary Latin America. The earthly goals change and are not sacred. What does not change and is sacred is the means to eternal salvation that the Church provides—vocation and prayer, confession and penance. This in turn gives mundane pursuits vital to the survival of the Church the character of a holy mission. It is the holiness of the activities, not the activities themselves, that is constant across cultures and centuries. Within living memory, Jews have made dramatic shifts in what they have defined as success in this world, moving from rabbis and peddlers in Eastern European shtetls to doctors and Hollywood moguls in the United States and soldiers and politicians in Israel. What was constant, again, was a dedication to a sacred means, in this case a religious tradition that emphasized reading and writing, arguing and interpretation, skills that turned out to have considerable impact in the emerging culture of the twentieth century.

For survival among the elderly, our analysis is indifferent as to whether they keep or change their earlier goals but recommends that whatever their goals, they should pursue them with as much stubborn, cantankerous zeal as they can muster. Enthusiasm in the young may look like orneriness in the elderly, but it has no less survival value, and the difference in label may, to some degree, lie in the eye of the beholder.

A commitment to means rather than ends may seem irrational but less rational societies may have exercised more effective control than we do. Our improved health status comes primarily from our better ability to manage the general environment, for example, sewage treatment, and to treat illness, for example, sterilization in hospitals or inoculations. It does not come from an increased commitment by individuals to healthful behavior. On the contrary, as we have seen, we have not been very successful in getting people to stop drinking, smoking, overeating, and in general doing things that are dangerous to their own or other people's health. Yet certain groups have been remarkably successful in keeping their members from doing most or even all of these things. They are, of course, religious sects that prohibit such practices (see Saward & Sorensen, 1978). Unlike the medical profession, which prohibits these things in excess because of their bad consequences, sects prohibit them totally because they are bad in and of themselves. Abstinence as a good in itself is a more powerful basis of commitment than abstinence as a possible means to a desirable end state.

The absence in traditional cultures of a scientific language and direct concern for control has sometimes caused us to overlook the very real influence that the cultures exercise indirectly. They do this through a ritual language and a concern for commitment. Food taboos in primitive societies may help people avoid dangerous items, attain balanced diets, and perhaps conserve scarce sources of protein (McDonald, 1975). Traditional cultures are not ignorant of birth control, as some Western observers have implied, but rather justify birth control and fertility practices by myths and traditions rather than by rational arguments about population size and resources. Population control may be attained more effectively by premarital or postpartum sexuality taboos than by arguments about population control, especially in societies where there are powerful economic and political pressures on members to produce long lineages (see Dumond, 1975). Western medicine may lead to larger families not only by reducing infant mortality but also by undermining the traditional taboos that once controlled sexuality. A concern for the consequences of pregnancy is by itself a poor substitute for these taboos, as witnessed by the teenage birth and abortion rates in the United States.

If a high degree of meaning and commitment is needed to sustain a behavior, and if this sense of meaning and commitment comes only from the behavior itself, the behavior can suffer no exceptions. William James (1890) wrote eloquently on this point. The argument can be summarized quite simply as the necessity, above all things, never to lose a battle. A gain on the wrong side undoes the effect of many victories on the right. Ainslie (1975) regards the process of making and sustaining such commitments as one of bargaining with oneself, subject to the same principles that govern bargaining with others. "Instead of a person's showing evidence to other people that his behavior in a given situation will be limited by unique boundaries which he is not likely to change, he must show this evidence to himself" (p. 482).

One must allow for certain exceptions, according to Ainslie, but these should be strictly limited to rare and easily distinguished events that are either outside the person's control or so costly that the person would never arrange them just to skip the habit in question. When the commitment is against a behavior defined as addictive, such as alcohol or drugs, we are sympathetic or at least understanding toward the policy of no exceptions. In other cases, friends who do not share the same commitment are less sympathetic. People who refuse to make exceptions are seen as making their lives and the lives of others more difficult. Why can't a vegetarian friend have a dish with a touch of meat in it just this one time? Why can't my radical friend make what seems to me such a small compromise, in a dispute with the university administration over grading practices, which will keep him from being fired? Because the compromise is not small, or rather it seems small only to people who do not have a radical commitment, a vegetarian commitment, or a commitment to the kind of excellence that only practice will produce. The intensity and value of the commitment are established not by resisting easy temptations but by resisting the hard ones, by resisting temptations when the easy and popular thing to do would be to make an exception. Anyone will defend the freedom of people whose cause they admire; only a group that values freedom above all, like the American Civil Liberties Union, will defend the freedom of people they despise, like American Nazis marching through a town filled with concentration camp survivors. To allow freedom to be abridged in one case is to risk losing its symbolic value, to risk losing it altogether.

The political, economic, and social power available to people who can control themselves in the way described above is clearly enormous. This makes unlikely one of the more benign visions of a rational and scientific future society—Donald Campbell's. Campbell (1969) has pointed out how much we would gain by treating political and social reforms as experiments, rather than as panaceas or sacred enterprises that easily turn into sacred cows. Proposals for change are likely not to work or to have unexpected and undesirable side effects (see, e.g., McCord, 1978). They should be made tentatively, treated as hypotheses rather than certainties, and evaluated by an ongoing and objective assessment of their effects. As Campbell (1975) himself has noted elsewhere, the appropriate attitude with which to approach questions of social change is one of humility. But for better and for worse, people do not act on that basis, whether it is proposing change or defending tradition. We act on the basis of felt certainty, rightness, and confidence greater than can be justified by any calculations carried out in advance, or we do not act at all. We do so because this is functional. It is not only rationality but the limits on rationality that have been selected for in the evolution of the species.

UNBRIDLED WILL TO POWER: DANGERS OF PURE CONTROL

Unlike the cases discussed above in which individuals retained a sense of commitment often alongside control, a person may have external control over actions without the actions generating a sense of meaning that initiates the commitment cycle. This combination is represented by the lower left cell of Table 4-1. Just as people can become more aware of and concerned for commitment and meaning when control is lacking, they can become more aware of and concerned for control when commitment and meaning are lacking. The problem, under these circumstances, is a simple one. There is never enough control. For Hobbes, the philosopher, the more power we have, the more additional power we feel we need to protect the power we already have. With power come expectations and aspirations that readily outstrip any degree of power, especially as the person becomes accustomed to exercising that degree of power (Brickman & Campbell, 1971). With power also come responsibilities to and expectations from other people, which again readily exceed the power's might. An individual's power is satisfactory only if it is adequate to his or her expectations and responsibilities. From this perspective, as Slater (1974) points out, the President of the United States may be the most powerless man in the world. Vast as they are, his powers are pitifully inadequate to control the worldwide events for which he is held responsible.

Some individuals are especially concerned with a desire to control their environment. They are hard-driving, aggressive, and competitive and have a strong sense of urgency about what they do (Glass, 1977), a pattern that has been called Type A behavior (Friedman & Rosenman, 1974). Type A individuals work very hard and are often successful, but they have repeatedly been observed to work without joy. Instead, they work with a sense of anger, frustration, and struggle (Jenkins, 1975). From a health standpoint, they have been found to be more vulnerable to heart attacks, a discovery that has stimulated all this interest in them. Because Type A individuals are successful, because they feel the need for more success and more control, and because they attribute success to their continual hard-driving behavior, it is difficult to change their behavior even after a heart attack.

More control alone cannot resolve the ambivalence, anger, frustration, and suspicion of those who wield and thirst after control. Commitment and the acceptance of some lack of control is the only way out of an endless control cycle, the only escape from the consuming imperative of Neitzsche's (1973) will to power.

When people cannot derive meaning from their behavior and commitment to a line of action, alienation results. Alienation has typically been associated with powerlessness (Seeman, 1959), but in our analysis, alienation is not primarily a question about power but a question of individuals' feelings about their own behavior. These feelings may be more problematic for those who have power than for those who do not. As we have noted, people with power may be drawn ever more relentlessly and totally into the pursuit of power, encouraged by achieving some success, frustrated and goaded by not having achieved more. They profit in this pursuit from making only those choices that can be justified by the reward and the power they bring, thus increasingly cutting themselves off from choices that might have intrinsic value.

On the other hand, if people have a great deal of control over their environment and are content with it, this can cut them off from commitment and meaning in a different way. Power and wealth, by decreasing any obvious need for sacrifice or action, can dampen the commitment cycle. It should not be surprising to find the problem of meaning emerging as a major one for affluent individuals and societies. Psychiatrist Roy Grinker, Jr. (1977), who has treated disturbed children of the superrich, describes them as emotional zombies for whom treatment—which is very difficult—consists in learning how to suffer. Maddi (1970) sees what he calls existential sickness, caused by a sense of meaninglessness, as the dominant form of neurosis in the decades since the Second World War. Out of the lack of meaning comes either a life of empty routine or a reckless pursuit of stimulation or a combination of the two. We are not implying, however that the presence of wealth and power is more dangerous to one's health than their absence. The implication is only that the disorder caused by lack of meaning is not a simple question of lack of control that can be cured by the attainment of control.

Without the sense that the choices one makes are right, that they have meaning and value, the exercise of control is stressful and has none of the healthful consequences claimed by its advocates. Control without meaning is, in fact, so aversive that people will go to considerable lengths and make considerable sacrifices to avoid it. The desire to escape a meaningless freedom is what Erich Fromm (1941) saw as the driving force behind twentieth-century fascism. People who have what has been called the authoritarian personality syndrome (Adorno, Frenkel-Brunswick, Levinson, & Sanford, 1950) do not derive a sense of meaning from free individual choices. They prefer to see choices governed by rules or made by authority figures, and they respond less favorably to supervisors who ask their advice or try to involve them in decision making (Vroom, 1960). Authoritarian tendencies, which include a cynical view of human nature, hostility against out-groups, and a concern for power and toughness, have been found to increase following the stress of failure in an experiment (Sales & Friend, 1973) or economic depression in a society (Sales, 1973). It is clear that authoritarianism has something to do with people's concern with control and a perceived need for more control, even if it is control imposed from outside sources. Fromm (1941), however, indicates quite clearly that in his view it was lack of meaning in people's lives, the sense of self as disconnected and automatic, that produced this obsession with control.

Although, as we have seen, meaninglessness is often associated with a sense of powerlessness, it can also be experienced by those who command a great deal of power in their society. The wealthy and the powerful, as well as the disinherited, have played an important role in the history of fascism. Evidence like the foregoing has led to the notion of an optimal degree of control, with people experiencing distress if their control either exceeds or falls short of this optimal amount (French, Rodgers, & Cobb, 1974). However, that notion is flawed by the assumption that the only limit on the amount of control people desire is imposed by their competence in exercising control. It also fails to incorporate the understanding that individuals quite competent to exercise control might fail to find meaning in it and thus might be overly driven by concern for control or, alternatively, might find meaning by entering into relationships or activities in which they relaxed or relinquished the exercise of control.

There is one highly admired domain of human life whose essence consists in looking at things entirely stripped of any perception of their intrinsic value. This is the special secret and danger of science. Our understanding of the planets increased as we began to think of them as bodies moving in obedience to blind forces rather than spirits whose actions had meaning. Similarly, though there were substantial virtues to treating a medical patient as a whole person, effective medical knowledge accumulated only when we began looking at each organ—the heart, the liver, the pancreas—by itself. The disease and health of a person were perceived to be products of blind natural forces whose operation had no intrinsic significance. We are now becoming aware of the drawbacks of this approach, and we may someday look back on the period in which it dominated Western medicine as a difficult stage or transition. But even if we return to a more personal view of medicine and health in the future, we can expect to benefit from the knowledge accumulated through the scientific, impersonal study of the body—knowledge that could not have been acquired any other way.

Since the legends of Prometheus and Faust, people have always reflected an ambivalence about science. This ambivalence has rested in part on a fear that scientific power would be used for evil rather than good, a fear that has proven well founded. It has also rested on the belief that the discoveries of science would change people, undermine traditional values, and perhaps even incur divine anger. What has not been articulated is that this threat to intrinsic value comes not so much from any particular discoveries of science as from the general perspective essential to the development and use of science. It may be true that the search for scientific knowledge impairs the ability to use that knowledge wisely; the ultimate problem is not in the knowledge gained but in its use. Since the powerful new options made available by science have multiple and long-term effects on the environment and on ourselves, it is hard to know how to use the options wisely. It is easy to see science as a part of an endless struggle for control, in which the solutions discovered today become the problems that need solving tomorrow. In making food tasty and abundant, we change the composition of our soil and our bodies, creating a new need for scientific discoveries to combat pollution, falling water tables, cancer, and overweight. If dinosaurs were dumb, says biologist George Wald, it was not simply because they had small brains, but because their brains were small in relation to the powerful bodies they commanded. In the last century, through tanks, planes, and nuclear weapons, through physics, chemistry, and biology, people have vastly increased the power they control without having increased the size of their brains at all. We are, according to Wald, in danger of becoming the new dinosaurs, lumbering our way to extinction, but doing so much more quickly because of the greater power we have. Perhaps computers will help redress the imbalance between human brains and power, though computers too are a power whose use must be carefully considered. One thing can be said with confidence. To the extent that people cannot meaningfully use the control made possible by science, and to the extent that people cannot even comprehend what is involved in this control, science will not make lives happier or the world a better place.

LIFE AND GROWTH: COMMITMENT IN THE ABSENCE OF CONTROL

We will start our explorations of the virtues of commitment by facing one of the focal concerns of human inquiry and thought—the suffering of pain. As Bakan (1968) puts it:

> No experience demands and insists upon interpretation in the same say. Pain forces the question of its meaning, and especially of its cause, insofar as cause is an important part of its meaning. In those instances in which pain is intense and intractable and in which its causes are obscure, its demand for interpretation is most naked . . . (pp. 57–58)

Against the stark landscape of pain and suffering, the virtues of commitment can be seen most clearly since the experience of pain represents forcefully a major breakdown in the ability to control reinforcements.

Distraction and Denial

One typical way of dealing with pain is through distraction and denial. The essence of distraction is that the person turns his or her attention away from the pain by focusing on another stimulus or activity. Kanfer and Seidner (1973), for example, showed that subjects could endure ice water better when distracted by travel slides, and they could endure it especially well when they could advance the slides at their own rate. Yet distraction does not imbue a negative situation with meaning or enhance people's commitment to enduring or coping with that situation. This point is clearly illustrated in a study by Lukas that is cited in Klinger (1977). In a survey of various locations in Vienna, people at the famous Prater amusement park complex were least likely to be able to name a source of meaning in their lives. Entertainment, in general, is a source of distraction, not meaning.

As a coping strategy, distraction, like denial, has two major disadvantages. First, by drawing individuals' attention away from their situation, it may cause them to miss potentially useful information that they could use to craft an adaptive solution. Second, with no adaptive solution, the situation remains noxious, ready to break through the distraction at any time. Distraction is hard to sustain over time, and the devices used to do so often have destructive consequences of their own. Distractions such as alcohol, drugs, or television provide only intermittent relief and must be continually reapplied, often in increasing doses. Furthermore, they make people less alert, both when under their influence and as a consequence of repeated use.

Quitting, Collapse, and Persistence in the Absence of Control

Times of stress should bring on greater concern about meaning because with the control cycle broken, behavior will break down without commitment. Paraplegics who have a firm expectation that they will recover work diligently and cope superbly until this expectation breaks down, at which point they may become apathetic and hard to manage (Litman, 1962). Paraplegics who have accepted their accident and their situation as meaningful continue to cope better (Bulman & Wortman, 1977). Parents of children dying of leukemia who denied the imminent prospect of their child's death and continued to center their energies on their child's survival coped less well with the last days and the mourning than parents who concentrated their energies on the meaning of the last days (Chodoff, Friedman, & Hamburg, 1964). This meant involving themselves in the activities of the moment, such as eating dinner with their children, talking to them, or trying to get them to a movie, all designed to enhance the quality of the present. People who have had the greatest ability to control their environments in the past and who have been most invested in that control are often least well-equipped to accept suffering as meaningful and most likely simply to blame themselves when things go wrong. Thus, individuals with higher social status, and a stronger sense of their own competence and internal responsibility for success and failure, are more likely to commit suicide when they lose control and the things they value are threatened (Gold, 1958).

Coming to terms with life involves coming to terms with pain and death. We will come back to this point, since it is one of the central themes of this section. On a more mundane level, in our work and in our relationships, we face lesser forces that are still beyond our control. The lesson is the same from both the extraordinary and ordinary. Only a structure of meaning and commitment sustains behavior in the absence of control. On the mundane level, this is very much what is meant by internalization—that is, individuals performing and accepting a behavior because it is congruent with their existing values (Kelman, 1958). In the previously mentioned study by Miller, Brickman, and Bolen (1975), children who were convinced by their teacher that they were neat and tidy people maintained the behavior of putting their litter in the garbage can and picking up after others even when the teacher ceased to comment on this behavior. Other children, who were initially persuaded to stop littering by their teacher's arguments that they should be neat and tidy, returned to their old habits when the teacher stopped praising neatness. Perhaps most interesting is that a behavior that is internalized may grow stronger, not weaker, when it is under stress or attack. Kiesler (1971) found that subjects who had three occasions to use a particular game strategy, thus perhaps developing a commitment to it, were even more likely to choose it again when it was subsequently attacked. In contrast, subjects who had one or no previous occasion to use the strategy were less likely to use it after it was attacked.

Making Pain and Suffering Endurable

Fundamentally, it is the structure of commitment that makes pain and suffering possible to endure. In Tolstoy's *The Death of Ivan Ilych* (1960), the pain of cancer devastates Ivan only after he realizes how meaningless his life has been. Erikson (1950) writes that it is not frustration that children cannot bear, but meaningless frustration. Some of the literature reviewed earlier (e.g., Bulman & Wortman, 1977; Langer et al., 1975) offers empirical, even experimental support for the function of commitment and meaning especially in times of difficulty and distress. But perhaps the most compelling evidence that a capacity to create meaning and forge commitments has survival value comes from the observation and self-observation of people in extreme circumstances. Victor Frankl (1963), founder of what is called logotherapy, or meaning therapy, is worth quoting at length on this point.

> Whenever one is confronted with an inescapable, unavoidable situation, whenever one has to face a fate that cannot be changed, e.g., an incurable disease, such as an inoperable cancer, just then is one given a last chance to actualize the highest value, to fulfill the deepest meaning, the meaning of suffering. For what matters above all is the attitude we take toward suffering, the attitude in which we take our suffering upon ourselves.
>
> Let me give a clear cut example: Once, an elderly general practitioner consulted me because of his severe depression. He could not overcome the loss of his wife who had died two years before and whom he had loved above all else.

Now how could I help him? What should I tell him? Well, I refrained from telling him anything, but instead confronted him with the question, 'What would have happened, Doctor, if you had died first, and your wife would have had to survive you?' 'Oh,' he said, 'for her this would have been terrible; how she would have suffered.' Whereupon I replied, 'You see, Doctor, such a suffering has been spared her, and it is you who have spared her this suffering; but now, you have to pay for it by surviving her and mourning her.' He said no word but shook my hand and calmly left my office. Suffering ceases to be suffering in some way at the moment it finds a meaning, such as the meaning of a sacrifice. . . . (p. 179)

It is especially noteworthy to see how Frankl, who had himself suffered in a Nazi concentration camp, calls for the transformation of unavoidable suffering into suffering that is chosen, accepted, affirmed as having significance and meaning, a source of pride rather than shame, strength rather than weakness. Frankl's concern was not with whether he and his comrades would survive the camp but whether "all this suffering, this dying around us, has a meaning."

Bettelheim (1943), another psychologist who spent some time in a concentration camp, observed that the people who coped worst with the shock of being sent to the camp were law-abiding, politically uneducated members of the German middle classes who were unable to explain to themselves why they had been sent to the camp or to question the wisdom of the law and the police. Many of those who coped best, on the other hand, were prisoners who felt that they had been sent to the camps as representatives of a certain political or economic group and who felt they were enduring for the sake of this group. Bettelheim also observed that the Gestapo engaged in tactics that were as much designed to disrupt the inmates' sense of meaning as their sense of control. Prisoners were never told why they had been imprisoned. Although some tasks represented productive labor, many others were deliberately designed to be nonsensical and humiliating, such as carrying heavy rocks back and forth between two places. Both Bettelheim and Frankl note a grim choice made between meaning and control by many prisoners. Those most concerned with control were most likely to cheat on their fellow prisoners, identify with the guards, and do other regrettable deeds.

It is interesting that Frankl (1963) quotes with approval two phrases of Nietzsche's, "That which does not kill me makes me stronger" and "He who has a why to live for can bear with almost any how." Nietzsche's conception of what is valuable in human life is almost totally different from Frankl's, glorifying as it does the idea of a superman and power over others. Yet along with Kierkegaard, the first major philosopher to confront the question of meaning without God, Nietzsche formulates and addresses questions of interest to all existential thinkers that follow.

Commitment in the absence of control rests not on changing the environment but on changing oneself, or even of keeping oneself from unwanted change. As T. S. Eliot said in a moment of renunciation combined with affirmation, "For us there is only trying. The rest is not our business" (cited in Coles, 1978, p. 122). Though not the master of one's fate, one may still be captain of one's soul.

Personal enlightenment. There are two major sources of meaning, and so commitment, in situations one cannot control. The first is a personal, perhaps idiosyncratic, sense that there are redeeming or enlightening features to the situation (see Curtis, Smith, & Moore, 1984). As one of the authors, Philip Brickman, once remarked, "Though I might well give them up if I did not have to do them, I have come to the conclusion that exercises I do every day for lower back pain are amply compensated for by the fact that they give me at least a minimal degree of muscle tone at times when I would not otherwise have it." Beecher (1956) found that soldiers wounded at Anzio required less medication and reported less pain than civilians undergoing comparable surgery. These differences may be partially accounted for by the fact that the medical trauma had two redeeming features for the soldiers that were generally absent for the civilians: The wounds had been incurred in a worthwhile cause, and they were accompanied by a relief at being removed from the dangerous battle zone. A more extreme example of injury with redeeming properties is religiously inspired self-mutilation. Participants typically claim that such injuries are not painful, and observers report that the injuries heal quickly and cleanly without any medication at all. This is in sharp contrast to psychosomatic or guilt-produced symptoms, which linger despite any amount of medication—a contrast reminiscent of the distinction between feeling an injury is deserved and feeling it is meaningful.

To feel that an injury is deserved is simply to feel that one has behaved badly in the past, a belief that does not endow the injury with any redeeming features. Chodoff, Friedman, and Hamburg (1964) and Bulman and Wortman (1977) found that this response among the victims they studied was rare and not helpful to their mourning or healing. When this kind of self-blame occurs, merely removing the pejorative implications of the disability may promote healing. This is exactly what Storms, Denney, McCaul, and Lowerly (1979) found for insomnia. Convincing people troubled by insomnia that insomniacs are more mentally active than most other people and have higher levels of autonomic activity, that they are not maladjusted or unable to handle stress, was expected to make insomniacs feel better regardless of whether it gave them greater control over falling asleep. As it turned out, subjects given this nonpejorative explanation reported that they fell asleep faster and more easily than did a control group. This analysis also helps explain why, like wounds, other problems picked up in the service appear easier to deal with than comparable problems developed in civilian life. A drug habit acquired in Viet Nam was more likely to be seen as a normal, externally justifiable response to the situation than a personal craving with pejorative connotation, an interpretation which made the habit easier to kick when veterans returned home (Robins, 1974).

The ultimate redeeming factor of pain, on a personal level, is that it enables the sufferer to see life more clearly. Bettelheim, Frankl, and Gandhi are only a few who made use of their time in prison for this purpose in a way that shaped the rest of their lives. Gibran (1936) writes, "Your pain is the breaking of the shell that encloses your understanding" (p. 60). Observers have noted the determination of cancer patients and victims of chronic pain not to go back to what they see as phony former life-styles if they recover (LeShan, 1964). The most austere version of the connection between suffering and enlightenment is the vision of Greek tragedy, which emphasized the terrible price unwilling humans paid for this gift of the gods. Aeschylus wrote:

> God, whose law it is that he who learns must suffer.
> And even in our sleep, pain that cannot forget,
> Falls drop by drop upon the heart;
> And in our own despite, against our will,
> Comes wisdom to us by the awful grace of God.

A modern existential vision makes people more responsible for the attainment of their own enlightenment but describes the process as exactly the same terrible confrontation with despair that the Greeks understood. The confrontation, terrifying and challenging, usually involves death. "For Heidegger, death presents the great opportunity to the willing seeker, the confused man who wants to know before he draws his last breath what at rock bottom he can consider his 'own most,' because it has been rescued from the everydayness of his life" (Coles, 1978, p. 106). Rescued from everydayness, in our terms, means being rescued from empty habit, rescued from the pressures of control. People facing death are free, if they choose, to act on the purest form of intrinsic motivation, to discover the essence of commitment and meaning in their lives.

Altruism.   The second source of meaning and commitment in situations one cannot control is the sense that one's pain or negative experience may benefit others, if not oneself. One can still help others when one can no longer help oneself, if only by example. Part of the secret of self-help groups is that they are peer help groups. People with cancer can find some meaning in their suffering by sharing their experiences and helping both patients and the public cope with the disease (Wortman & Dunkel-Schetter, 1979). The well-being of long-term hospital patients is improved by programs in which they take some responsibility for making their own beds and helping care for other patients who are too ill to care for themselves (Kornfeld, 1971; Taylor, 1979). Soldiers suffering from war neuroses do better if they are given some meaningful work around the hospital, especially if this work is related to the war effort (Grinker & Spiegler, 1945).

Our analysis suggests that this can be generalized to many other forms of suffering that seem beyond our control. On a more mundane level, there is the case of a colleague who transformed his going to conventions from a lonely experience, beset with painful social comparisons (Brickman & Janoff-Bulman, 1977), into something rich and pleasurable. He did this in a wholly admirable way, by becoming concerned with the field as a whole, devoting his energy to helping young people get ahead and supporting worthy causes, rather than obsessively worrying about his place in the field. In such cases, the sting of not being able to accomplish everything one wants fades in the commitment to helping other people accomplish things. This also helps prevent people from obsessively reviewing the past, dwelling on lost reinforcements and agonizing over why they were lost, something that characterizes depression accompanying divorce (Harvey, Wells, & Alvarez, 1978) or bereavement (Marris, 1958).

All of this suggests that, at least in extreme situations, altruism has a functional value for its carrier that has been ignored by previous theorists. It has long been recognized that commitment, caring, and altruism by parents may be a vital factor in the survival of children. As Bronfenbrenner (1977) puts it, "There has to be at least one person who has an irrational involvement with that child, someone who thinks that kid is more important than other people's kids, someone who's in love with him and whom he loves in return" (p. 43). As previously mentioned, sociobiologists have pointed out that it may also be in the parents' biological self-interest to sacrifice themselves for their children if this increases the chance that some of their genes will survive (Wilson, 1975). Sacrificing oneself for other than close kin cannot have survival value on a genetic basis, they argue, because the genes of individuals who displayed such a tendency would gradually disappear in favor of the genes of more selfish individuals. Our analysis establishes one set of conditions in which altruism may have direct survival value for its carriers. It may enable them to carry on when more selfish motives will not serve and no other sources of commitment and meaning remain.

Children, Astronauts, and Spies

Sometimes, in uncontrolled situations, meaning is so readily available that we are hardly aware of its urgency. Children appear to find meaning easily. This accounts partially for the fact that they are more resilient and less vulnerable to depression than adults despite being less able to control their environment. Virtually the only experiment that even indicated that people will see an activity in a more positive light when it leads to negative consequences that are totally unforeseen used children as subjects. This is Brehm's (1959) demonstration that children who were induced to eat a disliked vegetable and then told that their parents would be informed that they actually ate it increased their liking for the vegetable. In the domain of moral judgment, as Piaget (1948) showed, children are more likely than adults to hold a person responsible for an accident that has serious consequences. This may simply be another expression of a child's tendency to assume that all behavior is intentional and hence meaningful, that nothing happens without some essentially human or at least animate cause. If everything is intentional or meaningful, it makes sense that dropping a large number of cups should be treated as a more serious offense than dropping a small number of cups. From this perspective, it also makes sense that a major characteristic of regression in stressful times is the attaching of a seemingly exaggerated significance to minor events, and the enactment of fixed ritualistic behavior patterns. It should not be surprising that childlike forms of behavior may have great value in enabling people to adapt to situations they cannot control.

Where meaning is easily available, lack of control passes unnoticed among both adults and children. Astronauts and spies, for example, have remarkably little control over their lives without suffering breakdown or despair. The fate of astronauts in fact lies in the hands of thousands of scientists, engineers, and technicians, any one of whom can make a mistake that will cost the astronauts their lives. Furthermore, astronauts can do very little on their own initiative, aside from smuggling a few souvenirs on board. They are as tightly programmed and scheduled as their computers. Similarly, the fate of spies in the field lies in the hands of controllers who either keep them in the dark or actually mislead them about the purposes of their assignments.

Both spies and astronauts accept conditions that ordinary men and women would find intolerable in their everyday lives. They hardly notice the lack of control, and neither do we, because both they and we accept them as necessary and meaningful features of a chosen line of activity. Again, commitment makes the absence of control acceptable and even unremarkable. The orientation of astronauts and spies is not unusual, as it precisely parallels the orientation we all bring to any collective enterprise, including being a member of society. There are many problems that are totally out of any person's control, like pollution. In cases such as these it is often rational for the individual to behave in such as way that makes such problems worse rather than better. This, as we have seen, is called the tragedy of the commons (Hardin, 1968; Platt, 1973), in which individuals maximizing their self-interest in the short term create greater problems for the collective and themselves in the long term, whether it is circumventing pollution controls on one's car to improve performance or planting in semiarid regions crops that fetch higher prices but drain the local water supplies. No single individual is totally responsible for the problem, and neither can any individual single-handedly solve the problem. Only by acting collectively can people solve these problems. But—and this is the critical point—a collective solution, even when successful, does not give people the same psychological sense of control as an individual solution does. Collective solutions require us to trust the actions of many other people. The way to solve common problems, to escape from social traps such as the tragedy of the commons, may be to instill a sense of commitment among individuals to a collective solution that has personal meaning for each individual.

Voting, too, can be seen as an exercise of commitment rather than control. If people vote in a certain way, they may succeed in electing a candidate who will implement programs they favor. But few people have the sense that in voting they are exercising any kind of psychologically meaningful control over either the electoral process or the subsequent behavior of politicians. We may attach value to the voting process itself as symbolic of democracy; we may vote as an act of loyalty to a country, a party, or friends who are involved in an election; or we may vote as a pure expression of our attitudes and feelings. But, unless we are personally rewarded for voting by precinct workers, we do not control our environment by voting. Not voting, incidentally, is likewise a symbolic expression either of trust that the political process will take care of itself or distrust that it can be made to work fairly. As Coleman (1973) notes, although individuals may gain benefits by joining a guild, a union, or a professional association, they do so by giving up a measure of their direct, personal control over these benefits. They are induced to do so because joining and remaining a member of such a group comes to have commitment and meaning in itself. Successful utopian communities in nineteenth-century America achieved their greater longevity not by giving members a greater sense of control, but by inducing in them a greater sense of commitment (Kanter, 1972). Members established their commitment by renouncing outside interests, contributing goods and services to the commune, and participating in communal ceremonies, all activities that involved relinquishing rather than enlarging control in their lives. Nor, it should be added, is it only followers who make sacrifices for collective interest. Though leaders may sometimes be exempt from sacrifices, they are often equally involved in making sacrifices far greater than those expected of ordinary group members. This is equally true of revolutionary leaders and politicians. Many spouses and families of politicians well know how they too must give up control over much of their lives for the sake of pleasing and impressing constituents.

Like astronauts or spies, hospital patients are required to relinquish control over a great part of their lives. Moreover, they do so for essentially the same reason: to make collective control of the whole enterprise more efficient and effective. This requires people to follow rules and carry out isolated bits of routine activity regardless of how they feel about it at the time or even whether they understand what they are doing and why. Yet there is good evidence that hospital patients, already under stress for their injury or illness, are made to feel worse by what they experience as the further humiliations inflicted upon them by impersonal hospital routines (Goffman, 1961; Lorber, 1975; Taylor, 1979). Because both astronauts and hospital patients relinquish control, the difference in their feelings must lie not in lack of control itself but in the circumstances and significance of lack of control. The difference is one of commitment and meaning.

There are at least five different reasons why it should be harder for hospital patients than for astronauts to find meaning in their lack of control. First, people rarely choose to go to the hospital, and we have already seen how important choice is in the creation of meaning. Second, even if people do choose to go to the hospital, they are (except in rare cases) choosing strictly for personal reasons or for the benefits they anticipate from going, rather than for the more social or altruistic reasons that may govern the choice of other roles. We have already seen the importance of perceiving benefit for others in the creation of meaning. Third, unlike astronauts or spies, hospital patients are not trained for their role. Fourth, this lack of training in turn contributes to patients' inability to understand why things are happening to them or what they mean, even if hospital staff take the time to try to explain, which they often do not or cannot. Finally, it should not be forgotten that the role of the bedridden hospital patient is an unusually inactive one, with long boring stretches in which he or she has nothing to do. Since commitment and the meaning it depends on come from activity, this too makes it hard to get involved or find meaning of the role. With ingenuity, the role of hospital patient can be redefined in a way that is much more conducive to health (Taylor, 1979). Because there are limits to the amount of control ill patients can exercise—as there are for healthy people—it is fortunate that the key question is one of meaning and commitment rather than control.

Commitment Without Control:
The Path Through Life

By now it should be clear that the task of sustaining commitment and meaning in the absence of control is not one that falls only to the unfortunate, the victimized, or the inept. The task is inherent in the universal questions of life and death. Maturity can be defined as the ability to face the uncontrollable without despair. This makes meaning and commitment the essence of maturity. And it is in this sense that Erikson (1950) speaks of ego integrity, the fruit and culmination of his eight stages of life. Ego integrity and maturity lie as much in one's orientation to the past as to the future. To have integrity means to accept one's life as something that had to be the way it was and to show a lack of despair in the face of a coming death.

But the universal demand for commitment in the absence of control is not only a matter of reconciliation with the past or with death; it also is very much a task of dealing with the future, with life growth, and with creation. Organisms that are living, growing, and creating do not know and cannot know exactly where they are going or how they will get there. As Slater (1974) pointed out, an organism with complete control has no possibility of learning anything new. The more control we have, the more we ourselves determine what feedback we receive, the less chance the environment has to tell us that we have adopted a wrong, perhaps fatal, solution or overlooked a new opportunity. As Heidegger's (1963) critique of knowledge suggests, we do not know objects by controlling them or exercising our will over them. Understanding comes from allowing objects to reveal themselves as what they are as they are (Barrett, 1958). To the extent that people are at home in the world, they are at home not through dominating but through caring (Mayerhoff, 1971). Living creatures cannot shut themselves off entirely from the unknown, but they can retreat a good way from it through a relentless search for control, through locking themselves insofar as possible into a world that is secure and self-contained. One can stifle people's creativity simply by making them sufficiently concerned with control, with their success at meeting a certain criterion, or with winning a certain reward (Lepper & Dafoe, 1979; McGraw, 1978). This can be done simply by promising them a reward for every problem they solve rather than letting them work, or play, at the problems for their own sake. Creativity involves the ability or willingness to follow a line of thought through associations that are increasingly remote from the original stimulus; this may seem, to someone more concerned with control, like a wandering of attention away from a logical focus on the task (Wallach, 1970). Creativity involves a tolerance for ambiguity (Safan-Gerard, 1978) and an interest in discovering problems rather than solutions (Csikszentmihalyi, 1975; 1978). It involves a willingness to suspend dominant or familiar structures of thought even though they have worked well in the past and may continue to work well (Luchins,

1942; Rokeach, 1968). It involves, in short, a relaxation of the concern for control. Creative individuals describe themselves as having less self-control or less control of their impulses and less interest in making a good impression on others (Barron, 1957). To become a scientist, a person must learn to demand an extraordinary degree of control over the conduct of thought, manipulation, and measurement and to be critical of research in which this control is not achieved. Some very bright people internalize such strict scientific superegos that they lose (in Donald Campbell's phrase) the tolerance for their own sloppiness that would enable them to be creative.

We can, and perhaps must, stake out for ourselves limited areas of control in our lives. We can limit ourselves to these areas and pretend that they are all of life, but they are not. The general pathway through life follows commitment in the absence of control. It is an uncertain path, but there is no other.

CHAPTER FIVE
THE DEVELOPMENT
OF COMMITMENT

Philip Brickman
Christine Dunkel-Schetter
Antonia Abbey

Our fundamental model of commitment is a dialectic one in which instigating determinants of action are integrated with opposing forces. Only if the forces that oppose a line of action are reconciled can an actor proceed in the commitment indefinitely. Enduring lines of action thus require persistence in the face of difficulties because opposing forces cannot be made to disappear. They must be made compatible with instigating forces by some process of reinterpretation—that is, by integration. Once opposing forces have been integrated with instigating forces, their negative effects are neutralized. Indeed, as we have seen, the end product of this integration represents a stronger form of commitment, accompanied by stronger motivation than was present prior to the appearance of the opposing forces. Moreover, the commitment is also stronger than it would have been had the negative forces not been integrated with the positive ones.

Our fundamental postulate is that this integration, or *bonding*, of positive and negative elements cannot remain unchanged for long. It is continually subject to new forms of challenge or stress that ultimately lead either to a new integration or an unraveling of the commitment. In other words, commitments are completely rationalized or stable only momentarily, and then new inconsistencies or contradictions emerge. There are no final stages, solutions, or end points. Thus, the *development* of a commitment is seen here as a dialectical process, and a commitment itself is seen as a dynamic and ever-changing phenomenon.

THEORETICAL ROOTS FOR
A THEORY OF DEVELOPMENT

Dialectical Theories

The notion of a dialectical process in philosophy is at least as old as Plato. We must, however, be careful to distinguish between the dialectical nature of the evolution of ideas and the dialectical nature of development of behavior in the real world. Here we follow the distinction between "dialectical contradiction" and "real opposition" discussed by Colletti (1975). At a philosophical level, the principle of dialectical contradiction implies that two logically contradictory ideas can exist at the same time. Indeed, to assert that A is true is also to assert, at some level, that not-A is also true. One cannot comprehend the existence of beauty without also comprehending the existence of ugliness. Each of these two notions is incomplete without its opposite, and a full understanding of the two requires their integration into a still more complex idea—which will, in turn, involve the assertion of the logical contradiction of that idea. Although this kind of philosophical dialectic is a valid description of thought, clearly it cannot account for the relationship between instigating and inhibiting forces in connection with commitment. Colletti (1975) stated clearly that the dynamic of change in historical materialism involves the *real opposition of contending forces* rather than the logical contradiction of incompatible ideas. Although it contrasts with a number of previous Marxist interpretations, that is the notion of dialectics that we shall use here.

Inhibiting forces in commitment development are not necessarily logically contradictory with instigating forces. They are forces that work toward a contrary direction or line of action. The existence of instigating forces in the real world does not imply that inhibiting forces also exist. However, both occur together as part of the process of developing a commitment, and both are necessary. The model of commitment is incomplete without a full understanding of the two.

There are many other models in psychology that postulate that behavior is governed by an ebb and flow of contending forces. Schneirla (1959), for example, argued that a great deal of animal behavior could be explained by a biphasic process in which approach tendencies and withdrawal tendencies were alternately dominant. Shontz (1975) has claimed that the sequence of steps by which victims adapt to trauma is characterized by a continual shifting between cognitive confrontation (encounter with the crisis) and retreat (withdrawal from thinking about it). Atkinson and Birch (1970) have developed an elaborate series of equations to describe how persistence in a form of behavior is determined by the relative strength of different forces. Some of these forces are functions of the length of time since the individual engaged in that behavior (the instigating force, which increases motivation to engage in that behavior). Other forces are functions of the amount of time the individual has spent engaging in that behavior (the consummatory force, which decreases motivation to engage in that behavior). None of these models qualify as dialectical, however, because none of them consider the question of how contending forces may be integrated and qualitatively transformed or how the integration of contending forces at one point in time may serve as the basis for a new round of conflict at a later point in time.

One model in psychology that has more in common with our approach than any other is Solomon and Corbit's (1974) opponent-process theory of motivation, which has received considerable attention in experimental psychology. It will be discussed in greater detail than those mentioned above, although it is not truly dialectical either. Opponent-process theory comes from the observation that many affective sequences seem to involve two opposite states: an initial state, which is either positive or negative, and a second state, which is opposite to the initial state. The essential idea of opponent-process theory is that all primary affective reactions, whether positive or negative, arouse a secondary process that opposes and supresses the initial hedonic state. The opponent process is opposite to the initial process and is slow to begin, slow to build to its maximum intensity, and slow to decay. The affective state of the organism at any point in time is a function of the difference between these two yoked processes. Opiate addiction is the example used most frequently to illustrate the positive-negative sequence: Individuals feel good during the presence of the drug-induced stimulation and bad after this stimulation stops. Fear reactions are the examples used most frequently to illustrate the negative-positive sequence: Individuals feel bad anticipating or experiencing an aversive stimulus (e.g., an electric shock for dogs), and relieved or good after the stimulation stops.

With the addition of a second powerful postulate, opponent-process theory is able to explain the rather dramatic changes in affective tone that occur with repeated exposure to certain forms of stimulation. Solomon (1980) and Solomon and Corbit (1974) postulate that the opponent reaction becomes quicker, stronger, and longer lasting the more frequently it is elicited. Since the strength of the initial affective process that elicits it does not change, the overall quality of the experience comes increasingly to resemble that of the opponent process. The intensity of the initial affect is weakened, and the intensity of the opposite reaction is strengthened. For example, in the case of addictive drug use, the intensity of the initial positive reaction is reduced, and the intensity of the subsequent negative reaction (withdrawal) is increased. With electric shocks to dogs (or parachuting or using saunas for people), the initial experience of terror or discomfort becomes less intense, and the subsequent experience of exhilaration or relief becomes more intense.

There are many attractive features to opponent-process theory from our point of view. It calls attention to the mixture of positive and negative elements involved in the pursuit of behavior and to the gradual shift in orientation or motivation underlying a pursuit; in this general sense, it is similar to our model. The major points of difference derive from the fact that we are concerned with how people take action and make decisions, whereas Solomon and Corbit are concerned with an automatic process invoked by exposure to stimuli. Since the opponent process has not been experienced prior to exposure to the stimulus, it cannot serve as a source of ambivalence in the minds of individuals over whether to expose oneself to the stimulus the first time.

Within opponent-process theory, the initial decision to seek stimulation is determined by the valence of the initial state. People tend to seek out stimulus experiences whose initial impact is positive (including drug experiences)—unless restrained by other forces—and to avoid stimulus experiences whose initial impact is negative (including exposure to saunas or fear-inducing experiences like parachuting)—unless compelled by other forces. Over time, however, the increasingly intense opponent process can serve as a powerful source of additional motivation that will cause individuals to change the basis on which they approach the activity. If the opponent process is increasingly aversive, increasingly difficult to avoid, and more and more potent in canceling the initial positive effects of the primary reaction (e.g., pleasure from drug use), individuals will need to justify their continued pursuit of this behavior. Thus, for Solomon and Corbit, addiction is simply the result of repeated exposure to a certain form of stimulation that elicits an initial positive reaction and, over time, an increasingly intense yoked negative reaction. For us, addiction is something else in addition: a sense of commitment to seeking this form of stimulation, and a series of steps involved in continuing to do so despite the increasing costs associated with seeking the stimulation.

If the initial reaction to an activity is aversive—for example, the intense fear experienced by novice parachutists (Epstein, 1967)—the change in the opponent process makes people feel thrilled and exhilarated afterwards. In this case, the decision to continue pursuing the activity may be easier because the positive component rather than the negative component is being strengthened. Nonetheless, people must do so despite the continued presence of some initial negative motivation, and without the external support (e.g., hand-holding, encouragement, or teasing by friends) that may have seen them through the first few episodes. Thus, here too we would see the continued pursuit of a line of action despite the presence of negative elements as requiring commitment and a series of steps in continuing to do so. In the case of parachuting, this might involve the accumulation of moral, spiritual, and physical value attached to the sport—forms of justification that are hardly necessary when an activity does not have an aversive side to it. In other words, a negative-positive sequence like parachuting can lead as strongly to what behavior observers would call addiction as can positive-negative sequences like opiate use. It is ostensibly the second element in each sequence that is being strengthened over time. A similar process may take place for jogging enthusiasts.

Both opponent-process theory and our model of commitment can explain these addictive processes, but in our view, there is more ambiguity in the exact sequence of positive and negative elements than opponent-process theory allows. In the case of parachuting, for example, prior to the fear upon actually climbing into the plane for one's first jump, there is an extended period of interest and excitement that permits the person's recruitment to the activity in the first place. In the case of drug addiction, there are many instances (alcohol and cigarettes are two well-known examples) in which initial reactions are not positive at all but only gradually become so.

Opponent-process theory, in summary, assumes that all affective reactions elicit opponent processes. This means that all motivation involving a repeated exposure to stimulation will necessarily undergo an evolution. Our model makes similar predictions and on a similar basis: Most (but not necessarily all) outcomes involve the experience of both positive and negative elements, and the quality of the experience changes as these elements change. But we will not assume that the elements occur in fixed sequence, that one is necessarily yoked to the other (i.e., they may have independent sources), that only the yoked element changes over time, or that the transformation of motivation is the same in all cases, involving nothing more than the algebraic sum of a fixed initial reaction and a growing opponent process.

In our analysis, the nature of subsequent motivation depends on what kind of integration of prior contending forces the individual has been able to achieve. There is no such dialectical element in opponent-process theory, where the two states are never brought together into any kind of overall synthesis, and where indeed the intensity and quality of the initial reaction is assumed never to change. In contrast, we argue that the fact that parachutists become less intensely fearful before jumping as they grow more experienced (and also experience their fear at an earlier point in their preparation to jump; Epstein, 1967) is not merely an automatic result of a strengthening antifear or relief response but is a contingent product of an increasing commitment to jumping. The stressful experience of the period before jumping is qualitatively transformed or integrated with the episodes that follow—the actual descent and the emotional aftereffects. Meaning and value is attached to activities that were mechanical or uncertain before. Preparatory activities become both reassuring to experienced jumpers who better comprehend their significance and expressive of the personal significance attached to jumping. Of course, not all jumpers achieve their bonding of positive and negative elements; thus, not all jumpers continue jumping. The governing dynamics of the process are not merely the algebraic sum of two automatic emotional reactions (even if these reactions exist exactly as Solomon and Corbit posit) but include the manner in which the individual experiences these reactions as part of a larger whole. In consequence, an individual sees himself or herself as either committed or not committed to the entire sequence.

Structural Models

Whenever psychologists have been concerned with structures, dialectical models have appeared. Structures are by definition resistant to change. To be adaptive, however, a structure must eventually incorporate new information to respond to altered circumstances. Most structural models in psychology have dealt with cognition rather than affect. Thus, we have dialectical elements in the structural theories of Neisser in perception, Piaget in cognitive development, and Kuhn in the history of scientific thought. According to Neisser (1976), perception involves a kind of dialectical process in which anticipations interact with often conflicting information to in turn create new anticipations or schemas. For Piaget (1970), the fundamental movements of thought are those in which the individual is trying either to assimilate information to an existing structure or to change the structure to accommodate information that cannot be assimilated. Structures resist change until they are no longer capable of assimilating the information they are called to face. Children pass from one developmental stage to another when they begin to experience contradictions that did not theretofore bother them (e.g., inconsistencies in their judgments about which of two quantities is larger). Each new stage thus represents the synthesis of the previous structure with new information that had come to be experienced as contradictory with it.

Scientific revolutions, according to Kuhn (1962), represent a similar process in which previous knowledge is integrated with an accumulated series of facts that could not be accounted for by existing theory. (It should be noted, by the way, that the new structures need not retain all the elements of either the previous structures or the conflicting observations but may be built selectively out of those elements of each that best fit together.) Contradictory evidence may accumulate slowly and imperceptibly, whereas a change in structure is substantial and dramatic. Thus, dialectical processes of this sort tend to superimpose discontinuous or structural change onto a process of continuous change or accumulation of evidence. This may explain why we sometimes experience things in our lives as taking a sudden leap forward when in fact their development has been quite gradual but has only captured our attention after a certain critical point was passed (e.g., childrens' growth, work accomplishments).

The major theory that has postulated emotional or affective structures, Freudian psychoanalysis, is curiously devoid of a dialectical element. This is perhaps because the major elements of personality in psychoanalytic theory are unconscious, and the unconscious can tolerate inconsistencies. Conflicting impulses and wishes can exist side by side in the id or the superego without requiring any change. Only the ego, the sole element of personality that is predominantly conscious and predominantly concerned with adaptation to its environment, is sensitive to contradiction. Not surprisingly, as ego theory has developed in the hands of Erikson (1950), it has taken on the aspects of a dialectical process. Successful passage through each of Erikson's eight major stages of development requires the resolution of a polar conflict between two opposing potential identities (e.g., trust versus mistrust).

COMMITMENT AS A
DIALECTICAL PROCESS

Commitment is conceptualized here in dialectical terms as conjoined cognitive-affective change. An initial orientation to an object is a *thesis*. Emerging evidence that tends to oppose, weaken, or cancel this orientation is an *antithesis*, and the orientation that emerges to integrate the opposing forces is a *synthesis*. Contradictions are the drive behind the development of a commitment—that is, they are essential for its growth.

Contradictions to a Line of Action:
Antitheses

Contradictions to a line of action or a decision are often imposed by external events. The pursuit may be made unpalatable by difficulties or negative consequences that had not been foreseen or that the individual had hoped to avoid. New options, temptations, or choices may also arise. As people go through different life stages, they become sensitive to issues and elements that they were quite oblivious to before. These events may change the calculus of the balance of forces affecting one's actions (Riegel, 1975).

However, it is our view that antitheses to a decision will emerge even in the absence of external stresses; in fact, they are inevitable. If Solomon and Corbit (1974) are indeed correct that any positive state is eventually followed by a negative one, this suggests that individuals eventually have something to regret about their decisions, however good they may be. But the same conclusion can be reached without making assumptions nearly as demanding as those of opponent-process theory. It is enough to understand that humans, like all species, are not entirely coherent in their own internal wiring. It is impossible to make a decision that will not, eventually, have negative reverberations somewhere else in the psychic system. Human intelligence is not the result of a master circuit or chip, designed all at once and tested for consistency and reliability in all its components and combinations. It has evolved through a series of improvisations and a patchwork of adaptations. It is built not only to tolerate error but, in some curious sense, to produce and profit from error as well. As usual, the biologist Lewis Thomas (1979) is especially eloquent on this point:

> We could never have [evolved human intelligence] with human intelligence, even if molecular biologists had been flown in by satellite at the beginning, laboratories and all, from some other solar system. We have evolved scientists, to be sure, and so we know a lot about DNA, but if our kind of mind had been confronted with the problem of designing a similar replicating molecule, starting from scratch, we'd never have succeeded. We would have made one fatal mistake: our molecule would have been perfect. Given enough time, we would have figured out how to do this, nucleotides, enzymes, and all, to make flawless, exact copies, but it would never have occurred to us, thinking as we do, that the thing had to be able to make errors. . . .
>
> To err is human, we say, but we don't like the idea much, and it is harder still to accept the fact that erring is biological as well. We prefer sticking to the point, and insuring ourselves against change. But there it is: we are here by the purest chance, and by mistake at that. Somewhere along the line, nucleotides were edged apart to let new ones in; maybe viruses moved in, carrying along bits of other, foreign genomes; radiation from the sun or from outer space caused tiny cracks in the molecule, and humanity was conceived. . . . (pp. 28–30)

Another way to understand that our actions contain an element of internal contradiction may be through the paradox that freedom is consumed by use. Freedom of choice is always an element of initial commitment and is one basis on which we know that some positive element is present in the situation. But the freedom to choose alternatives is sacrificed by any consequential choice, though new forms of choice may open up in the future. To speak of the road not taken does not mean that it could be traversed at any time if the person chose to, but that it can no longer be taken because that option—that career, that relationship—is no longer available. This sacrifice of other options may eventually be experienced as a loss, an emergent antithesis, even if the chosen option and its consequences are entirely successful and without further negative elements. Some evidence indicates that we can justify our choices only to the extent that we can say to ourselves that we could reasonably foresee their consequences (Wicklund & Brehm, 1976). Since we can only foresee a limited way into the future, there eventually comes a point at which our current outcomes no longer seem to us to have been predictable when we made choices long ago—and hence it is no longer fully possible to justify our choices or to experience ourselves as committed to them.

In general, it takes psychic energy to integrate negative elements with positive ones and to maintain the sense that an ambivalent decision is justified. Like all stress adaptation processes (see Selye, 1957), this level of effort or energy can only be supplied for a limited time. What is needed to sustain a choice or decision, we suspect, is not a continual effort to justify that decision but a subsequent flow of smaller choices or decisions, each built on the last, each requiring its own effort and energy and each serving to dissolve the tensions that have arisen since the previous decision.

The dissonance literature already contains some evidence to this effect. Perhaps the best known of these is Walster's (1964) study of shifts in army draftees' ratings of chosen and rejected job assignments at various points in time after having made their decision (immediately, four, fifteen, or ninety minutes after the decision). Walster obtained evidence of dissonance reduction (i.e., enhanced rating of the chosen job relative to the rejected one) only at the 15-minute point. By the end of the 90-minute period, there was no longer any evidence of dissonance reduction. However, from the point of view of the present analysis, there was a very special feature to the Walster study. After making their decisions, subjects were simply left alone until the time of the posttest. Thus, they had no occasion to do any of the things that individuals ordinarily do in the moments after making such a decision— go to pick up further information or other material relevant to their prospective assignment, explain the reasons for their choice to a friend, or take any of a number of other small steps, each of which would serve to confirm or bolster the initial decision. Compare this with the procedure in a well-known study (Freedman, 1965) that obtained effects of dissonance reduction that endured over a period of two months. Children who had been induced to avoid playing with certain attractive toys under mild (rather than severe) experimenter pressure continued to avoid these toys in a posttest two months later. Note, however, that in the initial treatment in this experiment, not only did the children make a decision (at least implicitly), but they then went on to repeatedly behave in a way consistent with that decision in the time that followed (i.e., choosing to play with a variety of other toys rather than the tempting one that had been forbidden). Thus, the change in their view of themselves and their preferences can be thought of as based not on just one decision but on a sequence of behaviors calling for a series of mutually reinforcing decisions.

Repeatedly reinforcing a decision may simplify the structure and content of that choice in much the same way that repeatedly telling a story reduces the story to a simple structure of essentials (Bartlett, 1932). To be sure, in the work on story transmission, the simplification occurs through the actions of different message transmitters, each of whom understands the story in a slightly different way, thus dropping details that are perceived to be irrelevant. In the present context, the analogy is one of a single actor going over a particular "story" (a decision and its rationale) on different occasions. The story will be reduced to simple structure by repeated telling in this case as well, if only because the source and audience are familiar with it. Thus, a few simple cues can serve to stand for the whole. There is, moreover, strong evidence in work on memory indicating that what people remember is not the details of the original stimulus but their encoding of that stimulus (Higgins & King, 1980, Study 4; Lingle & Ostrom, 1979; Srull & Wyer, 1980).

The fact that social psychology has such a vast literature on impression formation based on first impressions and so little, relatively speaking, on subsequent impressions and their relationships to behavior may represent a profoundly misplaced emphasis. The direction may be set by a first impression, but it is what follows that anchors or does not anchor the impression. Similarly, simply exposing people to persuasive communications has surprisingly little effect, and what effects do obtain typically decay over time (Cook & Flay, 1978). On the other hand, alternative procedures, such as placing subjects in a situation in which they are required to make a series of decisions based on initial information (e.g., in the Luchins water jar problem) or to elaborate reasons for an impression (Ross & Lepper, 1975) or to interpret a range of their subsequent behavior consistently with the persuasive message they have received (Miller, Brickman, & Bolen, 1975), have effects that are surprisingly persistent. The key, once again, is to embed the persuasive messages in an ongoing stream of subject behavior, with the messages influencing the interpretation of the behavior and the behavior (and the decisions it involves), giving life and strength to the messages.

Some classic studies of first impressions have merely involved giving subjects some initial information about another person and then having them observe and judge that person in a standard situation, like a classroom (e.g., Kelley, 1950). More recently, experiments have given subjects information that is allegedly about a target person and then had them interact with this target, who is actually a naive other subject (see, e.g., Snyder, Tanke, & Berscheid, 1977; Snyder & Swann, 1978). We would predict that, if these studies were conducted over time, whatever the effects on the target person, subjects' commitment to their own impressions, and the persistence of these impressions, should be greater in the latter set of experiments than in the former.

Many things that appear to be single decisions turn out, upon closer examination, to represent the cumulative process of a series of steps, choices, or decisions,

each of which involves encountering and surmounting some form of stress or negation. For example, most religious conversions are actually reconversions or recom-
mitments (Argyle & Beit-Hallahmi, 1975) involving a series of steps. Another
example is an enduring marriage. There is universal agreement in the marriage and
family literature that successful couples continue to invest energy in their relationship to counteract the centrifugal forces that beseige all bonding. Such couples
seem to undergo periodic difficulties and resolutions resulting in greater commitment.

Characteristics of Commitments
as Syntheses

It is useful to think of a synthesis as a solution, resolution, or answer. It is, in
a sense, an answer to the question, What is to be the relationship between the thesis
and the antithesis? A good synthesis thus has the properties of a good answer. Perhaps the most important property of a good answer is a structure that is coherent,
preferably simple, and readily apparent and that allows for few alternatives. Garner
(1970) shows that good patterns in this sense are high in redundancy; that is, they
have many interconnections between their elements:

> Perhaps now we can understand why circles and squares are good patterns,
> whereas ink blots are not; there are very few ways in which circles and squares
> can be made, but many ways in which ink blots can be made. This smaller
> number of ways circles and squares can be made is the same thing as redun-
> dancy, and thus there is a direct relation between pattern goodness and
> redundancy. To summarize, poor patterns are those which are not redundant
> and thus have many alternatives, and the very best patterns are those which
> are unique, having no perceptual alternatives. (p. 42)

In semantic or thematic materials, good answers, patterns, stories, or schemas
will have the property of assimilating or absorbing into themselves elements that
might otherwise be perceived as incongruent or susceptible to alternative interpretation. Allport and Postman (1947) listed a variety of ways in which this process
would occur to make rumors simpler and better in the retelling: assimilation to the
principal theme (everything is made more consistent with the main point, and
irrelevant or inconsistent details are dropped out), assimilation by condensation
(elements are combined into fewer units), assimilation to expectation (elements are
made consistent with general expectations for such a situation), and assimilation to
the storyteller's individual interests and prejudices.

Answers, integrations, or syntheses also have a compelling quality. Once
people know the answer to a question, it is not only hard for them to think of
alternative answers but also hard for them to believe that they did not know this
answer all along. Fischhoff (1977, 1980) has repeatedly demonstrated that subjects
overestimate how likely they would have been to come up with the correct answers
to questions once they have been told these answers. One of the consequences of
this hindsight bias is that it makes past events seem more inevitable than they
appeared before they happened.

It is ironic that the very process that gives us the feeling that we understand the past—the knowledge of outcomes, and the construction of categories based on these outcomes to represent what came before—may deny us access to the past and reduce our ability to learn from it (Fischhoff, 1980). A great deal of recent work has been devoted to demonstrating the ways in which current states and needs determine individuals' memory for the past. Past behavior that is incompatible with current attitudes is remembered as less likely to have occurred. For example, when people are persuaded that brushing their teeth has negative consequences, they report having brushed their teeth less frequently in the past (Ross, McFarland, & Fletcher, 1981). People also remember themselves as less committed to past sexual partners than they are to current ones. The farther back in time the experience, the more they feel this is so (Jedlicka, 1975).

Perhaps the most dramatic evidence of the way in which properties of current syntheses may block access to the past is the recent research on mood and memory (Bower, 1981). When people are happy, they are more likely to recall happy words from lists of words they have memorized, happy episodes from daily diaries they have filled out, or happy childhood experiences. When they are sad, they are better able to recall unhappy elements from the past. Such selective memory may make the present seem inevitable. The perception of something as inevitable may in turn be an important form of commitment to it, especially if the person sees himself or herself as having played a critical role in making it inevitable. This may have some adaptive value in enabling the person to get on with the future. There is, for example, some evidence that people try to come to terms with heart attacks by restructuring their autobiographies in order to see the attack as something that followed from previous events and lifestyles such that it could have been anticipated, and thus future attacks can be prevented (Cowie, 1976). This process of draining the surprise from our perceptions of the present makes it inevitable that we will again be surprised by the future.

If a synthesis represents the integration of many different parts, it will make it not only more difficult to think of alternative integrations, but also will make it harder to think of the constituent parts of the synthesis in isolation. Hayes-Roth (1977), in her theory of knowledge assembly, postulates the transformation of many memory elements into a single unit that is activated in an all-or-none process. Once a knowledge structure has acquired a unitary representation, its constituent parts can be retrieved only if the unitary representation is activated and decomposed. This leads to the interesting and somewhat unobvious prediction that it may take longer for subjects with such an integration to access the constituent parts of memory than subjects without such an integration, and also that it may be harder for such subjects to retrieve parts of their knowledge structure than to retrieve the whole. Considerable evidence supports this theory. Horowitz, Day, Light, and White (1968), for example, found that subjects could turn an incomplete version of a unitized stimulus into a complete version twice as fast as they could produce the part that was needed to complete it. In addition, subjects can identify words faster than they can identify their constituent letters (Johnson, 1975). Langer (1979) has argued that when a task has been sufficiently overlearned, it may be impossible for people to retrieve the isolated movements and skills that go into their performance.

The masking of constituent elements within syntheses represents a critical issue in commitment, since it involves the masking of ambivalence. If people are really committed to something, they are unlikely to report that it has many negative elements, even though their commitment may in fact rest upon their having processed and integrated such negative elements. In processing them, however, they will come to experience them as no longer so negative, perhaps no longer negative at all. The difficulty, of course, lies in knowing whether ambivalence has been surmounted (or transformed) or simply never existed in the first place—two very different states of psychic reality. In longitudinal research, this information may become available as we track the ebb and flow of subjects' feelings during their pursuit of an activity (Folkman & Lazarus, 1984). In addition, it may be possible to get some contemporaneous measures of subjects' ambivalence by using two different versions of questions: a direct format, in which subjects are asked how they feel about some features of their situation, and a quasi-projective format, in which subjects are asked how they think other people would feel about this feature. The presumption is that if subjects think that something could or would be negative for other people in that situation, they understand, at some level, that it could be negative for them as well. But the question of comparing how ambivalent subjects could be (or could have been) about some activity with how ambivalent they actually are remains an important challenge for future research on commitment.

The syntheses involved in commitments are like answers in another way: the process by which they come into people's heads. They do not have nearly the same quality if they are given to people or imposed upon people that they have if they are generated by people themselves. It now appears, from an outpouring of recent research, that answers are more like commitments (i.e., are better retained by subjects) if subjects play an active role in generating them. Slamecka and Graf (1978), for example, found generally better memory by subjects for words they were asked to generate (given a general rule and a first letter) than for the same words (and the same rules) given to subjects in their entirety (see also Cosden, Ellis, & Feeney, 1979); Erdelyi, Buschke, & Finkelstein, 1977; Hamilton, Katz, & Leirer, 1980). Subjects are especially likely to remember stimuli that they have been asked to judge with reference to themselves (Rogers, Kuipers, & Kirker, 1977) or with reference to someone else they care a lot about, like their mother (Bower & Gilligan, 1979). Cognitive theorists have preferred to interpret these last findings as due to the fact that judgments involving self (or other familiar and highly involving concepts) are more likely to be tied into an elaborate and well-differentiated memory structure, and thus are more likely to be available for retrieval by a variety of different and well-established routes. These results, however, are also quite compatible with the idea that judgments with reference to self are more likely to lead to effort to come up with what is experienced as a "genuine answer" than are judgments with reference to abstract entities.

Participating in the process of generating answers or explanations causes subjects not only to remember them better but also to believe in them more strongly, even in the face of disconfirming evidence. This is the "belief perseverence" effect studied by Ross and Lepper and their colleagues. An initial study (Ross, Lepper, & Hubbard, 1975) showed that simply telling subjects after an experiment that the feedback during that experiment had been arbitrary was in no way sufficient to remove subjects' conviction that the person they had seen repeatedly receive such feedback (either themselves or someone else) was in fact good or poor at the task in question. Subjects had implicitly involved themselves in explaining or rationalizing this feedback, and it was these self-generated explanations that proved resistant to subsequent attempts by the experimenter to discredit the observations.

In a later study, Ross, Lepper, Strack, and Steinmetz (1977) examined this phenomenon more directly. Subjects were asked to explain particular events in the later lives of clinical patients whose case histories they had read, and then to estimate the likelihood of the events in question. The task of identifying potential antecedents to explain these events uniformly caused subjects to increase their estimates of the likelihood of these events. Anderson, Lepper, and Ross (1980) found that subjects could be induced to convince themselves that there was either a positive or a negative relationship between the quality of riskiness and success as a firefighter simply by being told that there was such a relationship (by reading one of two case studies) and then asked to explain it. Once they had done so, subjects were resistant to experimenters' attempts to indicate that there was, in fact, no such relationship or that the opposite relationship was equally plausible (see also Sherman, Skov, Herritz, & Stock, 1981).

There is another way in which syntheses come into a person's head like good answers. They are not predictable or obvious in advance, however right and inevitable they may appear in retrospect. Our model for this property is the ideal solution in the game of Twenty Questions wherein the object is to stump the others. This answer is something that no other player can think of in the course of the game, but something that everyone immediately recognizes when it is revealed. Likewise, the most compelling ending to a novel or a play is one that cannot be foreseen in advance but that seems eminently right, foreseeable, and even inevitable in retrospect.

The property of not being obvious in advance is as much a phenomenological property of answers to difficult questions as is the property of seeming obvious in retrospect. This will be the case especially when the syntheses can, in some sense, be thought of as emergent goals (see Csikszentmihalyi, 1975; March & Simon, 1958) or structures that have been created out of the matrix of previous actions rather than structures that existed from the start. Insofar as part of the purpose of a line of action is discovered during the course of the action, and the observation of its consequences and adaption to these consequences takes place subsequently, it can hardly have been predictable or knowable in advance.

There has always been some debate in the dissonance literature about whether negative consequences to an action had to be foreseen or known in advance in order to elicit dissonance and dissonance reduction. In our analysis, and in the most recent versions of dissonance theory, the critical question is instead whether or not the subject accepts responsibility for these consequences. It appears to be sufficient that the consequences were foreseeable rather than actually foreseen (i.e., things that people feel they could have anticipated given the information they had at hand, even if they did not). Thus, Goethals, Cooper, and Naficy (1979) compared subjects' reactions to having a counterattitudinal speech they had prepared sent to the college admissions board under one of three conditions. In the foreseen condition, subjects knew their speeches might be sent to the board; in the foreseeable condition, they knew their speeches might be sent to other interested groups but did not specifically know that the admissions board was such a group; and in the unforeseeable condition, they did not know that their speech might be sent to other groups. It should be noted that the quality of foreseeability—that an event seems to follow from or make sense in terms of some previous events—is present in both the foreseen and the foreseeable conditions. As predicted, self-justificatory attitude change was found in both the foreseen and the foreseeable condition, but not in the unforeseeable condition.

The present analysis suggests that the evolution of a good synthesis may involve some of the same stages as have been postulated for various problem-solving or creative processes. Wallas (1926), for example, hypothesized that creative thinking involved several stages: preparation (preliminary work is done on the problem); incubation (mental activity may be occurring outside of awareness, but there is no conscious attention or perceptible progress on the problem); illumination (the solution pops into awareness); and verification (the solution is tested for adequacy, generality, and stability against a variety of known facts). In one version or another, similar stages of intellectual activity have been postulated in a wide variety of models of thought (see Nisbett & Wilson, 1977).

For purposes of our discussion at this point, the most noteworthy feature of these models is their consensus that the answer appears suddenly in consciousness in the form of an insight, a new idea, a shift in figure/ground focus. There is even some fascinating evidence that people will better remember solutions that come to them after an initial period of incomprehension than those that are obvious to them from the start. This has been called the "aha" effect (Auble & Franks, 1978). It no doubt works in part on much the same basis as the experiments that we described earlier, on the role of active processing by subjects. But it highlights a feature of active processing we did not note in that earlier discussion: Such processing involves a period of challenge or frustration, a period in which what will later be the "obvious" answer has not yet appeared.

Zajonc (1980) has recently argued that affect may be independent of and exist prior to cognition, based on evidence that people are sometimes able to tell that they like or do not like something without being aware of the properties on which these feelings are based, or without even being able to recognize the stimuli that are flashed before them in a microsecond display. By our analysis, individuals are often in situations in which they are attempting to complete their understanding of some experience toward which they have feelings but whose exact nature and meaning is unclear to them (e.g., career events, a relationship, or a brief visual stimulus). The intensity of their affect will come, in part, from the effort they make to supply themselves with this understanding when in the midst of the challenge.

In summary, syntheses are relationships between theses and antitheses. They vary in quality; good ones are coherent and simple, allowing for few alternatives and effectively absorbing or assimilating incongruent elements. Syntheses have properties like answers or solutions: Once they are developed, it is hard to think of alternatives and to believe the solution was not known all along. Good syntheses are not obvious in advance but seem predictable or inevitable in retrospect, and memory is thus affected by syntheses. It is difficult to think of constituent parts of a synthesis in isolation, because this involves the masking of ambivalence and reinterpretation of negative elements as no longer so negative. Syntheses are stronger if people have active roles in generating them. Finally, the emergence of a synthesis involves stages like those in problem solving and creative processes, particularly a period of challenge or frustration.

ESCALATION AND CHANGE IN COMMITMENT: THE PROGRESSIVE IRREVERSIBILITY OF CHOICE

Justifiable Increments and Unforeseeable Consequences

Dialectical processes differ from purely circular or cyclical ones in that new syntheses are not merely repetitions of old ones but are different in systematic ways. The cumulative effect of these differences may be a state vastly different from the initial state, one perhaps not at all anticipated at the initial point.

Over and over again, people wind up demonstrably more involved in situations or more committed to lines of action than they had intended or foreseen. We have already discussed a number of examples of this in our chapter on rationality. The most dramatic of these, such as the Staw (1976) study of responses to unsuccessful investment decisions and the Brickman (1972) investigation of subjects' decisions about when to stop in situations in which outcomes are getting progressively better or worse (see also Shapira & Venezia, 1981), indicate a strong tendency by subjects to try to recoup their losses, and thus (under unfavorable circumstances) to wind up losing far more than they had initially considered risking. This seems to be especially true in conflict situations, and it illustrates the dynamics of escalation that occur in most commitments.

In the famous Deutsch and Kraus (1962) trucking experiment, the two subjects wind up blocking each other's routes and costing each other money simply because each responds to perceived provocation by the other. Likewise, in the previously discussed dollar auction game (extensively researched by Teger, 1979; and Brockner, Shaw, & Rubin, 1979), subjects continue investing money both in order not to lose what they have already put up and to keep their competitor from profiting from his or her own stubborn refusal to quit. As the behavior escalates, moreover, the rationalizations or justifications for the behavior also escalate and subtly shift in quality.

A poignant and pointed example of this process is provided by the physicist Freeman Dyson (1979) in his recollection of the explanations he gave himself for his progressively greater involvement in World War II—an eminently justifiable involvement on some levels, and yet one he found ultimately touched with great ambivalence:

> At the beginning of the war, I believed fiercely in the brotherhood of man, called myself a follower of Gandhi, and was morally opposed to all violence. After a year of war, I retreated, and said, 'Unfortunately, nonviolent resistance against Hitler is impracticable, but I am still morally opposed to bombing.' A couple of years later, I said, 'Unfortunately, it seems that bombing is necessary in order to win the war, and so I am willing to go to work for Bomber Command, but I am still morally opposed to bombing cities indiscriminately.' After I arrived at Bomber Command, I said, 'Unfortunately, it turns out that we are, after all, bombing cities indiscriminately, but this is morally justified, as it is helping to win the war.' A year later, I said, 'Unfortunately, it seems that our bombing is not really helping to win the war, but at least I am morally justified in working to save the lives of the bomber crews.' In the last spring of the war, I could no longer find any excuses [since even this last had been called into question]. (p. 56)

It should not be thought, however, that such progressive involvement is characteristic only of negative actions. Goldstein, Davis, and Herman (1975) conducted a study in which subjects were given a graded series of positive reinforcements and were asked to administer these to a learner at any level they chose. These subjects tended to give more and more intense degrees of reward over time. Subjects in another condition, who had available to them a graded series of punishments, tended to give more and more intense degrees of punishment over time. Indeed, the progressive escalation of involvement through gradual and sometimes imperceptible steps appears equally characteristic of the most highly valued and positive life involvements as it does of various forms of conflict and pathology. Both marriages and careers seem to follow this pattern. For example, Rusbult (1980) reports that students see themselves as more committed to a romantic relationship simply as a function of the more things (including time) that they have put into that relationship. Waller (1938) long ago reported that the decision to marry was less a dramatic episode than something that appeared to unfold gradually in the eyes of both the couple and various others in the couple's lives (see also Rubin, 1973). Masters and Johnson (1974) describe a case history that illuminates this point, in which a wife who is dissatisfied with her marriage but unwilling to leave it deliberately sought out a lover with whom she would have as little as possible in common, thus minimizing level of commitment. The lover did not even speak the same language. However, the tenderness they discovered despite these barriers became highly involving over time, and eventually the wife left her husband for her lover.

Careers often follow the same pattern of unexpected changes in the basis of involvement. For example, J. Q. Wilson (1962) describes the process by which newcomers to politics gradually find the initial reasons for their involvement in politics (i.e., idealism and ambition) replaced by a more professional set of concerns, in particular the concern with playing the game and winning. Ginzburg, Ginzburg, Axelrod, and Herma (1951), like Becker (1960), see career commitment as a consequence of having received job training as well as the cause of having sought that training in the first place. After training the individual must justify the time, effort, and money spent and therefore becomes acutely aware of the costs that would be incurred in switching careers.

With increasing concentration on one set of skills may come a progressive loss of interest (and ultimately aptitude) for work or recreation in other areas. Charles Darwin's confession of his loss of taste for poetry is one of the most famous examples of such a change. In many of these instances, to be sure, part of what may be happening is simply that a longstanding goal—a goal present right from the start— is simply coming closer, and the person's concern for this now highly salient goal is accordingly heightened (see Brown, 1951; Atkinson & Raynor, 1974). Distraction or disruption at this point will be more aversive and more strenuously resisted than distraction when the sequence of behavior had just been begun.

In other instances, it may make more sense to speak of new goals as having emerged and been attached to a sequence of behavior to which they were initially quite irrelevant. In his analysis of the case histories of four famous American abolitionists, for example, Tomkins (1965) makes it clear that none of them set out with the goal of becoming famous abolitionists in the first place. Though there were certain predisposing factors—all were deeply Christian, all had parents concerned with public service, and all were physically active and extroverted—the critical events that turned them into committed reformers were largely unanticipated. These lay in the vigorous and hostile public reactions to their early statements and in their manner of response to this opposition. Society's need for an abolitionist crusade, and their personal needs to participate in it, were things discovered rather than known from the start. In another era, on another side of a very complicated fence, Arthur Jensen's career as a vigorous defender of the validity of IQ tests and the heritability (on both individual and group levels) of IQ differences may be understood in part as his own response to what he has confessed was the quite unexpected fury that his 1969 *Harvard Educational Review* article aroused.

Deviant careers are launched and consolidated into personal identities in much the same incremental and incidental way as conventional careers. However, the point at which a deviant identity is publicly recognized may involve a more dramatic change than the same point in the history of a conventional career. Few people decide to become criminals as their first choice of career. Rather, as Matza (1964) indicates, most criminals start with minor offenses, get into trouble with the police, continue in this vein for a while, and then find it increasingly difficult to convince the straight world that they have abandoned their deviant behavior pattern even when they have (at least temporarily) actually done so (cf. Ray, 1961, for a parallel discussion of drug addicts). Women working in massage parlors typically begin without any commitment to sexual manipulation of customers (and are not necessarily required to do so by owners), but they gradually accede to more and more customer wishes because doing so is profitable and because there seems little difference between the next step and the step just taken (Velarde, 1976).

In the history of deviant careers, there may occur a special process that allows individuals to take a major irreversible step with little awareness of the consequences. Lofland (1969) has called this process "encapsulation." All attention is focused on the actor's immediate troubles and how to get out of them. This foreshortening of the time span over which consequences are considered makes actors discount the possibility of future detection and punishment even more sharply than usual. The deviant act may be, privately, relabeled and reinterpreted. This is most elegantly illustrated in Cressey's (1953) study of embezzlers. Cressey found that this crime would not occur unless the person went through a period of rationalizing the act without calling it embezzlement so that it seemed more like taking a loan or some other justifiable form of using someone else's money. Only in retrospect do they realize that they must have been kidding themselves by thinking that they would or could repay the money they took.

The major crimes and atrocities of this century can also be understood as a process wherein each precipitating event was just a small step to the perpetrators— and sometimes to the victims—when it was committed. When people first heard about Watergate, for example, an initial reaction was often to say, "How could they have been so stupid? Why would Nixon's people want to take the risks involved in breaking into the Democratic National Headquarters, and how could they have thought they could get away with it?" The answer, as subsequent revelations made clear, was that the Nixon administration had been running similar illegal covert operations in a variety of contexts for years and getting away with them quite nicely. Watergate was just the next step. One of the reasons the Nixon people may have been so puzzled by the public outrage over Watergate (assuming that their reaction was not entirely a matter of self-presentation) is that they knew it was no big deal compared to other things that had been happening all along and to which they (though not the public) had adapted.

The mass suicide at Jonestown is even more baffling to observers. How could people be led to poison their children and then themselves? Once again, it is critical to realize that the suicide plan was not something that was sprung on cult members all at once at the last moment. Accounts of events at the People's Temple (see Osherow, 1981, for a social psychological analysis) make it clear that the suicide ritual was something that had been repeatedly rehearsed, at first jokingly or at least light-heartedly, and gradually with increasing seriousness, elaboration, justification, and reality. Moreover, the willingness of Jones's followers to comply with this desperate measure had been previously prepared by a long series of steps in which they had been induced to comply in lesser forms of cruel or degrading acts—witnessing the beating of a child, for example, or participating in some form of sexual humiliation. Still earlier, Temple members had been induced to cut their ties with outsiders, invest their worldly goods in the Temple, participate in more ordinary forms of church services, and take many of the steps that build loyalty to a communal group (Kanter, 1972).

A very similar account can be given of the events leading up to the massacre at My Lai (Hersh, 1970). The soldiers of Charlie Company, like those of many similar units in Vietnam, were often exhausted, upset, angered by the deaths of their buddies, and frustrated or enraged by an enemy they could not seem to find. The first ventings of these feelings might be simple vandalism. Then would follow the beating and terrorizing of suspected Vietcong. Some members of Charlie Company later assaulted innocent women and old people. In the absence of social control by equally frustrated platoon leaders, other soldiers who had been initially reluctant to engage in these minor acts of violence eventually came under pressure from peers to participate as a means of establishing their own loyalty to the company. Each of these additional acts of coercion and violence was accompanied by additional reasons and justifications, which cumulatively led to a perceived justification for massacre just as the previous acts led to the massacre itself.

Similarly, Fein (1979) makes clear that the concentration camps in Nazi Europe did not spring into existence full-blown with their mission and machinery of death in place. They were the product of a long and complex process in which minorities, and in particular Jews, were gradually separated from the mass of citizens, first by symbolic means (e.g., the donning of yellow stars), then by economic and political restrictions (e.g., limitations of where they would work), and finally physically. Only then were the deportations ready to begin. In a number of instances in which the process of isolating and derogating Jews was stopped before this point (Denmark being the most famous example), the local population was unwilling to participate in deportations and murders. On the other hand, once the first of the irrevocable murders had begun, no goodwill in the world could have reversed the action or the pressure to understand and justify it.

There may be something special about the first episode of violence. However mild and limited it is, it marks the crossing of a line that all parties had hitherto been able to count on as a limit on the extent to which their conflict would escalate. Schelling (1960) has defended the ban on the use of tactical nuclear weapons in just these terms. The weapons themselves may be no more destructive than conventional weapons, and they may well shorten the particular battle or give significant advantage to one side. However, a clear rule well understood by both sides has much merit: no nuclear weapons. Once this rule is breached, there is no subsequent barrier to the incremental use of more numerous and more powerful nuclear warheads.

In the memory of participants in Synanon, one event stands out as a turning point in the decline of that organization from a harsh but high-minded community dedicated to rescuing drug addicts to a bizarre cult in which members perpetrated violence on each other and on outsiders. The group had always featured a strict prohibition against physical attack, even though brutal verbal attacks on what were regarded as self-serving and self-defeating lies by fellow addicts were common and marathon group encounter sessions were used to dismantle these life stories. But Charles Dederich, Synanon's leader, violated this one day simply by getting up and pouring a glass of root beer over the head of a woman whose carrying on he had found to be too much. The group was shocked by this act, yet years later they were no longer shocked by beatings of children and attempts to murder outsiders who threatened to reveal what had occurred in the group. The literature on spouse abuse attaches a similar significance to the first act of violence. It is not nearly as easy to have confidence that the event will not recur (perhaps even in worse form) as it was to believe that it wouldn't happen in the first place.

One of the things that has always puzzled students of family and cult violence as well as historians of the Holocaust and similar tragedies is why victims so often remain in vulnerable situations when they would seem to have ample opportunity to leave. Once again, the key is to understand how the psychological reality of this opportunity to leave can be progressively blocked by an escalating process of commitment to stay and by justification of this decision. In the early stages, victims are often encouraged to remain in the situation by deliberate deception on the part of others. When cult members are recruited, for example, there is often no indication in the early stages of what they will be asked to do later on, such as give up all outside contacts, endure privation and hardship, or demonstrate unquestioning obedience. The initial contact between women and rapists is often quite ordinary and gives no cause for alarm. Jews in World War II were encouraged, right to the end, to believe that they were being shipped to resettlement camps in the East rather than extermination centers.

In each case, there comes a point before anything terrible has actually happened when the victims become apprehensive about the true purposes and potentials of the situation. Psychologically, it may be very difficult to break away at this point. Conceivably, they may be motivated to believe that the worst will not happen. In addition, norms of polite and civilized behavior, reluctance to create the kind of disturbance that would often be involved in escaping, and obligations to others who appear kind and helpful in many ways may all be operating to inhibit action. By not taking any step, despite inner and outer signs that one should do so, however, individuals remain at risk and slowly are transformed into victims—compliant victims, if not willing ones.

People acquire what they later feel are bad habits, like drinking, smoking, or eating too much, by the same graded series of steps. In interviews with a dozen smokers, Ken Abosch and Chris Millen (working with Brickman) found that 11 of them had started smoking for extrinsic reasons, such as to gain acceptance, to imitate parents, to feel grown up, to have something to do in social situations, or simply to experiment with something new. Virtually all respondents reported that these reasons became unimportant as time progressed. When asked what smoking currently meant to them, smokers tended to reply that they simply enjoyed either the taste, the relaxing effects, or the feeling of smoke running down their throat. By that time the people were committed to the behavior itself because of the physiological effects or its role in their life-styles.

As Lemert (1962) and Coates and Wortman (1980) make clear, similar cycles are involved in locking people into paranoid or depressive identities. Once a person has fallen into such an identity—for whatever personal or historical reasons—he or she makes desperate attempts to gain reassurance from others, to feel that others are not avoiding, rejecting, or being angry or hostile toward him or her. However, these attempts are so unpleasant to others that they begin to avoid and reject the person (at least covertly) in a way that confirms the person's worst fears. This outcome leaves everyone more convinced than ever that the person is in a state from which he or she cannot recover.

People get involved in movies, books, games, and just about everything else in the same way. In an undergraduate honors thesis done under the supervision of Brickman, Eric Teplitz had subjects watch Hollywood feature films in five-minute segments and rate after each segment how they felt about the movie and then choose either to go on with that movie or to sample the next segment from another movie. Over time, subjects were less likely to switch movies and more likely to indicate their commitment to (and interest in) the movie they were watching. Introducing still another alternative movie that they could watch if they chose had no effect on subjects' subsequent tendency to switch away from their current favorite, although they were more likely to try the new alternative when it was introduced early rather than late in the process.

Brickman (1978), in an analysis of what makes games and other situations real for the parties involved, emphasizes the point that all roles (i.e., in a game, in an experiment, or in the outside world) are unreal at first and become progressively more real through people's own behavior and other people's responses. They do not start out feeling real. For example, it is only over time that people come to feel that they are really members of a profession or are really married. The manner in which they do so is by engaging in behavior that has consequences ("external correspondence" of behavior) and that elicits feelings ("internal correspondence" of behavior). As another example, the famous Zimbardo prison simulation (Zimbardo, Haney, & Banks, 1973) may have been quite different in many ways from an actual prison, but the processes by which participants came to treat that prison experience as real—including, among others, being punished by other participants for not taking it seriously enough—may be quite similar to those by which participants in other prisons come to treat their experiences as real.

There is considerable overlap between the concept of phenomenological reality (Brickman, 1978) and our definition of commitment. For the purpose of establishing links with other literatures, commitment is a more useful way to describe the phenomena of interest than phenomenological reality. However, based on the earlier analysis, we propose that commitment helps to establish the very sense that a situation is real for a person, and the absence of commitments establishes a sense of unreality.

The cumulative nature of behavioral involvements may be summarized as follows: Particular acts lead to other acts in a manner that extends and intensifies the motivation inherent in the earlier acts. Moreover, there is a sense in which each act in the sequence is incomplete in itself, or is complete only momentarily, but soon comes to serve as a kind of lead-in to the acts that follow. These acts tend to finish, justify, and place into perspective the earlier acts and also to extend them in a way that motivates still further developments. We are engaged by our own behavior in somewhat the same way we can be engaged by soap operas or comic strips. In isolation, each episode of a soap opera, a comic strip, or a baseball season is meaningless. After a while, however, each episode serves to answer a question left over from a previous episode and, soon, to pose a question that will need answering in the next episode. The fact that there is a delay between episodes (as there is between most episodes of the same behavior) may raise the tension level involved in this process and enhance its overall effectiveness (Auble, Franks, & Soraci, 1979).

Behavior, in this sense, is a chain in which the last link is always open, and the next link is often an imperceptible addition. It may be quite rare, in life, that there is a Rubicon to cross. More often, as C. S. Lewis has noted, there are no milestones on the road to hell, or perhaps on any road, until we look back on it and give it structure with the advantage of hindsight. Though each step seems small and builds only slightly on the previous one, when one looks back over many changes, the shifts may seem dramatic. The fact that the change from each episode to the next is in itself minor, together with the fact that each episode tends to call forth the next, gives behavioral sequences the property of momentum we have endeavored to display in this chapter. Brockner, Shaw, and Rubin (1979) have shown that subjects are more likely to stop a process of escalation if they are required to make a series of explicit decisions to continue than if they are not. Most sequences in life resemble the latter condition, in which subsequent events occur readily unless the person makes an active effort to stop them or to withdraw from the situation. There is a saying that single steps begin the longest journeys. The usual purpose of this aphorism is to remind people that they must start somewhere, in however modest a way, if they wish to accomplish anything great. For our analysis, however, the saying has another point. It is that within that single, first, small step may begin a journey of unknown length and consequence.

Not surprisingly, many of the most dramatic and influential experiments in social psychology have focused on this kind of commitment process, especially in the area of obedience or compliance. In all cases, subjects wind up agreeing to do something that observers find astonishing, something far more costly than most people would be expected to do. In all cases, the dynamics of the experiment involve getting subjects to agree to a variety of lesser things without knowing what will later be requested or what the implications of their earlier actions for this later request will be. Thus in the Milgram (1965) study of obedience, subjects accept money from the experimenter, accept their role assignment (as teacher) in the experiment, and administer a substantial number of initially mild but increasingly painful shocks to another person before they are confronted with the fact that they are inflicting pain and suffering on this other person. By the time a subject has administered a shock of, say, 170 volts to the confederate, and it has become clear that the confederate does not want to go on, the subject is no longer in the same psychological position as someone reading about the study, who has incurred none of the obligations and has not rationalized the behavior.

In the Freedman and Fraser (1966) research on the "foot-in-the-door" effect, subjects were more likely to agree to display a large, ugly sign on their lawn if they had earlier been induced to agree to a lesser request (to display a smaller window sticker). DeJong (1979), reviewing the many subsequent studies on the foot-in-the-door technique, concludes that the procedure is reliable and that it is most likely to work under conditions that maximize the chances that subjects will see themselves as having made a commitment when they agreed to the initial request. The initial request must be large enough to cause people to think about the implications of their own behavior (Seligman, Bush, & Kirsch, 1976) but not so large as to cause them to refuse to do it (Miller & Suls, 1977). And people must feel that their having agreed to the initial request was the result of their own free choice, not the result of coercion or pressure (Uranowitz, 1975; Zuckerman, Lazzaro, & Waldgeir, 1979).

Two other recent studies have established that there can be considerable advantage in simply masking the actual cost of carrying out an action from subjects until after they have agreed to carry it out. Cialdini, Cacioppo, Bassett, and Miller (1978) have called this the "low-ball procedure," named after a technique in which car salesman first get customers to agree to buy a car at a good price and then later report that they cannot actually get it for them at that price but can at a somewhat higher figure. Cialdini et al. (1978) found that subjects were more likely to agree to take part in an inconvenient experiment (one that required them to show up at 7:00 A.M.) if they were informed of the starting time after they had initially said that they would participate than if they were informed before making the decision to participate.

Transformations in Motivation and Affect

The idea that motivation is transformed over time is embodied in Gordon Allport's (1937b, 1961) principle of functional autonomy. Allport wished to call attention to the fact that the bases on which a behavior is started may be quite different than the bases on which it is continued, and to make clear that we should not mistake understanding of one for understanding of the other. Put simply, the principle of functional autonomy states that any activity or behavior may become an end or a goal in itself, whatever its original purpose may have been. (Cases in which behavior is originally pursued for one instrumental reason and later pursued for another instrumental reason—as when one hunts first in order to eat, or to express one's inborn aggressive instincts, but never just for the sake of hunting itself—would not be considered examples of functional autonomy, Hall & Lindzey, 1957, but could represent some of the processes that work to build commitment in our sense.) Allport went on to distinguish two kinds of functional autonomy: perseverative behavior (such as addictions, routines, or simple motor patterns like scratching that might persist beyond the point of receiving any reinforcement) and propriate behavior (new patterns of interests, values, and sentiments, which might derive from the exercise of an ability that was initially acquired for strictly instrumental purposes). Allport's formulation remained fuzzy in the eyes of his critics because he would not call upon an array of experimental (or naturalistic) observations to demonstrate both the generality and the limiting conditions of the processes that lead to functional autonomy. Although he alluded to a number of processes he felt were relevant to an understanding of how functional autonomy developed, he could not, in the end, specify either the cognitive and behavioral mechanisms or the adaptive advantages that would have made the idea of functional autonomy fully credible. Indeed, Allport ultimately preferred what he calls nonmechanical explanations of functional autonomy, which, taken together, "amount to saying that functional autonomy comes about because it is the essence or core of the purposive nature of man" (Allport, 1961, p. 250). There may be some truth to this, but it is clearly unsatisfying as a scientific explanation without a very clear link to a specification of instances, limiting conditions, mechanisms, and function.

On one level, our survey of commitment may help to supply these missing elements. Unlike Allport, however, we do not view the kind of functional autonomy supplied by commitment as necessarily good, individualizing, conscious, adult, or mature, as the previous examples of this chapter should make clear. The unduly rosy or optimistic qualities attached to the development of functional autonomy is another reason that Allport's formulation has been unacceptable to many psychologists and limited in the amount of research it has generated.

Nor does the idea that people become more involved in situations over time, that behavior over time becomes more functionally autonomous or intrinsically motivated, mean that individuals necessarily become more satisfied or happy over time. First of all, much of happiness, or at least pleasure, is located in extrinsic reinforcements whose subjective value declines as they become more familiar over time (Brickman & Campbell, 1971) or as opponent processes are set more strongly in motion over time (Solomon & Corbit, 1974). A level of praise or an amount of money that is quite gratifying the first time it is received may eventually seem routine and may come to be expected or taken for granted. It is also possible that people may become satiated with behavior that is intrinsically motivated, at least under circumstances in which this behavior is not done with any strong sense of purpose (Klinger, 1977, pp. 126–127).

The archetypical or paradigmatic sequence is one in which idealized, romanticized, and optimistic initial expectations are shattered and reshaped by contact with reality. As usual, we can document this proposition with data from the two major domains of lifelong commitment, careers and marriage. Lawler, Kuleck, Rhode, and Sorensen (1975) studied a sample of 431 accounting students while they chose jobs and during their first year on the job. Although after the job choice the chosen firms increased in attractiveness and the rejected firms decreased in attractiveness, after a year of employment subjects rated all firms lower in attractiveness than they had before they applied for jobs. Vroom and Deci (1971) also found that young managers rated both the attractiveness of the organization they worked for and its perceived instrumentality for goal attainment markedly lower after a year on the job, and they maintained these low ratings for at least the next two and one-half years. Bray, Campbell, and Grant (1974) found that the expectations of a group of newly hired managers at AT&T dropped every year for the first five years, though there was an upturn in the sixth and seventh years for the better performers.

Hall and Schneider (1973) describe new priests, following the joy of ordi- nation, as experiencing reality shock on four different levels: They move from being rather idealistic to being more realistic about the priesthood; they become aware of the interpersonal or political aspects of the priesthood; they come to appreciate how difficult it will be to make changes they are enthusiastic about because of the rigidity of church rules and procedures or because of the resistance of their pastor; and they experience dismay at the low level of challenge and the underutilization of their competencies in their first job. Wanous (1976) found similar declines in expectations for intrinsic organizational rewards among both MBA students and telephone operators. The decline of idealistic and humanitarian motives among medical students over the course of their years in school has been repeatedly noted (e.g., Becker, Geer, Hughes, & Strauss, 1964; Coombs & Boyle, 1971), although there is controversy over whether some of this idealism returns after graduation. It may be affected by the physician's specialty (Gray, Newman, & Reinhardt, 1966).

In a study of 120 Loyola University undergraduates carried out by Philip Brickman, Robert Chave, and Joshua Fox, year in school was found to be negatively correlated with the belief that one's major is valuable as a stepping stone toward a career or as something that pleases one's family (both measures of extrinsic value), indicating that the choice of major had been rationally made. However, year in school was positively associated with commitment to and interest in the major (intrinsic value).

Many of these issues are dramatically illustrated in the movie *Serpico*. The movie tells the true story of a rookie policeman in New York City, Frank Serpico, who decides not to go along with the widespread corruption he finds in the depart- ment. The explicitness of the corruption and threat of violence make this story different and more extreme than the other career examples we have been reviewing, but it involves the general theme of a young person who discovers that current practices in a profession are quite different from what he or she expected. This gap between the beliefs and values that draws one into a profession in the first place and the reality encountered may be universal.

A variety of studies illustrate within our romantic relationships effects similar to those described in careers. Kerckoff and David (1962), for example, found that more negative adjectives were used to describe partners in long-term than short-term relationships. Burgess and Walter (1968) found that couples, and especially male partners, tend to rate each other less physically attractive after marriage than before. Hobart (1958) found evidence of postmarital disillusionment, especially in the areas of personal freedom, marital roles, children and in-laws, neat- ness, money, and attitudes toward divorce. Much survey research indicates that marriages seem to become gradually less satisfying, on the whole, over at least their first 20 years (Blood & Wolfe, 1960; Campbell, Converse, & Rodgers, 1976; Hicks & Platt, 1970). According to Pineo (1961), the drop is not only large but most significant in such vital areas as sharing of interests and activities, frequency of intercourse, consensus, and sense of permanence and love. Many of these changes no doubt represent the effects of the different issues that couples face over the course of their lives and not simply the process by which initially attractive incentives gradually lose their power. Nonetheless, the data certainly make the point that increased commitment does not necessarily imply increased satisfaction and happiness. Increased happiness, as we shall see in our chapter on mental health, depends on the form the commitment takes. It should also be mentioned that changes of the sort we have been describing are not limited to marital relationships. Pollis (1969), for example, compared respondents who differed in their degree of emotional involvement with their dating partners. Subjects, again especially males, were less likely to idealize their partners the more involved with their partners they were.

The initial motivation for action must almost by definition be extrinsic: If the action itself has not yet been experienced, motivation can hardly spring from the action. As Blau (1964) writes, "Although men may want to associate together exclusively for the sake of sociable fellowship and have no interest in deriving any extrinsic advantage from their social relations, they must prove themselves attractive to each other by demonstrating qualities that make them preferable to other possible associates, qualities that must be comparable and that consequently are, in a relative sense, extrinsic" (p. 38). These attractive qualities may in the end be neither necessary nor sufficient for the relationship to endure, but they are necessary for it to begin. The problem comes when people either believe that this initial idealized motivation or the incentive value of these initial attractions can endure, or they mistake it for commitment. Thus one can be led into decisions that cannot be sustained and might otherwise not be made.

Interestingly enough, experts in human change are suspicious of what seems to them to be premature commitment or enthusiasm. Linda Brownell and Naomi Tabachnik, working with Philip Brickman, conducted interviews with four rabbis in the Chicago area involved in either sponsoring or teaching converts to Judaism. By virtue of their role, these rabbis were especially sensitive to the question of whether the motivation brought to the conversion would lead to a successful and enriching commitment to Judaism or an unsuccessful and superficial one. Most potential converts are female, and most are doing it for the sake of either a prospective or current marital partner. Although the rabbis were uniformly suspicious of potential converts who seemed to be interested for strictly opportunistic reasons— to "catch" the Jewish spouse or pacify his family—they were also suspicious of converts whose initial reasons seemed too abstract, intellectual, or even religious. As one said:

> If an individual comes to me on a very abstract, objective, intellectual plane, that person may or may not follow through. The conscious, intellectual,

rational approach is not a guarantee of a real commitment. Those who come for many reasons which in the traditional sense may be the wrong reasons, those may turn out to be the most efficient motivational factors.

The best predictors of conversion were simply such things as repeatedly attending services, joining a congregation, following Jewish customs, and so forth. Some of the rabbis were willing to vary what they required of converts, provided that the approach of the converts is active, "positive, and honest." In a rather different yet also similar context, Brehm and Cohen (1962) found that the Chinese Communist captors of American soldiers in Korea were unwilling to trust early claims of sympathy for the Communist cause until the prisoners had gone through a series of visible steps—participating in group discussions, confessing errors, preparing and signing documents—that made their own conversion something concrete and tangible in both their own eyes and those of their fellows.

One of two kinds of things can happen when early extrinsic motivation fades: People can find alternative intrinsic motivations, or they can increasingly attend to past or anticipated future extrinsic reward. If they follow the second path, then it is these future extrinsic rewards that they are committed to, not the actual activity. Regarding the former path, Hall and Schneider (1973) find that after an initial period of declining self-image and satisfaction, priests undergo a marked increase in both of these respects. In general, beyond the period of reality shock discussed above, job satisfaction is correlated with seniority (Salancik, 1974). However, this finding is hard to interpret because those who are most dissatisfied are most likely to leave, and in addition, seniority is generally associated with at least some increase in tangible and intangible benefits. Nonetheless, evidence on intrinsic interest over the life of a career is relevant.

Shepard and Herrick (1972), for example, asked workers how often they left work with the good feeling that they had done something particularly well. The percentage saying "very often" to this item rose sharply with age. In jobs that workers described as having little or no variety, older workers were much less likely than younger ones to say that this lack of variety bothered them. Similarly, salary was less related to satisfaction for university faculty who had tenure or who had been with the organization for a long time than it was for younger faculty (Pfeffer & Lawler, 1980). Thus in at least some instances, the absence of conventional extrinsic rewards is made up for by the addition of an array of unique, private satisfactions.

In romantic relationships, there is some evidence that the basis of love may change over time in a way that provides new satisfactions as some of the earlier incentives fade. Driscoll, Davis, and Lipetz (1972) showed that love was more highly correlated with trust and acceptance for married couples than for unmarried ones—marking what they suggested was a shift from "romantic love" to "conjugal love." Parental interference in the couple's relationship was positively correlated with romantic love—driven, in part, by the couple's enhanced sense of commitment if they stayed together despite the parental opposition—but not for married couples.

For the latter, the corrosive effect of continued parental interference on trust—now a more important component of love—was likely to cancel any beneficial effects it might have had on the couple's earlier sense of intrinsic motivation to their relationship. In interviews with freshmen and seniors from five Northwestern University sororities, Kathy Krasovec and Melinda Stolley, working with Philip Brickman, found that freshmen regularly mentioned the prestige of the sorority and the opportunities it afforded for new experiences, while seniors stressed only their interpersonal ties and feelings for other members.

When actors do experience this kind of increase in intrinsic motivation, it is often imperceptible to observers. A continual theme running through the eloquent testimony of individuals in many walks of life in Studs Terkel's (1975) book *Working*, is that their jobs were less extrinsically rewarding (paid less well, brought less prestige) and more intrinsically rewarding (demanded more skill, brought more satisfactions from achievement) than outsiders realized. In a study carried out by Jolene Galegher and Philip Brickman, the nature of students' career choices was rated both by the students themselves and by people the students had nominated as knowing them well. Actors were more likely than observers to say that they chose their prospective career because it seemed interesting and challenging and because it offered an opportunity to contribute to society. They were also more likely to say that they made their plans to please themselves rather than to please others and that their plans had a special meaning for them. They were less likely than observers to say "why not—nothing better to do" described their reasons for choosing their career plans. Similar findings occur in other areas, including instances in which the observers are professional helpers. Wikler, Wasow, and Hatfield (1981) found that parents of retarded children were more likely than social workers working with such parents to say that the parents' experiences with their retarded child have made them stronger rather than torn them apart. Parents were also likely to say that social workers could best have helped them by encouraging them to be strong, whereas social workers were likely to say that parents could best be helped by giving them permission to be weak.

Alternatively, people come to experience their involvement as increasingly coercive and to attend more and more to fading past extrinsic rewards or hoped-for future ones. They see themselves as no longer having a choice; they psychologically undo or regret their initial choice and would quit the line of activity if they could or felt they could. This is not at all uncommon. In response to a request on the topic, Ann Landers received a vast outpouring of mail from parents, the majority of whom indicated that they were sorry that they had had children. Similar anecdotes have been reported about couples who have been married many years; many express doubts as to whether they have married the right person. The studies we reviewed earlier showed that glamorized initial expectations and the shock of actually entering a career or a relationship can lead to an involvement that is ultimately experienced as coercive if there are not changes in either the nature of the activity or the person's orientation to the activity.

The word *burnout* has recently become popular (e.g., Maslach, 1976; Cherniss,

1978) to describe the state of helping professionals who lose their ability to care about and feel for client populations they once cared for tremendously. These professionals once felt they could help, but, eventually, they were overwhelmed by a system that seemed immune to every effort to make it more humane or more effective. If people under these or similar circumstances are unable to find instrinsic satisfactions in their activity to replace their fond initial hopes or the initially attractive extrinsic incentives, it follows that they should focus more and more on whatever fragments of extrinsic reward are available. It is then these extrinsic rewards, in fact, whose value may be enhanced.

We argue, as a key proposition, that one must become increasingly committed to *something* as a line of action is pursued. But this something does not necessarily have to be the value of that action per se. If healing the sick seems insufficient to justify the grueling hours and bureaucratic controls that characterize life as an intern and yet the person persists in his or her medical career, then perhaps the prospect of financial reward will take on added value. If love disappears from a marriage yet the couple stays married for the sake of their children or their social status, then it is the couple's commitment to these factors that will be progressively enhanced. In an analysis of survey data from a wide variety of occupations, Gruenberg (1980) found exactly this: Extrinsic rewards became more important in situations where workers felt that intrinsic rewards were unavailable. A great deal depends on whether people retain the sense that they have chosen and are choosing the line of activity they are pursuing. If they do, as Pfeffer and Lawler (1980) found for university faculty, then extrinsic rewards like pay play a relatively small role in determining their satisfaction. If they do not, high pay is an important determinant of whether they are motivated and productive workers (Folger, Rosenfield, & Hays, 1978).

We have now only the vaguest understanding of what individual and situational differences cause people to wind up in one of these two states rather than the other, but there are certainly individual differences. Teplitz, in the honors thesis referred to earlier, found that subjects who described themselves as inclined to make commitments were more likely to become interested in the movies they watched. But for now, all we aim to establish is that behavior must eventually emerge into one of two progressively more distinct absorbing states. In looking back, people say either that they really wanted to or that they really had no choice. Each of these represents a form of commitment. The former represents a commitment to the activity; the latter, a commitment to something other than the activity. Alternatively, the former represents a commitment to the activity as an end itself; the latter, a commitment to the activity as a means to some other end. Each is also a form of illusion, since there is usually both some element of choice and some element of coercion or external force in all behavior. What happens is that one of these elements comes to dominate the psychological field in which the activity is experienced, and the activity is thus felt as either entirely free or entirely coerced. Children may sometimes need reminders to do their chores and sometimes not need reminders, but as time goes by, they are progressively more likely (by this analysis) to settle into one of two relatively stable states: a state in which they almost never need reminders, having developed their own sense of commitment to the activities, or a state in which they almost always need reminders, having developed a sense that the activity is alien to them and one they continue solely as the result of external pressure. If disillusioned with the activity early on, people can easily disengage (this will be described in the next section), but once commitment processes have been fully engaged, there is eventually no region of noncommitment left. The person is either committed to doing the activity or committed to not doing it; he or she can no longer have neutral feelings about the activity.

The recently developed language of catastrophe theory, briefly described in the chapter on value, provides a powerful representation of this process. Two good descriptions of the application of catastrophe theory to social psychological problems are provided by Flay (1978) and Tesser (1978), and the present account draws on both of them. In its simplest form, catastrophe theory represents the strength of a behavior as a function of two variables with different properties. One variable is called the normal factor; as in our previous discussion, the normal factor is the instigating force that motivates the individual to pursue the behavior. The second factor in catastrophe theory is called the splitting factor. In our analysis, this is the inhibiting force or the force that makes the individual prefer not to do the behavior. The critical postulate of catastrophe theory under these circumstances is that when the inhibiting force is strong, no moderate or intermediate form of behavior is available. The individual will enact either approach behavior or avoidance behavior in extreme form and may shift suddenly from one to the other as the balance of forces changes even slightly in a critical region. This model describes our discussion to this point if we just make the assumption that inhibiting forces (the splitting factor) can, for all practical purposes, be represented as increasing (perhaps in a negatively accelerated manner) as a function of time. As time goes by, any line of action or any relationship is encumbered with additional costs in the form of investments, pressures from public opinion, residues of past conflicts, and so forth. These do not mean that the activity or the relationship must be discontinued, but they do mean that neutrality toward that activity or relationship becomes increasingly impossible. If the strength of positive forces is sufficient, the individual will experience a high degree of commitment to that relationship. If the strength of positive forces is not sufficient, the individual will experience a high degree of alienation from that relationship. In either case, according to a catastrophe theory representation, there will be a strong inertial tendency that makes people's commitment change more slowly than the underlying positive forces. But if the change does come, it will be rapid and drastic beyond their expectations.

In summary, commitments are formed by small and unique, nonrepetitive increments, the consequences of which are often unforeseeable and unintended. Examples drawn from conflict situations, from positively reinforcing contingencies such as marriage, and from careers are illustrative. Escalation in commitment occurs in two ways: through heightened concentration as goal attainment is closer and through the emergence of new goals. Many psychological, social, political, and historical phenomena (e.g., deviant careers, Watergate, Jonestown, violence and victimization, addiction, depression, and simple leisure activities) can be understood in light of an analysis of incremental change and commitment development.

The gradual development of a commitment implies transformations in the bases of both motivation and affect. Increased commitment, however, does not imply greater satisfaction or happiness; the archetypal sequence is early idealism and later reshaping in light of reality. Careers and romantic relationships are particular examples of this. As developed further below, we believe that the initial motivation for action is generally extrinsic but that it is soon replaced with imperceptible increases in intrinsic involvement, an involvement that steadily grows with time.

STAGES IN THE DEVELOPMENT OF COMMITMENT

The Importance of Negative Elements

It is clear from the foregoing that we believe that early extrinsic motivation is bound to fade, and when it does a new motivation must be found if commitment is to fully develop. In this section, we will argue that the development of a commitment follows a characteristic pattern in which an early, unreflective positive motivation is challenged and eventually replaced by a different form of motivation that integrates the negative elements of the challenge. In theory, the same end result could be achieved through the integration of initially negative elements with positive elements that followed. We will discuss an important special case in which this might occur. In general, however, if the initial elements of the stimulus situation are negative, the individual will not embark on action in the first place. One reason that bystander intervention in emergencies may be surprisingly rare (as Latane & Darley's 1969 famous research has shown) is that such situations immediately confront people with highly salient negative elements—risk of danger, the prospect of time-consuming delay, the possibility of being embarrassed. Extrinsic incentives for helping in such circumstances are much less salient. Furthermore, unless the individual has a history of action to generate intrinsic motivation or commitment, there are also no strong internal forces to induce action. On the other hand, people will make remarkable sacrifices to help others if the need for help occurs later in the sequence of events, after earlier interactions have established the motivation on which this help can draw.

If no negative elements or contradictions to the decision become salient, we do not think of it as a commitment. A simple example to illustrate this point is the phenomenon called functional fixedness (see e.g., Adamson, 1952). Subjects learn a moderately complicated rule necessary to solve a series of logical or perceptual problems. Sometimes this rule is simply the residue of past experience with an object (e.g., a paper clip or a hammer). Then the subject is confronted with a problem that can be solved by a much simpler rule, or a problem that can be solved only if the familiar object is used in a novel way. Typically, without some further cues from the experimenter, subjects will continue using the complicated rule or continue trying to use the familiar object only in the familiar way. Functional fixedness is generally discounted as an example of commitment because subjects are usually not aware of, and may never have been aware of, alternatives to their present habits in these problem-solving situations. Nor are they aware of the fact that these habits now involve substantial costs in their current situation. In that sense, we could predict that unlike true commitments, these habits would be quite vulnerable to any event that either made salient their costs or made available attractive alternatives, and this is indeed the case. Even subtle cues from the experimenter, which subjects do not remember receiving, may be sufficient to cause them to change their approach to the problem completely. The situation thus also resembles McGuire's (1966) findings on naive bases of belief and vulnerability to persuasion. If subjects have believed certain things simply as truisms (for example, brushing one's teeth is good), without ever having examined their premises or considered possible pro and con evidence, they are surprisingly vulnerable to persuasion that their belief has been mistaken. They are much less vulnerable to such persuasion when they have previously been led to consider (in weakened form) such counterarguments.

It is possible—and, we suggest, not at all unusual—to have both a favorable first impression of someone or something and a favorable second (or enduring) impression and still pass through an interval in which the positivity of the first impression has faded and the positivity of the second impression has not yet emerged. This has, in other analyses (e.g., Festinger, 1964), been called the period of regret, during which elements contradictory or antithetical to the first impression have accumulated and not yet been integrated into a synthesis. Several previous authors have made the point that the development of commitment in interpersonal relationships appears to have these three general phases. Thibaut and Kelley (1959) call the critical intermediate period one of commitment testing, and they suggest that during this time stress on the relationship is sometimes introduced deliberately by one partner in order to test the extent to which the other person is genuinely serious about the relationship and willing to make sacrifices for it. It should be noted, by the way, that one can test the seriousness of one's own commitment as well as the seriousness of the other person's commitment in this manner.

Merton (1949) has suggested that in the context of science, it is the element of discipline that carries the researcher over the barren periods after which the early excitement has faded and no answers are in sight. C. S. Lewis (1964) has suggested that such a stage in any worthwhile enterprise is actually part of God's plan for ensuring that people take responsibility for their actions rather than simply being led to do good by divine power. According to one of Lewis's devils, this period of disappointment or anticlimax that follows each endeavor (e.g., joining a church) is a rich opportunity to work evil:

> The Enemy [God] allows this disappointment to occur on the threshold of every human endeavour. It occurs when the boy who has been enchanted in the nursery by *Stories from the Odyssey* buckles down to really learning

Greek. It occurs when lovers have got married and begin the real task of learn-ing to live together. In every department of life it marks the transition from dreaming aspiration to laborious doing. The Enemy takes this risk because He has a curious fantasy of making all these disgusting little human vermin into what He calls His "free" lovers and servants—"sons" is the word He uses, with His inveterate love of degrading the whole spiritual world by unnatural liaisons with the two-legged animals. (Lewis, 1964, p. 17)

Our major addition to this theoretical outline is to postulate the existence of a second crisis point, called into existence by the very solution to the first crisis, or the success of the first synthesis, and to show that the character of the commitment or synthesis emerging from this second period of testing is demonstrably different from the commitment forged by the first crisis. We will also define, in more detail than has been done previously, the nature of each of these stages and the evidence that bears on them, their relationship to the breaking as well as the making of com-mitments, to the problem of mental health, and to the question of awareness.

Description of the Five Stages
of Commitment

For quick descriptive reference, Stage I commitments may be described as *exploratory*. People are exploring a potential activity or relationship, in either a cautious or carefree manner, but in general with concern only for what positive ele-ments are present that might make further exploration worthwhile. What we are calling Stage I commitments can be thought of as precommitments because they generally involve an unreflective positive orientation toward the potential object of commitment. This is also, in a different way, true of Stage II commitments, which involve the emergence of negative elements but not yet the existence of a synthesis (the first true commitment). But these first two periods are so important to our understanding of the commitment process that it seems both silly and un-necessarily cumbersome to call them precommitment stages. In addition, these processes have generally been referred to as stages in previous discussions of the growth of commitment (e.g., Thibaut & Kelley, 1959). One's actions during these stages foreshadow and shape the nature of the commitment to come (if it does) even if only in ways that are largely implicit and unrecognized. Earlier in this chapter we reviewed many of the studies that characterize beginning commitments as positive and unreflective.

Stage II commitments can be described as *testing*. Negative events of some sort have been encountered, and people assess their willingness and ability to accommodate these events. People may also be involved in testing their environ-ment, such as the willingness of a partner to make concessions or the prospects that a task can be solved. Clearly, Stage II commitments, like Stage I commitments, involve information search, but in Stage II the search is about the nature of nega-tive rather than positive features and is therefore more troubled. The orientation in Stage II is external or environmentally focused. The crisis at this time is one of encountering unfamiliar and perhaps unexpected events and the threat of not achieving goals or fulfilling wishes. The threat subjects experience is from something outside themselves; it is a threat to something that has, at that moment, primarily extrinsic value for them. In all of these features, as we will note in a moment, it contrasts with the Stage IV crisis.

Stage III commitments can be described as *passionate*. There may have been numerous minor and essentially unnoticed syntheses earlier, but this stage is marked by the first major synthesis of positive and negative elements and by the first recognition of the entire process as a commitment. Stage III commitments have two striking features: They are fiercely and unrelentingly positive—the existence of negative features is virtually denied—and they are highly self-conscious. Fanatical commitments are Stage III commitments, as are commitments that involve a rigid adherence to a certain behavioral schedule without exception and without regard to costs (Ainslie, 1975).

Stage IV commitments can be described as *quiet*. This stage emerges slowly as the energy needed to maintain a Stage III commitment fades and as the intensity of the ambivalence, which contributed to the need for this level of energy, likewise fades. With this fading, however, comes another kind of crisis or antithesis. The crisis is posed not by the prospects of failing to get the object of commitment or to sustain the commitment but by the actuality of having attained the object of commitment and of having sustained the commitment. The crisis is slowly and insidiously posed by familiarity and expectedness, not unfamiliarity and unexpectedness. In contrast to Stage II, the orientation of people in Stage IV is internal. The threat subjects experience is from something inside themselves, and the threat is to something that has, at this point, primarily intrinsic value for them. It can be thought of as the crisis of boredom.

Stage V commitments can be described as *integral*. They represent a higher level of integration of positive and negative elements, but integration more complex and flexible than the earlier bonding. The structure now absorbs the periodic emergence into awareness and fading from awareness of a variety of positive and negative elements without losing its basic form. Indeed, the entire commitment may move into and out of awareness. The cognitive and emotional quality of the commitment at this point depends markedly on whether it is in or out of awareness. We argue that cognitive complexity is lost when things are put out of awareness. Thus an increasing ability to put things out of awareness means an increasingly simple cognitive structure. Similarly, increasing awareness is paralleled by increasing cognitive complexity. Rational consideration of the pros and cons of the object of a commitment is typically done in awareness.

Emotional complexity, on the other hand, is lost when things are held in focal attention or focal awareness and competing impulses are excluded. Thus we suggest that an increasing ability to hold things in focal awareness means an increasingly simple emotional structure, and that putting things out of awareness enhances emotional complexity. Emotional working through of conflicting feelings, as well as the creative association of previously unattached thoughts and feelings, is usually done out of awareness. As commitments evolve over time, individuals come to have both a greater capacity for keeping them out of awareness and a greater capacity for keeping them in awareness. Thus, during Stage V individuals have the capacity to treat their commitments in a cognitively simple or mindless way, simply acting out of habit or following a well-known script. They also have the capacity to treat their commitments in an emotionally simple or single-minded way: They resurrect the Stage III passion. Both of these simplifications allow actions to be relentlessly followed without either cognitive or emotional ambiguity, which could make such dedicated pursuit difficult to maintain. Commitment could not continue, however, if cognitive and emotional complexity (doubts) were also not sometimes salient. Furthermore, we hypothesize that with time, individuals make transitions from one of these states to the other more easily.

Further Differences
Among the Five Stages

Table 5-1 summarizes the preceding description of the five stages as well as the discussion to follow of several further distinctions among the five stages. The stages differ in the major tasks involved, whether the positive or negative elements of the object are salient, the primary basis of motivation (intrinsic or extrinsic), and whether the commitment is in focal awareness.

As elaborated shortly, the five stages also differ importantly in dialectic form and in rate of growth or change. Also, it is speculated that individuals in different stages of a commitment differ in perceptions of control, feelings of playfulness, experience of freedom, and categorization of the commitment in stimulus or response terms. Finally, the stages are suggested to differ in the slopes of the approach or avoidance gradients. It is hoped that the speculative comparison of these properties of the five stages help to illuminate how the stages are qualitatively different from one another.

Differences in the stages in dialectic terms. The five stages can be described in the language of the thesis-antithesis-synthesis model of commitment. Stage I represents the initial statement of the thesis or approach motivation; Stage II represents the initial emergence of the antithesis or avoidance motivation; Stage III represents the initial emergence of a synthesis of these two, which we have characterized as a rigid synthesis; Stage IV represents the emergence of a second antithesis, produced by strains from within the initial synthesis rather than threats posed from outside; and Stage V represents the evolution of a higher-level synthesis, which we have characterized as more open and flexible.

Of course, this is a macroscopic view of the commitment process. Beginning with the first acknowledgement of negativity in Stage II that is somehow dealt with (i.e., synthesized), countless syntheses occur throughout the life of a commitment. Commitments are dynamic; they are constantly being challenged and transformed. There may be structure to enduring commitments, but it is changing rather than stable. As Giele (1976) writes concerning relationships:

TABLE 5-1 Description of Stages in the Commitment Process

| | STAGE | | | | |
	I	II	III	IV	V
Descriptive term	Exploratory	Testing	Passionate	Quiet	Integral
Major task	Information search about the positive	Information search about the negative	First major synthesis of positive and negative (rigid)	Crisis due to familiarity of object of commitment (boredom)	Second major synthesis (flexible)
Salient elements of commitment	Positive elements	Negative elements	Positive elements	Negative elements	Positive and negative elements
Basis of motivation	Extrinsic	Extrinsic	Intrinsic	Intrinsic	Intrinsic
Commitment in focal awareness	No	No	Yes	Yes	Off and on
Dialectic form	Thesis	Antithesis	Synthesis	Antithesis	Synthesis
Rate of growth	Slow growth	Break in this growth	Rapid growth and change	Erosion of growth	Growth and erosion fluctuating
Perception of control	Illusion of control	Confronted with lack of control	Illusion of no control	Recognition of past control	Realistic sense of partial control
Playfulness	Playful	Uncertain and ambivalent	Serious	Uncertain and ambivalent	Playful and serious
Type of freedom	Predecision freedom	Unfree (perception of external constraints)	Postdecision freedom	Unfree (perception of internal constraints)	Pre- and postdecision freedom
Approach/avoidance gradient	Avoidance gradient steeper; unambivalent approach	Avoidance gradient steeper; avoidance activated	Approach gradient steeper; approach	Approach gradient steeper; avoidance activated	Approach gradient steeper; approach and avoid
Stimulus or response categorization	Readily accessible stimulus categories (ambiguity reduction)	Not readily accessible stimulus categories (ambiguity reduction)	Readily accessible response categories (ambivalence reduction)	Not readily accessible response categories (ambivalence reduction)	Idiosyncratic response categories (ambivalence reduction)

> There is no holding a relationship to a single form. . . . A good relationship has a pattern like a dance and is built on some of the same rules. The partners do not need to hold on tightly because they move confidently in the same pattern, intricate, but gay and swift and free, like a country dance of Mozart's. . . . The dancers who are perfectly in time never destroy the 'winged life' in each other or in themselves. (pp. 69–86)

It is the nature of the particular antitheses and syntheses that distinguishes one stage from another. Figure 5-1 provides a schematic representation of this process. Each peak in the intrinsic motivation curve represents a synthesis. Extrinsic motivation is hypothesized to rise rapidly during Stage I but then to gradually decline throughout the life cycle of the commitment (except in special cases in which one's commitment shifts to the extrinsic factors, as discussed earlier). In contrast, intrinsic motivation develops slowly but increases dramatically during Stage III with the occurrence of the first large synthesis within awareness. During the Stage IV crisis, intrinsic motivation gradually erodes, but it rises again to at least the Stage III level when this crisis is resolved by the synthesis that initiates Stage V. Levels of intrinsic motivation closely parallel the individual's sense of how committed he or she is. Extrinsic motivation is not insignificant in commitments, as we define them. It can serve important functions, particularly in times of crisis. However, intrinsic motivation is the essential ingredient in a commitment in our formulation.

Differences in stages in rate of growth.   As can also be seen in Figure 5-1, the five stages represent very different rates of growth and change. Stage I involves a slow, often imperceptible change in sentiments. Stage II represents a break in the Stage I process of growth. Stage III is a period of rapid growth, even sudden change. Stage IV represents an erosion of the achievements of Stage III growth and Stage V, finally, is a dynamic equilibrium in which lesser versions of previous changes are reenacted in a basically stable structure.

Differences in stages in perceived control.   Stage I commitments feature the illusion of control. The exploration of the new object, activity, or person appears to be entirely under one's control, though the individual is actually under at least partial control of extrinsic motivators at this time. In Stage II commitments, individuals confront this and experience a lack of control. The consequences of choices already made become more apparent at this time. Greater knowledge of the object of commitment and its inherent negative features leads the person to recognize that he or she is not in control. The object is unlikely to change in any fundamental way, and one must come to terms with this. Stage III commitments are characterized by the illusion of "no control." That is, the person feels swept along by impulses, events, and inevitabilities that must be followed whether he or she wishes to or not. This is the stage in which people will say that they *have* to do something (i.e., invest more resources in a war, pursue an addiction) because they really have no choice. Although the person maintains some degreee of control at

182

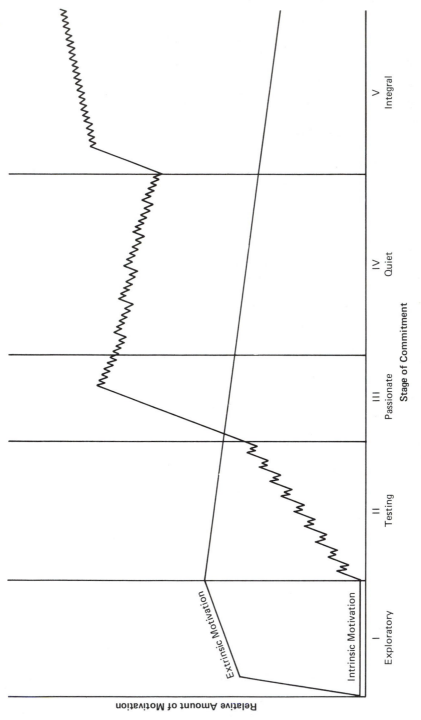

FIGURE 5-1 Levels of Intrinsic and Extrinsic Motivation During Commitment Stages

this stage, as at every stage, one's perception at this stage is of being out of control. Stage IV commitments involve a confrontation with what we may call "over control," or the recognition of past control. Individuals come to realize how large a role they have in fact played in determining events and must struggle to come to terms both with that fact and with the fact that their feelings about these events may no longer be what they once were. Stage V commitments bring individuals to a more realistic sense of partial control. Some actions have been and will be the individuals' own doing, and others have been imposed on them by events, and it is the function of commitment at this point to accommodate both of these facts.

Differences in stages in playfulness.   Stage I commitments could be described as playful, Stage III commitments are typically very serious, and Stage V commitments are, at different points, both serious and playful. Stage II and IV commitments are both uncertain and ambivalent.

Stage I commitments are flirtations; for example, in developing interpersonal relationships, requests and offers made at this point are deliberately lighthearted so that they can be refused without anyone's not yet fully engaged feelings being hurt. Stage III commitments, in this analogy, represent a later and much more serious stage of courtship, with feelings very much on the line in every offer and request. Stage V commitments are more like established marriages—the parties are aware of the external problems that are unknown at Stage I and the internal stresses that are unknown at Stage III, but they are capable of dealing with each of them in turn with aspects of previous orientations. It is, in a sense, as if seriousness were a necessary solution to the questions posed by Stage II ambivalence, while a return to playfulness is a necessary solution to the questions posed by Stage IV ambivalence. Seriousness represents the drive needed to conquer external obstacles; playfulness represents the flexibility and relaxation needed to dissolve the tensions of an overly rigid internal structure. Commitments that survive into Stage V must thus have the capacity for both seriousness and playfulness.

Differences in stages in freedom.   Stage I, Stage III, and Stage V commitments also involve significantly different orientations to freedom. Understanding the differences in people's experience of freedom at these different points in time will help up grasp not only the nature of freedom but the nature of commitment and the relationship between the two. Thus we will describe these different aspects of freedom before describing how they differ in importance at the various stages.

There has been considerable debate over what freedom means in both psychology and philosophy (see Adler, 1958, or Dewey & Gould, 1970 for reviews of this vast literature). Much of the debate has been over the relative importance of two different components or types of freedom: people's ability to make choices among alternatives without being subject to external constraints, and people's ability to achieve for themselves satisfactory outcomes. Ordinarily, these two might seem to be the same, since people who can choose freely among outcomes will ordinarily be expected to choose for themselves a satisfactory outcome. But what is their state if they can choose freely but there are no truly satisfactory outcomes available? Alternatively, what is their state if there is a highly satisfactory outcome available but it is the only one, thus precluding the objective possibility of choice? Writers have differed as to whether people are truly free, or will feel free, in these two conditions. Variations of these two conditions have also been used to describe what authors have felt were two different kinds of freedom. For example, Berlin's (1969) notion of negative freedom is largely freedom from constraint, while his notion of positive freedom is largely freedom to achieve positive outcomes. Steiner's (1970) conception of decision freedom is primarily freedom from constraint on choice (in this case, constraint imposed by differences in the actual value of the alternatives, which would serve to make the choice predictable), whereas his conception of outcome freedom is primarily freedom of access to desirable outcomes.

A number of recent conceptions of freedom, however, have tended to dissolve the distinction between these two aspects in a manner that follows from our analysis of the origins of meaning and value. To establish whether an outcome is valuable or desirable to any particular individual, it is necessary to know not simply the objective properties of that outcome but the subjective state of that individual: what he or she feels, wants, and desires. As we have seen, the outcome will be experienced as meaningful and valuable by the individual to the extent that the individual feels he or she has chosen it and is committed to it. Thus the first element of freedom (the experience of choice or the sense of having chosen the outcome) is necessary for the second element of freedom (the experience of the outcome as subjectively of value). Conversely, it is probably also true that outcomes cannot be indefinitely experienced as chosen without also being felt to be desirable. People feel free, in this general sense, when they feel that their actions and their consequences are their own, flowing from their own selves. Thus, according to Bergman (1977), the making of a choice does not in and of itself give rise to the feeling of freedom but does so only if the actor identifies with what he or she perceives as the agency that does the choosing (i.e., regards the thought processes that made the decision as truly his or her own) even if it has been conditioned or influenced by external forces. Dworkin (1970) describes an individual as acting freely if and only if the act in question is performed for reasons the individual does not mind. Kruglanski and Cohen (1973) and Trope (1978) have both shown that subjects view actors as free to the extent that they see these actors as behaving in a manner congruent with their personal disposition, or with the manner in which they could be predicted to behave in the absence of external pressures to behave otherwise. Thus, in the Trope (1978) study, actors were seen as more free when the rewards present in the choice situation (joining a painting club or an electronics club) were biased in favor with what the actor already wanted to do than when they were biased against what the actor wanted to do.

With this as background, we want to offer a distinction between two kinds of freedom. The distinction is related to elements of the foregoing discussion of freedom but rests primarily on a temporal shift and avoids, we think, some of the analytical confusion in previous distinctions. We think it is worthwhile to distinguish between the freedom people may experience before they make a decision (predecision freedom) and the freedom they may experience after they have made a decision (postdecision freedom). In each case, the match between the person's inner state, a line of action, and an outcome is the critical concern, but in predecision freedom we are talking about a number of possible lines of action and a number of prospective outcomes (if these are indeed available), whereas in postdecision freedom we are talking about a single (chosen) line of action and, eventually, a single (obtained) outcome. The reason that the number and quality of alternatives and the ability to choose among these alternatives without constraint are important in the consideration of predecision freedom is, in this view, simply because an increase in any of these raises the probability (in actors' or observers' eyes) that a course of action can be selected that will lead to a satisfactory outcome (an outcome congruent with the person's inner dispositions). Once a decision has been made, however, the number and quality of alternatives other than the one chosen and the ability to choose among these alternatives without constraint should be much less relevant. The experience of postdecision freedom, we suggest, will depend only on whether the particular course of action chosen corresponds to the person's inner dispositions and self-perceptions.

This issue has not been salient in past analyses, in good part because past analyses and most lay thinking about freedom have focused on the question of making (rather than enacting) decisions or on predecisional states. Moreover, most past analyses have not drawn another distinction alluded to earlier in this paragraph, namely, between the choice of a behavior and the choice of attainment of an outcome. If choosing a particular alternative automatically means obtaining the particular outcome associated with that alternative, many of the issues we have been concerned about here—and elsewhere in this book—become moot. People will obtain that outcome regardless of the extent to which they are committed to the line of action designed to lead to it, or regardless of how effectively they pursue that line of action. In most important cases, however, people choose only lines of action whose ultimate value will depend upon how successfully and vigorously they pursue them. Under these circumstances, feeling that such a line of action was freely chosen and that it represents enthusiastic rather than reluctant mobilization of inner energies will have functional value. As Csikszentmihalyi and Graef (1979) write, lack of what we call postdecision freedom "produces a split in consciousness: part of one's attention is concentrated on the task at hand because one has to deal with it, but part of one wishes to be elsewhere doing something else" (p. 98). On the other hand, when Martin Luther said "Here I stand; I can do no other," he was clearly experiencing no split in consciousness. In this most famous example of postdecision freedom, Luther indicates complete oneness with his action, an identification enhanced rather than diminished by his assertion that—for him, at that point—nothing else was possible.

If we identify Stage I commitments with predecision freedom and Stage III commitments with postdecision freedom, it will come as no surprise at this point that we feel Stage V commitments require elements of both predecision and postdecision freedom for their sustenance. In Stages II and IV, people do not feel free. Stage II begins with the erosion of Stage I's sense of predecision freedom, or the increasing perception of some form of external constraints. Stage IV begins with the erosion of Stage III's sense of postdecision freedom, or the increasing perception of some form of internal constraints that make impossible the indefinite continuation of Stage III's enthusiasm. In an enduring Stage V commitment, people need and seek a sense of predecision freedom, not so much because they are in fact interested in revoking their current choice or in pursuing alternatives but because they need to revive the sense that this is possible in order to retain the feeling that they are indeed committed to their current state and not just trapped by it—that is, that they have postdecision freedom. Maccoby (1977), in his analysis of corporate gamesmen, notes that these talented, enthusiastic executives, who play the corporate game for its own sake and are most effective in this role, regularly need to reassure themselves that they could leave the corporation they are working for any time they wanted to—despite the fact that they are usually highly committed to the corporation and never do leave it. In our analysis, it is the very fact that these executives are so strongly pressed to maintain such a high level of dedication, enthusiasm, and loyalty (which include heavy emphasis on team play and conformity) that requires them to try to maintain the prerequisite for such feelings—a strong sense of postdecision freedom. This requires, in turn, a periodic infusion of the sense of predecision freedom. In the variety of programs designed to renew or revitalize the commitment of participants, such as Marriage Encounter weekends or retreats for stressed and potentially burned-out helping professionals, the fact that participants have options, however scary, are always either an explicit or implicit part of the agenda.

In an unpublished study on actor-observer differences, Galegher and Brickman found some strong indications that the determinants of predecision freedom are different from the determinants of postdecision freedom. Northwestern University students were surveyed about their career interests and plans. Two different questions about freedom were asked: how free people felt to choose among possible careers, and how free they felt to carry out their choice. We were interested in the extent to which these perceptions could be predicted from two other variables—the number of career alternatives people felt they had, and the extent of their commitment to a particular career alternative. People who felt they had a large number of career alternatives rated themselves as significantly freer to choose among alternatives than did people who felt that they did not have a large number of alternatives. This variable was unaffected by degree of commitment to a particular career. On the other hand, feeling free to carry out a career choice was unrelated to the number of career alternatives people felt they had. It was, instead, positively and significantly related to the degree of commitment people reported having to a particular career choice.

Differences in stages in approach-avoidance gradients. Our commitment stages can also be articulated within the framework of approach and avoidance gradients first carried out by Miller (1948), although the later stages require a reversal of Miller's assumption that the avoidance gradient is steeper than the approach gradient. Miller made this assumption, and carried out his entire analysis of goal gradients, in part to explain the fact that rats running toward an object about which they were ambivalent (e.g., a food box at which they would get shocked) ran more slowly as they got closer to the goal. This could be understood if the rat had independent bases of approach and avoidance motivation—hunger and fear, respectively—and if hunger were relatively constant regardless of whether the rat was close or far from the goal box, while fear increased sharply as the rat got closer to the box. In our view, the first two stages of commitment can be described as analogous to these two regions of a graph in which an avoidance gradient is steeper than an approach gradient. Stage I commitments feature unambivalent approach because the object is distant and the avoidance motivation that will be aroused is weak. Stage II commitments begin when avoidance motivation becomes more imminent, salient, and perhaps restricting (Eidelson, 1980). Avoidance then begins to seriously challenge approach motivation, perhaps even overwhelming it.

Stage III begins with a cognitive and affective transformation of a more fundamental sort, which changes the relative steepness of the approach and avoidance gradients so that the approach gradient becomes steeper. In the earlier stages, forces operate to push subjects to an intermediate position—to move away if they get too close (because when subjects are close, avoidance motivation is stronger than approach), and to move closer if they get too far (because in the relative safety of distance, approach motivation is stronger than avoidance). Once the gradients have been transformed by that first commitment synthesis, forces operate to push subjects to one of two extreme positions: extreme closeness if they are somewhat close (because their approach motivation gets still stronger), or extreme distance if they are somewhat distant (because their avoidance motivation gets still stronger). This is another way of representing the fact (which we have discussed at length earlier) that once commitment enters the picture (as it does in Stage III), regions of effective neutrality become inaccessible. Stage III commitments can be pictured as states in which subjects are close to a goal in a situation where the approach gradient is steeper than the avoidance gradient, hence the passionate, unrelenting plunge toward the goal. Similarly, Stage IV commitments emerge when events—including those triggered by simple exhaustion or satiation—move subjects further away from the goal, hence the potential for the dissolution of the commitment. Stage V commitments involve some kind of slow and relatively stable oscillation between these two regions. During most of Stage V, approach is predominant. During each period of doubt or hesitation (i.e., emergence of a new antithesis), however, avoidance will predominate until resolution (i.e., a new synthesis) occurs.

Differences in stages in stimulus versus response categorization.   Still another way of characterizing our commitment stages, this time in the domain of social cognition, is to suggest that in our first two stages people think in terms of stimulus categories and in our last three stages they think in terms of response categories. In Stages I and II, in other words, people are thinking primarily about positive and negative features of the stimulus. They are considering only the attractiveness of their partner or their job. In Stages III and IV, they are thinking primarily about positive and negative features of their own response—that is, their enthusiasm towards their partner or their job. Within each framework, the stages may occur in the order they do in part because positive categories are more readily accessible and more likely to be recognized and reported than negative categories, as the literature on memory and judgements of self and others has repeatedly shown (e.g., Zajonc, 1968b). Thus initial impressions are based on readily accessible stimulus categories, and Stage II impressions are based on less readily accessible stimulus categories. Stage III impressions are based on readily accessible response categories, and Stage IV impressions are based on less readily accessible response categories. Stage V thinking, we suggest, involves a mixture of the foregoing, by which point the person will have evolved idiosyncratic personal categories for thinking about the commitment. Some antitheses and syntheses will involve the resolution of new stimulus features (e.g., use of a new text in a course), and others will involve new response features (e.g., boredom after teaching a course for the fifth time).

It should be noted that a breakdown of cognitive processes at the different stages thus places the twin tasks of ambiguity reduction and ambivalence reduction (Newman & Langer, 1981) at two different points in time. Ambiguity reduction, or trying to figure out what kind of a person or situation the individual is dealing with, is the dominant concern of the first two stages. Ambivalence reduction, or trying to figure out and manage what conflicting forms of motivation the individual has about the situation, is the task of subsequent stages.

Evidence consistent with the stages.   There are no studies in the literature that offer a direct test of all five of these stages. There are, however, many highly provocative works of research on the development of dyadic relationships, which collectively offer some suggestive evidence for the distinctions we are making. Our theory is equally relevant to the development of commitment in groups, but with a few exceptions (e.g., Bales, 1950; 1951; Schutz, 1958; Tuckman, 1965), there is no relevant research to review. What we would most like to show through a considera-tion of past studies is that there are two points of decline in the development of commitment, corresponding to our Stage II and Stage IV crises. A study of Eidelson (1980) and another by Braiker and Kelley (1979) provide evidence for the first crisis.

Eidelson (1980) hypothesizes that relationships develop under the influence of two conflicting motives, affiliation and independence, and that, moreover, the intensity of the conflict between these motives is likely to peak at a point partway through the process of relationship formation. Before that point, the individual can satisfy his or her need for affiliation in the relationship without yet encountering any restrictions or limitations on his or her independence. After that point, if the individual decides that the relationship is still worth pursuing despite the restrictive costs it entails, these costs are assumed to lose their salience by a process in which the individual redefines his or her independence and adopts a new frame of reference in which the relationship is now taken as a given. These points correspond nicely to our first three commitment stages, with the reorganization at the last point representing what we have called the first major commitment synthesis.

Eidelson interviewed university freshmen at two-week intervals for periods of five or six weeks. Participants' degree of involvement in each of the friendship relationships they rated was calculated as a function of the proportion of interpersonal time the person spent with that friend during successive time periods. Relationships were classified at each point in time as having one of four levels of involvement. Two separate comparisons were conducted. One compared subjects' feelings about many different relationships that differed in their level of involvement. The other compared subjects' feelings about a single relationship as a function of fluctuations in involvement over time. The same pattern was found in both studies. Satisfaction with the relationship rose from level one to level two involvement, dropped from level two to level three, and rose again from level three to level four. We, of course, would look eventually for a further drop and rise in relationship satisfaction, occurring for different reasons and with different consequences.

Braiker and Kelley (1979), on the other hand, had newlywed couples rate retrospectively the various stages of their courtship. A factor analysis identified four dimensions of relationship development: love, or the extent of belongingness or attachment; conflict, or the amount of negative affect and overt argument; maintenance, or the degree of mutual self-disclosure and discussion about the relationship; and ambivalence, or the degree of confusion or uncertainty about the future of the relationship. As we would expect in successful relationships, especially when viewed in retrospect, scores on the love and maintenance dimensions showed a pattern of linear (or at least monotonic) increase over all stages of courtship. In a pattern very similar to that uncovered by Eidelson's (1980) quite different approach, Braiker and Kelley found that reports of conflict increased from the period of casual to serious dating but leveled off afterwards. Most interesting of all, from the present point of view, was the ambivalence factor. Overall, ambivalence tended to decrease over the stages of the relationship. In addition, however, its meaning seemed to change. In the early stages, ambivalence was associated with the conflict factor, suggesting a crisis associated with (from each partner's perspective) external factors, or our Stage II crisis. Later, however, ambivalence was associated with the love factor, and in particular with waning feelings of love, suggesting a crisis associated with what each partner would experience as internal factors, or our Stage IV crisis. Very similar results have been reported in another study of courtship and marriage by Huston, Surra, Fitzgerald, and Cate (1981).

Finally, we might remind ourselves in this context of the shift in the correlates of romantic love reported in the study discussed earlier by Driscoll, Davis, and Lipetz (1972). In the period of courtship, romantic love was associated with the resolution of conflict and stress (e.g., parental interference), or external factors reminiscent of Stage II crises. Later in marriage, love was more strongly associated with trust, whose presence is more strongly suggestive of internal peace, or the resolution of a Stage IV crisis, than it is of romantic tension and passion. The Driscoll, Davis, and Lipetz (1972) finding on the changing relationship between love and trust over time has been replicated by Dion and Dion (1976).

We ourselves have conducted three studies of the evolution of commitments over time. The first, carried out by Abbey and Dunkel-Schetter (1979), was a longitudinal study of changes in students' feelings about courses they were taking over the entire quarter. All students participating in the study were enrolled in an introductory social psychology class, but the courses they chose to rate covered a wide variety of academic disciplines (i.e., they were not required to rate the social psychology class, and only a few did). Thus, the patterns that emerged can be considered to generalize across a wide variety of different university courses.

Among other things, students were asked to rate each week the extent to which each of the following words described their involvement with their class at this moment: exploring/tentative; testing/challenging; passionate/intense; placid/quiet; and complete/fulfilled. They also rated how anxious they felt about their class at that moment, how happy they felt about it, how much they thought about it, and whether they had come to any new conclusions about it. The pattern of students' self-descriptions of their involvement with their classes provided suggestive evidence for our five distinct stages. Students were significantly more likely to describe themselves as exploring during the first three weeks of the class than at any subsequent time. They were more likely to describe their orientation as one of testing during weeks three through five than during any time either before or after that period. Week five was a very special week in this pattern—it was the week in which subjects were significantly more likely to use the word passionate or intense in describing their involvement than they were at any other time. Week five was also one of two points at which subjects were most likely to describe their involvement as complete or fulfilled. The other such point was week ten, the end of the data collection and end of classes (though not exams). In between these two points, in weeks six through nine, none of these descriptive adjectives was especially salient, thus implying (by negation) a period in which commitment was relatively dormant. Thus, subjects' unfolding involvement in their courses seems to pass through periods possibly akin to each of the five stages we have outlined.

The pattern of change on other weekly variables paralleled this discrimination. Subjects moved from a period in the first three weeks, in which they were relatively happy and not terribly anxious, to a period in weeks four through six in which they were both anxious and happy. In weeks seven and eight they were primarily anxious, and in weeks nine and ten they were again happy yet still anxious (especially in week nine). The exploratory stage was thus, as expected, one of relatively pure positive affect; the next two stages were characterized by growing anxiety; then followed a stage in which happiness eroded, and a final stage in which positive affect again emerged. It is interesting that students' reports of spending time thinking about the class peaked at week five, the point at which the first major commitment synthesis emerged. This was also (along with week two, during the exploratory period) the point at which the largest percentage (44%) of students reported having reached new conclusions about the class.

Clearly, many of the particular features of this pattern have to do with the rhythm of classes at a university, such as the fact that midterms and the associated stress typically fall midway through the course and that the course has a known termination date. It has never been our contention, however, that the episodes in the development of commitment are entirely internally paced. Like all responses, they are paced in part by the occurrence of external events, to which they are a response.

Another such data set, collected by Hamilton and Jacque (1977) with Brickman, maps (in a cross-sectional design) students' commitment to and enthusiasm about academic life and personal success over their four years in college. Commitment and enthusiasm were both high in the freshman year, dropped during the sophomore year, rebounded during the junior year, and tailed off again during the senior year. The first three years correspond nicely to what we have come to expect from Stage I through Stage III commitments: an early period of unconflicted and somewhat naive positivity, superseded by a growing awareness of what sacrifices it will take to succeed, followed by the emergence of that we have called the first major commitment synthesis, and in this instance, the acquisition of new skills and experiences relevant to this commitment. The drop-off in the senior year is harder to interpret, however, since it could represent either the fading of motivation (as the major goals of undergraduate work have been achieved and the time of graduation approaches) or some kind of anticipatory disengagement from a path and a way of life that will, for most of our sample, soon be abandoned for other pursuits. (We will turn shortly to a discussion of the processes involved in breaking or undoing commitments.) In the present data set, some erosion of the peak of commitment in the junior year seemingly takes place. We cannot say whether this represents a new ambivalence, which would eventually have to be restored by a new synthesis, or a reorientation to what subjects expect will be the end of their involvement in academic life.

Another data set that supports our commitment stages is from a large study conducted by Silver and Dunkel-Schetter (1981). They gave a medical career questionnaire to a cross-sectional sample of doctors and prospective doctors at nine different points in their medical careers: high school students, college freshmen and juniors, seniors enrolled in an honors program, first-year medical students, third-year medical students, interns, residents, and practicing physicians (alumni).

Subjects' commitment to their medical career was assessed by an index of seven items.[1] The results for this index are displayed in Figure 5-2. As can be seen, the fit of this study with our hypothesized five-point model is dramatic. College freshmen were moderately highly committed to medical careers; juniors were more ambivalent; first year medical students displayed a peak of commitment, which began to drop off by the third year of medical school; interns reported an all-time low in commitment; while residents and practicing physicians showed a return to the same level of commitment as the freshmen, although of a qualitatively different sort. It was, for example, both more tense and angry, and more content and satisfied than that of the freshmen.

This pattern of results may be interpreted as consistent with a naive Stage I commitment, a passionate and intense Stage III commitment, and a relatively modulated and mature Stage V commitment. It also reveals two dramatically different commitment crises occurring at just the points where we would expect them in this sequence. The Stage II crisis occurred during the junior year in college, and the Stage IV crisis occurred among interns. It should be noted that ratings of stress were highest among juniors and among interns. Otherwise, however, the crises have quite different correlates. Juniors were lowest in how free they felt to determine the *course* of their medical career (see Figure 5-3). Juniors also represented the major dip in the curve regarding feeling *in control* of their success or failure in becoming a doctor. In other words, juniors were at the point where they had already worked hard to become doctors and were quite aware of how much they had given up and how much of their college lives they had sacrificed in this quest, and yet they had no assurance that any of these efforts would be worthwhile. They had not yet been admitted to medical school and did not know if they ever would be. Interns, on the other hand, were not affected by these issues. They were lowest in how free they felt to determine their *everyday activities*. They were also highest in feeling that the pursuit of a career in medicine *conflicted* with other areas of life, such as friends and social life; love relationships; home responsibilities; hobbies, sports, and recreation; personal time or time to oneself; and development of new interests. (An index comprised of these six items is shown in Figure 5-4.) Interns were not wondering about whether they could become doctors; they were wondering about whether they could *stand* having become doctors. The Stage II crisis is about whether something *can* be achieved; the Stage IV crisis is about whether it

---

[1] The seven items were: (a) To what extent are you dedicated to your career in medicine no matter what stands in your way? (b) To what extent are you dedicated to your career in medicine no matter what impact it has on the rest of your life? (c) To what extent are you open to alternatives to a career in medicine at the present time? (This question was reverse-scored) (d) Within the last three months, have you felt like giving up your career in medicine? (This question was reverse-scored) (e) To what extent do you feel that it might be possible for you to give up your career in medicine right now? (This question was reverse-scored) (f) Given what you know now, would you choose medicine again as a career? (g) Considering all aspects of your life at the present, from the most important to the least important, how important is your career in medicine to you? Not all of these items were applicable to high school students; therefore, this group does not appear in Figure 5-2.

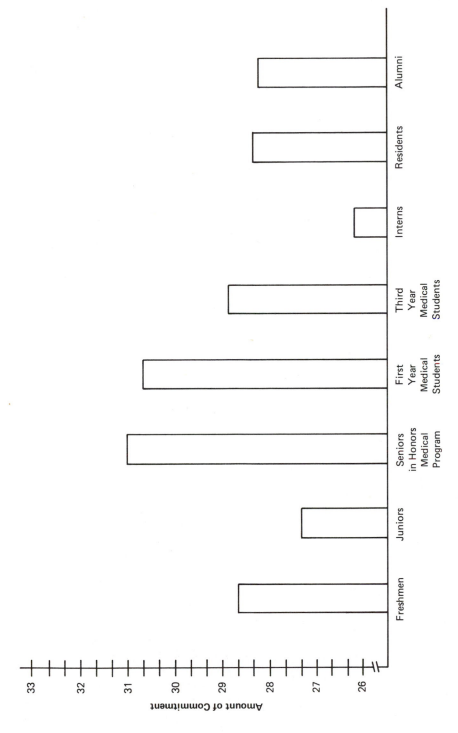

FIGURE 5-2 Group Differences in Commitment

194

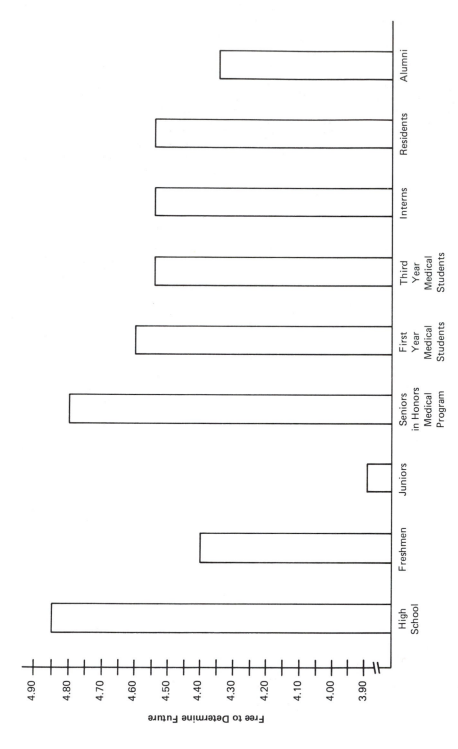

FIGURE 5-3 Group Differences in Freedom

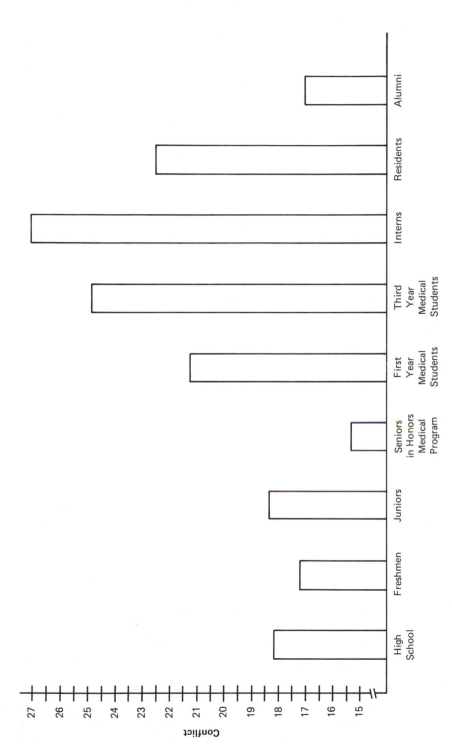

FIGURE 5-4 Group Differences in Conflict

195

was *worth* achieving and whether it should be *sustained*. The pattern across groups on the commitment index (in Figure 5-2) was quite similar to patterns on related measures such as *intrinsic motivation*. This was measured by endorsement of various incentives, such as the opportunities to contribute to medicine, society, and humanity, to care for and help others, and to experience intellectual challenge. Juniors and interns were lowest in intrinsic motivation. They were also most likely to say that medicine had changed them as persons.

Finally, on theoretical grounds, we expected that commitment would be greatest when respondents indicated that the negative aspects of their chosen career were necessary to that career (rather than being some form of arbitrary impediments). Subjects were asked to describe the most negative and second most negative aspects of continuing their careers at the present time and to rate how necessary each of these was. Juniors and interns once again represent dips on this curve. Sacrifices were generally seen as more necessary by respondents earlier in their careers, with the middle of medical school—and, no doubt, the accumulation of a substantial financial debt (Abbey, Dunkel-Schetter, & Brickman, 1983)—representing the general breaking point in this curve.

Only some of the main findings from this data set relevant to the course of commitment over time have been presented here. Data concerning subjects' affect, coping styles, the specific conflicts they experienced with their medical careers, and the effects of all these things on the development of their commitment to medicine are beyond the scope of our discussion. Nonetheless, the preliminary findings from this study and from the other literature discussed earlier conform to our ideas about the stages of commitment. Much more research is clearly needed, especially longitudinal research, and especially research addressing the predictive utility of knowing that subjects are in one stage of commitment or another, in order to provide a definitive assessment of the validity and significance of this conceptualization.

Variations in the Sequence

Although we hypothesize that the order of the stages is invariant, the pace at which people progress through them, and their awareness of each stage, is not. It may sometimes seem that Stage I has been skipped, for example, since the events that constitute it are often minor, pleasurable, and without conflictful or tension-inducing properties that would propel them into focal awareness. Or else these events may have been spread out over such a long period of time as to escape notice. Sometimes, for example, someone undertakes a course of action with highly salient negative features, such as risk or danger, that are apparent right from the start. Most people may avoid helping a bystander in an emergency—as we discussed earlier—but some will charge right in even when potential costs are high. We argue that this would only happen when people have been quietly prepared by a long prior history of socialization to make this commitment. That is, through previous actions or training they have come to accept an image of themselves, whether they have realized it or not, that enables them to encounter and work through a Stage II crisis without the ambivalence (or simple avoidance) that would be elicited in someone without this prior history.

Sometimes, of course, people are forced to make a choice whose negative features are salient right from the start because a better choice is not available. This happens, for example, when people must take their second choice of a job because they are not offered their first choice. If the element of coerciveness is high enough, this is of course not a commitment at all. If the restriction of freedom involved is only moderate (e.g., if there are third- and fourth-choice jobs the person refuses), the job still represents a commitment. It is, however, one in which the person is forced to confront elements of a Stage II crisis sooner than would ordinarily be the case. It should be noted, however, that our previous review of the literature on the fate of early idealism in jobs and relationships makes it clear that everyone will arrive at such a crisis eventually.

More rarely, it may appear that both Stage I and Stage II have been skipped. This seems to be true when a passionate commitment seems to emerge full-blown, as in the case of religious conversions. Students of conversion, however, are generally agreed that the event of conversion is preceded by a period of ambivalence and turmoil in the convert's life, though perhaps in domains far removed from the explicit concerns of religion (Downton, 1979; Frank, 1963; Lofland & Stark, 1965; Underwood, 1925). Indeed, the early steps in many conversion strategies call for proselytizers to locate and intensify sources of ambivalence in the potential converts' lives, as is done, for example, in est training. It is relatively rare for Stage II to proceed outside of awareness; if there is ambivalence, the "agony of Saint Augustine" is more common than the apparently unconflicted pursuit of an opposite commitment like that of Saint Paul, who was an active persecutor of Christians until his sudden conversion on the road to Damascus. This type of conversion, however, is possible. One question for future research is what the consequences are of passing through Stage II with greater or lesser awareness for the future development and stability of the commitment. Without a direct and considered confrontation of the potentially negative elements, a commitment may be formed with weaker roots. Thus, a commitment that approaches Stage II gradually and passes through it thoughtfully may have better prospects for lasting than one that moves through it quickly and dramatically. For example, Starbuck (1912) found that 87% of 92 revival converts reverted within six months, whereas only 40% of a group of gradual converts lapsed in the same period.

It is also true that any of these stages can be prolonged, in some cases to the detriment of the commitment ultimately formed. Stage I can be prolonged simply because there is no negative element to challenge a line of behavior and force a commitment or an exit. It can also be prolonged by persons trying to avoid making a commitment. Procrastination, indecisiveness, buck-passing, disclaiming, perpetual joking, denial of responsibility, and callousness may all be understood—and explored in future research—as devices to this end. Stage II is prolonged when it is not possible for a person either to reach a solution to his or her ambivalence or to exit from the situation. This can be an intensely painful experience. Classic animal studies by Pavlov (1927) and Masserman (1943) have shown that animals become paralyzed and highly emotional when confronted with a discrimination they must make (e.g., to escape shock) but which has gradually been made too subtle for them to make. The classic psychoanalytic definition of neurosis is essentially a prolonged Stage II crisis in which one element of the conflict (either an unacknowledged fear or an unacknowledged impulse) is unconscious. As we see below, in our discussion of Weiss's (1975, 1976) analysis of ambivalence in separation, the prolongation of a Stage II crisis while the commitment dissolves is extraordinarily painful.

Stage III is prolonged when a residual tension remains to energize the commitment or when the commitment is not allowed to relax because the ambivalence that preceded it cannot be fully absorbed. Commitments fixed at this stage look like pathological rigidity or fanaticism (issues to which we will return in the next chapter). Commitments of this form may sometimes be sought as desirable, as in the case of romantic passion, and deliberate efforts may be made to prolong them. As celebrated (and lamented) in literature and song, these efforts typically involve the introduction into the relationship of new challenges, tests, and difficulties— which may sustain or rekindle passion but may also place the relationship in new peril.

Stage IV is prolonged, like Stage II, when it is not possible for a person either to reach a new synthesis or to exit. A prolonged Stage IV crisis takes the form of persistent boredom and self-absorption. Finally, the attainment of Stage V does not, of course, mean the end of change. Over the years, numerous new negative elements will demand new syntheses that in turn evolve their own antitheses, as in the dialectical process we discussed in opening this chapter. New crises may return a commitment to all the turmoil and uncertainty of Stage II, although this is less a case of regression than it is the experience of an analogous stage in what can be understood as a further commitment cycle, or even a decommitment cycle. One of the leading questions for future research is how the handling of different sorts of positive and negative elements, alternative commitments, and so forth differs according to the maturity of the existing commitment or the number of previous syntheses on which this commitment rests. For example, we hypothesize that long-term Stage V commitments may eventually accumulate so much intrinsic motivation and meaning that they become overwhelming. Some kind of pruning or reduction of this meaning and value may be necessary for the commitment to survive. Research on couples who have been married twenty or more years or individuals in the same job for similar lengths of time would provide fascinating evidence on this issue.

To summarize, we hypothesize that the formation of commitment involves a five-stage process. Commitments begin when positive, extrinsic rewards encourage individuals to pursue a particular activity. Eventually, negative aspects of the activity become salient; at this point individuals either withdraw from the activity, and a commitment never forms, or they continue. If they continue, they do so because they have somehow created intrinsic meaning by integrating these negative elements with positive elements. Such syntheses involve not a denial of negative factors but their transformation into something positive; we love our partner because of his or her flaws rather than in spite of them. After this synthesis, there is a stable period, but eventually a new crisis evolves. Whereas the first major antithesis involved external factors, this second major antithesis involves internal factors. Now that the desired activity is achieved, individuals begin to question if it is really what they want. This crisis of familiarity must be resolved for the final stage to be achieved. In the final stage, commitments are not static; instead, they involve a continual ebb and flow in which negative elements are raised and resolved. It is our contention that negative elements inevitably arise, due to either external or internal forces. Thus commitments are always growing and evolving—just as the individual who holds the commitment continually grows and evolves.

The five stages are distinguished by differences in the rates of change occurring, perceptions of control, degrees of playfulness and freedom, approach-avoidance orientations, and cognitive categorization. Progression through the stages is invariant, but the pace is not, nor is an individual always aware of his or her progression. Stages may appear as if they have been skipped, and they may also be prolonged. The extent of such variation is a fascinating issue for future research.

THE DISSOLUTION OF COMMITMENTS

There are two apparently contradictory elements in people's experience of breaking commitments or losing objects of commitment. The first is the unexpected suddenness with which desirable commitments may end, often triggered by a seemingly minor event in a manner that appears to catch one or both parties by surprise. The underpinnings of the commitment had apparently been eroded without at least one party having been aware that this had taken place. This can refer either to the person's own commitment ("I awoke one day and suddenly I realized that the feeling was gone") or to the perception of another person's commitment ("I had not realized that her feelings had changed until one day she told me that she was leaving").

The second puzzle concerning the breaking of commitments is the agonizing slowness with which undesirable commitments seem to fully dissolve. Years later, someone who has left the church or lost a marital partner may encounter situations or stimuli that remind him or her of this past commitment and cause him or her to reexperience in miniature the entire process of grief and emotional loss (Weiss, 1975). In the more immediate aftermath of a major commitment, people may feel that they have done the right thing in relinquishing that commitment and that there was nothing they could have done to prevent the loss of that commitment. Yet they find themselves engaged in an endless, obsessive review of past events, a review they know to be fruitless and punishing but are still unable to avoid. Our analysis provides a clue to both of these puzzles. The apparent slowness with which commitments are eroded, and the apparent suddenness with which the feelings associated with them vanish, refer to different stages of the process of commitment withdrawal—a process which, in its essentials, seems quite parallel to the process by which commitments are established in the first place, though the affective quality of the different stages is in general more turbulent, intense, and painful. Such stages in the ending of a commitment are explored in a preliminary fashion in the following section.

Stages in the Dissolution of a Commitment

Stage I in the process of ending a commitment is a stage in which the basis of the commitment is gradually, often imperceptibly eroded. A person carries out a series of small actions that are increasingly discrepant with the nature of the commitment or observes a series of such actions carried out by a partner. For example, a married individual may become progressively more and more involved in an extramarital affair, but in tiny, inconspicuous increments. Ordinarily, in strong commitment systems, these actions are defended against (either before or after they occur) by psychological reactions of guilt or jealousy, which serve to flag them, inhibit them, or motivate people to try to undo them after they have occurred (emotional means of defending commitments will be discussed at greater length in the next chapter). If the defenses or inhibitions against discrepant acts fail, however, there will nonetheless usually be no immediately dramatic emotional consequences. This process is one of small but unresolved antitheses accumulating over time. As in our catastrophe theory representation, feelings are at this point relatively stable and inelastic. This leaves people unprepared for the fact that with further discrepant acts they will move into a region in which their feelings change suddenly or catastrophically. The image is of rolling down a gentle slope and then over a cliff.

In the first phase of commitment dissolution, like the first phase of commitment formation, there is no hint of this point of discontinuity. In a series of economic and political illustrations, Hirschman (1970) notes that consumers or voters may grumble for a long time (exercising "voice," if there is anyone to hear their complaints) before taking the much more drastic and decisive step of switching the product they buy or the party they vote for ("exiting"). The loyalty of at least a substantial number of such consumers or voters, and the attendant inertia in their behavior, has the functional advantage of giving the company or the party some lead time to correct its mistakes before it loses its entire membership. This, of course, requires that people (or at least some people) be sensitive enough to the problem to report it while they (or others, in our collective example) simultaneously are insensitive enough to it to persist in their present relationship.

Stage II in the ending of a commitment is the discovery of renewed ambivalence and reentry into the associated state of emotional turmoil. There is a kind of shock to this stage, and also a general intensification of behavior designed to protest, deny, or ward off the loss. This stage thus corresponds to the invigoration stage of Klinger's (1975) analysis of the process of disengagement from incentives, and to the protest stage of Bowlby's (1960, 1973) theory of attachment and loss. Freudenberger (1974) and other students of burnout among helping professionals report that immediately prior to burnout there is often a period in which the volunteer or the professional increases his or her investment in the halfway house, working longer hours, assuming more and more responsibility for the fate of clients. More generally, the person alternates between periods of intense effort to sustain or repair the commitment and periods of collapse or escape. One of the most painful aspects of this process is the switching between times of hope and times of despair and the cost of being on an emotional roller coaster. As Weiss (1975) notes, it is the joy of repeated reconciliations that intensifies the agony of subsequent disappointments, quarrels, and estrangements, while of course the agony of the latter likewise intensifies the pleasure of the former. Novelist John Fowles (1977) describes this "hopeless downward progression" with great poignancy:

> Such changes in a person's character, and in the character of a relationship, don't announce themselves dramatically; they steal slowly over months, masking themselves behind reconciliations, periods of happiness, new resolves. Like some forms of lethal disease, they invite every myth of comforting explanation before they exact the truth. (p. 90)

There is considerable evidence that high expectations, which are ordinarily conducive to success, may lead to pathological forms of persistence and costly life disasters when the goal being sought is in fact impossible to obtain (Janoff-Bulman & Brickman, 1981). And no expectation is likely to be stronger than the one people hold for something they have always been able to expect, and to get, in the past. At the same time, however, as the object of their commitment becomes more frustrating and remote, people tend to become both attracted and repulsed by it. One kind of evidence for this growing ambivalence is the alternately detached and clinging behavior exhibited both by young children (Bowlby, 1973) and young monkeys (Kaufman, 1969) when reunited with their mothers after a period of separation. They are both angry at their mothers for having left, happy that they have returned, and fearful that they will leave again—a complex set of emotions that has no simple behavioral expression. This stage in decommitment is one of a slowly developing major crisis, much like a slow growing tumor.

The third stage in the breaking of commitments involves the dismantling of the perceptual field that was created when the commitment was formed and has existed and sustained the commitment since that time. The shuttling back and forth between attraction and repulsion of Stage II is superseded by a stable anticommitment, a strong and coherent negative orientation to the former object of commitment. In catastrophe theory terms, this is the state that exists after people have completed their tumble from the prior positive orientation. Stage II may be thought of as a period in which people are caught in the process of tumbling, trying to and at times succeeding in scrambling back, but in general caught in the turmoil of change. Stage III corresponds to Klinger's (1975) stage of aggression or Bowlby's (1973) stage of anger as reactions to the loss of the commitment object. This stage represents the orientation of zealous ex-converts, who are now as active in proselytizing against the sect or cult they have left as they once were in proselytizing for it. If the passage through Stage II of commitment withdrawal has been brief, it may seem as if the person has suddenly switched from being committed one way to being committed another. This is also the period in which people undertake that process of reconstructing the past to make it compatible with (and, indeed, a component of) their new commitment orientation. What were once seen as minor flaws in a relationship, for example, will now be seen as fatal weaknesses that were found, sooner or later, to disrupt the relationship. Since there is a quality of new synthesis to Stage III, it might be seen as one involving integration toward a new state or object of commitment.

Stage IV in commitment dissolution sets in with the erosion of the emotional anticommitment. Anticommitment, in turn, is even more difficult to sustain than most Stage III passions, since it must fight against and overcome what is (if the past commitment has been strong) an extensive and unruly residue of attachment. As the negative commitment erodes and some ambivalence reasserts itself, feelings of sadness, loss, and grief set in. In Stage II of commitment loss, attachment to the commitment object was still dominant, and the ambivalence centered on the newly recognized negative features of that object (e.g., disinterest or hostility on the part of a relationship partner). In Stage IV of commitment loss, detachment from that object is now dominant, and the ambivalence centers on newly recognized positive features of that object that are incompatible with the negative Stage III anticommitment.

Weiss (1976) describes the often unexpected persistence of attachment in this period as "echo effects" of the lost commitment. Separated or divorced couples are often taken aback by how much they not only miss one another but still enjoy—at least for brief periods—one another's company, which may lead, for a while, to a strange situation:

> Having told their family and their lawyers how much they have suffered at each other's hands, a husband and wife can hardly admit that they now look forward to evenings together. As a result, some couples may temporarily adopt a bizarre variation of the marital practice of hiding fights from public view; now they may be estranged in public but affectionate in private. (Weiss, 1976, p. 44)

Divorce lawyers are regularly frustrated by what appear to be clients' irrational changes of mind during this period of obsessive, interminable review by people of what went wrong, including a search for causes or explanations (Harvey, Wells, & Alvarez, 1978), especially explanations that provide some reassurance that the same thing will not happen again in the future. Much of the terror and loneliness that characterize this stage in the loss of a major life commitment derive from the fact that the person has lost a major source of meaning and value in his or her life and hence must cope not only with inner feelings of ambivalence about and grief for the loss, but also with a sense of inner emptiness that makes the beginning of a search for alternatives all the more difficult. This stage, like the previous ones, has been described for people coming out of religious cults (Singer, 1979) in a manner strikingly similar to the manner in which they have been described for people coming out of marital relationships (Weiss, 1975, 1976). Stage IV in the decommitment process clearly corresponds, in its affective tone, to the stage of depression or apathy in the analyses of Klinger (1975) and Bowlby (1973).

If the positive feelings for the commitment object have been lost, slowly and then drastically, in Stages I, II, and III of commitment loss, it may appear something of a puzzle to determine what fuels the sense of loss or grief of Stage IV. We explain much of it as the encounter with the sense of emptiness that has replaced the earlier emotions (both positive and negative). Weiss (1976), however, also draws an instructive distinction between attachment and love:

> Most people would seem to think of love as a condition combining positive regard for another with urgent desire to maintain the other's accessibility. Rubin (1973) has shown that love is ordinarily a syndrome including a number of components such as trust, idealization, and liking which can exist independently of one another. Attachment would be one such component. It would appear that in unhappy marriages most of the components of love fade, sometimes to be replaced by their opposites. In this way trust may change to mistrust, idealization to disrespect, liking to disdain. Attachment, however, seems to persist. It appears that most components of love are modifiable by negative experience, but that attachment once developed can be sustained by proximity alone and fades only slowly in response to absence. (pp. 138–139)

The fifth and final stage in the commitment dissolution process involves a gradual decline in the importance of the old commitment accompanied by an increasing occupation of the person's life space by new or alternative commitments. This is most akin to the process of beginning a commitment but with a new target. There is a sense in which old commitments, like old soldiers, never die; they just fade away. The person may appear to achieve a return to indifference toward the object of commitment, but this indifference is more apparent than real; it has within it elements that make it quite different from the kind of indifference the person might have felt before the involvement. It is an indifference sustained by the stable capacity to look away, stay away, and find meaning and value in other domains and other commitments, rather than an indifference of no interest or no repulsion at all.

In this sense, recovery from the loss of a vital commitment, like the recovery from any major life trauma, is never complete, and, as Silver and Wortman (1980) make clear in their review of the literature on coping with undesirable life events, any stage theory that implies that it is complete in this sense is dangerously misleading. Similarly, one can recover from an injury or an operation and function as well as or better than before, but scars will remain, sensitive when touched. "At anniversaries, for example, or when an old friend comes to call unexpectedly or when a forgotten photograph is discovered in a drawer all the feelings or acute pining and sadness return and the bereaved person goes through, in miniature, another bereavement" (Parkes, 1970b, p. 464). At first, any small reminder may be sufficient to trigger some such reaction. Eventually, it may take a fairly strong or prolonged exposure to trigger a reaction. One couple known to one of the authors had come to the following understanding of their relationship years after separation. "We are still friends, but we have learned that we can have about five good hours together. After that, we start getting on each other's nerves again." (See also Weiss, 1976). They tried to make good use of this time together when they could and not to ask for more. The reaction to the ex-commitment object, depicted in this fashion, is allergic. There may be no feelings in its absence, and fond feelings in its anticipation or early contact, but eventually there are elicited some of the feelings—either irritation or sadness—that accompanied the commitment itself, and which mark the person experiencing them as different from someone who had never had that commitment. This stage is clearly analogous to Klinger's (1975) recovery stage.

If the commitment involved has been minor, this entire set of stages may be swept through without incident, or with only minor emotional work. For example, if a person is unable to see a movie that he or she had especially wanted to see, all of the above steps may be triggered: a period in which the events that make this impossible occur without the person's awareness, a point of ambivalence when this is realized, a moment of anger, a feeling of loss, and a turning to other activities. In this case, the object is so unimportant, and the number of satisfactory alternatives so great, that the recovery stage may be quite transient. Nonetheless, we would still expect such a person to feel differently about the missed movie than a person who had never intended to see it in the first place or who didn't care one way or the other.

The Role of Alternatives in the Ending of Commitments

Since the role of making alternative commitments is so important both to the unraveling of existing commitments (the alternatives representing the discrepant acts that in Stage I begin to undermine the existing commitment) and to the repairing of damage once commitments have been unraveled, it is clear that we need research that focuses on the relationship between growing and declining commitments. What difference does it make to the growth of a new commitment—the pace with which it passes through various stages, the nature of the difficulties it encounters—whether it begins when an old commitment is still intact or when an old commitment has partially or completely unraveled? What difference does the stage of a commitment that is being completed make to the process by which any new commitments may develop? Marriages and careers are both marked by a series of smaller commitments that gradually overlap and replace one another, even when the marriage or career retains its essential shape. The process by which marital partners accommodate their commitment to children or to each other, to a new career interest on the part of one of them (or the process by which researchers test out later career involvements in teaching, editing, or administration) should be fertile grounds for the investigation of these questions. The process by which adolescent children leave home, of which there are many variations, some even peaceful (Goleman, 1980), is another example. Goleman's discussion of work in this area seems to indicate that the difficulty of the transition is related not so much to the strength of the initial commitment to home life but to the quality and nature of the conflicts embedded in that commitment. Adolescents who are most conflicted about leaving home—both pulled to leave and pulled to stay—have the hardest time making the transition. In our terms, they are most likely to be trapped in Stage II or Stage IV emotions.

One study that sheds some light on the process by which new commitments supplant old ones is the senior honors thesis done by Philip Brickman (1964) on how Harvard students move closer to what they perceive to be Harvard norms rather than the norms of their home town, family, and high school. This study found that the event of going home for Christmas vacation was an important episode in this change process, with students rating themselves as closer to Harvard norms after they returned than before they went. Upon arriving at Harvard earlier in the fall, students were no doubt made highly aware of features in their accents, background, training, and dress that were characteristic of their places of origin. Thus their initial experience of Harvard made them more, rather than less, conscious of their prior identity—and, we hypothesize, more committed to that prior identity, both in reaction to pressure to change and out of nostalgia for valued elements of their past that were now out of reach. Ironically, at the same time, small changes were taking place that in fact represented the beginnings of the acquisition of an identity as a Harvard student. These changes only surfaced in awareness, in many instances, when students returned home, perhaps full of nostalgia and happy to be back, only to be told by the folks at home, "What happened to you? You're so different! Harvard has changed you." Small characteristics, habits, and possessions that were undistinguishing at Harvard are highly noticeable badges of identity in home territory. Furthermore, the act of displaying and defending such new characteristics may enhance one's commitment to them. Thus we can isolate certain processes of commitment change that take place in the absence of the object of commitment and others that take place in the renewed presence of that object. The former are likely to be small and imperceptible; the latter are those that entail the emotional consequences of recognizing and reacting to the former. This same dynamic, we think, is part of what makes it hard for even the best-intentioned and most loving couples to survive long periods of separation (as is regularly shown, for example, by postwar divorce statistics). Even as they are missing one another and feeling more loving than ever before, they are changing in small ways that may prove irreconcilable when they get back together again.

Can a broken commitment, like Humpty Dumpty, but put back together again? Yes, but not in its original form. The reconstructed commitment must have, as one of its constituent elements, the knowledge that it has been broken and can always be broken. With this additional history, it is therefore like a new commitment. Some commitments thus pass through a more extended cycle in which they alternately are made and broken, as do those of couples who (at least for a time) repeatedly break up and make up.

Variations in Patterns
of Commitment Endings

There are two important variations in the circumstances under which commitments are dissolved, in addition to the usual pattern described above. The first is the case in which an object of commitment is taken away—through the departure, death, or failure of some sort by the person—before any of the psychological processes involved in relinquishing that commitment have begun. The loss of a commitment object can result, for example, from a sudden, unexpected, and traumatic accident. In this case, the psychological commitment may be intensified rather than diminished by the loss. Although we would expect people to still pass through the decommitment stages we have outlined before that commitment is relinquished, their journey through these stages may be delayed or otherwise altered in ways that can only be tested in future research. The fact that the object of commitment has been definitively and decisively lost at the start in a manner that cannot be altered by any future behavior would certainly have implications for decommitment.

The second variation is when the end of a commitment is anticipated long in advance, perhaps even from the point at which the commitment is initiated. These are time-limited or *temporary commitments*. In such cases, people might prefer to hold back their emotional investments because they know what it will cost to relinquish such investments. Time and again, however, people find that what they had entered into as temporary arrangements draw them in much further than they had anticipated—as amply demonstrated by our review of the literature on the cumulative effects of choice. A case in point is an instance in which a couple sets a deadline for parting—the end of a summer, the end of a year, a time when one or another party would have to go back to another job or another relationship. This termination date seems reasonable and agreeable to both parties at the time it is set, but it eventually places a tremendous burden on the relationship. One party encounters unexpected and increasing distress as the end approaches, and the other becomes increasingly irritable and withdrawn in response. Even people who know, rationally, that the end of a current situation would be a good thing, and who have been anticipating the end for a long time, may find themselves reacting with panic and dismay as the end actually approaches. In political science, the phrase "terminal horror" has been coined to describe the response of voters who, at the last minute, wind up voting for the incumbent president rather than an opposition candidate whom they have supported all along. The incumbent is a known quantity, however unattractive, whereas the opposition candidate raises the prospect of unknown levels of change. It is well known in prisons and mental hospitals that some inmates exhibit more unruly or disturbed behavior as the time for their release approaches, expressing indirectly their ambivalence about leaving and sometimes compelling the institution to keep them longer.

With regard to time-limited commitments, or commitments that are known to be temporary right from the start, the critical difference is whether people enter into them because they are temporary or in spite of the fact that they are temporary. Many tasks, for example, are ones that people are willing to make a commitment to doing precisely because they know they will be completed, and can be forgotten, in a reasonable period of time. The commitment, in this case, is to the completion, rather than the continuation, of the task. The well-known Zeigarnik effect (see Chapter 3) describes the fact that, in such instances, people are extraordinarily aware of the task until it is completed, and eager to return to it if interrupted, and quite unmindful of it—unable to recall details, uninterested in it—afterwards. The original observation of this was of German waiters in a particular restaurant, who kept all customers' tabs in their heads until the customers had paid their bills, then promptly forgot them. People go to see movies knowing they will end, eager to see how they end, and comfortably aware of the fact that other movies and comparable opportunities will be available upon their completion of the current one.

The initial effect of knowing and welcoming the fact that a commitment is temporary, we hypothesize, will be to reduce conflict about getting involved and facilitate passage through Stage II ambivalence. Costs, like the commitment itself, are known to be temporary. On the other hand, accepting a commitment as temporary may also make it less likely that people will experience a Stage IV crisis, precipitated by their being forced to consider the nature and extent of their intrinsic motivation to continue the commitment. They may be able to bypass this question simply by knowing that the commitment will soon be over. Finally, accepting a commitment as temporary makes it most likely that people will experience a strong goal gradient effect, or an intensification of motivation (and an increasing degree of upset at being interrupted) as the goal approaches. (This is in contrast to the pattern of motivation we expect for commitments reluctantly accepted as temporary, as discussed subsequently.)

A good example of this pattern—together with a good example of a rather different pattern—is the way in which undergraduates, as opposed to graduate students, get involved in research projects with faculty. In general, it never occurs to undergraduates that their involvement is other than temporary; in most instances, they are committed only to doing well, learning something, and acquiring a credential. For graduate students, on the other hand, a career and an identity rest in part on the project, and they have a keen sense that their involvement is likely to be open-ended rather than limited. Undergraduates thus get involved more quickly and with less ambivalence, less subsequent questioning of the intrinsic value of the experience, and more eagerness to finish.

Accepting a commitment in spite of the fact that it is temporary, on the other hand, should lead to a very different pattern of involvement. It should first delay involvement and escalate ambivalence, as people weigh not only the usual costs of involvement but the additional cost of knowing the benefits they might like will not continue indefinitely, or that the value of their adaptation will only be temporary. When they do get involved, however, we would expect their involvement to be all the more intense because it represents the surmounting of this intensified ambivalence. This helps account for some of the heightened, idyllic, bittersweet quality of summer romances or vacation experiences in general. The commitment itself is likely to end before a Stage IV crisis, or a questioning of intrinsic motivation, has arisen. But there is a sense in which the approaching end of the commitment provokes something like a Stage IV crisis, but one in which subjects are oriented to relinquish, rather than overcome, their motivation to continue, because they know that continuation is impossible.

This may also account for the characteristic inverted U-shaped curve found to depict the involvement of sojourners in foreign cultures (e.g., Gullahorn & Gullahorn, 1960) or prisons (Wheeler, 1961; Clark, 1976) or colleges (see the earlier discussion of the study by Hamilton & Jacque, 1977). The peak of involvement by travelers with their host country, its norms and habits, is intermediate in their stay; likewise, the peak of involvement by prison inmates with what has been called inmate culture (featuring, especially, antiguard norms) seems to be intermediate in their term of imprisonment. Before this, newcomers do not know enough to become effectively involved with the local culture and may be hesitant to become involved both because of their ignorance and because of their fear of losing valued past identities. Later, as the end of their stay approaches, sojourners begin to anticipate returning to the world from which they came, shedding some of the new values and customs they have acquired in anticipation of this return. Nonetheless, when they do return to this world, the Brickman study (1964) suggests that they will be further surprised to discover how much their travel has changed them in small ways that they did not even recognize. Thus, although accepting commitments because they are temporary speeds up the process of involvement, allows involvement to be more casual, and causes involvement to peak as the end approaches, accepting commitments in spite of the fact that they are temporary delays involvement, forces involvement to be more serious, and causes involvement to peak part way through the sequence of events and to decline as the end approaches.

In summary, two elements of the experience of ending commitments have been highlighted. One is the unexpected suddenness with which desirable commitments appear to end and the other element is the agonizing slowness with which undesirable commitments typically seem to dissolve. The dissolution process is proposed to parallel the process by which commitments are established. Stages in the ending of commitment that are suggested are as follows: first, a stage of gradual erosion; second, a stage of growing emotional turmoil and ambivalence; third, a stage of dismantling the perceptual field; fourth, a stage of lessened emotional attachment but parting grief and loss; and finally, a stage of the fading away of the importance of the object.

The role of conflicting commitments in supplanting existing ones was explored. Also, two variations on the standard pattern of commitment dissolution were explained, one in which the object of the commitment is taken away or lost, and the second in which the commitment was always temporary, having occurred either because of this or despite it.

COMMITMENT THROUGHOUT
THE LIFE CYCLE

There is a developmental sequence not only to individual commitments but to the manner in which people make and sustain commitments over the course of the life cycle. The clue to the characteristic difference between commitment in adults and children can be found in what each group envies about the other. Children envy adults' predecision freedom, while adults are nostalgic for children's postdecision freedom. Children see adults as having many choices or many options that are not available to them. They have to wait until they are older before they can stay up as late as they would like, go places on their own, and in general do all the desirable things they perceive adults as able to do. Adults, on the other hand, often remember childhood as a time when they had a sense of freedom they have now lost or now experience much more rarely. This freedom, they believe, came from the ability to feel free in relatively impoverished environments, to make do with a few simple things, to be enthusiastic about a particular activity without regard for the fact that other activities might also be competing for time and attention. In the language of Brickman's (1978) essay on what makes people treat things as real, children take for granted internal correspondence (that their actions correspond with their feelings) and work to achieve external correspondence (that their actions will have desired or appropriate consequences on their environment). Adults are better able to assume external correspondence and more likely to have to struggle for internal correspondence.

We are socialized to ambivalence: to think first, not act first; to anticipate consequences, difficulties and conflicts; to remember past courses of action and where they went wrong; and to deal with possible objections that may be raised to our choices by an inner observer (the internalized other) who represents all those people who have praised and criticized us in the past. As children grow older, they become more aware of contradictions between their judgements at one time and their judgements at another time, and they become more concerned with avoiding these contradictions (Piaget, 1972; Kohlberg, 1969). They become more aware of discrepancies between the kind of person they would like to be (ideal self-image) and the kind of person they actually are (real self-image; see Katz and Zigler, 1967). They become more aware of the extent to which situations are ambiguous, the extent to which human knowledge is limited, and even the extent to which their own mastery of the knowledge that exists in a particular field is limited—a process Fox (1979) has eloquently discussed as one of the explicit aims of medical education.

All of these things make choice harder. Where there is more ambivalence— more complex alternatives and consequences to be considered—it is more difficult to select a single course of action as best. This is especially true, as Mann and Taylor (1970) have shown in a study of college women's choices among paintings, when the decision is understood to be irrevocable and one that they would later have to justify publicly. More decisions appear to have this quality as individuals grow older. As children grow older, they come to attach more qualifications to the inferences they make about themselves and others (Leahy, 1976). They also become more reflective and less impulsive in their problem-solving style, for example, in taking more time to decide which of six closely related stimuli is the correct answer to a question (Mussen, Conger, & Kagan, 1974). If images are related to simple and unconflicted decision making, these changes may also be related to the fact that children seem more likely to use imagery than adults (Kosslyn, 1976).

And yet we are also socialized not only to act in the face of this ambivalence but to act in a consistent, persistent fashion that other people can predict and count on (Becker, 1960). As children grow older, they are more likely to be rated by teachers as showing self-control—keeping promises, maintaining a steady quality of work, being patient, working for long-range goals, sticking to one thing (Kendall & Wilcox, 1979). Older children are more likely to choose moderately difficult tasks to work on, whereas younger children choose easy tasks (Veroff, 1969). Some of this more consistent and persistent quality of behavior is achieved by routinization and practice. People do things repeatedly, become good at them, come to like them, and then do not have to make many conscious choices in doing them (as we saw in our earlier discussion of mindlessness). Another part of developmental change, however, refers to a more self-conscious awareness of making commitments, of seeing future events as contingent on present decisions, and of accepting the implications of this awareness. Both components contribute to a growing perception of a part of the self as constant, immovable, or nonvolitional—that is, fixed by past habits, past obligations, and past choices. Part of the self thus becomes experienced as part of the world, and the difference between awareness of self and awareness of the world (what Wicklund and Duval, 1971, call objective and subjective self-awareness) decreases.

Thus, if adults have a greater capacity for commitment, they also have a greater need for it. Because they have more ambivalence to overcome, they have a greater need for their actions to have symbolic justification. We hypothesize that as children have less ability to delay gratification (to postpone the time at which they will receive a reward in order to receive a larger reward), adults have less ability to delay justification (to postpone coming up with reasons for their behavior in order eventually to come up with better reasons or better understanding).

In general, adults also have less pure motives but better reasons for their behavior. Some of this is very nicely illustrated in the developmental literature on changes in individuals' orientations to friends and friendship. In a pilot study carried out by Brickman with Lisa Fritz and Lynn Paxton, six third and fourth graders and six high school seniors, all females, were interviewed about their best friends. The younger children were uninhibited and enthusiastic in explaining their friendship choices in extrinsic terms: The friend has nice toys, the friend lives close by, the friend is nice, the two of them are a club. The older subjects uniformly used a very different language: I trust and appreciate her, I love her, I dare to act myself with her, we understand each other, we can confide in each other. All six of the older subjects said they loved their best friend; none of the younger subjects did. Selman and Selman (1979) report that younger children are more likely to see friendship as justified by the fact that it satisfies the separate self-interests of each participant and as reasonable to end when this is not the case; older children are more likely to see friendship as collaboration with others for mutual and common interests, including the sharing of plans and feelings; still older subjects are aware of the risks, uncertainties, and commitment involved in friendship. Berndt (1981) found that older children were more likely to mention intimacy, trust, loyalty, and faithfulness as aspects of friendship. Horrocks and Mussman (1973) and others found that altruistic wishes increased with age (and materialistic ones declined).

The literature on friendship has generally interpreted these findings as indicating that children acquire a richer, more internal, and more differentiated conception of friendship with age. Our analysis does not contest this development, but it offers a somewhat different view of what it means. Adults and older children are not necessarily less aware of or less concerned with what benefits they get from friendship or what extrinsically desirable features their friends have. They are, however, more aware of what friendship costs and what investments are required to maintain a friendship. A simple cost-benefit accounting is not sufficient to sustain commitment to a friendship through difficult times, nor is it sufficient as a public account or explanation of that friendship. The more psychological, symbolic, and intrinsic language with which older children and adults describe friendship derives, in our view, from developmental changes in their own complex and ambivalent motivations toward other people.

One thing that enables adults to sustain often conflicting commitments in the face of considerable ambivalence is their acquired ability to compartmentalize, ignore, lie, delay, and procrastinate. Older children are better than younger children at focusing their attention on one thing and tuning out other things that would be distracting (Lane, 1980; Zuckier & Hagen, 1978). This is, of course, a critical element in the capacity for commitment and self-control. It is also, according to Newman (1976), a critical element in adults' ability to manage conflict in interpersonal relationships by smoothing over or ignoring uncomfortable episodes (see also Goffman, 1961). Children's friendships are more volatile—best friends today are enemies tomorrow and friends again the day after—in part because children are more wholeheartedly involved in each episode as it occurs. Once adults do get involved in a negative episode, on the other hand (e.g., taking sides in a fight between their own children and those of a neighbor), the conflict is much more likely to have enduring consequences, again because of the greater tendency of adult behavior to require and involve substantial commitment.

At what age do children begin to have the capacity to make commitments in our sense? Certainly some parts of what we regard as commitment are present in very young children. Gunnar-Vongnechten (1978) has shown that children as young as a year old are reassured by having the ability to determine when a potentially frightening mechanical toy started, a process that in part rests (as we have argued in the control chapter) on their ability to make a commitment to seeing the toy move. There is also a definite sense in which learning to walk and talk are commitments, ones that are highly programmed to succeed in the face of difficulties, falls, errors, and other setbacks. Yet these are relatively unconflicted commitments, as we can recognize by the very fact that they are so highly programmed to succeed. Except in the most unusual of cases, there are no important alternative attractions, no serious temptations not to learn to walk or talk, and no important opposition to walking or talking by parents or other sources.

The first great Stage II crisis is the crisis of toilet training, thumb-sucking, table manners, or some other such primary battle of socialization. Two sources of gratification are pitted against one another: the pleasure of bodily impulses or uninhibited behavior and the pleasure of parental love, warmth, and approval. Virtually all developmental theorists (e.g., Ilg & Ames, 1981) have postulated that it is out of this primary conflict that the child first comes to acquire some sense of responsibility and some sense of self. This sense of responsibility and self is defined, in the first instance, by the child's ability to say no to parental demands. But whether the child defends his or her own impulses and resists parental pressures or seeks parental approval and relinquishes the pleasures of being dirty or sloppy, he or she must in either case make a significant commitment to the chosen line of behavior because that line of behavior involves abandoning another important source of gratification. The child can make a choice—indeed, must make a choice—that involves both positive and negative elements, and he or she will be held responsibile for that choice and its consequences.

Eventually, out of the child's need to justify his or her ambivalent abandonment of instinctual pleasures (including, according to Freud, the impossible wish for sexual gratification with the opposite-sex parent) comes the first major commitment synthesis: the internalization of the parents as the resolution of this crisis. The period of inner conflict is settled with the arrival of a stable solution in which identification with parental wishes, prohibitions, and attributes is given great symbolic value, and contrary impulses are denied or repressed.

In general, we think that children are most likely to make what look like Stage I commitments. As we saw in our discussion of friendship, they are most likely to focus on the extrinsic properties (and indeed the overt physical characteristics, Livesley & Bromley, 1973) of others. They prefer to view real, physical rewards rather than symbolic or pictorial representations of these rewards, even when the presence of the real rewards makes it harder for them to wait the required period of time needed to obtain these rewards (Yates & Mischel, 1979). Their perceptual processes have been described as stimulus bound rather than internally (or socially) regulated. Thus Mackworth and Bruner (1970) write that visual search must develop from a point at which gaze is controlled by the stimulus object and its features to one in which it is actively directed by the perceiver in the service of his or her own aims. Gibson (1969) describes attention as something that changes from being captured to being exploratory as children mature. At a symbolic level, the social judgments of younger children (e.g., of the appropriate length of sentence for a transgressor; see Saltzstein, Supraner, & Sanvitale, 1976) are more subject to direct attempts to influence them than are those of older children. Harter (1981) found that younger children are more likely to rely on the teacher's judgment in classroom situations and less likely to have internal criteria for success and failure. Children's behavior is, in general, more volatile and changeable—again, exemplified by their orientation to friends. This is what we would expect of behavior that has not in general been confronted with the task of mastering and integrating Stage II ambivalence. Children are probably more curious than adults, but their curiosity does not have the disciplined, purposeful, systematic quality that marks that of adults. There is much to be said for playful curiosity as opposed to worklike activity, but nothing is gained by pretending that there is no difference between the two.

Adolescents are most likely to make Stage III commitments, passionate and intense and extreme. Ambivalence is at its most intense at adolescence, when differentiation has outstripped integration. Adolescents have become aware that they are different people in different situations and relationships and that each of these makes different demands and offers new opportunities, and yet they have no sense of how to resolve these disorienting pulls and pushes. The carefree way in which roles are tried on just for fun and fantasy in childhood is replaced by a more self-conscious, agonized awareness of the costs, benefits, and ambiguities involved in each choice (Douvan, 1974). Not the least of the conflicts in adolescence are those between the personal solutions evolved in childhood—the childhood personality—and the pressures for very different forms of behavior. These pressures arise both from biological maturation and from often drastic shifts in cultural expectations (Benedict, 1938). Thus, once again, the adolescent is caught between a desire to maintain the pleasures of childhood ways and social pressures to abandon these ways for mature forms of behavior, with both tendencies blurred and confused by an emerging and ambivalent sexuality.

So adolescence is a period of exploring alternatives, testing limits, and struggling for identity and freedom. Of all age groups, adolescents are most likely to be immobilized, to feel unable to act, and to worry (Gurin, Veroff, & Feld, 1960; Veroff, 1978). When they do act, their actions—as we would expect—are most likely to take extreme forms. These extreme forms can be quite contradictory, and the same adolescent can move from one variety to another. Thus, Kenniston (1960, 1968) has found adolescents embodying both the most intense forms of personal and social alienation and the most intense forms of active involvement and commitment to a political cause. Adolescents are both idealistic and cynical about friendship (Douvan & Adelson, 1966). Their need for identity or for some unification of their disparate fragments is so great, according to Erikson (1959), that if they cannot achieve a positive identity (i.e., one that conforms to norms valued by society, such as achievement in school), they will seek out a negative identity (i.e., one that deliberately flouts and challenges these norms, such as delinquence; Gold & Petronio, 1980). Most religious conversions occur during adolescence (Argyle & Beit-Hallahmi, 1975), and a fair number of persons report more than one conversion. Some religious sects, such as Meher Baba, may be a means used by adolescents to rescue themselves from entanglements with previous life-styles (e.g., drug culture) that have proved undesirable but are hard to abandon (Robbins & Anthony, 1972).

Among the sources of ambivalence in adolescence, it should be noted, is commitment itself. Some of the apparent rebelliousness, alienation, cliqueishness, conformity, and idealism of adolescence may in fact be understood'as protection against the possibility of more realistic but premature commitments (Douvan, 1974). By embarking on a starry-eyed romance with an unattainable movie star or older and married teacher, adolescents can protect themselves against the possibility of involvement with someone nearer to their own age with sexual implications they are unprepared to handle.

Adults are best able to reach Stage V commitments; they evidence less of the high anxiety that drives Stage III commitments. Reviewing a variety of studies of the transition from youth to young adulthood, Neugarten (1972) concludes that the transition is marked by a stabilization of social roles and a concomitant increase in feelings of autonomy, competence, and stability, along with more equilibrium in mood and more integration of ego processes with impulses. The process continues from young to middle adulthood. Roles become more consistent, and according to Maccoby (1976), people derive more of their energy from a sense of coherent re-latedness than from the inner upwellings that marked earlier periods of life.

Adult life, too, has important stages, whose properties have recently become much better known through the work of such people as Gould (1972), Levinson (1977, 1978), and Vaillant (1977). According to Levinson (1977), the periods of adult life divide into stable periods (e.g., settling down) and transitional periods (e.g., midlife transition). The movement from one stable period through a transi-tional period to another stable period corresponds quite well with our understanding of the dialectical manner in which commitments evolve. In a stable period, people make certain crucial choices, such as the career they will pursue or the family they will have, and seek to attain their goals and values within the chosen structure. In a transitional period, the choice and structure are partly or completely called into question, reviewed, and often terminated. Contradictions are recognized, possibili-ties for change in the world and the self are explored, and tensions are experienced that propel the person toward new choices that will form the basis for a new life structure and another stable period. We suggest that our stages of decommitment and recommitment can be usefully applied to understanding the steps, and the asso-ciated emotional changes, whereby the stable structure of one period is undermined and eventually replaced by the stable structure of the next period.

There is, indeed, a useful sense in which the entire drama of a lifetime, the psychological drama of adult life, can be understood as the discovery, unfolding, and coming to terms with a single major commitment, called by Levinson (1978) "the Dream." What makes the midlife crisis as inevitable and powerful as it appears to be is that in it a person deals with the fate of this dream, whether this fate has been success or failure:

> From our study of the lives of 40 men—biologists, novelists, executives, work-ing men—we have concluded that many young men have a Dream (we will use the capital to emphasize our specific use of the word) of the kind of life they want to lead as adults. The Dream in its primordial form is a vague sense of self-in-the-adult-world. It has the quality of a vision, an imagined possibility that generates excitement and vitality. The meaning is the one Delmore

Schwartz intended with the title of his book of poetry *In Dreams Begin Responsibilities*.

The fate of the Dream has fundamental consequences for a man's life. A few men by their early 40s have achieved all or most of what they had set out to do; they feel that they have truly succeeded and are assured of a happy future. Others find themselves seriously disappointed and unable to avoid the conclusion that the satisfactions and peace of mind they thought success would bring were an illusion. Those who have fallen short of their Dreams, on the other hand, may come to believe that they have failed in a profound sense, that they have been found wanting and without value not only in their work but also as persons.

According to Levinson, the major tasks of male adult life up to this point of reconsideration and reevaluation involve pursuit of this Dream, though the connections may not seem evident at the start. One such task is forming a mentor relationship with an older person in the same field who serves as a kind of guide, teacher, counselor, and guru—a substitute father figure, in many ways, who provides in early adult life many of the same grounds for confidence that the man's actual father did in an earlier period. Another task, according to Levinson's research, is forming an intimate relationship with a special woman. Although this relationship ordinarily involves sexual, romantic, and loving feelings, it also turns out to be a kind of mentoring relationship, in which the woman facilitates the man's entry into the adult world and helps him shape and live out the Dream. The special woman supports his pursuit of the Dream while still accepting his dependency, insecurity, and juvenile tendency to idealize her. She is, in many ways, a substitute mother figure, just as the mentor is a substitute father figure, and the coming of the midlife crisis is in part marked by a recognition on the part of all these critical figures—the mentor, the special woman, and the person himself—that they have contributed all they can to the pursuit of the Dream and that it is now time to take stock, to come to terms with what has and has not been achieved, and to move on to other developmental tasks and new kinds of relationships. Whereas Levinson considered only males, others have examined both women's and men's lives from a life course perspective (e.g., Sales, 1978). Career choices made by men and women are sometimes timed differently, but both sexes go through similar periods of commitment to a life goal, ambivalence and reexamination of this goal, and renewed enthusiasm for a revised goal. Thus, our examination of parallels between Levinson's stages and our theory of commitment development will consider both men and women.

Levinson's major stages of early adulthood and early middle adulthood correspond rather elegantly to our five stages of commitment. The first stage according to Levinson, Entering the Adult World, has many of the elements of a Stage I commitment. It extends roughly from about age 22 to 28. In this period, the young adult, though still concerned with keeping eyes and options open, makes first choices of careers and relationships that will form the basis for adult life. The period is, in general, a time of adventure and excitement, though not without confusion and uncertainty as well. The end of this period is marked by a Stage II crisis, the Age-Thirty Transition, which lasts from about 28 to 33. This is a period in which people wonder whether they have made the right choices or whether they have unduly constricted themselves and thus prematurely foreclosed their access to some of the things they will need to pursue their dream. There is a peaking of marital problems and divorce, various kinds of occupational changes, and psychotherapy at this point. The next phase, Settling Down, has many of the properties that we recognize as characteristic of Stage III commitments. This period lasts from 32 or 33 to about 39 or 40. The doubts of the Age-Thirty Transition are worked through and individuals now turn seriously to their youthful aspirations for work, family, friendship, leisure, or whatever is most important to them. The major tasks of this period, according to Levinson, are establishing a niche (developing a skill and a place) and "making it." These are serious tasks, and they are pursued seriously. The culmination of this period is the point at which the person passes beyond junior status, perhaps with a mentor relationship, to a senior position in which he or she has "become his or her own person"—or, alternatively, realized that this is not to be.

The Mid-Life Transition, which occurs between the ages of 40 and 45, is in many ways a Stage IV crisis. It is at this point that people ask what they have done with their lives, whether they are truly using or wasting their talents, what they are getting from (and giving to) their jobs and their families, and what it is that they truly want for themselves and others. This is, of course, a questioning of the intrinsic value of what they have achieved. It is not a cool, rational process, but a time of emotional turmoil and despair. It is a time when people recognize that many of their long-cherished assumptions and beliefs about the world, and about themselves, are illusions. Levinson calls this a period of "de-illusionment." The Mid-Life Transition is in part precipitated by a return of the repressed, a reawakening of inner voices calling attention to lost opportunities, alternative identities, and parts of the self that have in general been ignored or overlooked in the pursuit of the Dream. There is some especially interesting evidence that this is the case with regard to traditional sex-role specialization. Older males tend to show more traditionally feminine characteristics (see, e.g., Hyde & Phillis, 1979; Schaw & Henry, 1956)—for example, being more oriented to inner rather than outer worlds—and older females tend to show more traditionally masculine characteristics. These changes have been most extensively described by Guttman (1975):

> The transcultural data make it clear that, by contrast with younger men, older men are on the whole less aggressive: they are more affiliative, more interested in love than in conquest or power, more interested in community than in agency. . . .
> We also find, across a wide range of cultures, that women age psychologically in the reverse direction. Even in normally patriarchal societies, women become more aggressive in later life, less sentimental, and more domineering. They become less interested in communion and more turned toward agency. (p. 171)

It is parental roles, according to Guttman, that have traditionally called forth the sharpest sex-linked behavior: nurturant roles in women and provider roles in men, with associated differences in how close to home they stay, how oriented they are to assertiveness or security, and so forth.

> Men, the providers of physical security, give up the need for comfort and dependency that would interfere with their courage and endurance; and women, the providers of emotional security, give up the aggression that could alienate their male providers or that could damage a vulnerable and needful child. . . .
>
> As parents enter middle age, and as children take over the responsibility for their own security, the chronic sense of parental emergency phases out, the psychological structures established by men and women in response to this crisis condition are in effect dismantled, and the sex-role reversals that shape our transcultural data occur. . . . (M)en begin to live out directly, to own as part of themselves, the passivity, the sensuality, the tenderness—in effect, the "femininity"—that was previously repressed in the service of productive instrumentality. By the same token, we find, transculturally, the opposite effect in women, who generally become domineering, independent, and unsentimental in middle life. Just as men reclaim title to their denied "femininity," women repossess the aggressive "masculinity" that they once lived out vicariously through their husbands. (pp. 180–181)

We need not and do not subscribe to the view that these stereotypical sex roles have the biological imperative Guttman implies, even in early adult life, or that such a psychological division of labor is unchanging. What we offer is a generalization of Guttman's thesis. Whatever form the major commitment of adult life—the Dream—takes, we are structured to invest in it heavily for the almost 20 years that define early adulthood. During this period, negative elements, antitheses, and other selves are pushed aside or integrated into the major synthesis. Eventually, however—with either the definitive achievement of the goal of this commitment, the clear failure to achieve it, or the simple exhaustion of the time span allotted to the attempt to achieve it—the energy that sustains this life commitment wanes. Negative elements and other selves once again become visible, and the person is faced with the new developmental task of asking which of these various elements he or she wishes to reassemble in a new and more flexible synthesis, a synthesis that may recognize limitations and impossibilities that are not theretofore acknowledged.

Out of this period of turmoil the individual emerges, eventually, into Middle Adulthood (ages 40 to 65), a period we can in many ways recognize as a Stage V commitment. The life structure of this period varies greatly in how satisfactory and viable it is. For some, it is a period of constriction and decline, of coming to terms with the defeats they have suffered earlier in life and finally and irrevocably recognized in the Mid-Life Transition. Others continue with their lives, keep busy, and fulfill their responsibilities, but without the sense of self and inner peace that would have been produced by a successful new synthesis. For many, however, Middle Adulthood is reported as the fullest and most creative season of life: they are free of the tyrannies of youthful ambitions, instincts, and illusions, yet still in full command of their powers, more secure in themselves and also more attached, in a mature way, to others.

Finally, in old age, we hypothesize that individuals come full cycle to return, on a very different basis, to Stage III and Stage I commitments. The basic effect of age on psychological functioning, according to Neugarten (1972), is a movement from an active, combative, outer-world orientation to a more adaptive, conforming, inner-world orientation. The loss of the capacity and energy to generate commitments under these circumstances seems analagous, on a psychological level, to the loss of resilience in many physiological structures. Many commitments will, of course, be carried over from earlier points in life. As internal and external resources for supporting these commitments dwindle, the commitments may become more rigid and extreme—that is, more, once again, like Stage III than Stage V commitments. Older parents who are unable to make many changes in their own lives and whose energy must be increasingly devoted to maintaining their own functioning, may be less able to adapt and change the form of their love for one of their children as the circumstances of this child's life change (e.g., through divorce or illness). New commitments, on the other hand, tend to be limited not only by this constriction of resources and new inward orientation but also by a shortened time span and (as a consequence of all of the above) a reduced ability to make substantial investments or side bets on behavior (Becker, 1960). Thus new commitments in old age are more likely to look like Stage I commitments, hedged and foreshortened before Stage II crises can be reached.

New commitments in the elderly will differ from comparable Stage I commitments in children, however, because they embody less energy and also because they represent a stage that might be called postambivalent rather then (as in children) preambivalent. There is some sense in which the elderly, like the young, can act in a less conflicted fashion, although for very different reasons. The young have not yet been socialized to ambivalence. The elderly have, in some sense, come to terms with the dominant forms of ambivalence in their lives during the processes of turning inward, renewing emotional awareness, and life review just mentioned. The solutions and the resolutions may not be entirely satisfactory, though the elderly appear, on the whole, less dissatisfied than most age stereotypes would lead us to expect (Campbell, Converse & Rodgers, 1976; Klinger, 1977; Neugartern, 1972) but the energy that fuels the remaining conflict is, in any event, less than it once was.

It should also be noted that the elderly, through the loss of life roles and life partners through retirement and death, are much more heavily engaged in dealing with decommitment processes; this will absorb a considerable portion of their available psychic energy. It may be hypothesized that turning inward is an adaptive response, in many ways, to a world that now contains fewer external incentives (Klinger, 1977). Langer (1979) has claimed that even an extreme form of turning inward—senility—predicts longer, rather than shorter, survival in nursing homes (if physical diagnosis is held constant). This is so, Langer claims, because senility actually represents an active psychic process—involving, in our terms, repeated commitments to a significant inner world—rather than merely a passive process of decay. Senility is thus preferable to a realistic but passive accommodation to the completely monotonous and unchallenging external environment characteristic of nursing homes.

Our analysis of change in the form and quality of commitments over the life cycle suggests an answer to a question that has repeatedly puzzled observers of relationships between the generations. Commentaries by the older generation on the behavior and character of the young read in a surprisingly similar manner whether taken from yesterday's newspaper or speeches in ancient Greece. The common lament is over the loss of standards, the loss of moral character—in our terms, the perceived loss of commitment—by the young. In general—and certainly in times of prosperity—the young are seen as having it easier than the older generation did, as not having had to sacrifice as much, and as not appreciating what they have. (This is true, by our informal observation, even for the judgments of younger siblings by older ones.) The older generation may not wish to go back to the material standards of past times, but they uniformly regret the loss of what they feel were moral standards of those times. In our view, this characteristic pattern represents less a perception of any actual historical reality than a shift in perspective with age. The older generation has indeed made more sacrifices, accumulated more commitments, and come to see the world more in terms of intrinsic value. The fact that the young have not makes them appear extrinsically oriented, amoral, or even immoral. It is not that the young have lost commitments. Rather, they have not yet gained them—at least not in the full measure dictated by the passing of Stage III commitments into Stage V commitments, by the accommodation to the fate of a Dream, and by the acquisition and resolution of conflicting commitments in a variety of life domains.

There should be no presumption, by the way, that the changes we have been talking about in capacity and inclination for commitment over the life cycle are biological rather than social. They may be due equally to changes in the ways people are treated at different points in life and to changes in the internal worlds of these people. For example, both children and the elderly may be actively discouraged from making commitments by others who treat them as though they do not have the requisite capacity for independent judgment. Commitments, by our definition, involve the perception of choice, some sense of ambivalence, and the recognition of responsibility for the consequences of choice. Our discussion has primarily traced changes in the extent and quality of commitment as a function of changes in the extent and quality of the ambivalence a person confronts at different points in his or her life. Ambivalence, whatever its sources, is primarily located within the individual. But people also differ in how much freedom they are allowed and how much responsibility they are assigned at different points in life. Commitment cannot begin unless people see themselves (in consequence, perhaps, of being seen by others) as free to make choices and take risks. As we have noted, limits on this freedom may constrain the extent to which commitments can develop in the very young and very old. Commitment cannot progress to its higher stages unless people see themselves as responsible for the consequences of their choices—for overcoming obstacles to their pursuits, and for coming to terms with inner dissatisfactions with their results. If, as seems likely, social roles entail the most intense assignment of responsibility to people during the middle years of adult life, we thus also expect the most elaborate development of commitments at this point in their lives.

Our discussion of developmental changes in the extent and quality of commitments has been speculative because there is little research that directly assesses how commitment processes change over the life cycle. As we have seen, however, there is some related literature that lends itself surprisingly well to interpretation as a special case of change in the predisposition or capacity to make commitments. Thus, we mentioned evidence that children acquire greater capacity for self-control and selective attention as they grow. In a related vein, there is a body of literature indicating that people tend to acquire a greater belief in their capacity to control reinforcements, or in their sense of themselves as causal agents influencing environmental events, as they grow older (Lifshitz, 1973; Nowicki & Duke, 1974), at least until age 50 or 60 (Bradley & Webb, 1976; Lao, 1974; Penk, 1969). From childhood to adolescence there is an increase in the sense of the self as an existential, individuating, self-determining actor (Montemayor & Eisen, 1977). There is a parallel increase in the tendency to see other people as personally responsible for their actions rather than seeing these actions as environmentally caused—that is, to see actors as choosing things because of properties in themselves rather than properties of the thing chosen (Ruble, Feldman, Higgins, & Karlovac, 1979). All of these various findings imply the development of the three elements we have considered preconditions of commitment: the sense of oneself as making choices, the awareness that these choices have both positive and negative consequences, and the acceptance of responsibility for these choices and their consequences.

Likewise, children's apparent progression through Kohlberg's six stages of moral judgment (Kohlberg, 1972; see also the fine presentation in Brown & Herrnstein, 1975) can be understood as regular increases in people's perception that the children are choosing actions as a function of the intrinsic value of these actions rather than as a function of the material (preconventional) or social (conventional) rewards and punishments attached to these actions. To make higher-level moral judgments, in Kohlberg's sense, an actor must be aware that individuals (or societies) make difficult choices (that are affirmed despite the fact that the intended goal of these choices may be impossible to demonstrate (i.e., that moral values are not givens or absolutes). The goal is for the choices to be internally consistent and universally applicable. Making choices of this sort clearly involves the capacity to make commitments. Thus, Kohlberg's argument that young children have not developed the cognitive capacities to make these higher-level moral judgments strongly suggests that such children have not developed the capacity to make commitments. They could, to be sure, have developed the capacity to make commitments but not yet applied it in the sphere of moral judgment, but we regard this as highly unlikely, since moral judgment, and evaluative judgment in general, would seem to be one of the first domains in which one would make commitments. Incidentally, the one anomaly in the data bearing on Kohlberg's hypothesized developmental sequence— that a substantial number of adolescents make more primitive moral judgments than they did earlier (see Trainer, 1977)—is itself highly supportive of our developmental analysis. We have suggested that adolescence is a time when Stage III commitments, which are relatively rigid and intense, are undertaken for reasons that have much more to do with social and affective development than with the cognitive factors Kohlberg emphasizes. If this is so, and if rigid Stage III commitments are incompatible with the progression from conventional to principled thought, we then have an explanation for the otherwise puzzling interruption in Kohlberg's sequence of moral development.

Although we are encouraged that this wide variety of literature on developmental changes in cognition, affect, and social behavior is eminently compatible with our theory of commitment, studies designed for other purposes can never be adequate to test the critical hypotheses of a given theory. We need a generation of studies that will directly assess the quality of the commitments experienced by people of different ages and how these commitments evolve over time.

CHAPTER SIX
COMMITMENT AND MENTAL HEALTH

Philip Brickman
Dan Coates*

What is the relationship between commitment and mental health? Do we need commitment in order to be happy, well-adapted individuals? Can commitment lead us into psychological distress and self-destructive behavior? The solution we propose for these questions, and the basic argument of this chapter, is that commitment is a necessary but not sufficient condition for full mental health. Given earlier discussions of the role commitment plays in enhancing perceived control and providing meaning and value, it will perhaps not be surprising to learn that commitment can make a positive contribution to mental health. We will begin this chapter with a review of evidence indicating that commitment benefits psychological adjustment by directly promoting subjective well-being, improving our ability to cope with stress, and enhancing our adaptive functioning. We will suggest some of the mechanisms by which commitment can have these positive effects, and we will argue that, in some ways at least, commitment is necessary for full mental health.

However, commitment does have its dark side, and being committed is no guarantee of good psychological adjustment or adaptive functioning. In the second part of this chapter, we will contend that guilt, jealousy, and depression can all result from commitment. But even these forms of distress are not the most serious threat that commitment carries for mental health. Although they can be quite devastating for the individuals experiencing them, guilt, jealousy, and depression,

*The preparation and writing of this manuscript was supported in part by NIMH Grant #RO1 MH39529-02 to the second author.

when they are handled properly, can also be the stepping stones to enhanced personal growth. A commitment is most threatening to mental health when it becomes so stringently demanding, so all-encompassing, that it leaves no room for other goals or commitments in a person's life. Such destructive commitments, we believe, are most likely to occur when people are in situations that do not offer clear choices or real opportunities for fulfillment. So, in the final section of this chapter, we will consider how certain problems produced by conditions of abundance and scarcity can interfere with the commitment process and lead people to make commitments that are less than optimal.

COMMITMENT AND
PSYCHOLOGICAL ADJUSTMENT

Earlier in human history, the question of whether people need commitment in order to be well-adjusted simply would not have been raised. Traditional society surrounded its members with a web of commitments and an associated structure of meaning and value (Singer, 1962). People's marriages, occupations, and residences—virtually all aspects of their lives—were largely arranged for them, almost completely determined by family and societal position. Individual choice and freedom—and the possibility of questioning traditional commitments—has been expanded in the last few centuries, slowly but significantly, by that combination of processes known as capitalism, protestantism, science, and democracy.

In the twentieth century, psychology—from Freud's argument that civilization is based on represssion to Maslow's call for individuals who will maximize their independent, higher-order selves—has played a considerable role in championing and justifying the liberation of the individual from traditional constraints. Commitments came to be seen as infringements on freedom rather than the fulfillment of freedom. The culmination of this movement has been the belief that all commitments are based on neurotic fears or pathological cultural conditioning. On the topic of marriage, for example, Bardwick (1979) writes:

> This reasoning begins with the idea that neurotic, dependent people are insatiably needy for affection and commitment, and therefore healthy people are the reverse, are independent. While independent people may enjoy relating to others, the reasoning continues, they do not *need* to be loved or remain within a relationship. Moreover, since autonomous people are secure in themselves, they do not need legal permanence and do not need to possess their partner or limit their partner's experience. A relationship, from this prospective, is healthy when it is made up of two autonomous people, whose commitments are first to themselves and secondarily to their partner or children. (p. 123)

Applying similar reasoning, Bach (1974) sees the marital commitment as a security trap, fostering regressive tendencies toward possessiveness, jealousy, and dependency in both men and women.

The rational ideal has always been controlled caring: to become involved with others but not too involved, to be attached but not unreasonably so. It has never been recommended that a person should withhold feeling or not care at all about others, for this would be insensitive or exploitative and would cut one off from many reciprocal pleasures. On the other hand, a person should also not let his or her feelings get out of control, for passion of this sort leads to demands for permanence and exclusiveness that are unreasonable or impossible and thus painful. The preeminent rational hero of our times, Bertrand Russell (1930), has described the experience of love as the best life has to offer. But he has also made it clear that for rational people, if a marriage is solid and substantial in its affectionate basis, it has nothing to lose if it permits outside sexual relations. The ideal of having many relationships, each of which is growth enhancing and none of which is constricting, is also found in such diverse modern creeds as the Playboy philosophy of life and feminist critiques of the family (Bardwick, 1979).

These sensible views of the world do not take into account human limitations—that people may not be able to be this rational or to measure out and control their feelings with such precision. We may agree, for instance, that having sex with a person one merely likes instead of loves is still pleasurable, as was pointed out in the film *Annie Hall*:

Diane Keaton: Sex without love is an empty experience.
Woody Allen: Yes, but as empty experiences go, it's one of the best. (Allen, 1982, p. 65)

On the other hand, we would also agree that having sex with a person one does not like is probably going to be self-destructive and ultimately distressing. The problem, then, is simply keeping a clear distinction between people we like and people we do not like. This is precisely what is difficult to do without commitment. Without commitment, liking changes as the other person's behavior or the situation changes. No one is likable all the time. There are unlikely to be grounds—without commitment—for sustaining a consistently or fundamentally positive orientation toward someone else—or expecting them to do the same. That space in which people find others that they like enough to care about but not so much as to become dependent on them or committed to them may be a very small space indeed, and one that is impossible to stay in for very long.

The 1980s have seen a reaction against the "Me Decade" of the 1970s, with its self-centered pursuit of fulfillment and opposition to all constraints on that pursuit. Commenting on this narcissistic society, Bradwick (1979) writes:

> The ideal of the autonomous self, someone so intact and mature that he or she does not need anyone else, is, in this context, an ideal of a painless existence in which one can avoid the great hope and the awful pain that become possible when one allows oneself to need another. I have never met someone so autonomous as not to need anyone; I have met many who were so vulnerable that they could not allow themselves to act on their needs for someone. (p. 127)

Yankelovich (1981), reviewing the results of a number of surveys of changing American values, writes:

> Among people I interviewed, many truly committed self-fulfillment seekers focus so sharply on their own needs that instead of achieving the more intimate relationships they desire, they grow farther apart from others. . . . They are caught in a debilitating contradiction: their goal is to expand their lives by reaching beyond the self, but the strategy they employ constricts them, drawing them inward toward an even-narrowing, closed-off 'I'. (p. 40)

In the remainder of this section, we will argue that people are more fulfilled and better adjusted when they are involved in some type of commitment. It has been proposed that the capacity to make commitments to activities and relationships is necessary in order to exercise effective control and to see these things as having meaning and value. Here, we will consider whether and how commitment contributes to our subjective well-being, our ability to cope with stress, and our general adaptive functioning.

Commitment and subjective well-being. Commitment appears to enhance subjective well-being, first of all, by helping people to feel more content and happy with their lives. People who are engaged in what have traditionally been recognized as overarching, lifetime commitments are generally happier than those who are not. Being married has been the single best predictor of happiness and life satisfaction in several large surveys (Andrews & Withey, 1976; Campbell, Converse, & Rodgers, 1976; Glenn & Weaver, 1981; see also Kessler & Essex, 1982, for a reivew). In general, religious belief and participation have also been associated with greater happiness and less distress (see Batson & Ventis, 1982; Hadaway, 1978; Moberg & Brusek, 1978, for reviews). Further, there is evidence that commitment in particular life domains is related to greater satisfaction in those domains. For example, Blood (1969) studied the relationship between an index of job satisfaction (including measures of satisfaction with work, supervisor, people, pay, and promotion) and endorsement of a Protestant work ethic (making a symbolic commitment to work, as measured by agreement with such items as "Hard work makes a man a better person" or "Wasting time is as bad as wasting money"). Among both students and workers in a variety of unskilled positions, agreement with the Protestant ethic was positively correlated with job satisfaction. In his famous longitudinal study of gifted children, Terman (see Goleman, 1980) found that those who were ultimately most satisfied with their occupations were those who reported an early liking for their work and a feeling at age 30 of choosing one's career rather than drifting into it. In the interpersonal domain, Hetherington (1976) studied how commitment to a partner was related to sexual satisfaction among divorced people. For both men and women who did have such an intimate commitment, frequency of intercourse was positively correlated with happiness at every point in time (two months, one year, and two years after divorce). Among men and women who did not have such an intimate commitment, frequency of intercourse was negatively correlated with happiness at all points in time—significantly so for females at all three points, and for males at the one-year and two-year points. Apparently, sex contributes to our happiness only when it is part of a romantic commitment. In an unpublished study by Binns, Stowell, and Brickman, undergraduates who were involved in a romantic relationship were asked to rate how free they felt to do what they wanted in the relationship, how responsible they felt for what happened in the relationship, and how satisfied they were with their relationship. Those who were more committed to the relationship—feeling both greater freedom and greater responsibility—were also more satisfied with the relationship.

How is it that commitment has this beneficial effect on people's feelings of satisfaction with their lives? First of all, it is clear that it is not a particular set of beliefs or activities that produces this effect. Despite wide variations in types of beliefs and practices, there is no evidence that belonging to one religion is any more beneficial than belonging to another (Batson & Ventis, 1982; Cutler, 1976). Indeed, religious belief in general is not a sufficient or necessary condition for happiness. Batson and Ventis (1982) review evidence suggesting that religious participants who are less committed to their beliefs—those who hold an extrinsic orientation to religion—are more likely to be dissatisfied and distressed than nonbelievers. In a nationwide survey of religion, health, and happiness among 65,000 readers of *Redbook* (Safran, 1977), some very interesting results were obtained. Women who described themselves as very religious were more likely to say they were happy, less likely to report feelings of anxiety, tension, or worthlessness, less likely to suffer from headaches or stomach upsets, and more likely to find sex continuing to be interesting and pleasurable. Women who were moderately or slightly religious scored less favorably on all these items. On the other hand, women who said they were not at all religious or were antireligious were just as happy and healthy as women who said they were very religious. The author suggests that it is the courage, rather than the content, of one's convictions that counts:

> According to our survey, it is the woman who feels certain that she has an answer to the mysteries of life—either as a strong believer or a strong nonbeliever—who is healthiest and happiest. The woman who is still struggling with her doubts is the one with headaches. (p. 217)

In a similar way, while adovcating the need for some genuine belief in order to be happy, Bertrand Russell (1930) points out that no particular belief is required:

> Belief in a cause is a source of happiness to large numbers of people. I am not thinking only of revolutionaries, socialists, nationalists in oppressed countries and such; I am thinking also of many humbler kinds of belief. The men I have known who believed that the English were the lost ten tribes were almost invariably happy, while as for those who believed that the English were only the tribes of Ephraim and Manasseh, their bliss knew no bounds. I am not suggesting that the reader should adopt this creed, since I cannot advocate any happiness based upon what seem to me to be false beliefs. For the same reason I cannot urge the reader to believe that men should live exclusively

upon nuts, although, as far as my observation goes, this belief invariably ensures perfect happiness. But it is easy to find some cause . . . and those whose interest in any such cause is genuine are provided with an occupation for their leisure hours and a complete antidote to the feeling that life is empty. (p. 92)

Happiness, then, does not result from some special beliefs or set of adherences. Rather, it appears to spring from the confidence of one's beliefs, a sense of conviction that whatever one has chosen is important and worthwhile. Happiness (like love, power, and so many other fundamental human concerns; see Brickman, 1980) may be ultimately undefinable, and it is certainly, in its particulars, different things to different people. Yet we venture the following as a distinguishing characteristic that all happy people have in common: They know what they want to do and are doing it. They have a visible enthusiasm, vigor, or zest for their lives.

To know what one wants to do and to be doing it means that a person is not greatly troubled by the thought that there might be more attractive alternatives that have been missed or rejected and, indeed, is no longer very much concerned with alternatives. Discovering what one wants to do, by our previous analysis of meaning and value, comes about through choosing alternatives and overcoming obstacles. Doing what one likes, likewise, involves resisting the distraction of potentially more attractive alternatives, as well as some measure of luck and skill. Because these steps require commitment, their inclusion as elements in the definition of happiness implies that happiness involves commitment. Happiness involves the enthusiastic and unambivalent acceptance of activities or relationships that are not the best that might possibly be obtained. In one sense, it means having people acting as what March and Simon (1958) call a satisficer, who settles for merely adequate solutions rather than mounting the ideally rational search for the best possible solution. In another sense, however, happiness requires people to think of themselves as optimizers, or as having found what is—at least for them—the best possible solution. To be happy, we have to believe that what we are doing or have done is or was the best alternative, even though we can never do all we would like to do or find worthwhile doing. Without commitment, which enables us to turn costs such as forgone possibilities into enhancement of the chosen option, complete happiness may not be possible.

When people are able to forget about alternatives and become intensely committed to some course of action, they can experience great euphoria. At certain moments, people may become physically and psychologically involved in what they are doing to such an extent that all conflicting tendencies or distracting stimuli are completely shut out. As was extensively discussed earlier, Csikszentmihalyi (1975) calls the sensation people experience when they act with total involvement "flow," and considers it to be—by the reports of chess players, mountain climbers, dancers, composers, and surgeons—life's peak experience. According to participants, this exalted state has the following characteristics: the activity has the person's undivided attention; all potentially intruding stimuli (including feelings of self-consciousness) are kept out of awareness; the person feels in control, or at any rate is not worried about the possibility of lack of control; the environment contains coherent, noncontradictory demands for action and provides clear, unambiguous feedback; and finally, the activity is autotelic, or self-motivating, appearing to need no goals or rewards external to itself. Surgeons are, of course, highly rewarded by society, but according to Csikzentmihalyi, they are no more likely than chess players or dancers to refer to these rewards in explaining their involvement.

On the other hand, when people cannot settle into a course of action because they are constantly tempted by attractive alternatives, they are likely to feel less happy. Freedman (1978) found that people who are unequivocally oriented to either one sex or the other (exclusively homosexual or exclusively heterosexual) are happier on many dimensions than people who are conflicted in their sexual orientation, or bisexual:

> At least for those people in our samples, homosexuals differ little from heterosexuals in their levels of satisfaction and happiness; while those with mixed preferences are worse off.... It is tempting to speculate that in sex as in many other things in life conflicting values or tastes are difficult to deal with. It is hard to be a little homosexual, and apparently harder still to be a little heterosexual. Those who have taken a firm, unambiguous stand on the matter can concentrate on getting as much satisfaction and happiness out of sex and love as possible. But those who have mixed preferences may have trouble reconciling them—they cannot settle into a homosexual life because they occasionally are attracted to the opposite sex; they cannot settle into a heterosexual life because sometimes same-sex people attract them. And perhaps a difficult aspect of this is that no one in the world is entirely, automatically neutral in terms of sexual attraction. (p. 71)

An inability to accept and become committed to some course of action may lead not only to unhappiness but to more serious forms of psychological distress as well. Neurosis may be thought of as a special case of the failure to make and enforce an effective choice. According to Freud (1935), neurotics are characterized by powerful ambivalence or conflicting motives, simultaneously desiring and fearing some important activity, such as sex. Neurotics cannot resolve such a conflict because one of the competing motives is hidden from awareness:

> The pathogenic conflict in a neurotic must not be confounded with a normal struggle between conflicting impulses all of which are in the same mental field. It is a battle between two forces of which one has succeeded in coming to the level of the preconscious and conscious part of the mind, while the other has been confined on the unconscious level. That is why the conflict can never have a final outcome one way or the other; the antagonists meet each other as little as the whale and polar bear in the well known story. An effective decision can be reached only when they confront each other on the same ground. And, in my opinion, to accomplish this is the sole task of the treatment. (Freud, 1935, p. 376)

An inability to reduce ambivalence and forge commitments also seems to underlie two other important sources of distress in people's lives—shyness and alienation. Shy people find it difficult to initiate certain types of activities (Zimbardo, 1977; Zimbardo, Pilkonis, & Norwood, 1975), whereas alienated people find it difficult to sustain them (Kenniston, 1960, 1968; Kobasa, 1984; Maddi, Kobasa, & Hoover, 1979). For shy people, instead of a Stage II crisis developing gradually over time, the crisis appears to be implicit in the very first approach, thus tending to paralyze action. Shy people are caught between the dissonant beliefs that they both desire and fear social interactions and relationships (Zimbardo et al., 1975). If shy people choose one alternative or the other, they can either become more socially involved and overcome their shyness or can find value in being alone and the unique opportunities it provides. Indeed, it might be expected that initially shy people would become strongly committed to whichever alternative they chose, by virtue of the very difficulty or high level of dissonance they have to overcome in making that choice. However, when shy people continue to avoid any commitment and the dissonance goes unresolved, they are lonely and unhappy, feeling too incapable and frightened to do what is necessary to get the social stimulation they feel they need (Zimbardo et al., 1975).

By contrast, alienated people appear to find it easy to initiate activities and relationships, they just do not stay with them for very long. Kobasa and Maddi (Kobasa, 1984; Kobaska, Maddi & Pucetti, 1982; Maddi, Kobasa, & Hoover, 1979) define alienation as the inability to maintain enthusiasm and involvement in important activities, such as work. In his classic study, Kenniston (1960) found that alienated students often threw themselves wholeheartedly into new projects or relationships (easily overcoming Stage II crisis), but then, in complete contrast to Csikszentmihalyi's description of flow, felt trapped or bored and withdrew (Stage IV crises). They appear to burn and then burn out, their motivation an exhaustible rather than replenishable fuel. Their feelings decay rather than consolidate with the pursuit of an activity. Indeed, the very intensity of their impulsive initial investments may be part of what breeds their fear of commitments as all-consuming and irrational, and their unwillingness to admire anything for fear of being swallowed up by it (thus the characteristic cynicism and aloofness of the alienated). Perhaps because they experience so little ambivalence in making their initial choices, these choices also generate little commitment for the alienated.

Clinical depression, in our analysis, involves both a general inability to initiate action and a general inability to experience any action elicited by external forces as truly rewarding. In this sense, it combines the symptoms previously discussed in connection with shyness and alienation. Like shy people, depressed people have trouble making choices, so much so in fact that they tend to put off decisions altogether or try to get other people to make the decisions for them (Billings, Cronkite, & Moos, 1983; Billings & Moos, 1984; Coyne, Aldwin, & Lazarus, 1981). Like alienated people, depressed people have trouble sustaining activities (Seligman, 1975). But this is probably because depressed people avoid making choices altogether, rather than making them too easily and quickly, as alienated people do. To the extent that the inability to make and maintain commitments leads to depression, it may also underlie many other serious disorders; research indicates that symptoms of depression are common to many forms of psychopathology (Depue & Monore, 1978; Gotlib, 1984).

Depressed people's problems in making choices and initiating commitments may stem from what some observers have seen as a tendency on the part of the depressed to set unrealistically high, idealistic standards for themselves (Rehm, 1977). When they have to make a decision, depressed people appear to get stuck at the stage of considering alternatives, unable to comfortably choose any option because no real solution can ever be ideal. Rather than deciding on an adequate solution and enjoying the benefits of the dissonance reduction this would allow, they continually search for the optimal, perfect answer and take no constructive action at all. Miller and Lewis (1977) found that elderly depressed patients lose points on memory tests and are sometimes subsequently misdiagnosed as senile because they are unwilling to guess unless they feel very certain they are correct. Abramson, Alloy, and Rosoff (1981) found that depressed students were less willing to predict when a light would come on if they had to generate a hypothesis about when the light would come on by themselves rather than select the correct hypothesis from a short list provided by the experimenter. For nondepressed students, the requirement of generating their own hypotheses made less of a difference in their performance.

In other studies, investigators have tested the responses of depressed people to problems or demanding situations in their daily lives. For example, Billings, Cronkite, and Moos (1983) compared the self-reported coping behaviors of a large group of patients entering psychiatric treatment for unipolar depression with those of a demographically matched, nondepressed control group. Compared to the controls, the depressed patients were significantly more likely to report using the coping strategy of information seeking—that is, trying to find out more about a demanding situation and obtaining guidance from others. Apparently, as part of their search for the perfect solution, depressed people may often seek advice from others and, in that process, let those others make the choices for them. The nondepressed, on the other hand, are more likely to report engaging in some specific problem-solving activity. In a later study, Billings and Moos (1984) found that this same type of information seeking was the most common coping strategy among a group of 424 depressed patients. Coyne, Aldwin, and Lazarus (1981) also investigated the coping behavior of depressed and nondepressed people, and they too found that when faced with a problem depressed people, unlike nondepressed people, continue seeking information and helpful direction from others rather than taking direct action to solve the problem themselves. These investigators also found that depressed people were less likely than nondepressed people to agree that some negative situations have to be accepted, supporting the notion that the depressed are unwilling to settle on anything less than an ideal solution. In some ways, it is quite rational to very carefully consider all relevant information and alternatives and to hold out for the best possible answer, but it is apparently not very satisfying or adaptive. As cognitive behavior therapists have indicated (Meichenbaum, 1977), too much internal dialogue over the possible pros and cons of a line of action kills assertive possibilities by making too much seem to be at stake in the first steps that can be taken. The tendency of the depressed to seek information and counsel rather than choosing some course of action is another example of how the depressed engage in cognitive processes that are apparently sensible or accurate but are ultimately less functional than those of the nondepressed (Alloy & Abramson, 1979; Lewinsohn, Mischel, Chaplin, & Barton, 1980; Roth & Ingram, 1985; Sackeim, 1983).

In avoiding decisions or choices or in having others make decisions for them, depressed people also decrease the possibility of gaining satisfaction from any course of action in which they become involved. Any dissonance that arises or problems or difficulties that are encountered will not be resolved into greater valuing of the activity if the person does not feel he or she has chosen the activity. As Coates and Wortman (1980) point out, depressed people may fail to derive much benefit from any nondepressed behavior they engage in because they attribute it to others' desires or wishes rather than their own. Subsequently, the depressed, like the alienated, feel trapped, bored, and inclined to withdraw from activities. While not usually attributing it to a failure in the commitment process, many observers have noted that depressed people have trouble sustaining any activities. The tendency of the depressed to give up is a hallmark characteristic of the disorder according to some theories, such as learned helplessness (Abramson, Seligman, & Teasdale, 1978; Raps, Peterson, Reinhard, Abramson, & Seligman, 1982; Seligman, 1975; see, also, Coyne & Gotlib, 1983, for a review of helplessness theory and related research). There appears to be general agreement that a lack of interest and persistence, if not a central component of the disorder, is at least commonly associated with depression (American Psychiatric Association, 1980). Of course suicide, the ultimate withdrawal from all of life's activities, is a considerable danger with depressed people (Copas & Robin, 1982; Morrison, 1982; Pallis, Barraclough, Levey, Jenkins, & Sainsbury, 1982; Slater & Depue, 1981).

So there does seem to be quite a bit of evidence indicating a relationship between the avoidance of commitment and depression. But we should note here that avoiding commitment is only one way to be without commitment. People can also lose commitments they have already formed, and later we will discuss how such loss can contribute to the development of depression. For the time being, our main point is that people who fail to make effective choices and stick with them tend to be depressed.

In leading us to choose certain activities and to find those activities valuable and worthwhile, commitment does not only enhance our happiness and enable us to avoid some potentially devastating forms of distress. It also contributes to another important component of subjective well-being: self-esteem. Previous research has revealed a consistent relationship between the capacity to make commitments and high self-esteem. In studies of cognitive dissonance theory, subjects who show the strongest dissonance reduction also tend to be the ones who think most highly of themselves. Malewski (1962) gave subjects a choice between two alternatives that they had earlier indicated were almost equally preferable. As predicted, only subjects with high self-esteem exhibited the dissonance reduction effect of increasing the attractiveness of the chosen alternative and decreasing the attractiveness of the rejected alternative. Subjects high in self-esteem are more likely than those low in self-esteem to subsequently rate a counterattitudinal speech they had made as worthwhile, that is, as indicative of their current true attitudes (Greenbaum, 1966). Gerard, Blevans, and Malcolm (1964) found that only subjects who were told that they had high ability in judging designs showed the dissonance effect of attaching greater value, after making a choice, to the design they had chosen. Korman (1966, 1967) found that individuals low in self-esteem were more likely to choose occupations that they perceived as unstaisfying and not consistent with their self-perceived characteristics. To some extent, people must have a fairly high opinion of themselves in order to make commitments in the first place. They have to feel they can make good choices and attach value to the choices they make. But people also need commitment in order to maintain their self-esteem. People will continue to think well of themselves only if they continue to believe the activities and relationships they have chosen are valuable and worthwhile.

Commitment and coping with stress. People who are more committed may also enjoy greater subjective well-being because they are able to cope more successfully with life's inevitable unpleasant and stressful events. No research has directly investigated the relationship between reactions to stress and the capacity for commitment. But past research has shown that several factors that would be expected to correlate with such a capacity are also associated with more positive responses to negative events. In the chapter on meaning and value, we pointed out that choice and responsibility are the necessary preconditions for commitment, and they appear to be similarly important preconditions for successful coping. In general, people feel less anxious and respond more adaptively to negative events when they believe they have more choice, either concurrent or retrospective, about encountering those events and the circumstances leading up to them (Bulman & Wortman, 1977; Corah & Boffa, 1970; see also Averill, 1973; Thompson, 1981, for reviews). People who have an internal locus of control, and who would therefore be expected to take more responsibility for the consequences of their choices, are less likely than those with an external locus of control to become seriously distressed or ill following negative events (Houtz, Tetenbaum, & Philips, 1981; Hunter & Locke, 1984; Johnson & Sarason, 1978; Lefcourt, Miller, Ware, & Sherk, 1981; Sandler & Lakey, 1982; Wise & Rosenthal, 1982). Taking personal responsibility for negative events, at least in some forms, has also been shown to be related to better adjustment to those events (Abramson & Sackeim, 1977; Bulman & Wortman, 1977; Janoff-Bulman, 1979; Lerner, 1980; Miller & Porter, 1983). Taking responsibility for negative events in a way that denies choice—attributing the event to unchanging and unchangeable aspects of ourselves—leads to poorer coping (Abramson, Seligman, & Teasdale, 1978; Janoff-Bulman, 1979).

Other research has come closer to measuring something like a general capacity for commitment, rather than its components, and its relation to coping with stress. Survey studies suggest that people who have a moderate number of multiple identities—roles, relationships, and activities to which they are committed—are better able to maintain their psychological well-being in the face of negative events than those who have very few identities (Moss, 1973; see Thoits, 1983, for a review). Kobasa and her colleagues have conducted an impressive line of research indicating that individuals who are high in the personality characteristic of hardiness are less likely to respond to stress by becoming physically ill (Kobasa, 1979a, 1979b, 1982a, 1984; Kobasa, Maddi, & Courington, 1981; Kobasa, Maddi, & Kahn, 1982; Kobasa, Maddi, & Pucetti, 1982; Kobasa & Pucetti, 1982) or psychologically distressed (Kobasa, 1982b; Ganellen & Blaney, 1984). Hardiness has been conceptualized and measured as consisting of three dimensions: perceived control, the ability to see change as a challenge rather than a threat, and commitment. Kobasa's definition of commitment is not too different from our own: "Commitment is defined as the ability to believe in the truth, importance, and interest value of what one is doing" (Kobasa, 1982b, p. 708) and "a generalized sense of purpose that allows people to identify with and find meaningful the events, things, and persons of their environment" (Kobasa, Maddi, & Kahn, 1982, p. 169). Although all three dimensions of hardiness are related to one another, measures of the commitment factor appear to be particularly important predictors of physical and psychological health in the face of stress (Kobasa, 1979b, 1982a; Ganellen & Blaney, 1984).

How does commitment enable us to cope more successfully with negative events? First, and perhaps most important, it provides meaning for stressful or unpleasant experiences. It seems obvious that any particular negative event will seem less negative if we can see it as necessary to some larger purpose, as unimportant in itself, or as symbolic of something positive. Following from the evidence presented in the chapter on meaning and value, commitment provides meaning by enabling us to bond the negative elements of life to more positive ones. As a result, we experience those negative elements as less devastating and more tolerable. Many previous authors have suggested that being able to find meaning in our suffering allows us to cope more successfully with that suffering (Antonovsky, 1979; Bulman & Wortman, 1977; Frankl, 1959, 1963; Lifton, 1968; Silver, Boon, & Stones, 1983; Silver & Wortman, 1980; Taylor, 1983). These authors typically view meaning more broadly than we do here, as making sense, somehow, of the bad things that happen to us. However, the kind of meaning that helps people to accept and adapt to life events both small and large may require that they perceive their pain as directly serving some larger goal or higher purpose. And this is precisely the type of meaning that commitment would be expected to produce.

One of our favorite examples of finding meaning in life's problems comes from a pregnant colleague and dear friend who rejoiced when she vomited in the morning because it indicated that she was still pregnant. In a related way, to get more enjoyment out of their leisure, vacationers are advised to connect the inevitable frustrations of their trip to some better purpose: "If you are waiting on a long line to get into an attraction, you can make a friend. If it is raining, you can explore shops, museums or go antiquing instead of sitting around, sulking about the weather. If your companion is complaining, you can use that to establish a deeper intimacy"

(Sleed, 1980, p. B-4). Seeing suffering as producing at least some advantages or positive aspects has also been associated with better coping among people confronted with more severe negative events. Silver and Wortman (1980) review suggestive evidence that victims who are able to find value in their harrowing experiences are calmer and less distressed. For example, Natterson and Knudson (1960) report that among parents facing the death of a child, those who could link that experience to a desire to help all children were in a less agonized state of mind. Similarly, Weissman and Worden (1976) found that cancer patients who were able to find something favorable in their illness were the least distressed by it.

Other researchers have more directly investigated the effects of meaning on adjustment to serious negative events. Taylor and her colleagues have conducted a number of studies on the cognitive adaptations people make in response to developing cancer (Taylor, Lichtman, & Wood, 1984; Taylor, Wood, & Lichtman, 1983). In summarizing this work, Taylor (1983) notes that some of the patients saw their suffering as essential to some larger purpose, such as putting their lives in perspective, enabling them to gain greater self-awareness, or changing their priorities to focus on the really important things. These patients, who felt they were suffering at least in part for some greater good, were better psychologically adjusted than those who found either no meaning or what Taylor refers to as other types of meaning in their disease. Silver et al. (1983) studied the search for meaning among adult women who had been victims, in most cases, of father-daughter incest. Those women who could make some sense out of this experience were less distressed and better adjusted socially and had higher self-esteem than those who could not. In interpreting their results, Silver et al. report that only about 20% of the women who made sense of the incest did so by tying it to some positive feature of their own lives or some personal goal of theirs. However, this seems an underestimate of the number of women who found meaning in their incest by bonding it to something better in their lives. The remaining 80% of these women explained the incest by forgiving their fathers, attributing his behavior to mental illness or situational constraints, such as the death of the mother or her unwillingness to engage in sexual activities. It appears, then, that most of the women who found meaning in their incest did so by relating it to a more positive feature of their lives, specifically their remaining favorable feelings for their fathers. Together, these studies indicate that the type of meaning commitment provides—enabling us to see our suffering as necessary or important in accomplishing or maintaining some cause, goal, or valued relationship—is the type of meaning that may best enhance coping and adjustment to stressful events.

Recent research on the effects of life events on physical and mental health provides further support for the proposition that the bonding of positive and negative elements through commitment enables us to cope successfully. Although life event research has traditionally focused on rather negative occurrences (see Monroe, 1982; Schroeder & Costa, 1984, for reviews), some studies have investigated the impact of more positive events as well. The effects of these positive events seem to be rather mixed. For example, Lewinsohn and his associates have found that depressed people tend to engage in fewer pleasant activities and that increases in the depressed person's pleasant activities are associated with improvement in mood (Lewinsohn & Graf, 1973; Lewinsohn & Libet, 1972). Cohen and Hoberman (1983) found that among students who reported experiencing a high number of negative events, those who also reported a high number of positive events were less likely to score as physically ill or depressed on health scales. These studies indicate that positive events lead to less distress and better coping, but other studies have not found this to be the case. Lazarus and his colleagues have investigated the effects of "hassles" and "uplifts"—minor negative and positive events—on psychological and physical health (Delongis, Coyne, Dakof, Folkman, & Lazarus, 1982; Kanner, Coyne, Schaefer, & Lazarus, 1980; Lazarus, 1981). These studies have shown that hassles are good predictors of poor health, better in some ways than more major negative events (see, also, Eckenrode, 1984). However, uplifts are not related to better health overall, and among women at least, more uplifts are associated with greater reported distress. Similarly, Miller, Ingham, and Davidson (1976) and Sweeney, Schaeffer, and Golin (1982) also found no relationship between reported pleasant or positive events and depression level.

From a commitment perspective, these inconsistent results are not very surprising. Positive events will make negative ones more meaningful only when the two types of events are connected by commitment. Pleasant activities and outcomes must represent goals we are committed to in order to absorb and neutralize our negative experiences. The preconditions of commitment—choice and responsibility—also appear to be necessary for positive events to have beneficial effects on coping. Hammen and Glass (1975) report two studies in which one group of depressed subjects was instructed by a therapist to increase their pleasant activities. Control groups of depressed subjects received no such instruction. The people who were told to engage in more pleasant activities did so for several weeks, but they were no less depressed at the end of this period; and in one study, they were more depressed than the controls. Both Blaney (1977) and Coates and Wortman (1980) explain these results as a consequence of the attributions the depressed subjects were probably making. They attributed their increase in pleasant activities to the therapists' demands rather than their own choice, and so they experienced these activities as extrinsically motivated chores rather than intrinsically motivated fun. Survey research by Reich and Zautra (Reich & Zautra, 1981; Zautra & Reich, 1980) has shown that subjective well-being is related to the experience of positive events that people feel responsible for (what the authors call "Positive Origin Events") but not to their experience of equally positive events for which they do not feel responsible (what the authors call "Positive Pawn Events"). More recently, Reich and Zautra (1983) have found that pleasant events that they call "Desires"—activities that are freely chosen and intrinsically motivated—are related to greater subjective well-being and better psychiatric health, especially among college students who are experiencing high levels of stressful events. Taken together, these results suggest that positive events must be seen as part of a commitment in order to counteract or neutralize our negative experiences.

Finding meaning in negative events may require seeing them as directly related not only to positive elements but to positive elements that are somehow bigger, more important, or more significant than the negative experiences. When this is true, minor negative events may not even be perceived, or may not be perceived as negative. The very fact that they are perceived, coded as negative, and experienced as hassles (at least with any high degree of frequency) may signify that something is wrong with, or missing from, the major life commitment in that domain. Nietzel and Barnett (1979) found that the more minor problems subjects had with spouses, such as, "spouse monpolized bathroom," the less happy they were with their marriages. However, the number of similarly minor but positive behaviors that spouses performed, such as, "spouse packed my lunch," was not related to marital satisfaction. Although the irritations and the kindnesses of a spouse would probably be seen as closely related, the favors a spouse provides may not be sufficient justification for the problems he or she causes. Such minor irritations may need to be seen as sacrifices we tolerate for something larger, such as love. Kessler and Essex (1982) found that dissatisfaction with housework was strongly related to depression for nonmarried women, less so for married women, and not at all for married women who had loving, intimate relationships. Major, overarching commitments, such as an intense romantic relationship or adherence to a religion, can absorb many of the negative events we experience because they directly connect so many domains of our lives to a larger, more significant purpose. Research has shown that sincerely committed religious believers do report a strong sense of purpose in life (Crumbaugh, Raphael, & Sharadar, 1970; Paloutzian, 1981). Freedman (1978) found that people who believe their lives have greater purpose or meaning in general are more satisfied with almost every aspect of their lives—the recognition they get, their finances, their home, job, romantic life, friends, and even their own physical attractiveness. They are also less frequently anxious, tired, guilty, lonely, or fearful.

As we saw in our chapter on control, the ability to commit oneself to a particular course of action, and to justify that commitment, does not necessarily mean that the course of action is easy. On the contrary, greater commitment is associated with a course of action that is seen as difficult, demanding, and perhaps problematic. Thus, it should not be assumed that seeing the positive aspects of stressful situations means ignoring or glossing over the real difficulties these situations involve. Viewing a problem as meaningful does not necessarily cancel out all unhappiness or distress about the problem. Some studies have shown that people who can find meaning in their pain are less upset and unhappy than those who cannot (Silver, 1983; Silver & Wortman, 1980; Taylor, 1983), but it does not follow that these people are completely happy and content. Silver (1983), for example, points out that even those incest victims who could make sense of their sexual violations scored worse than the general population on measures of psychological distress. Likewise, in a research review, Coates and Winston (1983) report that participants in peer support groups often come to find their victimization more meaningful after belonging to such a group, particularly because the group enables them to discover and help similarly afflicted others. However, they are not usually any less depressed after participating then victims who have not been involved in such groups.

It is not the presence or absence of distress, in our view, which is crucial, but whether or not this distress is converted into positive motivation to pursue a helpful line of action. Some distress may be necessary to kick this line of action into gear in the first place. Eventually, however, effective coping will be best sustained if people can see an unpleasant situation, as well as the action it has called forth, as having redeeming or intrinsically valuable features of its own. Finding meaning in adversity may help more with some aspects of the coping process than others (see Folkman, 1984). Specifically, it may not help people eliminate all the psychological disturbances that negative events can bring, but it should help them see the negative event as at least tolerable rather than catastrophic, as a challenge rather than a defeat. Consistent with this reasoning, laboratory studies have shown that when people have more choice over encountering mild stressors, such as electric chocks or loud noise bursts, they do not usually rate the aversive stimuli as less painful than people with less choice do, but they are usually willing to endure them for much longer (see Thompson, 1981, for a review). Similarly, Lipowski (1970–1971) has argued that when people can connect their illness to some positive goal, they may continue to feel bad about being sick, but they are more likely to engage in active coping methods rather than becoming passive and helpless. On the other hand, when negative events are seen as meaningless and unintegrated with anything positive, even relatively minor losses can trigger major depression, as Adamson and Schmale (1965) found was the case for more than one-third of their sample of psychiatric patients.

The capacity for commitment may help us to cope with stress not just by allowing us to find meaning for the stress but also by enabling us to benefit more from social support. Research has generally shown a positive, even causal, relationship between availability and quality of social support and physical and mental health (see Billings & Moos, 1982; Leavy, 1983; Wortman, 1984, for reviews). It seems to follow almost by definition that people who are more inclined to make commitments are more likely to have ongoing relationships with friends and family, a social network (Mitchell, 1982) to which they can turn in bad times as well as good. But as suggested in the chapter on control, a greater capacity for commitment should also enable people to make better use of whatever support is available. Research indicates that the stress-buffering effects of social support are greater for people with an internal locus of control (Sandler & Lakey, 1982; Lefcourt, Martin, & Saleh, 1984) and people who score higher on the hardiness scale (Kobasa, 1984; Kobasa & Pucetti, 1982). Since these variables are positively related to capacity for commitment, we would also expect a stronger capacity for commitment to have similar effects. This finding has often been interpreted as indicating that internal or hardy individuals are less likely to succumb to the passivity and dependency that strong social support can breed (Kobasa, 1984). The more others do for us, the harder it may become to do things for ourselves, especially when we are coping with other stresses and strains (Burgess, 1969; see also Brickman et al., 1982; Coates,

Renzaglia, & Embree, 1983, for reviews). The best way of avoiding such traps could be by increasing the contributions and sacrifices we make for others. In other words, we may best use social support at stressful times by becoming generally more committed to available relationships. This is, of course, what people with a greater capacity for commitment would most likely do.

The beneficial effects of social support are most often seen as coming from what others give to the distressed person—for example, helpful information or needed goods and services (see Barrera & Ainlay, 1983; House, 1981; Silver & Wortman, 1980; Wortman, 1984, for reviews). Consideration is seldom given to the fact that supportive relationships are reciprocal ones, in which people are expected not only to receive but to give. The commitment interpretation significantly differs from traditional perspectives on social support, which view supportive others as the critical, active agents and the recipient as essentially passive. Our emphasis is just the reverse. Social support may have its most favorable effects on coping by providing distressed people with relationships they can make contributions to rather than just get services from. High degrees of social support have been associated with more, rather than less, activity on the part of the recipient. For example, Stephens, Blau, Oser, and Miller (1978) found that as informal social support increased so did planned engagements, involvement in leisure pursuits, and a variety of other activities done with friends. To be effective, supportive relationships may have to require sacrifices from all the parties involved. In an interesting study comparing unmarried adults who lived alone or with others, Hughes and Gove (1981) found that those who lived alone were no worse off on most measures of mental health and psychological well-being, and they were actually better off on some. People who lived alone reported feeling irritated less often and also said they were more satisfied with their home lives. However, Hughes and Gove did find that people who live alone are more likely to use alcohol and other drugs. They suggest, therefore, that the primary benefits we derive from having others around are the sometimes irritating daily obligations and responsibilities that living with someone involves. Such obligations or sacrifices can keep us from our own self-destructive tendencies—we are less likely to stay out all night drinking, for example, when there is someone at home who is expecting us to fix breakfast, let the dog out, help with the cleaning, or just be there. Further supporting the notion that it is what you give rather than get that is important, research on recipient reactions to aid has consistently shown that those who help, rather than those who receive help, benefit most in terms of greater self-esteem and perceived self-competence (see Brickman et al., 1982; Coates, Renzaglia, & Embree, 1983; Fisher, Nadler, & Whitcher-Alagna, 1982, for reviews). Similarly, supportive relationships may best enhance coping by giving us something to work and sacrifice for, something to be obligated and committed to and derive meaning from.

Commitment and adaptive functioning. Commitment, of course, has to do with more than subjective well-being, as we saw in the chapters on rationality and control. It also has to do with the capacity for sustained, effective action, and thus the ability of an individual or species to survive. Commitment contributes to survival indirectly through its enhancement of subjective well-being. Commitment also contributes to survival directly by enabling us to persist in activities even when they carry costs or sacrifices that can make us unhappy and even when there is little evidence for some ultimate reason to go on.

It is by enhancing our ability to engage in effective action, rather than by making us happy and satisfied, that commitment has its primary adaptive value. One cannot argue that evolution is designed to make people happy, or that a particular adaptation would be selected for simply because it made those who possessed it happier than those who did not (Ghiselin, 1974). Indeed, it can be argued that a restless and somewhat dissatisfied creature would be continually motivated to seek more rewarding and presumably more favorable ecological niches. But as it turns out, subjective well-being also contributes to our ability to initiate and maintain the types of activities that are most likely to promote survival.

Other authors have noted that being able to maintain a positive mood and optimistic outlook facilitates effective action and problem solving (Lazarus, Kanner, & Folkman, 1980; Seligman, 1975; Taylor, 1983). Linsenmeier and Brickman (1978) review a vast body of literature dealing with the effects of expectations on performance, and they conclude that people with higher expectations usually perform better (although they are also more upset and disappointed if they learn they have performed poorly). Hopelessness, the antithesis of optimism, appears to be an important predictor of suicide, the antithesis of adaptive functioning (see Petrie & Chamberlain, 1983, for a review). Sackeim (1983) reviews several studies indicating that people perform more effectively when they are happier, even if their happiness is based on unrealistic, positively biased interpretations of the world. A number of experiments have shown that nondepressed people expect to perform better than objective conditions warrant in a chance situation, but depressed people do not (Alloy & Abramson, 1979, 1980, 1982; Golin, Terrell, Weitz, & Drost, 1979). Putting people into better moods makes them feel like they have more control over outcomes (Alloy, Abramson, & Viscusi, 1981), which presumably leads to greater persistence. In general, then, happiness and subjective well-being appear to promote and maintain effective action.

Subjective well-being may also contribute to our ability to sustain activities and survive by making us physically healthier and better able to overcome illness or injury. Hinkle (1968) found that telephone operators who liked their work, their families, and their associates were generally healthier than those who did not. Terman and Sears (see Goleman, 1980) found similar results in their longitudinal study of the gifted. Several recent literature reviews reveal a consistent and positive relationship between subjective well-being and physical health (Okun, Stock, Haring, & Witter, 1984; Zautra & Hempel, 1984). Maintaining a positive outlook may be particularly important in the health recovery process. Silver and Wortman (1980) review several studies that indicate that quadriplegics and paraplegics who believe they can improve their condition through their own efforts, even if this is unrealistic, show better emotional functioning and coping. In her work with cancer patients,

Taylor has repeatedly emphasized the extent to which these patients positively distort bad aspects of their situations, which she views as promoting favorable psychological and physical outcomes (Taylor, 1983; Taylor, Lichtman, & Wood, 1984; Taylor, Wood, & Lichtman, 1983). Lazarus (1983) reviews several studies indicating that people who have suffered heart attacks, spinal cord injuries, and strokes show better adjustment and decreased mortality when they remain hopeful and optimistic despite their illnesses.

So by promoting greater satisfaction and subjective well-being, commitment also contributes to adaptive functioning and survival. But as we saw in earlier chapters, commitment contributes to our capacity for effective action in other ways than by making us happy. Indeed, in an attempt to safeguard their happiness or self-esteem, people may avoid commitment. Because commitments always involve costs and risks, and because it takes energy to make and sustain the decisions on which they are based, it is understandable that people should have a well-developed set of skills for minimizing their commitments. Minimizing what one is committed to automatically minimizes what one can regret if things do not work out. People are especially likely to exercise their ability to avoid commitments when they anticipate that they cannot succeed in making a commitment that will have a satisfactory outcome. They may even have a stable agenda of things they have decided not to decide (a commitment of sorts, of course). In her catalogue of ways of avoiding decisions, Corbin (1979) generally assumes that decisions are only being postponed (e.g., for better deliberation, further information, current need to attend to other things) rather than being put aside altogether. But if it appears that a satisfactory decision cannot be made and implemented, people are likely to be happier if they can put it aside altogether.

Of course, even when people do not feel ready to do so themselves, they may be pressed by others to make decisions and commitments. Following from work on reactance theory (Brehm, 1966), people may be particularly inclined to respond to such pressure by working even more diligently to avoid commitment. In passing, it may be worth clarifying here a distinction between reactance and commitment. There are times when people will react to pressure from an influence agent by increasing or decreasing their commitment to a recommended line of action. When parents attempt to discourage the romantic involvements of their children, for example, this has the paradoxical effect of increasing that involvement—the Romeo and Juliet phenomena (Driscoll, Davis & Lipetz, 1972). Commitment—or the avoidance of commitment—is not the same thing as reactance, however, but rather only one possible way of restoring the actor's sense of freedom in the manner that reactance intends. The sense of having restored one's freedom may indeed require the actor to publicize a commitment of one sort or another (see our earlier discussion of freedom), but the motivation of reactance—to restore freedom—is quite different from the motivation for commitment—to establish a consistent line of action.

Even when people do decide to begin making a commitment, if initial costs to subjective well-being are high, they may do so tentatively, disclaiming the commitment to others and perhaps themselves. The problem of disclaiming commitment is particularly pressing when people have decided to engage in an activity that is embarrassing and thus threatens their happiness, self-esteem, and social standing. Goffman (1961) amusingly describes how children who are too old to ride a merry-go-round—an activity that is supposed to be interesting, exciting, or scary only for younger children—use smiles and looks of bored detachment to make it clear that they are only minimally involved with this activity (however much they may actually be enjoying it). An even more serious problem in this regard faces people attending singles' dances (Berk, 1977) because the mere fact of appearing at such a dance tends to stigmatize people as lonely, unattractive, or otherwise unsuccessful in love. Anyone who can possibly claim a reason for attending the dance other than to find a partner—for example, staff who are working there, researchers who are studying the phenomenon—does so as immediately and unsubtly as possible. Participants always claim to have come to the dance for the sake of a friend who needed company or because they just happened to be in the neighborhood or were curious about what such dances were like—anything other than having come to the dance for its own sake. Sometimes, to be sure, commitment to a line of action is not embarrassing in itself but threatens to become so if the commitment becomes excessive. This is the case with students studying for qualifying exams that may determine their entire future careers. Mechanic (1962) describes in great detail how graduate students in this situation use joking and humor to drain off some of the pressure and downplay some of the fiercer and more stressful elements of their own commitment. The joking is designed to communicate to others (and to oneself) that the commitment to passing should be serious but not overwhelming and that there are alternatives in life (often described with black humor) for people who do not pass. Maintaining subjective well-being and becoming fully committed to some course of action may therefore be in opposition to one another under certain circumstances.

It is precisely because of this opposition that commitment contributes to adaptive functioning in a way that the pursuit of immediate happiness and gratification cannot. Commitment enables people to act in ways that involve making sacrifices or taking risks that they are decidedly unhappy about but that they understand as being necessary to any possibilities of future happiness or success. The analogy suggested by Kiev (1979), in his discussion of how people can move away from comfortable but doomed patterns of self-defeating behavior, is that of a person leaving an oasis that is slowly drying up and setting out across a desert with no certainty of reaching another habitable spot. To stay at the oasis represents certain death in the long run, but to leave it requires both greater immediate discomfort and the uncertainty of not knowing whether there is a more desirable place. The courage or commitment that is required to act in these circumstances functions not as a means to happiness but as a device to enable people to surrender some portion of happiness in pursuit of a larger, more desirable goal.

Commitments typically involve greater threats to subjective well-being in their earlier than their later stages. For example, Callero and Piliavin (1983) describe how some people become committed to donating blood, and provide data indicating that variables like how much choice people have in coming for their first visit predict who becomes a regular donor. They also review other research indicating that first-time donors are more likely to complain about factors like the pain of the needle than are donors coming for subsequent visits. The beginning of a love affair may involve a level of infatuation that more developed relationships do not have (Rubin, 1973), but love relationships are also apparently more upsetting and stressful at first than they are in later, more assured and comfortable periods. For example, Klemper and Bologh (in Lobsenz, 1981) report that people in the early stages of romantic relationships are more likely than the average person to show signs of physical and psychological distress—to take more nonprescription drugs, to suffer more from minor illnesses like colds, headaches, and upset stomachs, and to be more likely to have sleeping problems. On the other hand, lovers whose relationships have lasted more than two years have fewer ailments than average. This suggests that commitments are more likely to be associated with enduring happiness at later, more mature stages than they are in earlier, more turbulent stages. Through commitment people can convert initial unhappiness into greater subjective well-being in the long run.

In the same way, by enabling us to keep going even in the face of inevitable unhappy outcomes, commitment makes a very important contribution to our survival. Even when no alternatives seem like good ones, when all the options promise regrets, decisions still often have to be made and actions taken. Confronted by a swooping hawk, a rabbit can fight, hide, or run away. None may bring escape, but the rabbit is much more likely to escape if it tries to do one of these rather than all three or none at all. Similarly, depressed people only make their problems worse by continually searching for the best solution rather than choosing and acting on any (Billings & Moos, 1984; Coyne, Aldwin, & Lazarus, 1981). To the extent the environment favors activity, it will favor wholehearted over halfhearted pursuit, sustained rather than interrupted or distracted action. By enabling us to turn the initial distress and problems encountered in some activity into enhancement of and persistence in that activity, commitment acts as a cybernetic mechanism (Carver & Scheier, 1982) to keep us on track when the going gets rough.

Commitment not only allows us to sustain activities and persist in tasks and relationships that are not immediately rewarding, it also enables us to go on in a much broader sense. In order to survive, humans need a purpose in life, a reason to go on; at a most basic level, an answer to the question of why they should get out of bed in the morning. Most people believe they have such an answer—their careers, their families, God, and so on. But these answers are fragile and imperfect at best. Much as we may believe that it will not happen to us, we do know that even very talented and motivated workers can become ill, injured, or otherwise forced to give up their careers. Convinced though we may be that our families will be together forever, we all know of once happy families who, due to one crisis or another, no longer see one another. Whatever our own stand on the matter, we all know that philosophers have been arguing for centuries about whether God really exists, precisely because there is no definitive or universally acceptable answer to this issue. And, much as we may not like to think about it, we all known that we are going to die, maybe not for years and maybe tomorrow. No matter what purpose in life we may have found, we can never know with rational certainty that the purpose is there now, or will be there for very long. To maintain a purpose in life, then, we need faith and courage, the enthusiastic willingness to accept as true something that cannot be proven as true—in other words, a commitment.

What would life be like if we were unable to find any meaning or purpose in it? Modern playwrights have been earnest in their attempts to acquaint us with such an existence. Beckett, Ionesco, Osborne, and Pinter all discard the amenities of dramatic construction—including recognizable plot, dialogue, and sentiment—in order to force their audiences to face what they feel is the void in which human lives are conducted:

> For Beckett, neither age, time, language, nor intelligence can help us. For Pinter, language only explores ignorance and uncertainty. Logic, reasoned discourse, discernable fact, knowledge, all dissolve into either laughter or silence. . . . (Beckett's) much-discussed grimness of outlook—the melancholy conviction that existence equals protacted pain and pointlessness; that all men's acts are circus turns performed over the void: risky, purposeless, irresistibly funny; that meaning is a preposterous fantasy—is maintained with a kind of irritable comic serenity and wry good humor that may be the only form of nobility left to us. . . . One can't go on, one goes on, with a brief laugh if possible. (Chapman, 1979, pp. 54-55)

Clearly, this meaningless world of "protracted pain and pointlessness," in which the best we can hope for is to recognize the bad joke of human absurdity, would be a devastating and debilitating world in which to live.

If we manage to avoid such a world though, it is not because we can ever know that it is in fact a better place, or one in which we have much control over our fates or circumstances. There is a genuine tension between the belief that human life—either individually or collectively—has some discernable purpose, and the lack of anything like scientific evidence for such a belief. Or, as Kant (1964) put it in the preface to *The Critique of Pure Reason*: "Human reason has this peculiar fate, that in one species of its knowledge it is burdened by questions which, as prescribed by the very nature of reason itself, it is not able to ignore, but, which as transcending all its powers, it is also not able to answer." To have a sense of purpose in life, therefore, requires not reason or intellect but faith, the maintenance of a belief in the absence of any rational or empirical evidence to support it. If people can continue to believe that their work, their families, their God will sustain them even in the face of evidence that such things can be very fragile and temporary, it is only because they are engaged in a commitment, a process that can build certainty out of contradiction.

The fruit of these commitments, and the measure of their success, is a sense of being at home and connected in the world rather than being alien or estranged in it. It is important to remember, as Mayeroff (1971) puts it, that the world becomes intelligible or meaningful to people in this sense not through the exercise of control, which can never serve to answer questions of meaning and value, but through commitment and caring. Mayeroff writes, "in the sense in which intelligibility means being at home in the world, we are ultimately at home not through dominating or explaining or appreciating things, but through caring and being cared for" (p. 76). Such caring, indeed, involves a relaxation of the need for control, which is in turn essential to allowing the person to be open to the experience or events to which he or she would like to be connected. There is an interdependence between the caring we feel, most of the time, for our work, our families, and the other sources of meaning in our lives, and our ability to forget, most of the time, that these things may in fact be quite vulnerable, ephemeral and out of our control. It is only through commitment that we can come to care so much about such delicate and possibly transient objects or allow ourselves to dismiss our fears and worries over losing what we care so much about.

The objects of these commitments may be—must be—imperfect, as are the imperfectly wired creatures who make them. Neither is coherent in themselves, neither is free of contradiction. But as we have repeatedly observed, the commitments themselves are grounded in these very imperfections and contradictions. Neither their state nor their fate keeps us from needing them, in the same way Woody Allen (1982) summed up how people need relationships in the closing scene of *Annie Hall*:

> I thought of that old joke, you know . . . this guy goes to a psychiatrist and says, "Doc, uh, my brother's crazy. He thinks he's a chicken." And . . . the doctor says, "Well, why don't you turn him in?" And the guy says, "I would, but I need the eggs." Well, I guess that's pretty much how I feel about relationships. You know, they're totally irrational and crazy and absurd . . . but, . . . I guess we keep goin' through it because . . . most of us need the eggs (p. 105)

The metaphor is misleading in that it implies that most of what people get from such engagements is provided by the partner (the eggs), rather than generated by their own involvement. We would agree, however, that the sense of purpose we get from commitments, like the eggs, is illusory, a product of belief rather than empirical fact. Of course, such a sense of purpose is not experienced by people as anything like a false belief, but rather as the basic truth of their lives, the justification of their sacrifice, suffering, and very existence. Without such self-generated illusions, people would find living very difficult indeed. It is interesting to note in this regard the mounting research evidence that shows, contrary to traditional views, that it is nondepressed people who tend to distort, deny, and misperceive reality—albeit in a positive direction—and depressed people who tend to see things, very reasonably and rationally, as they are (Alloy & Abramson, 1979; Lewinsohn, Mischel, Chaplin & Barton, 1980; see also Roth & Ingram, 1985; Sackeim, 1983; Taylor, 1983; for reviews). As Woody Allen suggests is the case with relationships, commitment more generally is a crazy, irrational process that works, after a fashion and for awhile, in holding us together and in the world.

The commitments people make are nothing less than a measure of their courage—that virtue so essential to all other virtues, as Samuel Johnson put it, that it is always respected, even when associated with vice. The basis on which we make commitments may change, as we become more aware of the uncertainty of our knowledge and the unknowability of certain elements of our fate. Perhaps, as Isiah Berlin (1969) reported, "to realize the relative validity of one's convictions . . . and yet stand for them unflinchingly, is what distinguishes a civilized man from a barbarian" (p. 172). Perhaps it is only a sophisticated modern awareness that faces inner as well as outer doubts, doubts about the reliability or trustworthiness of one's own inner world as well as doubts about the realiability of the outer world, whereas primitive awareness confronted mainly the latter. But the essential quality of courage, and commitment, remains: as Tillich (1952) put it, an affirmative response to the despair through which all must pass, the deepest most deeply.

Throughout this section on psychological adjustment, we have proposed several ways in which commitment contributes to mental health. Through commitment, we can feel more satisfied with our lives and ourselves, despite the fact that we often have to settle for less than optimal solutions. Further, we can derive meaning from adversity and hardship in a way that enables us to cope more successfully. And we can persist in our activities even if they make us unhappy and there is little evidence for some ultimate reason to go on. Without engaging in a process like commitment, which allows us to turn ambivalence and uncertainty, forgone alternatives, and other costs associated with some activity into greater valuing of that activity, it could be impossible to achieve these beneficial outcomes. In this way, then, commitment may be necessary for mental health. But commitment is clearly not a sufficient condition for mental health. As we have already noted, becoming committed can involve some very painful first steps, which likely detract, at least temporarily, from our subjective well-being. Most of us can name people who appear to be very committed to their jobs and families but are not very happy in them. Indeed, this would seem to describe the dominant flavor of work in the United States (Terkel, 1975). Commitments can also lead people to act in maladaptive ways. As Janoff-Bulman and Brickman (1981) have shown, dogged pursuit of a goal that has become impossible to obtain may lead to either real tragedy (as when the Jews of Europe could not believe that the passive strategies that had enabled them to survive with previous oppressors would not work with Hitler) or psychic tragedy (as when a spouse persists in trying to sustain a relationship that has become unworkable and irreparable). We will now turn to a consideration of this darker side of commitment, beginning with commitment-induced distress.

COMMITMENT-INDUCED DISTRESS

What happens when people make commitments which, for internal or external reasons, they are unable to pursue in what they regard as a successful or satisfactory manner yet are also unable to abandon? The experience of being caught or trapped in this manner will be painful. In Tomkins' (1965) language, sequences of positive and negative events will tend to be structured with the negative events bracketing the positive ones (which are thus seen as the intermediate ones or the exceptions), rather than positive events bracketing, absorbing, and defusing the negative ones. We are talking, of course, about the two faces of commitment discussed in chapter one, and about circumstances in which people experience the negative face rather than the positive one. The precise nature of the pain they experience, however, depends on the nature of the threat to their commitments and the means they have available to combat this threat.

One of the common ways that people experience problems in pursuing their commitments is through overcommitment. When people are overcommitted, one commitment cannot be carried out satisfactorily without detriment to another, equally important, commitment. Overcommitment is likely to be most serious, we hypothesize, when people are unwilling to relinquish alternatives, have no clear rules (their own or society's) for doing so, underestimate the time and energy needed for everything, and continue to try to do all things regardless of the conflicts involved. Overcommitment is fostered and encouraged by a social system that places people in many different roles (family, career, recreational, etc.) and rewards them for filling as many as possible as well as possible. Overcommitment is a form of disorder to which mature individuals—with well-developed capacities for commitment—are especially vulnerable. It is interesting that more committed, regular blood donors are less likely than first-time donors to complain about factors like pain but more likely to complain about the wait involved when they come to give blood (Callero & Piliavin, 1983). To the extent that people with a strong capacity for commitment are also inclined to overcommitment, it is to be expected that issues like waiting and wasting time would be primary concerns of theirs.

However, the inability to balance or set priorities on conflicting commitments can inflict severe costs. We may need friends and intimate relationships to sustain us in this world, but trying to meet all the demands and requirements of many such relationships can be exhausting and demoralizing (Turkington, 1985). A powerful set of conflicting commitments are set in motion by serious extramarital affairs, in which the actor cannot, almost by definition, provide each of the valued partners with all these partners want or expect. Bartusis (1978) reports that infidelity can generate a variety of psychological and physical symptoms in both the perpetrator and the injured party. Maybe the best example of overcommitment, or at least a strong sense of overcommitment, is represented by the Type A behavior pattern. Type A individuals are consistently described as time-conscious and always focused on maximizing personal productivity, even to the point of doing several things simultaneously—for example, working while eating, calculating while driving, or reading while shaving (Jenkins, 1975; Matthews & Brunson, 1979; Williams, 1984). People who exhibit this heavily overcommitted behavior pattern, of course, are substantially more likely to have heart attacks (Friedman & Rosenman, 1974).

On the other hand, if they are not completely incompatible or directly conflicting, multiple commitments can enrich people's lives, and may be actively sought out for precisely this reason. In recent decades, for example, many women have chosen to pursue both motherhood and a career, in some cases at least because they find these dual commitments more fulfilling than either by itself (Poloma, 1972). Of course, successfully conducting such dual commitments does require rather special organizational skills, and unfortunately, we need to know much more than we do at present about how people manage multiple commitments. Sometimes, it is possible to link two commitments and thus contribute to both simultaneously, as when husband and wife work together and so satisfy both career and marital commitments. In other cases, commitments can be better managed by compartmentalizing them or keeping them separate, and providing as little occasion as possible for gauging one against the other. In other cases, especially when commitments are in direct conflict, priorities must be set, with one commitment declared more important and carried out more conscientiously than the other, however painful this might be. Exactly when these or other management strategies will be most effective in reducing the tension among multiple commitments remains an issue for future research.

In any case, it is likely that even the best management strategies will not eliminate all the problems that multiple commitments bring, only minimize them. The more commitments we have, the more demands there are on our time and energy, and problems such as feeling overwhelmed by all we have to do become inevitable. But such problems, like other sources of stress, need not be devastating as long as we can see them as meaningful, as something we choose to endure for some higher good or purpose. Recent research indicates, for instance, that not all the components of Type A behavior are directly related to heart disease. A tendency to rapid speech, time-consciousness, and hyperactivity, all symptoms of over-commitment, are not related to premature death by heart attack except in people who are also cynical and inclined to see the world as hostile and meaningless (see Williams, 1984, for a review). Similarly, Kobasa (1984) reports that executives who score high on Type A measures but also score high on the hardiness dimension—which includes measures of the ability to become committed and find meaning in stress—are much less likely to get sick than Type A people who are low in hardiness. So while even very organized and effective managers may not be able to escape all of the strains that multiple commitments can bring, they can escape the negative impact of such strains as long as they see them as justified by the meaning and value their commitments provide.

Commitment can also lead, though perhaps less obviously, to more difficult forms of distress: jealousy, guilt, and depression. All three of these conditions have a common feature—to outside observers, they seem like irrational reactions, too intense for the situation that appears to prompt them. Jealousy has often been characterized as a sick or neurotic response, quite out of proportion to any real threat the jealous person faces (Freud, 1959; Mead, 1931; Peele & Brodsky, 1975). Guilt may appear to be irrational in a similar way, since it is often the people who are objectively most innocent of a transgression who feel most guilty about it (Gerrard, 1982; Gerrard & Gibbons, 1982; Mosher, 1973). When people suffer serious losses, others may expect some depression to follow, but even in these circumstances, those around a depressed person often see his or her distress as too intense, too complicated, and too enduring for the loss he or she has experienced (see Coates & Peterson, 1982; Coates & Winston, 1983; Coates & Wortman, 1980; Silver & Wortman, 1980, for reviews). The apparently unfounded intensity of all these disorders may indicate that they are indeed related to commitment. As we saw in the chapter on meaning and value, the components of intrinsic value in a commitment to a relationship or activity that has been pursued for some time are characteristically invisible to observers. Thus, jealous, guilty, and depressed people may act like there is more at stake than there appears to be, in reaction to the threatened or actual loss of intrinsic value that outsiders cannot see. Indeed, as we will discuss in more detail below, commitment, with the intrinsic value it provides, appears to be necessary for any of these disorders to occur.

Although we view jealousy, guilt, and depression as all related to commitment, we see them as related in different ways. People experience guilt and jealousy when they believe a commitment is threatened, whereas they experience depression when they believe a commitment has been lost. Previous researchers have noted that people respond to losses with depression and by expressing negative feelings, whereas they tend to respond to threats with anxiety and by searching for solutions (Finlay-Jones & Brown, 1981; McCrae, 1984; see, also, Lazarus & Launier, 1978). Similarly, we see guilt and jealousy as experiences people have when commitments can still be saved, whereas people experience depression when a commitment has been ended.

Threats to a commitment can be either internal or external. Guilt results when the obstacle to the commitment is internal—for example, an inability to resist temptations or transgressions that could keep a commitment from being fulfilled. While researchers have sometimes confused guilt with causal responsibility for a bad outcome, we will consider guilt as the result of moral responsibility attributions (Brickman et al., 1982; Heider, 1959), a distinction we will discuss in detail later. External threats to commitment can come in many forms, but in interpersonal relationships and achievement situations, such threats often derive from the more successful performance of a rival. Jealousy results when people perceive such an external threat to a commitment. In our discussion, we will focus on romantic jealousy—the type of jealousy that arises when a love relationship is threatened by the real or imagined interests of some outsider. This is the type of jealousy that seems to concern people most (Clanton & Smith, 1977), and it is also the type of jealousy that has most often been studied in the little research that is available on this topic. However, much of what is said here could probably be applied to jealousy that people encounter in other domains, such as their friendships or careers.

Earlier in this chapter, we indicated that depression is associated with an inability to make and sustain commitments. Thus, it may seem strange that we are now saying that commitment is a necessary condition for depression, but there is a logical consistency to this reasoning. Depression is seen as a state of being without commitment, or at least being without some important, unifying commitment. This state can therefore be brought about by the loss of commitment, just as it can be maintained by the inability to make new commitments. Indeed, it is precisely because commitment enables us to find relationships and activities worthwhile, meaningful, and important that we feel pain, regret, and remorse when these things are gone. In giving us something of value, commitment also gives us something to lose. If we did not care about some outcome, if we were not committed to it, we would not miss it. So by making it possible for us to be happy and fulfilled, commitment also makes it possible for us to experience emptiness and despair.

All three of these forms of distress—guilt, jealousy, and depression—can clearly be devastating and destructive. In all three, the search for meaning in the adversity is blunted by the fact that the very commitment that might ordinarily justify such distress is in doubt or already gone. But these forms of distress can also be quite functional, leading us to do what we can to save commitments that are still possible, and helping us to build new commitments when old ones are impossible.

Reactions to commitment threats: Jealousy and guilt. Most people would probably agree that jealousy is prompted by the perceived external threat of a rival, but they would perhaps be less inclined to accept that jealousy is a response to threat to commitment in particular. In a review of the literature on jealousy, Adams (1980) indicates that most researchers agree that jealousy is distinguished by "fear of losing to someone else," but not necessarily fear of losing a relationship or activity a person is committed to. However, in previous chapters we proposed that commitment is necessary for people to have such experiences as love and caring for another, and there appears to be some agreement that love is a necessary condition for romantic jealousy to occur. Traditionally, romantic jealousy has been associated with greater love, or deeper commitment, in a relationship. For example, in his play *The Miser*, Moliere tells us, "Only one who loves without ardor is never jealous." Similarly, in *Two Gentlemen of Verona*, Shakespeare writes, "For love, thou know'st, is full of jealousy." The medieval author, Capellanus, stated in his *Art of Courtly Love*, "He who is not jealous cannot be in love" and further, "True jealousy always increases the feelings of love." Some psychologists have also suggested that jealousy occurs only when people care about one another: "Who would want to live a life in which one cared so little about another, or the other was of so little value, that nothing he did, or who he went with, mattered. . . . If someone is precious to us, we must have a modicum of jealousy as a basic cement" (Seidenburg, 1967, p. 83). Even rational-emotive therapist Albert Ellis, who has argued that the total elimination of jealousy is the goal to strive for, admits that "if you were completely unjealous, we would suspect that you really didn't care very much for this partner" (Ellis, 1962, p. 173). So to the extent that loving and caring are the result of commitment, jealousy may be also.

However, there is another traditional view of jealousy, which at least indirectly suggests that jealousy is not the product of commitment. This is the view that the people who are most likely to get jealous are those who are exceptionally insecure and low in self-esteem (Berscheid & Fei, 1977; Clanton & Smith, 1977; Mead, 1931; Peele & Brodsky, 1975). There is some evidence supporting this view, especially when it comes to jealous men. White (1981b) found a negative relationship between measures of self-esteem and jealousy among men but not women. Women are more likely to say they would respond to jealousy by doing things to save the relationship, such as trying to make themselves more attractive to their partners, whereas men are more likely to respond to jealousy by doing things that would perhaps protect their self-esteem at the expense of the relationship (Adams, 1980; Shettel-Neuber, Bryson & Young, 1978; White, 1980). For example, men are more likely to say they would look for new relationships if they felt jealous (Shettel-Neuber et al., 1978), and in the rare case in which people respond in such ways, jealous men are much more likely than women to kill their wandering mates or their consorts (Adams, 1980). Earlier in this chapter, we pointed out that people need at least moderately high levels of self-esteem in order to form commitments, in order to believe they can make good choices and take responsibility for the consequences of their choices (cf. Gerard, Blevans, & Malcolm, 1964; Malewski, 1962). It would follow, then, that people chronically low in self-esteem would make fewer or weaker commitments. Thus, to the extent that jealousy is a result of commitment, men who are low in self-esteem should experience less jealousy. However, in the same earlier discussion, we suggested that people need commitment to continue seeing their relationships and activities as worthwhile and so maintain their self-esteem. Men may not get jealous because they are low in self-esteem but rather may experience low self-esteem because they are jealous and therefore doubtful about the future of a commitment that is an important source of their favorable self-image. In support of this, White found that for men, feelings of inadequacy as a partner occurred only after and not before a relationship had been disturbed by jealousy (see Adams, 1980).

Other research results provide further suggestive support for the proposition that commitment is a necessary condition for jealousy to occur. People are apparently more likely to experience romantic jealousy when they are more committed to a relationship, in the sense that they have greater perceived choice about continuing the relationship and make more sacrifices for the relationship. For instance, White (1981b) found, among women at least, that those who were most likely to be jealous were also most likely to agree that their threatened relationship "is about the best relationship I could hope to have with anybody." Aronson and Pines (see Adams, 1980) found that for both sexes, jealousy was most frequent among people who said they would not leave their partners no matter what alternatives were available to them, and among people who had themselves been unfaithful in a relationship. The most jealous people, then, seem to be the ones who see themselves as choosing the threatened relationship, even though they are quite likely aware of alternative relationships that are available to them. Similarly, in a review of survey data on attitudes toward infidelity, Bernard (1974) concludes that participants in nonconventional unions such as living together (in which people probably feel more choice about continuing their relationship) are more intolerant of infidelity than those in conventional unions such as marriage (in which extrinsic pressures limit people's choices about staying or going). Clanton (1981) also indicates that jealousy is a particular problem for people involved in nontraditional love relationships.

Other evidence suggests that jealousy is greatest among individuals who are most willing to sacrifice for a relationship. Research by White (1980, 1981a; see also Adams, 1980; White, 1982, for reviews) has fairly consistently shown that people who feel they are contributing more or are more involved than their partners in a relationship are also more likely to be jealous. Hansen (1983) found that among a sample of married men, those who were most jealous were also most likely to agree with statements like "I want desperately for my marriage to succeed and would go to almost any length to see that it does." Thus, when people choose to stay in and sacrifice for a relationship, they are also more likely to be jealous about the relationship.

Of course, in order for jealousy to occur, not only must people be committed to a relationship, they must also believe that the relationship may be lost through the partner's attraction to a rival. In support of this, people are more likely to feel jealous when they believe they cannot provide their partners with all a rival could (Adams, 1980; White, 1981a), or when they believe their partner is seeking a more permanent or intimate relationship with a rival (Hansen, 1982; White, 1982). In our culture, the trigger for romantic jealousy is usually sexual infidelity. White (1981b), for example, reports that the expectation of sexual exclusivity in a relationship is an important predictor of jealousy. But this may only be because in our culture, a partner's sexual activity with a rival usually also implies an important, intimate, or lasting relationship with that rival. Sexual infidelity, in and of itself, is neither sufficient nor necessary for romantic jealousy. It is quite common for a person to be jealous of the time his or her partner spends in other activities or relationships that have no sexual component at all but detract from time the person wishes they spent together (Hansen, 1982; Hansen, 1983; Lobsenz, 1975). On the other hand, in some relationships both partners agree to have outside sexual interactions, and jealousy does not result (at least as long as the norm of no serious involvement with these outside partners is followed; see e.g., Wachowiak & Bragg, 1980). Cross-culturally, there are many customary practices that might qualify as sexual infidelity in our culture but do not lead to jealousy in other societies because they are seen as enhancing rather than detracting from the primary marital relationship (Davis, 1936). For example, in some societies, the first person to have sexual intercourse with a new bride is not the groom but a priest or other respected, elder male. However, this is usually done to confirm that the bride is a virgin and, according to the beliefs of these cultures anyway, thereby insure that the marriage will be successful.

Guilt, like jealousy, is also a reaction to a perceived threat to the maintenance of a commitment. However, the jealous person does not feel that he or she has chosen to threaten the commitment—that choice was made by someone else, the partner or perhaps the rival. With guilt, it is the afflicted person who feels he or she has chosen the threatening activity. Guilt results, then, when people feel they have failed to live up to a commitment by making a choice that interferes or conflicts with the fulfillment of that commitment.

Most discussions of guilt do recognize it as the result or representation of an internal conflict. The classic psychoanalytical approach, of course, regards guilt as a punishment the superego inflicts not only for actions but even for impulses that conflict with its ideals (Freud, 1935). Guilt has usually been distinguished from shame on the grounds that guilt occurs when we fail to meet our own standards, whereas shame occurs when we fail to meet the standards of others (Erikson, 1950). Others have pointed out that we may feel guilty when we violate consensual or public norms (e.g., Schwartz, 1977), but only if we internalize those norms or standards and make them our own. To internalize rules or standards, of course, means that we choose, in most circumstances and most of the time, to abide by those standards (Schwartz, 1977). These standards, therefore, become a kind of commitment. Further, whenever we choose to follow some pursuit or goal, that commitment becomes a kind of internal standard.

The other element of guilt—the threat to the commitment—is also a product of choice. Guilt occurs when we choose, whether or not we enact that choice, to behave in ways that are detrimental to or inconsistent with a commitment we have made. The connection between choice and guilt seems tenuous at best if we see guilt as resulting from, or equivalent to, feeling that we have caused something bad to happen. People do blame themselves, in a causal way, for negative events or outcomes they would not choose—such as rape (Janoff-Bulman, 1979), accidental paralysis (Bulman & Wortman, 1977) and other afflictions (see Ross & DiTecco, 1975; Wortman, 1976, for reviews). People may even blame themselves for bad outcomes in a way that denies they could have had any choice—attributing the outcomes to stable, unchangeable, uncontrollable features of themselves, such as lack of ability or other characterological defects (Abramson & Sackeim, 1977; Abramson, Seligman, & Teasdale, 1978; Janoff-Bulman, 1979). Although such attributions perhaps do lead to reduced self-esteem, that is not the same thing as guilt. Guilt includes elements of self-blame and reduced self-esteem, but these reflect moral, not causal, attributions (Brickman et al., 1982). Some researchers recognize that guilt carries certain moral overtones—guilty people feel that they have failed to meet some standard they should have met, and sometimes even that they deserve to be punished for this failure (Mosher, 1966, 1973). The guilty person, then, is concerned not so much with questions of could or can, which causal attributions can answer, but with questions of should or ought, which only moral attributions can answer (see Heider, 1958).

Causal responsibility and moral responsibility, like control and choice (Thompson, 1981), can be difficult to distinguish because they are often correlated (Coates et al., 1983). But there are clearly situations in which causal information is unnecessary or irrelevant in the determination of moral responsibility. As Coates et al. (1983) point out, the classic example of such a situation is the legal defense of insanity. Everyone agrees the suspect is causally responsible for the crime—what they are trying to determine is whether the suspect can be held morally responsible for the crime, quite often by focusing specifically on the question of whether the person was capable of making reasonable decisions. As this example suggests, moral questions are questions of choice, which may have nothing to do with cause. It follows, then, that we will not hold ourselves morally responsible, or in other words feel guilty, for outcomes or events we did not, at least in some way, choose (see Brickman et al., 1982; Coates et al., 1983; Schwartz, 1977, for further discussion of moral responsibility). Guilt, then, is what we feel when we choose to do one thing that keeps us from doing something else that we believe is ultimately more valuable or important. It is the experience we have when we decide to stray from some activity, goal, or belief we are committed to.

Many of these ideas about the relationships among commitment, guilt, and jealousy received preliminary support in a study carried out for a senior honors thesis project by Aaron Janis under the supervision of the authors. Seventy-two undergraduates, 36 men and 36 women, were asked to rate how guilty or jealous a variety of common situations made them feel, and also to rate the number, intensity, and security of their commitments. Among subjects who indicated they were heavily committed, 64% reported often feeling jealous and 62% reported often feeling guilty, versus 22% and 19%, respectively, among those who reported being less committed. Of subjects who felt their commitments were threatened, 86% reported often feeling jealous and 72% said they frequently felt guilty. Among subjects who rated their commitments as secure, only 22% said they felt jealous and 26% said they felt guilty. All of these differences are highly statistically significant and clearly support the general proposition that guilt and jealousy result from perceived threats to commitments. Other significant findings support the hypothesis that these forms of distress result from different types of threats. Higher guilt was reported by people who said they frequently tested themselves, and in responses to situations in which the actors' commitments were threatened by the actors themselves. Higher jealousy was reported by people who said they frequently tested others and in response to situations in which the actors' commitments were threatened by someone else.

Jealousy and guilt can be devastating and intense forms of distress perhaps because they cannot be seen as meaningful in the usual way. For instance, it might be expected that when people run into difficulties or problems associated with their lovers but choose to stay with them anyway, they would resolve the ambivalence the problems create into greater love for their partners and stronger attachment to the relationship (cf. Driscoll, Davis, & Lipitz, 1972). But the jealous person who does this finds only greater pain in the fact that the partner appears to be getting ready to dissolve the relationship. Margaret Mead (1931) described jealousy as a "negative, miserable state of feeling," and Harry Stack Sullivan (1953) called it "poignant and devastating." Research suggests that jealous people are more likely than others to experience a whole range of negative emotions, including anger, anxiety, humiliation, shame, sorrow, and suspicion (Adams, 1980; Bringle & Evenbeck, 1979). Some jealous people, at least, are sufficiently distressed to seek professional help, especially from marriage counselors (Clanton & Smith, 1977; Lobsenz, 1975). Likewise, guilt presents unique problems in reducing ambivalence and thereby finding meaning in the distress. If people are tempted to sway from some goal they are committed to but choose not to give into temptation, they resolve the ambivalence created by the temptation into greater commitment to the goal (cf. Freedman, 1965). But when people choose the temptation, they create more dissonance, raising further doubts about the value or importance of the threatened commitment. Freedman (1978) found that except for relationships with the same-sex parent, guilt is the only characteristic of childhood that predicts adult unhappiness and dissatisfaction. People who often felt guilty as children are, as adults, more likely to experience fears, anxiety, insomnia, loneliness, feelings of worthlessness, mental breakdowns, and suicidal impulses.

Both jealousy and guilt, then, can lead to great distress, but like other forms of distress (Wortman & Dintzer, 1978), they can also motivate one to improve one's situation. Both jealousy and guilt appear to be designed, in many ways, to get people to do what they can to keep the threatened commitment alive. The same freedom that makes jealousy more likely in nonconventional relationships (Bernard, 1974) may also make it more necessary in these relationships because they do not have traditional, extrinsic pressures to hold them together. Jealousy does seem to lead people to value a threatened relationship more. According to folk wisdom, provoking jealousy in a partner is an effective means of increasing the partner's commitment to the relationship, and there is evidence that people do exactly that, especially when they lack the power to control the partner in other ways (White, 1980). As we noted earlier, despite the pain of jealousy, jealous people are more likely to say that they prefer the threatened relationship over others (Adams, 1980; White, 1981b) and, in some ways at least, even find their relationships more valuable and satisfying than less jealous people since they are more likely to agree that they would go to any length to save the relationship (Hansen, 1983). Jealousy also frequently promotes behavior that could help to maintain or enhance the threatened relationship, such as paying more attention and making oneself more attractive to a partner (Bringle & Evenbeck, 1979; Shettel-Neuber, Bryson, & Young, 1978), or aggressing against and, for that matter, even permanently eliminating a rival (Adams, 1980). Finally, Clanton and Smith (1977) note that jealousy can often provoke a constructive dialogue between mates about what they want from their relationship that can strengthen that relationship.

Guilt can similarly serve to enhance and maintain a commitment a person has chosen to stray from. Guilt would best protect commitments if it struck before people ever acted inconsistently, while they still only seriously considered doing so. By not acting on contrary impulses no matter how much they might choose or want to do so, people obviously create less of a threat to the commitment. There is some evidence that guilt does act in this way, since it is often the people who have not actually engaged in any transgression who feel the guiltiest. For instance, several studies have shown that people who engage less in sex are higher in sex guilt (Gerrard, 1982; Gerrard & Gibbons, 1982; Mosher, 1973; Mosher & Cross, 1971), suggesting that guilt keeps people from performing actions that would conflict with goals or beliefs to which they are committed. And guilt serves this commitment protection function very effectively—people who are higher in sex guilt express fewer sexually toned associations both in situations in which such expressions are socially approved and those in which they are not (Mosher, 1965; Gailbraith & Mosher, 1968).

Mackinnon (1933, in Murray, 1962) found that subjects who resisted a temptation to cheat in order to succeed on an experimental task generally exhibited a more intropunitive personality style (blaming themselves when things went wrong), whereas subjects who violated the experimental prohibition generally exhibited a more extropunitive style (blaming others rather than themselves). Thus again, the nonviolators showed more signs of guilt-related distress than the violators—in a situation in which the temptation to behave dishonestly was strong. Of course, guilt is not always this effective in inhibiting behavior, and people do sometimes choose and engage in commitment discrepant behaviors that make them feel guilty. But even then, the guilt may serve to convince people that they are still committed. If a person does something but does not enjoy it because of guilt either before or afterwards, his or her doing it was some kind of exception to a general rule of behavior rather than a basis for altering this rule. Guilt enables us to act immorally on occasion while still feeling that we are moral people because we punish ourselves for the immorality with the pain of guilt. In a similar way, guilt can help a person continue feeling committed in spite of contrary action because it was so painful to stray from the commitment.

Of course, if jealousy and guilt are successful in serving these functions, the threat to the commitment is removed, and people can find meaning for their distress in the usual ways. The pain the jealous person was put through can be converted into greater love for the partner who is going to stay in the relationship, and the pain the guilty person was put through can be converted into greater appreciation for the activity or goal he or she eventually chose to stay with or return to. However, with both jealousy and guilt, reintegrating this distress into the once-threatened commitment may require a rather special process, forgiveness. We can, of course, forgive ourselves as well as others, and we often need to. Forgiveness does not necessarily involve absolving ourselves or others of causal responsibility. We can forgive, even though we may never be able to forget, that a lover caused us great pain or that we caused ourselves to act in some reprehensible way (Gittleson, 1978). However, forgiveness may require absolving someone of moral responsibility, perhaps by convincing oneself that the person did not really choose, or at least would not choose again, to do such a thing. Most of the father-daughter incest victims in the Silver et al. (1983) study who could make sense of their sexual violation appeared to do so through a process of forgiveness that involved absolving moral responsibility by limiting perceived choice. These women attributed the incest to factors that clearly would have diminished their father's choice in the matter, his mental illness, or the lack of alternative sexual outlets. Snyder (1984) has suggested that when people cannot deny that they did something bad, they will attempt to obtain forgiveness by using "consistency-reducing" excuses, explanations for the failure that imply it is uncharacteristic of their usual behavior and unlikely to be repeated in the future. Denying our own or another's choice to engage in some undesirable behavior would obviously be a very good consistency-reducing excuse because it would imply that there is no commitment to such behavior. If we cannot somehow deny or limit the original offending choice, we may be able to forgive ourselves or others with the conviction that at least such choices would not be made again. Miller and Porter (1983) report that battered women sometimes distinguish between an "old self", who was in some way responsible for the beatings, and a "new self", who has learned from her mistakes or has corrected other defects. Miller and Porter suggest that battered women may be able to escape some of the more devastating consequences of self-blame through this distinction. They may be able to relieve any guilt they had by believing they would not repeat the same poor choices they made in the past.

Even if guilt and jealousy do not lead to the maintenance of the threatened commitment, we may be able to see these forms of distress as important first steps in developing new commitments and still find meaning in them. Although jealousy tends to stimulate more behaviors aimed at saving than ending a relationship, sometimes people respond to the pain and distress of jealousy by looking for new lovers (Adams, 1980). If the jealous person chooses to leave the threatened relationship, he or she will be inclined to devalue that relationship (cf. Brehm, 1966), and the misery of the jealousy should make that all the easier to do. As these people come to see their old relationships as less desirable, they will be more likely to initiate new ones, because more of the available relationships will look good by comparison (cf. Brickman, Coates, & Janoff-Bulman, 1978). Among a sample of divorced people, Berman and Turk (1981) found that those who were highest in a sense of autonomy—and who would presumably be most inclined to see themselves as making the important decisions in their lives—were most likely to be involved in new relationships, were generally more satisfied with their lives and their relationships, and were less likely to show serious mood disturbances. Hetherington, Cox, and Cox (1977) found that the most important predictor of a positive self-image among divorced men and women was the establishment of a new, satisfying heterosexual relationship. As these results suggest, the lessons we learn from a painful episode of jealousy could also help us to select new relationships that are less likely to fall prey to past mistakes. Albrecht (1979) found that people in their second marriages are generally happier than those in their first, and they report that they do not encounter the same problems in their second marriages as they had in their first. Since guilt always results from our choice rather than another's, it is probably even more likely than jealousy to lead us into new commitments. When people choose not to return to a threatened commitment, and repeatedly engage in some conflicting behavior, they are likely to stop feeling guilty and start finding meaning and importance in the new behavior or the course of action it is a part of. Thus, Reiss (1962) found that subjects who initially felt most guilty about intimate homosexual contact were also most likely to come to value this activity rather than give it up.

Guilt and jealousy are most destructive, obviously, when they lead to the loss of a commitment and interfere with our ability to make new ones. Jealous people may sometimes drive their partners into leaving. The misery of jealousy may be understandable, but several observers have noted that miserably jealous people are not very enjoyable company (Mead, 1931; Peele & Brodsky, 1975). Jealous people often do things to the partner—seek reassurance, express intense dysphoria, complain—that are very similar to the behavior of other distressed individuals whom people typically find very unappealing (see Coates & Wortman, 1980; Wortman, & Abbey, 1979; Coyne & Gotlib, 1983; for reviews). Furthermore, in what is perhaps the fatal error of jealous people, they are apparently likely to apply strong extrinsic pressure on their partners to get them to stay, ranging from demands that the partner live up to his or her "duty" (Clanton & Smith, 1977) to threats of physical violence against themselves (e.g., suicide threats; see Peele & Brodsky, 1975) or their partners (Adams, 1980; Peele & Brodsky, 1975). Such pressure is likely to minimize the partner's perceived choice and likewise decrease any chance that the partner will come to see his or her tolerance of the jealous person's obnoxious and unappealing behavior as a sacrifice he or she is making for the sake of the relationship. If the partner does decide to leave the relationship, the jealous person is not only alone but is likely to find it very difficult to form new relationships. In this case, the jealous person is being forced by the partner to give up an option he or she would otherwise choose—continuing the relationship— which is likely to lead to greater valuing of the withdrawn alternative (cf. Brehm, 1966). The jealous person then may come to see the lost relationship in idealistic terms, providing a standard by which the range of available relationships will fare very poorly. This, of course, makes it very difficult for the person to choose any of the available relationships. Research on marital separation and breaking up in romantic relationships shows that this is always a very painful process (see Harvey, Weber, Yarkin, & Stewart, 1982; Kelly, 1982; for reviews). But studies also show that people who feel they chose to leave, while still deeply pained, cope at least a little better with the loss (Goode, 1956; Hill, Rubin, & Peplau, 1976; Weiss, 1976).

Guilt is most destructive when it becomes chronic. If people choose to give up a behavior that makes them feel guilty, they will stop feeling guilty and become more committed to the activity or goal that was threatened; if they choose to keep engaging in the offensive behavior, they will stop feeling guilty and form a new commitment to that behavior. If, however, people try to avoid this choice altogether, they will remain chronically guilty. This is perhaps most likely to occur when people find themselves in conflicting commitments, where the efforts given to one commitment automatically detract from the pursuit of the other. Such conflicts may not become apparent until after people have been pursuing what they see as independent activities for some time and then realize that because each of these activities has become more demanding, continuing both of them will be very difficult. Examples of such conflicting commitments include the dilemma of family and career facing many women (Keith & Schafer, 1982; Poloma, 1972) or an innocent friendship that becomes a serious extramarital affair (Bartusis, 1978), or multiple commitments that become conflicted commitments when a person does not have the time, energy, or resources to do all he or she is committed to doing. Sometimes people can reduce the conflict between such commitments (Poloma, 1972) and pursue both without guilt, but this is often not possible. When the conflict cannot be reduced, as long as the commitments are in some ways mutually exclusive, people may have to give up, or at least postpone, one of them in order to escape their guilt. This is, of course, a painful choice because both commitments hold a lot of value. But once made, the choice makes it likely that all the benefits of dissonance reduction will favor the chosen commitment.

When people try to pursue both conflicting commitments, they will continue to feel guilty, because most anything they do will be inconsistent with one commitment or the other. And as they continue to pursue both commitments despite the guilt, both commitments will probably become all the more valuable. In addition, people are likely to lose one or both commitments anyway because the distress of the guilt and, more important, the fact that the commitments carry conflicting demands mean that they will not be able to uphold either very well as long as they try to uphold both. But under these circumstances, the loss of the commitment will not be the result of choice. The guilty person faces a problem similar to that of the jealous person whose partner chooses to leave: he or she will enhance the value of the lost activities or goals, making available activities and goals appear worse by comparison. The idea that commitments they did not choose to lose become idealized comparison points for chronically guilty people may help to explain why chronic guilt is often associated with unrealistically high internal standards (Erikson, 1950; Freud, 1935) and inhibited activity (Gerrard & Gibbons, 1982). It also explains how chronic guilt can interfere with people's ability to make new commitments. This ability may also be indirectly impaired because chronic guilt, like frequent jealousy (Adams, 1980), is likely to take a toll on self-esteem.

Of course, when they lead people to lose commitments and interfere with the ability to make new ones, guilt and jealousy become a much more serious form of distress—what people generally recognize as depression. The connection between this disorder and commitment will be discussed next.

Reactions to commitment loss: Depression. Clinical depression is a complicated disorder and a difficult one to define. According to the *Diagnostic and Statistical Manual of Mental Disorders* (American Psychiatric Association, 1980), depressed people typically experience affective symptoms (e.g., low mood, sadness, guilt, despair), cognitive symptoms (e.g., difficulties in concentrating and making decisions, beliefs that they are worthless, suicidal thoughts and fantasies), motivational symptoms (e.g., apathy, lethargy, lack of energy) and somatic symptoms (e.g., appetite disturbance, difficulties sleeping). There have been, however, a number of criticisms raised about the diagnostic criteria and categories used in the DSM-III (e.g., Eysenk, Wakefield, & Friedman, 1983; McLemore & Benjamin, 1979; VanPraag, 1982). It is clear that not all depressed people have all these symtoms. For example, some depressed people do not show low self-esteem (Abramson et al., 1978), and some, those who have atypical or nonmelancholic depression, do not even show the negative mood and profound sadness that most of us might consider the hallmark feature of depression (Beeber & Pies, 1983). One thing that all depressed people may have in common is a severe motivational deficit, a lack of interest in initiating activities and an inability to derive much satisfaction from activities that are initiated (Layne, 1980; Layne, Merry, Christian, & Ginn, 1982).

There may also be different routes to depression. Some researchers and theorists have distinguished between reactive and endogenous depression (e.g., Hirschfeld, 1981; Klinger, 1977; Paykel, 1979). Reactive depression is usually defined as resulting from some discernable negative event in a person's life; endogenous depression arises in the absence of any preceeding event, as the result of some genetic or biological process or the depressed person's pre-existing personality characteristics. Some authors (e.g., Klinger, 1977) have questioned the validity of this distinction, since endogenously depressed people sometimes report as many recent negative events as reactively depressed people do (e.g., Leff, Roatch, & Bunney, 1970), Paykel (1979) concluded that most depressions are reactive but there are a small number that have other causes. In our discussion here, we will focus on reactive depression. We do not mean to imply, however, that we are dismissing the concept of endogenous depression. Certain personality features that have been associated with depression—such as low self-esteem (Abramson et al., 1978), being too rational (Alloy & Abramson, 1979), or even just being too self-centered and selfish (cf. Roth & Ingram, 1985)—would also make it difficult to form commitments and so could also lead to the lack of commitment and subsequent depression in the absence of any loss.

Although much research has shown that negative events, both large and small, are associated with greater depression (see e.g. Billings & Moos, 1982; Bloom, 1984; Warheit, 1979; for reviews), it has also shown that not all negative events lead to depression in all people. In their review of the literature on life events and depression, Billings and Moos (1982) conclude that life events can only account for about 10% of the variance in depression rates. As an explanation for this sort of finding, other authors have specifically suggested that people only become depressed when they endure a negative event that is itself the loss of an important commitment or interferes with the pursuit of an important commitment (Folkman, 1984; Lazarus & Folkman, 1984; Klinger, 1977). The first step in understanding depression from a commitment point of view is to understand that the critical loss is the loss of intrinsic value, not extrinsic value. This is true even when the depression appears to be due to loss of money, loss of a love object, or loss of control over various external reinforcements. To be sure, some people who were financially ruined in the Great Depression killed themselves by jumping out of buildings. But many others did not. Loss of money is a fatal blow only if money has come to acquire a high degree of intrinsic as well as extrinsic value, to symbolize the extent to which one is an honorable person, a good person, a person with a life worth living. There is some research support for our general contention here.

Some unhappiness may follow the loss of any commitment, even minor, tangential commitments. Klinger (1977) writes that people get a little depressed after losing even something as small as a coin in a vending machine, if having the coin was important to them. However, the full syndrome of clinical depression probably occurs only when people lose a major, overarching commitment that gave meaning and value to many aspects of their lives. The loss of a love relationship or important friendship, which of course represents a central commitment in most people's lives, appears to be one of the most devastating events that people encounter (Lynch, 1979). When subjects are asked to rate the most stressful events on a long list of possibilities, death of a spouse is typically chosen as the worst of all outcomes, followed closely by divorce (Holmes & Rahe, 1967). The death of a spouse or dissolution of a marriage provokes a strong and lasting period of depression in most people (see Bloom, 1984, for a review). Some studies of clinical populations have shown that most people suffering from various forms of psychopathology have recently endured a large number of stressful events, but depressed people differ from those with other diagnoses in that depressed people have experienced more "exit events," losses of important or valued relationships (e.g., Jacobs, Prusoff, & Paykel, 1974; see also Monroe, Imhoff, Wise, & Harris, 1983). Even among depressed patients, those who have experienced more exit events, especially when they have fewer close relationships to start with, are more likely to attempt suicide (Slater & Depue, 1981). The loss of other types of commitments can also be depressing, as Schmitt (1979) suggests in discussing religious people who find they can no longer believe in God following some totally unjustified and inexplicable adversity in their lives. Other research indicates that negative life events are most likely to lead to depression when they interfere with a person's ability to maintain daily routines (Eckenrode, 1984; Kanner, Coyne, Schaefer, & Lazarus, 1981), and thus his or her ability to maintain many commitments. Pearlin, Lieberman, Menaghan, & Mullan (1981), for example, found that involuntary job loss was most likely to lead to depression among people for whom the termination produced the greatest role-strain (i.e., decreased their ability to pursue other commitments, such as supporting a family and keeping a home). Illness and injury can often lead to depression (see, e.g., Silver & Wortman, 1980), perhaps because they so often interfere with commitments.

Research on suicide also indicates that it is the absence or loss of a commitment and the intrinsic value it carries that often prompts this self-destructive behavior. Research reviews show that people who are involved in some type of commitment— religious participants, married people, parents, people who are engaged in intimate relationships, the employed—are generally less likely to kill themselves than people without such commitments (Lester & Lester, 1971; Stack, 1982a). People who are more committed may be less likely to even seriously consider killing themselves. Linehan, Goodstein, Nielsen, and Chiles (1983) asked people about reasons they found for staying alive when they were thinking about killing themselves, and they found that many mentioned commitment-related issues, such as family responsibilities and concerns for children. However, these researchers also found that people who had seriously considered or attempted suicide were less likely to endorse such reasons for staying alive than were people who had not seriously contemplated suicide. Further, the loss of commitment is associated with a higher probability of suicide. The unemployment rate is generally a good predictor of the suicide rate (Brenner, 1973); some studies show that people who have recently lost jobs are as much as 30 times more likely to kill themselves than employed people are (Stillman,

1980). Moving, with all the loss of commitments that it implies, is also strongly associated with suicide (Stack, 1980; 1981; 1982b). Divorce is another common correlate of suicide (National Center for Health Statistics, 1970), and some researchers have even suggested that the dramatic rise in teenage suicide since World War II is the result of broken families and disrupted parental commitments in their lives (Hendin, 1978). The loss of important commitments has also been seen as an explanation for why suicide among women peaks between the ages of 45 and 60 (when the traditionally important commitment of caring for the children ends), whereas suicide among men peaks after age 65 (when they retire from the traditionally important commitment of work; see Stack, 1982a). White men over the age of 65 continue to have one of the highest suicide rates of any demographic group, but it has been dropping in the last few decades, and time series analyses show that this decline is linked to increases in Social Security benefits (Marshall, 1978). Apparently, when retirement does not carry such heavy costs to men's commitment to being providers, they are less likely to respond to retirement by killing themselves. Conflicts in maintaining important commitments have also been associated with suicide. There is evidence that the strains produced by trying to have both careers and families are leading to a higher suicide rate among working-age women (Gibbs, 1982; Synder, 1977; Stack, 1982b), though as might be expected, there is also evidence that women who are able to pursue both commitments with minimal strain or conflict between them are less likely to kill themselves than women who are engaged in only one of these activities (Cumming; Lazer, & Lichisolm, 1975).

The loss of such a commitment, from our perspective, should be more tolerable if people can see themselves as having chosen to lose it. However, this sense of choice helps, primarily, by making it more likely that people will come to see their loss as meaningful, as ultimately serving some greater good. Perceived choice is not going to make the loss of commitment painless; meaning makes pain tolerable but does not eliminate it. Losing an important commitment and the intrinsic value it carries is painful under any circumstances. Research on the dissolution of romantic relationships and marital separation indicates that people who feel they have chosen to end the relationship generally do cope a little better, but they still typically find the separation excruciating (Goode, 1956; Harvey, Weber, Yarkin, & Stewart, 1982; Hill, Rubin, & Peplau, 1976; Kelley, 1982; Weiss, 1976). Depression can sometimes occur when people choose to give up a relationship or activity that was not obviously rewarding, without realizing the extent to which their internal economy and organization actually depended upon the pursuit of that activity and the value it generated. In chapter 4, it was pointed out in a discussion of Solomon and Corbit's (1974) opponent process theory that the pleasure derived from the presence of particular companions or the exercise of certain sports tends to diminish as the companion or sport becomes more familiar, while the distress produced by the absence of such companions or activities becomes more intense. Thus, people may be relieved by their retirement from a job they found draining, or an extra-curricular activity (like running cross-country or being in a play) they found unduly time-consuming, and yet at the same time feel saddened and adrift. Studies of bereavement indicate that people are deeply pained even by the loss of intimate relationships that were very disturbed and more punishing than pleasurable (see, e.g., Glick, Weiss & Parkes, 1974; Lopota, 1973; Vachon, Rogers, Lyall, Lancee, Sheldon & Freeman, 1982). In such situations, people may be surprised by their sense of loss and the ensuing depression, since in their prior state they were aware primarily of their neutral or negative feelings toward the object of commitment and unaware of the positive elements to which these were bonded. So even when people would choose not to keep a commitment, losing the commitment still hurts. This evidence further underscores the point that it is the loss of a commitment, even an unenjoyable commitment, and not merely the loss of pleasurable activities that triggers depression.

However, seeing ourselves as choosing to lose a commitment may save us from some of the more devastating symptoms of the ensuing depression. If we do not choose to lose a commitment, or perhaps if we are uncertain of whether we chose to or not, it follows from dissonance research (Brehm, 1966) that we will enhance and idealize the lost commitment. The idealization of the lost commitment makes it very difficult to find any available activities desirable or rewarding. This occurs in part, as we suggested earlier and other authors have noted (Lopota, 1973), through a comparison process. The lost commitment, and all the activities associated with that commitment, seem much better than any of the current alternatives. This could explain, in part at least, why depressed people have such high standards (Rehm, 1977), find it difficult to choose any available option (Billings & Moos, 1984; Coyne et al., 1981), and find no activities enjoyable enough to persist in (Seligman, 1975). According to the revised learned helplessness model, although people may experience other symptoms of depression under other circumstances, they are most likely to experience universal or personal helplessness when they attribute losses to factors they could not control and therefore could not have chosen. We agree that people are most likely to find new activities unappealing following unchosen losses, but we suggest this is a result of the idealization process rather than a lost sense of control.

This idealization of the lost commitment may also lead to attempts to preserve and honor it even when it is clearly gone. Depressed people tend to be preoccupied with the past, often reporting intrusive and repetitive thoughts about what has been or might have been. Ruminations and obsessions with the lost commitment are frequently described by the bereaved (Glick, Weiss & Parkes, 1974; Lopota, 1973; 1975; Parkes, 1970a; Zisook, Devaul & Click, 1982), by people who have endured the dissolution of their marriages and romantic relationships (Harvey et al., 1982; Kelley, 1982; Weiss, 1976), as well as individuals who have encountered other types of losses (Silver et al., 1983; Silver & Wortman, 1980). Singer (1979) has described very similar symptoms, along with elements of indecisiveness, passivity, and fear among ex-members of religious cults who are still trying to break their ties with the cult and reestablish a place in outside society.

Obviously, this focus on the past can make functioning in the present very difficult. To the extent that depressed people are trying to honor and preserve the lost commitment, any new activities or pursuits will seem like infringements on that commitment. These behaviors, without the lost commitment, seem like alternatives that used to be turned down and sacrificed for the commitment, so doing them now creates conflict and guilt. In this way, depressed people may not just see new activities as relatively unattractive compared to what they lost, they may actually be inhibiting themselves from engaging in any new activities. This helps us to understand why depressed people are so often chronically exhausted, despite the fact that they typically do not seem to do very much. It takes a lot of energy to maintain inhibitions against action at such a high level. These inhibitions in reactive depression are sustained not by the absence of motivation but by the highly charged and debilitating presence of motivations that cannot be acted upon—for example, motivations to interact with the lost object of commitment, or conflicting motivations to express versus not express anger at perceived causes of this loss (including the self). As Freud put it, it takes as much energy to break a cathexis as it took to establish it in the first place. Or, in more colloquial language, the distance to be travelled to come out of a commitment is proportionate to the distance travelled into it. The only way out of depression is the unspectacular, partially invisible, maddeningly slow ebb and flow of the dialectical process by which new commitments are created, like new civilizations built on the ruins of old. The work of depression is the suspension of activity until the old can be torn down to make room for the new.

The first step in moving from the old to the new is the excruciating process of shutting down previous action systems, preparatory to dismantling some of them, putting others in reverse motion, and building new ones. People do this only in desperate circumstances when the task of internal reconstruction is of overriding importance. It may only be through the profound pain of the depression itself that people are able to finally give up the lost commitment. The pain enables people to do this by reestablishing, precipitously, a lower baseline from which subsequent developments can be seen as upward steps rather than merely poor substitutes for the lost object. The total misery of depression, rather than the lost commitment, gradually becomes the comparison point, and new opportunities start to look more appealing. To use an analogy, loss can be seen as the partial draining of a full glass; depression is the mind's and body's response of draining the glass completely; the adaptive value of this response is that it enables the person to see the glass as half-full (a positive comparison) rather than half-empty (a negative comparison) when it is very slowly refilled with new activities and relationships. The pain of depression, along with opportunities and pressures in the environment, slowly lead the depressed person to make certain decisions that take him or her away from the lost commitment in favor of new ones. We try not to think about it, at least for tonight. Many people describe their thoughts about lost commitments as intrusive, implying that they would choose not to have them (see, e.g., Silver et al., 1983). We decide to try going out, even though we may feel guilty about it. In this way, we slowly start to find intrinsic value in new opportunities and engagements. The suicide fantasies so often associated with depression may serve a particularly valuable function in this regard. They remind people that no matter how bad things get, they do have the freedom to escape, they do not have to put up with it. When death seems like a reasonable alternative to a life of unrelenting misery (cf. Neuringer, 1979) but a person chooses to live anyway, he or she may be able to forge a powerful commitment to persisting in life despite the pain. Many depressed people contemplete suicide, but the vast majority choose to live (Copas & Robin, 1982; Keller & Shapiro, 1981; Morrison, 1982).

Other authors have also acknowledged that depression can serve positive or adaptive functions (Klinger, 1977), such as forcing people to relinquish the damaging and even life-threatening pursuit of unobtainable but costly goals (Janoff-Bulman & Brickman, 1981). But, by our present analysis, whatever other functions depression may serve, the experience of intense misery that depression brings is critical to the formation of new commitments. Silver and Wortman (1980) provide support for the idea that when we have experienced a significant loss, the full realization of the pain of that loss may be necessary for recovery, physical as well as psychological:

> In fact, there is even some recent evidence suggesting that reacting to a crisis with expressions of emotional distress may favorably influence a person's physical prognosis. Derogatis, Abeloff, and Melisaratos (1979) collected a variety of psychological measures on 35 women with breast cancer and correlated the results with length of survival. Interestingly, those women who reported higher levels of hostility, anxiety, and dysphoric mood at the initial assessment were likely to survive the longest. . . . Consistent findings were also obtained in a prospective study of patients with malignant melanoma (Rogentine, van Kammen, Fox, Docherty, Rosenblatt, Boyd, & Bunney, 1979). Respondents were asked to indicate how much adjustment was needed to cope with their disease. Those who reported that little adjustment was required, thus suggesting that their illness had caused them little distress, were significantly more likely to experience a relapse 1 year later. (p. 328)

However, if the pain of depression serves adaptive functions, it does so only when it is relatively short-lived. Depression becomes pathological when it fails to reestablish a base from which favorable comparisons and internal coherence can be derived; when it cannot be liquidated or lifted, so that what was intended to be temporary becomes permanent; when nonresponding becomes habitual instead of restorative, an end in itself instead of a means to other ends. As a remedy, depression is a desperate measure that can easily become worse than the situation to which it is a response. Depression lacks foresight. It triggers the withdrawal from what has become an unbearably painful situation, but without regard for the question that is fundamental to ultimate recovery—whether alternative, more attractive situations will become available in time for the individual to get involved and thus carried out of the depressive state. If nothing comes along to interrupt the cycle of mourning, recrimination and inactivity—or if the person is unable to appreciate the opportunities that do come along—the state of depression may establish itself as a chronic condition or life-pattern. While most people who suffer from serious victimization (see Coates & Winston, 1983; Silver & Wortman, 1980; for reviews), and most depressed patients (Keller & Shapiro, 1981; Shapiro & Keller, 1981;) recover from their depression within a year, anywhere from 25% to 50% do not, and relapses are fairly common (Keller, Lavori, Lewis & Klerman, 1983). Depression is self-limiting, in our analysis, only insofar as it is ordinarily interupted by new opportunities for commitment, which in turn accelerate the process by which the past is forgotten. It is not self-limiting in that it will vanish of its own accord. Depression represents the breaking of a set of bonds, not the forgetting of them, but it is forgetting that marks the return to normal activity. As Kierkegaard (1959) wrote in *Either/Or:* "If a man cannot forget, he will never amount to much." In more psychological terms, pyschiatrist George Vaillant (1977) summarized the overall conclusion he drew from his 40-year study of 95 Harvard men, some of them successful and happy and some not, in this way: "No whim of fate, no Freudian trauma, no loss of a loved-one is as devastating to the human spirit as some chronic ambivalent relationship that keeps us forever from saying goodbye."

If people can only escape depression by making new commitments, the environment obviously plays an important role in making this possible and shaping the kinds of commitments that people develop. When opportunities for new commitments are minimal, as when people have low social support and few relationships with others, depression is more likely to persist (Monroe, Bellack, Hersen, & Himmelhoch, 1983; Steinmetz, Lewinsohn, & Antonuccio, 1983). But even when people are involved in ongoing relationships, these relationships can themselves interfere with the process of making commitments. Although social support is often seen as protecting or curing people of pathology, there is a long tradition in clinical psychology that recognizes that important interpersonal relationships can also be the source of pathology (see, e.g., Bateson, Jackson, Haley, & Weakland, 1956).

If activities and opportunities are forgone for too long a period after the initial loss, depressed people may come to see themselves as committed to the feeling and experience of loss itself, with the unintended assistance of their friends and family. When a person's loss is obvious and significant—as in bereavement—a period of depression is not only tolerated but expected, as a gesture of loyalty, caring, and respect. The depression is understood by both the person afflicted and others to have a recognizable and acceptable cause. The danger arises when the depression overstays what people feel is its "legitimate" time, leading to the stated or unstated question: "It's been six months (or two years). Why are you still depressed?" Equally treacherous is a depression that appears to have no legitimate cause, as when a person is promoted to a new job in a new location and is expected to be happy but turns out to find the new job stressful and to miss the familiar routines and old friends he or she knew in the previous position. In circumstances like these, the sympathy and understanding of friends and family toward the depressed person give way to frustration and annoyance, as Coates and Wortman (1980) point out in their review of research on interpersonal reactions to the depressed. Attempts to reassure and help the depressed person are replaced by punishing outbursts of anger and strident demands for improvement. The pressure on the depressed person to stop acting depressed can become so intense that the afflicted individual attributes any nondepressed behaviors to others' demands rather than his or her own choice (see Coates & Wortman, 1980). Simultaneously, the depressed person comes to feel that he or she must be choosing to act sad and withdrawn, since everyone else clearly disapproves of such behaviors. Of course, once people believe they have chosen to be depressed, they are likely to become committed to being depressed. It is interesting to note that paradoxical therapists respond to depressed people in just the opposite way from how members of their social environments typically react. Rather than disapproving of depression, paradoxical therapy involves encouraging depressed people to experience and even practice their symptoms. And there is evidence that such a paradoxical approach is more effective in alleviating at least moderate depression—especially in the long run—than a directive counseling approach in which depressed people are told to stop their symptoms and encouraged to practice nondepressed behaviors (Beck & Strong, 1982; Feldman, Strong & Danser, 1982).

If people do become committed to being depressed, through a process like being forced to act nondepressed, it follows that their depression will be different in several ways from the depression people immediately experience in response to loss. An especially interesting example of committed depression is suggested by what Watson and Clark (1984) call Negative Affectivity (NA) and define as a disposition to experience negative emotional states. In their review of research on this personality characteristic, Watson and Clark suggest that it may develop from genetic or biological causes, but people who are high in NA have a number of attributes that would be expected from committed depressed people.

The depression triggered by the loss of an important commitment is experienced as singularly painful, a gaping wound in the structure of purpose and value in one's life. It is experienced as a state of meaninglessness. By contrast, a commitment to being depressed, like any commitment, should actually produce some meaning and value in a person's life. And people who are high in the NA characteristic apparently do find value and importance in their melancholy. In one study, high NA subjects rated symptoms of anxiety and depression as generally more desirable characteristics for people to have than low NA subjects did (Heineman, 1953). In another study, high NA subjects interpreted such symptoms in others as evidence that these people were serious about life and honest with themselves, while low NA subjects interpreted the same symptoms as evidence of psychopathology (Lefcourt, 1966). Watson and Clark (1984) further point out that while high NA subjects are usually in a bad mood, they differ from most depressed people in that they also report positive but nonmanic moods. Perhaps these more satisfied moments of high NA people derive from the meaning they find in practicing their depression.

Furthermore, once people become committed to being depressed, their depression becomes self-sustaining and can be very long lasting. While people can and do overcome the depression caused by loss—even serious loss, like the death of a loved one—within months, a committed depression may last for decades. High NA people do stay relatively depressed for very long periods of time, since in one study at least, NA measures predicted psychological distress levels 30 years later (Leon, Gillum, Gillum & Gouze, 1979). In this way, high NA people are similar to those with what may be another form of committed depression, nonmelancholic depression. Like those high in NA, nonmelancholic depressed people do experience positive moods but have many of the other symptoms of depression and tend to retain these symptoms for very long periods of time (Beeber & Pies, 1983). Watson and Clark (1984) also cite a number of studies indicating that high NA people are extremely resistant to influence attempts by others. This suggests that they may be holding onto their depression for so long, in part at least, because they are rebelling against the antidepression choice limitations that those around them are trying to enforce (cf. Brehm, 1966).

Committed depressions may also be long lasting because they leave little room for other commitments. Any meaning that people may derive from a commitment to being depressed is going to carry significant and important costs. A commitment to being chronically dissatisfied with the world and one's place in it makes it very difficult to become committed to anything else. Watson and Clark (1984) indicate that high NA people do have a very limited capacity for commitment to anything but their symptomatic behaviors. These reviewers interpret a study by Olson and Zanna (1978) as finding that, compared to low NA people, high NA subjects were less likely to show the expected dissonance effect of spending more time looking at paintings they had earlier chosen to take home with them. Once people are committed to being depressed, apparently, they fail to follow through or enforce other choices with their actions. They cannot allow themselves to become involved in other activities, since this would deny their commitment to being depressed. So, they fail to make any new commitments or escape their basically depressed state.

As our analysis here suggests, the interplay between the individual and the environment is extremely important in shaping commitments. In the next section, we will consider in a more general way how features of the environment can limit the nature and quality of the commitments the people make.

ENVIRONMENTAL LIMITATIONS ON COMMITMENT

Sometimes, various social systems or social environments have the explicit purpose of preventing people from sustaining commitments, especially to other people. The State Department regularly transfers its personnel to different countries in order to inhibit their development of a strong loyalty to any one country, whose interests might then be placed on a par with those of the United States. This goal is judged of sufficient importance to justify the costs involved in never having foreign service personnel become fully knowledgeable or completely at home in their host countries and thus never capable of rendering the most sensitive possible service. Club Med follows a similar policy for its employees, who are supposed to socialize with the ever-changing population of guests at the resort, but who quickly come to prefer each other's company if they are not routinely transferred to other resorts. Fraternities and sororities perform their function of preventing participants from premature commitment to an "inappropriate" member of the opposite sex (Scott, 1969) by developing elaborate formal and informal norms requiring members to attend to each other's opinions in such matters and to place loyalty to the peer group over loyalty to dates, at least until the dating relationship has become very serious. The most extreme case in which people are prevented from developing any sense of commitment to others is in the training of soldiers, prison guards, and similar groups to regard the inmates or enemies they deal with as less than human (Zimbardo, Haney, Banks, & Jaffe, 1973). This is not always easy to do because recruits to these roles have long histories of allowing ongoing relationships with others, even others in subordinate roles, to evolve into systems of mutual commitment. Once it is done, however, there is no limit to the torments those so trained will be willing to inflict on their victims.

More often though, the environment affects people's abilities to make and sustain commitments through the range of choices that it offers. Under conditions of abundance or high status, people have more choices available to them. Under conditions of scarcity or low status, people have considerably fewer choices. Pathologies of commitment can develop under either of these general circumstances, but the greater difficulty is presented by fewer choices. An inability to make commitments is one of the hallmarks of low status in society. As Becker (1960) points out, children (and the elderly and mental patients) are often not allowed to make commitments, not being considered enough in command of their faculties to bear full responsibility for their actions. The adaptation of perhaps the most down-and-out segment of American society, that of the black streetcorner man, is in part caused by and characterized by an inability to make commitments. Participant-observer of this underground world Liebow (1967) writes:

> The constant awareness of a future loaded with "trouble" results in a constant readiness to leave, to "make it," to "get out of town," and discourages the man from sinking roots into the world he lives in. Just as it discourages him from putting money in the bank, so it discourages him from committing himself to a job, especially one whose payoff lies in the promise of future rewards rather than in the present. In the same way, it discourages him from deep and lasting commitments to family and friends or to any other persons, places, or things, since such commitments could hold him hostage, limiting his freedom of movement and thereby compromising his security, which lies in that freedom. . . .
> On the streetcorner, the man chooses to forget he got married because he wanted to get married and assume the duties, responsibilities, and status of manhood; instead, he sees himself as the "put-upon" male who got married because his girl was pregnant or because he was tricked, cajoled or otherwise persuaded into doing so. . . .
> Conceding that to be head of a family and to support it is the principle measure of a man, he claims that he was too much of a man to be a man. He

says his marriage did not fail because he failed as a breadwinner and head of the family but because his wife refused to put up with his manly appetite for whiskey and other women. . . .

Society in general makes it easier for high-status people to feel committed to their activities and to see them as having meaning and value. Freedman (1978) reviews evidence that college graduates and noncollege graduates are about equally satisfied or dissatisfied with the financial aspects of their jobs, with their job security, with their fellow workers, and with the enjoyment and self-determination their job allows. The one big difference is that the college-educated viewed their jobs as much more worthwhile. Gruenberg (1980) found that extrinsic factors, such as pay, were a much more important determinant of overall job satisfaction among unskilled, semiskilled, or clerical workers than among skilled and professional workers, a finding he interprets as reflecting the fact that those in the latter group have much greater opportunities for intrinsic satisfaction in their work.

We previously discussed the psychological state of alienation as a condition in which people find little satisfaction in the activities they pursue. Social conditions can also produce alienation by giving people little choice over what they do. This is, of course, Marx's (1844/1932) analysis of the consequences of capitalist work organization for employees. Capitalism achieves its efficiency by breaking jobs down into smaller and smaller and simpler and simpler components, each of which can be done by workers with the least possible skill (and requiring the least amount of pay). The entire sequence of steps is carefully controlled by managers, while the product of all these steps is owned by the factory owners. So workers in a capitalist system have no choice over either the process by which they produce their goods or the goods themselves. The bulk of their days are thus filled with activities that allow little freedom, responsibility, or opportunity for commitment. In addition, in a Marxist analysis, working conditions often afford little opportunity for workers to form meaningful bonds and meaningful working-class or proletarian norms. Finally, due to repeated alienation in all these other domains, it is also argued that workers will experience a sense of alienation from themselves, a sense of self-estrangement (the last and most psychological of the five components of alienation postulated by Seeman, 1959; the others are powerlessness and meaninglessness, which were discussed in connection with workers' feelings about work organization; and normlessness and isolation, mentioned in connection with workers' feelings about fellow workers). In all of this, it should be noted, an important component of alienation is that the person also feels trapped into having a continuing relationship with the activity or the other people to whom he or she is no longer attached (Kanungo, 1979).

Of course, people usually do have some choice in their lives and therefore some opportunities for commitment, even in the most oppressive circumstances. But the choices can be very limited, either directly by the social system, or indirectly by stressful conditions that reduce the availability of alternatives. Under severe stress, individuals may be led to seek dependent commitments—commitments that they believe are beyond their capacity to handle alone. One such commitment is represented by an orientation to authority known as authoritarianism. The components of authoritarian personality are complex (see Adorno, Frenkel-Brunswick, Levinson, & Sanford, 1950, for a description), but their critical features include submission to authority, aggression against deviants or outgroups, impatience with feelings, emphasis on power and toughness, a cynical view of human nature, and a tendency toward superstitious or stereotypical thinking. From our point of view, every one of these features serves to suppress inner conflicts, doubts, and uncertainties and to justify strong and even violent action by reliance on the power and authority of an external agent. This is precisely the orientation we would expect people to seek in times of stress, when they doubt their own capacity to make and sustain successful commitments and to overcome hostile forces. And indeed, in a series of interesting studies, Sales has shown that indicators of authoritarianism in both experimental and historical situations increase when people are placed under stress. Sales and Friend (1973) showed that subjects who were led to believe that they had failed on laboratory tests of intelligence subsequently scored higher on a measure of authoritariansim and, in another study, were more willing to conform to an authority figure in an ambiguous situation (judging how far a light had ostensibly moved). Subjects who succeeded on the laboratory tests scored as less authoritarian. Sales (1972) also studied conversion to authoritarian and nonauthoritarian churches in good and bad times. Authoritarian churches were those that demanded absolute obedience either to the leadership of the church or to the divine, condemned heretics and disbelievers, and showed strong concern over sin. During economically bad years, the number of converts to authoritarian churches increased. During economically good years, the number of converts to nonauthoritarian churches increased. Similarly, Sales (1973) found that literary, cultural, or institutional indicators of authoritarianism increased during the Great Depression of the 1930s. For example, new comic strips were likely to emphasize power and toughness in their central characters, magazine articles were more likely to be cynical about human nature, states were more likely to pass loyalty oaths, and cities to increase police budgets. Mulder and Stemerding (1963) found that groups under stress were inclined to select a strong leader. Janis's (1972) famous analysis of "groupthink" in policymaking bodies under stress likewise makes it clear that individuals under stress are more likely to suppress doubt and dissent (including their own) and to insist on unquestioning loyalty to the group—leading, sometimes, to disastrous decisions (such as the decision to invade the Bay of Pigs in Cuba) that could probably have been avoided in a more open and less pressured discussion.

Other examples of dependent commitments of this sort are described by Brickman et al. (1982) as representative of one of four fundamental world views, each representing a particular combination of beliefs about whether individuals are responsible for the origins of their problems and whether they are responsible for the solutions to their problems. In one of these models, the enlightenment model, people are blamed for causing their problems but are not believed capable of solving them by themselves (with proponents of the model placing great emphasis on enlightening people about their true state, hence the name). These attributions require people to accept a strikingly negative image of themselves and, in order to improve, to accept a strong degree of submission to agents of social control. It is people's own impulses—to eat, drink, lie, cheat, steal—that are out of control. To control these impulses, people must submit to the stern or sympathetic discipline provided by agents who represent the authoritative moral (and, if necessary, physical) force of the community.

> The enlightenment model is the basis of coping whenever people are unable to control what they experience as undesirable behavior on their part. When a drug addict or an alcoholic tells people, for the forty-second time, that he has turned over a new leaf and is about to change his life, this claim of future responsibility is treated with understandable skepticism. With a repeated history of failures to change, addicts themselves may find it impossible to credit any more promises that rest on their own capacity for self control. The "Who are you kidding?" response may be short-circuited, however, if the troubled person can point to a powerful and respected external authority—God, a religious cult, a new set of duties—as the source of change, especially if this attribution is supported by others who also believe in this agency. Thus Malcolm X, St. Paul, or Charles Colson may be able to make their claims to have changed more credible by pointing to an irrestible external force as the basis of change. (Brickman et al., 1982, p. 374)

The commitment to change, under these circumstances, is a commitment to an external agency from whom the power to produce change will flow. Whether this is the case or not, however, is in turn presumed to depend on the intensity and purity of the person's commitment to this symbolic figure. This not only requires commitment to be maintained at an intense level but also concentrates great power in the hands of any one person to whom such commitments are made. A Charles Manson, Jim Jones, or Adolf Hitler may eventually require those who believe in him—and, in particular, believe that all good things in their own lives stem from their relationship to this charismatic figure—to commit the acts of murder or suicide that shock the world.

Authoritarian or submissive commitments are not, however, the only form of stress-induced commitments. The commitment to negative identities discussed by Erikson (1950) is another example. This is the case in which delinquents, blacks, Jews, or other minorities, blocked by society from the achievement of positively valued identities (through inability to get adequate schooling, jobs, or other prerequisites for status), adopt and display in exaggerated form the stereotyped negative characteristics attributed by society to their group. Delinquents may become scornful of the straight values or conventional routes to success that are closed to them, proud of their own tough alternative code, and provocative in their display of outsider status by the clothes they wear, the way they walk and talk, and the markings with which they identify their territory. According to Erikson, a negative identity is preferable to a diffuse identity or no identity at all; or, as La Rochefoucauld long ago put it, we would rather that people talk evil of us than not talk about us at all. The negative identity may be defiant rather than submissive, though some forms of negative identity, such as Uncle Tom or "poor helpless me" (see, e.g., Berne, 1964) involve behavior that is superficially passive and submissive while in actuality quite manipulative. But negative identities, like authoritarian submission, involve commitments made by people under conditions of stress, with what they see as relatively few choices and limited resources with which to make their choices.

Under conditions of abundance, people are more protected from stress, have more choices, and so tend to make healthier, less destructive commitments. But this does not mean that forming commitments is problem-free under such conditions or that commitments are any less important under such conditions. Interestingly enough, commitment may be more essential for happiness under conditions of abundance rather than scarcity—just when it might appear to be least necessary. Under conditions of scarcity, people have no trouble bringing themselves to pursue a reasonable or good alternative when one becomes available. Only under conditions of abundance are people likely to be torn from the pursuit of a good opportunity by the prospect (or hope) that a still better one will come along. One of the authors' students, for example, explained during a class discussion her difficulty in making a commitment to a current relationship. It was not that she could not be happy in this relationship, if she committed herself to it, or that she questioned whether or not commitment was necessary to being happy in this relationship. Rather, she was not sure that this relationship was the best she could hope for, and she did not want to foreclose other possibilities by deciding to be happy, once and for all, in the present situation. A number of authors have suggested that at least some of the problems of youth come from an overabundance of choice and scarcity of guidelines or a sense of limitation:

> One may postulate that some of the current problems of youth may be related to their inability to choose from too many alternatives. There is a collusion of two kinds of factors: on the one hand, patterns of upbringing that for various reasons result in the young people's high appetitive readiness . . . on the other hand, a social environment that offers an overabundance of attractive alternatives coupled with ambiguous values and norms of behavior, while exerting pressure to make choices. . . . The related anxiety and anger may lead to attempts to opt out of unbearable conflict by wholesale rejection of the existing social order and withdrawal into the autistic and largely passive pleasures of drug-induced altered states of consciousness. (Lipowski, 1970, p. 277)

Slater (1974) argues that choice is more exhilarating with fewer alternatives, because when there are many attractive possibilities that cannot be chosen, they may seem to dwarf the one that is:

> Choice tends to be liberating and exciting when it is dualistic—when one can either accept what appears to be one's fate or reject it. This is the situation facing those who first leave a stable community. But the life-space of most middle-class Westerners—in which any number of possibilities can, in fact, be realized—is considerably less joyous. If all options are equally pleasurable and

there are more than two choices, then on a purely mathematical basis more would be lost than gained with each decision. (p. 92)

The difficulty of simultaneously—or even sequentially—maximizing all possible valued states in a given domain is nicely illustrated by the difficulty of arranging one's life so that the experiences of privacy, intimacy, and community are all highly and easily accessible. Most people need and value all three of these states: privacy, defined as being alone and in communion primarily with oneself; intimacy, defined as a deep sharing with another person; and community, or the sense of belonging to and participating in a collectivity. But there is clearly a trade-off among them. If one arranges one's life so that privacy is always conveniently available, the opportunities for intimacy and community will necessarily be constrained. If intimate sharing with another person is one's primary commitment, there must be a large sacrifice of privacy and some degree of withdrawal from the broader community. If the value of community is foremost, privacy and intimacy needs may have to be tempered or even abandoned, as often appears to be the case with political leaders and activists of both Establishment and anti-Establishment persuasions. The value that each of the alternatives has for people will continue to be measured by what people give up for it, and not the less so as the number of attractive states it is possible to realize increases.

In hard times, it is possible to derive satisfaction from even simple achievements because of the struggle that even minor accomplishments require under such conditions. But in situations of abundance and privilege, only truly great outcomes require much effort or provide much satisfaction, and failure to achieve such satisfaction becomes all the more painful and personally consequential. Mark Vonnegut (1975), recounting what became his struggle with schizophrenia, writes:

> Clearing land, gardening, building the house was all just a front. I was into being good, being right. Truth, beauty, and saving the world, liberation, enlightenment, and salvation. I was playing for the highest stakes I could find. I had been given all the breaks anyone could ask for and more. Generations had spent their lives worrying about money so that I wouldn't have to. I didn't have to do anything. So the only way I could do anything was to do something very, very much worth doing. (pp. 170–171)

Here the problem is reminiscent of the University of Chicago or Harvard graduate students who cannot commit themselves to a dissertation unless it appears to be of Nobel Prize–winning quality, and hence either cannot commit themselves to any dissertation or must widely (and, in the end, dangerously) exaggerate the significance of what they finally do. If a person does pursue a fabulous goal and succeeds, another difficulty awaits: Lesser or more mundane pleasures pale by comparison, as Brickman, Coates, and Janoff-Bulman (1978) found was the case for state lottery winners, and continued pursuit of such mundane activities (however important they may be for mental health and balance) may be possible only if people go out of their way to find significance or symbolic value in their pursuit. Moreover, if one is located in an environment rich in opportunities and still fails to achieve happiness, it is difficult to escape the depressing conclusion that the fault lies within oneself. Here is singer John Denver talking about the suicide of comedian Freddie Prinze:

> He had everything in the universe. But in taking in all (those drugs), it had no meaning. If you've got everything you ever wanted—cars, women, drugs, whatever it is—and you're still not happy, then what reason is there for living? . . . There's none. So you blow your brains out. (Dangaard, 1977, p. 18)

When there are fewer external injustices but we are still unable to find much meaning in life, we are more likely to blame ourselves for that failure—perhaps accounting for the higher ratio of suicide to homicide among higher status parties—for example, officers versus enlisted men (Henry & Short, 1954; Gold, 1958) and older white males versus older black males (Stack, 1982a).

When people encounter severe problems in forming and sustaining commitments, as a result of either scarcity or abundance, they may turn to chemical agents that dissolve the need for commitment and dull the pain of being without meaning and purpose. It might seem surprising to suggest that drug abuse dissolves the need for commitment, since some people do become very committed, or addicted, to drugs. There is an important sense in which addicts and alcoholics are committed to their lifestyle as addicts, with the procurement, consumption and recovery from their preferred drugs being the pivot around which almost all aspects of their lives are oriented (cf. Klinger, 1977). We would argue that such addictions are most likely to occur when people have little else in their lives to be committed to, either because opportunities are very limited or because they come too easily. In their review of research on heroin addiction, Alexander and Hadaway (1982) conclude that heroin addiction only occurs when it "fills a hole" or serves some missing function in a person's life. Many people even use drugs that can create a psysiological dependence, like heroin, quite regularly without becoming addicts (Blackwell, 1983), or stop them fairly easily after becoming biologically addicted (Waldorf, 1983). In other situation, people become addicted to activities that create no direct physiological dependence at all. In an interesting review of work on addictions, Milkman and Sunderwirth (1982) point out that some people become addicted to activities like watching television (Winn, 1977), intimate relationships (Peele & Brodsky, 1975), or acquiring wealth (Slater, 1980). According to Milkman and Sunderwirth, a commitment to such activities becomes an addiction when the person involved in them gives up virtually all other alternative activities, even more promising or more enjoyable ones, for the sake of the chosen activity. In this way, then, drug addiction and alcoholism are no different from other overarching or single-minded commitments that crowd out all other human concerns.

But there is also a way in which the pursuit and use of these chemical agents is different from other commitments. Drug abuse not only pushes out concerns for other activities but makes it very difficult if not impossible to form other commitments, even to a limited degree or even if the addict is so inclined. Steele, Southwick, and Critchlow (1981) found that consumption of alcohol by subjects in a series of experiments involving the writing of counterattitudinal essays was sufficient to eliminate all the dissonance reducing attitude change ordinarily found in such experiments. Likewise, Cooper, Zanna, and Taves (1978) found that dissonance reducing attitude change—and the commitment it supports—can be eliminated by a tranquilizing drug that relieves the unpleasantness of dissonance. The practical implication is that drug abuse may evolve as an alternative means of reducing ambivalence—that is, as a device by which people can escape internal pressure to justify their behavior and sustain the commitments set in motion by such processes of justification (see also Cowan, 1983). Commitment to a drug, at the expense of all other commitments, is not likely to produce sufficient meaning in people's lives. Many researchers have noted a strong relationship between alcoholism or other drug addiction and depression (Croughan, Miller, Keopke & Whitman, 1981; Hatsukami & Pickens, 1982; Kosten, Rounsaville & Kleber, 1983; Rounsaville, Weissman, Kleber & Wilber, 1982; Steer, McElroy & Beck, 1982). Thus, we may see these chemical agents as commitment solvents. Not surprisingly, the folklore of bars and saloons indicates that they are often used by people who are trying to forget previous unsuccessful, but still fresh and painful, commitments.

While we may not find it surprising that people with little opportunity, such as the poor and oppressed, become drug addicts, we are always a little baffled by the rich and talented who are also so inclined—cases like Elvis Presley or William Burroughs. Likewise, researchers often comment on how irrational it is for the prosperous to become addicted to activities like work or intimate relationships (Peele & Brodsky, 1979; Slater, 1980). Under conditions of abundance, the commitments that people form, and the limitations that those commitments require, can appear particularly irrational precisely because there is no apparent need for such limitations. But people do need to struggle and sacrifice, and when the environment does not demand this, people tend to demand it of themselves.

There are numerous examples of people seeking out hardships, difficulties, and constrains in order to forge commitments, and the experiences commitments allow, in otherwise undemanding environments. Existential therapist Frankel (1978) considers sports to be one such example:

> [Modern man] artificially creates the tension that he has been spared by affluent society! He provides himself with tensions by deliberately placing demands on himself—by voluntarily exposing himself to stress situations, if only temporarily. As I see it, this is precisely the function carried out by sports! Sports allow man to build up situations of emergency. What he then demands of himself is unnecessary achievement—and unnecessary sacrifice. In the midst of a sea of affluence, islands of asceticism emerge! In fact, I regard sports as the modern, the secular, form of asceticism. (p. 96)

The seeking of what turns out to be a harrowing and violent wilderness experience in the book and movie *Deliverance* (Dickey, 1970) is a more extreme illustration of this drive—and the title of the book, with its religious connotations, is instructive. A striking feature of many modern religious cults like Hare Krishna (see Johnson, 1976) is the asceticism and discipline they impose on recruits who have typically come from prosperous middle-class homes. In Hare Krishna, clothes, money, and personal effects are surrendered; the hair of males is shaved; old names are given up; and strict prohibitions are placed on sex, gambling, and the consumption of meat, liquor, cigarettes, and drugs. The preparatory stage of such religious discipline, according to Johnson (1976), requires a constancy of motive, dedication to purpose, and degree of self-sacrifice comparable to the most rigorous medical or professional school in the land. Erhard Seminar Training (est) provides another example of a particularly manipulative form of unnecessary constraint and punishment sought out by the rich and middle class. It would be difficult to find a purer application of a commitment theory analysis of choice, suffering, and meaning. This program promises to send its adherents back to their old lives with a new sense of purpose and power. Est participants pay substantial amounts of money for two weekends of treatment that involves intense doses of verbal and physical abuse by both the staff and by fellow participants (Brewer, 1975). Participants are constantly reminded that they have chosen, not only the abusive treatment but everything about themselves. Graduates of est are amazingly active prosletyzers for the experience, working long hours without pay to gather new recruits, a form of dissonance reduction that has long been recognized by researchers (Festinger, Riecken, & Schachter, 1956). This last feature makes est a salesperson's dream, and the program was in fact founded by a man with considerable experience in high-pressure sales (Brewer, 1975).

As we have pointed out throughout this chapter, commitment is clearly not a sufficient condition for full mental health. Some of the most severely deranged commitments—the type that can lead to great tragedies like Jonestown—are most likely to occur when choices and opportunities are very limited. But even under conditions of abundance, commitment can be made difficult by the very fact that there are so many choices available, and the consequences of being without commitment can be all the more lethal. In addition, particularly under conditions of abundance, people may impose strict, constraining, and irrational limits on themselves in their efforts to build and maintain commitments. But the fact that people seek out such limiting commitments even when they are not forced to by external circumstances is strong testament to the basic human need for commitment. It is a process that can go wrong, but it is a process we can hardly do without. As Dostoyevsky put it in the *Brothers Karamazov:*

> For the secret of man's being is not only to live but to have something to live for. Without a stable conception of the object of life, man would not consent to go on living, and would rather destroy himself than remain on earth, though he had bread in abundance.

REFERENCES

Abbey, A., & Dunkel-Schetter, C. (1979). *A dialectical model of the life cycle of commitment.* Unpublished manuscript, Northwestern University.

Abbey, A., Dunkel-Schetter, C., & Brickman, P. (1983). Handling the stress of looking for a job in law school: The relationship between intrinsic motivation, internal attributions, relations with others, and happiness. *Basic and Applied Social Psychology, 6,* 111–129.

Abelson, R. P. (1976). A script theory of understanding, attitude, and behavior. In J. Carroll & T. Payne (Eds.), *Cognition and social behavior* (pp. 33–46). Potomac, MD: Erlbaum.

Abelson, R. P., Aronson, E., McGuire, W. J., Newcomb, T. M., Rosenberg, M. J., & Tannenbaum, P. H. (Eds.). (1968). *Theories of cognitive consistency: A sourcebook.* Chicago: Rand McNally.

Abelson, R. P., & Rosenberg, M. J. (1958). Symbolic psycho-logic: A model of attitude cognition. *Behavioral Science, 3,* 1–13.

Abramson, L.Y., Alloy, L.B., & Rosoff, R. (1980). Depression and the generation of complex hypotheses in the judgement of contingencies. *Behavior Research and Therapy, 19,* 35–45.

Abramson, L. Y., & Sackheim, H. A. (1977). A paradox in depression: Uncontrollability and self-blame. *Psychological Bulletin, 84,* 838–851.

Abramson, L.Y., Seligman, M. E. P., & Teasdale, J. (1977). Learned helplessness in humans: Critique and reformulation. *Journal of Abnormal Psychology, 87,* 49–74.

Adams, V. (1980, May). Getting at the heart of jealous love. *Psychology Today,* pp. 38–106.

Adamson, J. D., & Schmale, A. H. (1965). Object loss, giving up and the onset of psychiatric disease. *Psychosomatic Medicine, 27,* 557–576.

Adamson, R. E. (1952). Functional fixedness as related to problem-solving: A repetition of three experiments. *Journal of Experimental Psychology, 44,* 288–291.

Adler, M. J. (1958). *The idea of freedom.* New York: Doubleday.

Adorono, T., Frenkel-Brunswick, E., Levinson, D., & Sanford, R. (1950). *The authoritarian personality.* New York: Harper.

Ainslie, G. (1975). Specious reward: A behavioral theory of impulsiveness and impulse control. *Psychological Bulletin, 82*, 463–496.

Ajzen, I., & Fishbein, M. (1974). Factors influencing intentions and intention-behavior relations. *Human Relations, 27*, 1–15.

Albrecht, S. L. (1979). Correlates of marital happiness among the remarried. *Journal of Marriage and the Family, 41* (4), 857–867.

Alexander, B. K., & Hadaway, P. F. (1982). Opiate addiciton: The case for an adaptive orientation. *Psychological Bulletin, 92*, 367–381.

Alineky, S. A. (1972). *Rules for radicals*. New York: Random House.

Allen, W. (1982). *Four films of Woody Allen*. New York, Random House.

Alloy, L. B., & Abramson, L. Y. (1979). Judgements of contingency in depressed and non-depressed students: Sadder but wiser? *Journal of Experimental Psychology, 108*, 441–485.

Alloy, L. B., & Abramson, L. Y. (1980). The cognitive component of human helplessness and depression: A critical analysis. In J. Garber & M. E. P. Seligman (Eds.), *Human helplessness: Theory and applications* (pp. 59–70). New York: Academic Press.

Alloy, L. B., Abramson, L. Y., & Viscusi, D. (1982). Induced mood and the illusion of control. *Journal of Personality and Social Psychology, 41*, 1129–1140.

Allport, G. W. (1937a). The functional autonomy of motives. *American Psychologist, 50*, 141–156.

Allport, G. W. (1937b). *Personality: A psychological interpretation*. New York: Holt, Rinehart & Winston.

Allport, G. W. (1961). *Pattern and growth in personality*. New York: Holt, Rinehart & Winston.

Allport, G. W., & Postman, L.J. (1947). *The psychology of rumor*. New York: Holt, Rinehart & Winston.

American Psychiatric Association. (1980). *Diagnostic and statistical manual of mental disorders* (3rd ed.). Washington, DC: Author.

Anderson, C. A., Lepper, M. R., & Ross, L. (1980). The perseverance of social theories: The role of explanation in the persistence of discredited information. *Journal of Personality and Social Psychology, 39*, 1037–1049.

Andrews, F. M., & Withey, S. B. (1976). *Social indicators of well-being*. New York: Plenum.

Antonovsky, A. (1979). *Health, stress and coping*. San Francisco, CA: Jossey-Bass.

Argyle, M., & Beit-Hallahmi, B. (1975). *The social psychology of religion*. Boston, MA: Routledge and Kegan Paul.

Aries, F. (1962). *Centuries of childhood*. New York: Knopf.

Aronson, E. (1966). Avoidance of inter-subject communication. *Psychological Reports, 19*, 238.

Aronson, E. (1968). The theory of cognitive dissonance: A current perspective. In L. Berkowitz (Ed.), *Advances in experimental social psychology* (Vol. 4). New York: Academic Press.

Aronson, E. (1973, May). The rationalizing animal. *Psychology Today*, pp. 46–54.

Aronson, E., & Carlsmith, J. M. (1963). Effect of severity of threat on the valuation of forbidden behavior. *Journal of Abnormal and Social Psychology, 66*, 584–588.

Aronson, E., & Landy, D. (1967). Further steps beyond Parkinson's Law: A replication and extention of the excessive time effect. *Journal of Experimental Social Psychology, 3*, 274–285.

Aronson, E., & Mills, J. (1958). The effect of severity of initiation on liking for a group. *Journal of Abnormal and Social Psychology, 59*, 177–184.

Arrow, K. J. (1951). *Social choice and individual values*. New York: Wiley.

Arrowood, A. J., Wood, L., & Ross, L. (1970). Dissonance, self-perception, and the perception of others: A study in cognitive dissonance. *Journal of Experimental Social Psychology, 6*, 304–315.

Asch, S. E. (1951). Effects of group pressure upon the modification and distortion of judgment. In H. Guetzkow (Ed.), *Groups, leadership, and men* (pp. 177–190). Pittsburgh, PA: Carnegie.

Atkinson, J. W. (1964). *An introduction to motivation*. New York: Van Nostrand.

Atkinson, J. W., & Birch, D. (1970). *The dynamics of action*. New York: Wiley.

Atkinson, J. W., & Feather, N. T. (1966). *A theory of achievement motivation*. New York: Wiley.

Atkinson, J. W., & Raynor, J. O. (1974). *Motivation and achievement*. Washington, DC: Winston.

Auble, P. M., Franks, J. J., & Soraci, S. A., Jr. (1979). Effort toward comprehension: Elaboration or "aha!"? *Memory and Cognition, 7*, 426–434.

Averill, J. R. (1973). Personal control over aversive stimuli and its relationship to stress. *Psychological Bulletin, 80*, 286–303.

Bach, G. R. (1974). *The intimate enemy*. New York: Grove Press.

Bakan, D. (1968). *Disease, pain and sacrifice*. Chicago: University of Chicago Press.

Bales, R. F. (1950). A set of categories for the analysis of small group interaction. *American Sociological Review, 15*, 257–263.

Bales, R. F. (1958). Task roles and social roles in problem-solving groups. In E. E. Maccoby, T. M. Newcomb, & E. L. Hartley (Eds.), *Readings in social psychology*. New York: Holt, Rinehart & Winston.

Bales, R. F., & Strodtbeck, F. L. (1951). Phases in group problem solving. *Journal of Abnormal and Social Psychology, 46*, 485–495.

Bandler, R. J., Madaras, G. R., & Bem, D. J. (1968). Self-observation as a source of pain perception. *Journal of Personality and Social Psychology, 9*, 205–209.

Bandura, A. (1977). Self-efficacy: Toward a unifying theory of behavioral change. *Psychological Review, 84*, 191–125.

Bardwick, J. M. (1971). *Psychology of women: A study of bio-cultural conflicts*. New York: Harper & Row.

Bardwick, J. M. (1979). *In transition*. New York: Holt, Rinehart & Winston.

Barrera, M., & Ainlay, S. L. (1983). The structure of social support: An empirical and conceptual analysis. *Journal of Community Psychology, 11*, 133–143.

Barrett, W. (1958). *Irrational man: A study in existential philosophy*. Garden City, NY: Doubleday.

Barron, F. (1957). Originality in relation to personality and intellect. *Journal of Personality, 25*, 730–742.

Bartlett, F.C. (1932). *Remembering: A study in experimental and social psychology*. Cambridge, England: Cambridge University Press.

Bartusis, M. A. (1978). *Every other man*. New York: E. P. Dutton.

Bateson, G., Jackson, D., Haley, J., & Weakland, J. (1956). Toward a theory of schizophrenia. *Behavioral Science, 1*, 251–264.

Batson, C. D. (1975). Rational processing or rationalization?: The effect of disconfirming information on a stated religious belief. *Journal of Personality and Social Psychology, 32*, 176–184.

Batson, C. D., Coke, J. S., Jasnoski, M. L., & Hansen, M. (1978). Buying kindness: Effect of an extrinsic incentive for helping on perceived altruism. *Personality and Social Psychology Bulletin, 4*, 86–91.

Batson, C. D., & Ventis, W. L. (1982). *The religious experience*. New York: Oxford University Press.

Beck, J. T., & Strong, S. R. (1982). Stimulating therapeutic change with interpretations: A comparison of positive and negative connotations. *Journal of Counseling Psychology, 29*, 551–559.

Becker, H. S. (1960). Notes on the concept of commitment. *American Journal of Sociology, 66*, 32–40.

Becker, H. S., Geer, B., Hughes, E. C., & Strauss, A. L. (1964). *Boys in white*. Chicago: University of Chicago Press.

Beeber, A. R., & Pies, R. W. (1983). The nonmelancholic depressive syndromes: An alternative approach to classification. *The Journal of Nervous and Mental Disease, 171*, 3–9.

Beecher, H. K. (1956). Relationship of significance of wound to pain experience. *Journal of the American Medical Association, 161*, 1609–1613.

Bell, T. (1978, February 20). Whatever happened to the class of '68? *Chicago Daily News*, p. 19.

Bem, D. J. (1967). Self-perception: An alternative interpretation of cognitive dissonance phenomenon. *Psychological Review, 74*, 183–200.

Bem, D. J., & McConnell, H. K. (1970). Testing the self-perception explanation of dissonance phenomena: On the salience of premanipulation attitudes. *Journal of Personality and Social Psychology, 14*, 23–31.

Benedict, R. (1938). Continuities and discontinuities in cultural conditioning. *Psychiatry, 1*, 161–167.

Bennis, W. G., & Slater, P. E. (1968). *The temporary society.* New York: Harper & Row.

Bergmann, F. (1977). *On being free.* South Bend, IN: University of Notre Dame Press.

Berk, B. (1977). Face-saving at the singles dance. *Social Problems, 24*, 530–544.

Berkowitz, L., & Cottingham, D. R. (1960). The interest value and relevance of fear-arousing communications. *Journal of Abnormal and Social Psychology, 60*, 37–43.

Berlew, P., & Hall, D. (1966). The socialization of managers: Effects of expectations in performance. *Administration Science Quarterly, 11*, 207–223.

Berlin, Sir I. (1969). *Four essays on liberty.* London: Oxford University Press.

Berman, W. H., & Turk, D. C. (1981). Adaptation to divorce: Problems and coping strategies. *Journal of Marriage and the Family, 43*(1), 179–189.

Bernard, J. (1974). Infidelity: Some moral and social issues. In J. R. Smith & L. G. Smith (Eds.), *Beyond monogamy* (pp. 138–158). Baltimore: The Johns Hopkins University Press.

Berndt, T. J. (1981). Age changes and changes over time in prosocial intentions and behavior between friends. *Developmental Psychology, 17*, 408–416.

Berne, E. (1964). *Games people play.* New York: Grove Press.

Berscheid, E., & Fei, J. (1977). Romantic love and jealousy. In G. Clanton & L. G. Smith (Eds.) *Jealousy.* Englewood Cliffs, NJ: Prentice-Hall.

Berscheid, E., & Walster, E. (1974). A little bit about love. In T. Huston (Ed.), *Foundations of interpersonal attraction.* New York: Academic Press.

Berscheid, E., Walster, E., & Bohrnstedt, G. (1973). The body image report. *Psychology Today, 7*, 119–131.

Bettelheim, B. (1943). Individual and mass behavior in extreme situation. *Journal of Abnormal and Social Psychology, 38*, 417–452.

Billings, A. G., Cronkite, R. C., & Moos, R. H. (1983). Social-environmental factors in unipolar depression: Comparisons of depressed patients and nondepressed controls. *Journal of Abnormal Psychology, 92*, 119–133.

Billings, A. G., & Moos, R. H. (1982). Psychosocial theory and research on depression: An integrative framework and review. *Clinical Psychology Review, 2*, 213–237.

Billings, A. G., & Moos, R. H. (1984). Coping, stress and social resources among adults with unipolar depression. *Journal of Personality and Social Psychology, 46*, 877–891.

Blackwell, J. S. (1983, Spring). Drifting controlling and overcoming: Opiate users who avoid becoming chronically dependent. *Journal of Drug Issues*, 219–235.

Blaney, P. H. (1977). Contemporary theories of depression: Critique and comparison. *Journal of Abnormal Psychology, 86*, 203–223.

Blau, P. M. (1964). *Exchange and power in social life.* New York: Wiley.

Blood, M. R. (1969). Work values and job satisfaction. *Journal of Applied Psychology, 53*, 456–459.

Blood, R. O., & Wolfe, D. M. (1960). *Husbands and wives: The dynamics of married living.* Glencoe, IL: The Free Press of Glencoe.

Bloom, B. L. (1984). *Community mental health.* Monterey, CA: Brooks/Cole.

Bower, G. H. (1981). Mood and memory. *American Psychologist, 36*, 129–148.

Bower, G. H., & Gilligan, S. G. (1979). Remembering information related to one's self. *Journal of Research in Personality, 13*, 420–432.

Bowlby, J. (1960). Grief and mourning in infancy and early childhood. *Psychoanalytic Study of the Child, 15*, 9–52.

Bowlby, J. (1973). *Attachment and loss: Vol. 2. Separation: Anxiety and anger.* New York: Basic Books.

Bradley, R. H., & Webb, R. (1976). Age related differences in locus of control orientation in three behavior domains. *Human Development, 19*, 49–55.

Braiker, H. B., & Kelley, H. H. (1979). Conflict in the development of close relationships. In R. L. Burgess & T. L. Huston (Eds.), *Social exchange in developing relationships.* New York: Academic Press.

Bray, D. W., Campbell, R. J., & Grant, D. L. (1974). *Formative years in business*. New York: Wiley.

Brehm, J. W. (1959). Increasing cognitive dissonance by fait accompli. *Journal of Abnormal and Social Psychology, 58*, 379-382.

Brehm, J. W. (1966). *A theory of psychological reactance*. New York: Academic Press.

Brehm, J. W. (1972). *Responses to loss of freedom: A theory of psychological reactance*. Morristown, NJ: General Learning Press.

Brehm, J. W., & Cohen, A. R. (1962). *Explorations in cognitive dissonance* (pp. 192-200). New York: Wiley.

Brehm, J. W., & Leventhal, G. S. (1962). An experiment on the effect of commitment. In J. W. Brehm & A. R. Cohen (Eds.), *Explorations in cognitive dissonance*. New York: Wiley.

Brenner, M. H. (1973). *Mental illness and the economy*. Cambridge, MA: Harvard University Press.

Brewer, M. (1975, August). Erhard seminars training: We're gonna tear you down and put you back together. *Psychology Today*, pp. 35-89.

Brickman, P. (1964). *Attitudes out of context: Harvard students go home*. Unpublished undergraduate honors thesis, Harvard University.

Brickman, P. (1972). Optional stopping on ascending and descending series. *Organizational Behavior and Human Performance, 7*, 53-62.

Brickman, P. (1977). Crime and punishment in sports and society. *Journal of Social Issues, 33*(1), 140-164.

Brickman, P. (1978). Is it real? In J. H. Harvey, W. J. Ickes, & R. F. Kidd (Eds.), *New directions in attribution research* (Vol. 2). Hillsdale, NJ: Lawrence Erlbaum.

Brickman, P. (1980). A social psychology of human concerns. In R. Gilmour & S. Duck (Eds.), *The development of social psychology* (pp. 5-25). London: Academic Press.

Brickman, P., & Campbell, D. T. (1971). Hedonic relativism and planning the good society. In M. Appley (Ed.), *Adaptation level theory: A symposium*. New York: Academic Press.

Brickman, P., Coates, D., & Janoff-Bulman, R. (1978). Lottery winners and accident victims: Is happiness relative? *Journal of Personality and Social Psychology, 36*(3), 917-927.

Brickman, P., & Horn, C. (1973). Balance theory and interpersonal coping in triads. *Journal of Personality and Social Psychology, 26*, 347-355.

Brickman, P., & Janoff-Bulman, R. (1977). Pleasure and pain in social comparison. In J. M. Suls & R. L. Miller (Eds.), *Social comparison processes: Theoretical and empirical perspectives*. New York: Hemisphere.

Brickman, P., Rabinowitz, V. C., Karuza, J., Jr., Coates, D., Cohn, E., & Kidder, L. (1982). Models of helping and coping. *American Psychologist, 37*(4), 368-384.

Brickman, P., Ryan, K., & Wortman, C. B. (1975). Causal chains: Attribution of responsibility as a function of immediate and prior causes. *Journal of Personality and Social Psychology, 32*, 1060-1067.

Brickman, P., Shaver, P., & Archibald, P. (1969). American tactics and American goals in Vietnam as perceived by social scientists. In W. Izard (Ed.), *Vietnam: Issues and alternatives*. Cambridge, MA: Schenkman.

Bringle, R. G., & Evenbeck, S. (1979). The study of jealousy as a dispositional characteristic. In M. Cook & G. Wilson (Eds.), *Love and attraction*. New York: Pergamon.

Brock, T. C., & Buss, A. H. (1962). Dissonance, aggression, and evaluation of pain. *Journal of Abnormal and Social Psychology, 65*, 197-202.

Brockner, J., Shaw, M. C., & Rubin, J. Z. (1979). Factors affecting withdrawal from an escalating conflict: Quitting before it's too late. *Journal of Experimental Social Psychology, 15*, 492-503.

Bronfenbrenner, U. (1977, May). Nobody home: The erosion of the American family. *Psychology Today*, pp. 40-43.

Brown, G., Bhrolchain, N., & Harris, T. (1975). Social class and psychiatric disturbance among women in an urban population. *Sociology, 9*, 225-254.

Brown, J. S., & Farber, I. E. (1951). Emotions conceptualized as intervening variables—with suggestions toward a theory of frustration. *Psychological Bulletin, 48*, 465-495.

Brown, R., & Herrnstein, R. (1975). *Psychology*. Boston: Little Brown.

Bulman, R. J., & Wortman, C. B. (1977). Attributions of blame and coping in the "real world:"

Severe accident victims react to their lot. *Journal of Personality and Social Psychology, 35*(5), 351–363.

Burgess, E. P. (1969). The modification of depressive behaviors. In R. D. Rubin & C. D. Franks (Eds.), *Advances in behavior therapy*. New York: Academic Press.

Burgess, E. W., & Walter, P. (1968). Idealization, love, and self-esteem. In *Family roles and interaction: An anthology*. Chicago: Rand McNally.

Burnstein, E., & Vinokur, A. (1975). What a person thinks upon learning he has chosen differently from others: Nice evidence for the persuasive-arguments explanation of choice shifts. *Journal of Experimental Social Psychology, 11*, 412–426.

Calder, B. J. (1977). Endogenous-exogenous versus internal-external attributions: Implications for the development of attribution theory. *Personality and Social Psychology Bulletin, 3*, 400–406.

Calder, B. J., & Staw, B. M. (1975). Interaction of intrinsic and extrinsic motivation: Some methodological notes. *Journal of Personality and Social Psychology, 31*, 76–80.

Calder, B. J., & Staw, B. M. (1974). Self-perception of intrinsic and extrinsic motivation? *Journal of Applied Social Psychology, 4*, 62–93.

Callero, P.I., & Piliavin, J. A. (1983). Developing a commitment to blood donation: The impact of one's first experience. *Journal of Applied Social Psychology, 13*, 1–16.

Cameron, P., Titus, D. G., Kostin, J., & Kostin, M. (1973). The life satisfaction of non-normal persons. *Journal of Counseling and Clinical Psychology, 41*, 207–214.

Campbell, A. T., Converse, P. E., & Rogers, W. L. (1976). *The quality of American life: Perceptions, evaluations, and satisfactions*. New York Russell Sage Foundations.

Campbell, D. T. (1960). Blind variation and selective retention in creative thought as in other knowledge processes. *Psychological Review, 67*, 380–400.

Campbell, D. T. (1969). Reforms as experiments. *American Psychologist, 24*, 409–429.

Campbell, D. T. (1972). On the genetics of altruism and the counterhedonic components in human culture. *Journal of Social Issues, 28*(3), 21–37.

Campbell, D. T. (1975). On the conflicts between biological and social evolution and between psychology and moral tradition. *American Psychologist, 30*(12), 1103–1126.

Carder, B., & Berkow, K. (1970). Rats' preference for earned in comparison with free food. *Science, 167*, 1273–1274.

Carnegie, D. (1937). *How to win friends and influence people*. New York: Simon & Schuster.

Cartwright, D. (1973). Determinants of scientific progress: The case of research on risky shift. *American Psychologist, 28*, 222–231.

Carver, C. S., & Scheier, M. F. (1982). Control theory: A useful conceptual framework for personality-social, clinical and health psychology. *Psychological Bulletin, 92*, 111–135.

Chanowitz, B., & Langer, E. J. (1981). Premature cognitive commitment. *Journal of Personality and Social Psychology, 41*, 1051–1063.

Chapman, R. H. (1979, September–October). In the play pen: Contemporary drama cornered. *Harvard Magazine*, 54–60.

Cherniss, C. (1978). *Recent research and theory on job stress and burnout in helping professions*. Unpublished manuscript, University of Michigan.

Chodoff, P., Friedman, S. B., & Hamburg, D. A. (1964). Stress defenses and coping behavior: Observations in parents and children with malignant disease. *American Journal of Psychiatry, 36*, 463–476.

Cialdini, R. R., Cacioppo, J. T., Bassett, R., & Miller, J. A. (1978). Low-ball procedure for producing compliance: Commitment then cost. *Journal of Personality and Social Psychology, 120*, 743–749.

Clanton, G. (1981). Frontiers of jealousy research: Introduction to the special issue on jealousy. *Alternative Lifestyles, 4*, 259–273.

Clanton, G., & Smith, L. G. (1977). *Jealousy*. Englewood Cliffs, NJ: Prentice-Hall.

Clark, L. (1960). The effect of mental practice on the development of a certain motor skill. *Research Quarterly, 31*, 560–569.

Clark, N. T. (1976). Behavioral indicators of longitudinal inmate change in a maximum security prison. Unpublished doctoral dissertation, Northwestern University.

Coates, D., & Peterson, B. A. (1982). Depression and deviance. In G. Weary & H. L. Mirels (Eds.), *Integrations of clinical and social psychology*. New York: Oxford University Press.

Coates, D., Renzaglia, G. J., & Embree, M. C. (1983). When helping backfires: Help and helplessness. In J. D. Fisher, A. Nadler, & B. DePaulo (Eds.), *New directions in helping: Recipients' reaction to aid* (Vol. 1). New York: Academic Press.

Coates, D., & Winston, T. (1983). Counteracting the deviance of depression: Peer support groups for victims. *Journal of Social Issues, 39*(2), 169–194.

Coates, D., & Wortman, C. B. (1980). Depression maintenance and interpersonal control. In A. Baum & J. Singer (Eds.), *Advances in environmental psychology* (Vol. 2, pp. 152–182). Hillsdale, NJ: Erlbaum.

Coates, D., Wortman, C. B. & Abbey, A. (1979). Reactions to victims. In I.H. Frieze, D. Bar-Tal & J. S. Carroll (Eds.) *New approaches to social problems*. San Francisco: Jossey-Bass.

Cobb, S. (1976). Social support as moderator of life stress. *Psychosomatic Medicine, 38*, 300–314.

Coffin, W. S., Jr. (1977). *Once to every man: A memoir*. New York: Atheneum.

Cohen, S., & Hoberman, H. M. (1983). Positive events and social supports as buffers of life change stress. *Journal of Applied Social Psychology, 13*, 99–125.

Cohen, S. & Syme, S. L. (1985). *Social support and health*. New York: Academic Press.

Coleman, J. S. (1973). Loss of power. *American Sociological Review, 38*, 1–17.

Coles, R. (1978, October 9). The search II. *The New Yorker*.

Colletti, L. (1975). Marxism and the dialectic. *New Left Review, 93*, 3–29.

Collins, B. E., & Hoyt, M. F. (1972). Personal responsibility-for-consequences: An integration and extension of the "forced compliance" literature. *Journal of Experimental Social Psychology, 8*, 558, 593.

Cook, T. D., & Flay, B. R. (1978). The persistence of experimentally induced attitude change. In L. Berkowitz (Ed.), *Advances in experimental social psychology* (Vol. 11). New York: Academic Press.

Cooley, C. H. (1902). Human nature and the social order. New York: Scribner.

Coombs, D. T., & Boyle, P. B. (1971). The transition to medical school: Expectations versus realities. In R. H. Coombs & C. E. Vincent (Eds.), *Psychosocial aspects of medical training* (pp. 91–109). Springfield IL: Charles C. Thomas.

Cooper, J. (1971). Personal responsibility and dissonance: The role of foreseen consequences. *Journal of Personality and Social Psychology, 18*, 354–363.

Cooper, J., & Worchel, S. (1970). Role of undesired consequences in arousing cognitive dissonance. *Journal of Personality and Social Psychology, 11*, 199–206.

Cooper, J., Zanna, M. P., & Taves, P. A. (1978). Arousal as a necessary condition for attitude change following induced compliance. *Journal of Personality and Social Psychology, 36*, 1101–1106.

Copas, J. B. & Robin, A. (1982). Suicide in psychiatric in-patients. *British Journal of Psychiatry, 141*, 503–511.

Coppinger, R. M., & Rosenblatt, P. C. (1968). Romantic love and subsistence dependence of spouses. *Southwestern Journal of Anthropology, 24*, 310–319.

Corah, N. L., & Boffa, J. (1970). Perceived control, self-observation, and response to aversive behavior. *Journal of Personality and Social Psychology, 16*, 1–14.

Corbin, B. (1967). The effects of covert rehearsal on the development of a complex motor skill. *Journal of Genetic Psychology, 76*, 143–150.

Corbin, R. M. (1979). Decisions that might not get made. In T. S. Wallsten (Ed.), *Cognitive processes in choice and decision behavior*. Hillsdale, NJ: Erlbaum.

Cosden, M. A., Ellis, H. S., & Feeney, D. M. (1979). Cognitive flexibility, rigidity, repetition effects, and memory. *Journal of Research in Personality, 13*, 386–395.

Costello, C. G. (1972). Depression: Loss of reinforcers or loss of reinforcer effectiveness? *Behavior Therapy, 3*, 240–257.

Cottrell, N. B., & Wack, D. L. (1967). Energizing effects of cognitive dissonance upon dominant and subordinate responses. *Journal of Personality and Social Psychology, 6*, 132–138.

Cowan, J. D. (1983). Testing the escape hypothesis: Alcohol helps users to forget their feelings. *The Journal of Nervous and Mental Disease, 171*, 40–48.

Cowie, B. (1976). Accepting a heart attack. *Human Behavior, 5*, 30.

Coyne, J. C., Aldwin, C., & Lazarus, R. S. (1981). Depression and coping in stressful episodes. *Journal of Abnormal Psychology, 90*, 439–447.

Coyne, J. C., & Gotlib, I. H. (1983). The role of cognition in depression: A critical appraisal. *Psychological Bulletin, 94*, 472–505.

Cozby, P. C., & Rosenblatt, P. C. (1972, October). Flirting. *Sexual Behavior, 2*(10), 10–16.

Cressey, D. R. (1953). *Other people's money: A study in the social psychology of embezzlement.* Glencoe, IL: Free Press.

Croughan, J. L., Miller, J. P., Koepke, J., & Whitman, B. Y. (1981). Depression in narcotic addicts—a prospective study with a five-year follow-up. *Comprehensive Psychiatry, 22*, 428–433.

Crumbaugh, J. C., Raphael, M., Sr., & Sharader, R. R. (1970). Frankl's will to meaning in a religious order. *Journal of Clinical Psychology, 26*, 206–207.

Csikszentmihalyi, M. (1975). *Beyond boredom and anxiety: The experience of play in work and games.* San Francisco: Jossey-Bass.

Csikszentmihalyi, M. (1978). Attention and the holistic approach to behavior. In K. S. Tope & J. L. Singer (Eds.), *The stream of consciousness.* New York: Plenum.

Csikszentmihalyi, M., & Graef, R. (1979, December). Feeling free. *Psychology Today,* pp. 84–92.

Cumming, E., Lazer, C., & Lichisolm, L. (1975). Suicide as an index of role-strain among employed and not employed married women in British Columbia. *Canadian Review of Sociology and Anthropology, 24*, 462–470.

Curtis, R., Smith, R., & Moore, R. (1984). Suffering to improve outcomes determined by both chance and skill. *Journal of Social and Clinical Psychology, 2*, 165–173.

Cutler, S. J. (1976). Membership in different types of voluntary associations and psychological well-being. *The Gerontologist, 16*, 335–339.

Dahl, R. A. (1957). The concept of power. *Behavioral Science, 2*, 201–215.

Dangaard, C. (1977, November 20). Denver is on a Rocky Mountain high of hits. *Chicago Tribune,* pp. 2, 18.

Davies, J. C. (1962). Toward a theory of revolution. *American Sociological Review, 27*, 5–19.

Davis, J. H., Kerr, N. L., Atkin, R., Holt, R., & Meek, D. (1975). The decision processes of 6- and 12-person mock juries assigned unanimous and two-thirds majority rules. *Journal of Personality and Social Psychology, 32*, 1–14.

Davis, K. (1936). Jealousy and sexual property. *Social Forces, 14*, 295–405.

Davis, K. E., & Jones, E. E. (1960). Changes in interpersonal perceptions as a means of reducing cognitive dissonance. *Journal of Abnormal and Social Psychology, 61*, 402–410.

Deci, E. L. (1975). *Intrinsic motivation.* New York: Plenum.

Deci, E. L. (1980). *The psychology of self-determination.* Lexington, MA: D. C. Heath.

DeGood, D. E. (1975). Cognitive control factors in vascular stress response. *Psychophysiology, 12*, 399–401.

DeJong, W. (1979). An examination of self-perception medication of the foot-in-the-door effect. *Journal of Personality and Social Psychology, 37*, 2221–2239.

DeLongis, A., Coyne, J. C., Dakof, G., Folkman, S., & Lazarus, R. S. (1982). Relationship of daily hassles, uplifts, and major life events to health status. *Health Psychology, 1*(2), 119–136.

Depue, R., & Monroe, S. (1978). Learned helplessness in the perspective of the depressive disorders: Conceptual and definitional issues. *Journal of Abnormal Psychology, 87*, 3–20.

Deutsch, M. (1958). Trust and suspicion. *Journal of Conflict Resolution, 2*, 265–279.

Deutsch, M., & Krauss, R. M. (1962). Studies of interpersonal bargaining. *Journal of Conflict Resolution, 6*, 52–76.

Deutsch, M., Krauss, R. M., & Rosenaw, N. (1962). Dissonance or defensiveness? *Journal of Personality, 30*, 28–31.

Dewey, R. E., & Gould, L. J. (1970). *Freedom: Its history, nature, and varieties.* New York: MacMillan.

Dickey, J. (1970). *Deliverance.* New York: Houghton Mifflin.

Diener, C. I., & Dweck, C. S. (1978). An analysis of learned helplessness, continuous changes in performance, strategy and achievement cognitions following failure. *Journal of Personality and Social Psychology, 36*, 451–462.

Dion, K. L., & Dion, K. K. (1976). Love, liking and trust in heterosexual relationships. *Personality and Social Psychology Bulletin, 2*, 187–190.

Dollard, J., Doob, L. W., Miller, K. E., Mowrer, O. H., & Sears, R. R. (1939). *Frustration and aggression*. New Haven, CT: Yale University Press.

Dollinger, S., & Taub, S. (1971). Interaction of locus of control expectancies and providing purpose on children's motivation. *Journal of Research in Personality, 11*, 118-127.

Douvan, E. (1974). Commitment and social contract in adolescence. *Psychiatry, 37*, 22-36.

Douvan, E. (1977). Interpersonal relationships, some questions and observations. In H. Raush & G. Levinger (Eds.), *Close Relationships* (pp. 17-32). Amherst, MA: University of Massachusetts Press.

Douvan, E. (1979). The capacity for intimacy. In H. Chickering (Ed.), *The future of higher education*. San Francisco: Jossey-Bass.

Douvan, E., & Adelson, J. (1966). *The adolescent experience*. New York: Wiley.

Downton, J. U., Jr. (1979). *Sacred journeys: The conversion of young Americans*. New York: Columbia University Press.

Drachmer, A., & Worchel, S. (1976). Misattribution of arousal as a means of dissonance reduction. *Sociometry, 37*, 53-59.

Dreikurs, R. (1968). *A new approach to discipline: Logical consequences*. New York: Hawthorn Books.

Drenick, E. (1973). Weight reduction by prolonged fasting. In G. Bray (Ed.), *Obesity in perspective, Fogerty international series on preventive medicine* (Vol. 2, Pt 2, pp. 341-360). Washington, DC: U.S. Government Printing Office.

Driscoll, R., Davis, K. E., & Lipetz, M. E. (1972). Parental interference and romantic love: The Romeo and Juliet effect. *Journal of Personality and Social Psychology, 24*, 1-10.

Duenstbier, R. A., Hillsner, S., Lehnhoff, J., Hillman, J., & Valkenair, M. C. (1975). An emotion-attribution approach to moral behavior: Interfacing cognitive and avoidance theories of moral development. *Psychological Review, 82*, 299-315.

Dumond, D. E. (1975). The limitations of human population: A natural history. *Science, 187*, 713-721.

Dutton, S., & Aron, A. (1974). Some evidence for heightened sexual attraction under conditions of high anxiety. *Journal of Personality and Social Psychology, 30*, 510-517.

Dweck, C. S. (1975). The role of expectations and attributions in the alleviation of learned helplessness. *Journal of Personality and Social Psychology, 31*, 674-685.

Dworkin, G. (1970). Acting freely. *Nous, 4*, 367-382.

Dyer, L., & Parker, S. F. (1975). Classifying outcomes in work motivation research: An examination of the intrinsic-extrinsic dichotomy. *Journal of Applied Psychology, 60*, 455-458.

Dyer, W. W. (1976). *Your erroneous zones*. New York: Avon Books.

Dyson, F. (1979, August 6). Reflections: The world of the scientist—part I. *The New Yorker*, 37-61.

Eckenrode, J. (1984). Impact of chronic and acute stressors on daily reports of mood. *Journal of Personality and Social Psychology, 46*, 907-918.

Edwards, W. (1968). Conservatism in human information processing. In B. Kleinmuntz (Ed.), *Formal representation of human judgment* (pp. 17-52). New York: Wiley.

Egbert, L., Battit, G., Welch, L., & Bartlett, M. (1964). Reduction of post operative pain by encouragement and instruction of patients. *New England Journal of Medicine, 270*, 825-827.

Eglash, A. (1951). *Abnormal fixations*. Ann Arbor, MI: University Microfilms.

Eidelson, R. J. (1980). Interpersonal satisfaction and level of involvement: A curvilinear relationship. *Journal of Personality and Social Psychology, 39*, 460-470.

Ellis, A. (1962). *Reason and emotion in psychotherapy*. Secaucus, NJ: Lyle Stuart and Citadel Press.

Epstein, S. M. (1967). Toward a unified theory of anxiety. In B. A. Maher (Ed.), *Progress in experimental personality research* (Vol. 4, pp. 2-89). New York: Academic Press.

Erdelyi, M., Buschke, H., & Finkelstein, S. (1977). Hyperamnesia for socratic stimuli. The growth of recall for an internally generated memory list abstracted from a series of riddles. *Memory and Cognition, 5*, 283-286.

Erikson, E. H. (1950). *Childhood and society*. New York: Norton.

Erikson, E. H. (1959). Identity and the life cycle: Selected papers. *Psychological Issues, 1*, 1-171.

Eysenck, H. J. (1955). *The psychology of politics*. New York: Praeger.

Eysenck, H. J., Wakefield, J. A., & Friedman, A. F. (1983). Diagnosis and clinical assessment: The DSM-III. *Annual Review of Psychology, 34,* 167-193.

Fazio, R. H., & Zanna, M. P. (1978). Attitudinal qualities relating to the strength of the attitude-behavior relationship. *Journal of Experimental Social Psychology, 14,* 398-408.

Fein, H. (1979). *Accounting for genocide.* New York: Free Press.

Fein, R. (1979). From reform to relativism: Empirical validity and social equity. *Milbank Memorial Fund Quarterly—Health and Society, 57*(3), 353-357.

Feldman, D. A., Strong, S. R., & Danser, D. B. (1982). A comparison of paradoxical and non-paradoxical interpretations and directives. *Journal of Counseling Psychology, 29,* 572-579.

Festinger, L. (1950). Informal social communication. *Psychological Review, 57,* 271-282.

Festinger, L. (1957). *A theory of cognitive dissonance.* Stanford, CA: Stanford University Press.

Festinger, L. (1964). Behavioral support for opinion change. *Public Opinion Quarterly, 28,* 404-417.

Festinger, L., & Carlsmith, J. M. (1959). Cognitive consequences of forced compliance. *Journal of Abnormal and Social Psychology, 58,* 203-210.

Festinger, L., Riecken, H. W., & Schachter, S. (1956). *When prophecy fails.* Minneapolis: University of Minnesota Press.

Finlay-Jones, R., & Brown, G. W. (1981). Types of stressful life event and the onset of anxiety and depressive disorders. *Psychological Medicine, 11,* 803-815.

Fischhoff, B. (1975). Hindsight-foresight: The effects of outcome knowledge on judgment under uncertainty. *Journal of Experimental Psychology: Human Perception and Performance, 1,* 288-299.

Fischhoff, B. (1977). Perceived informativeness of facts. *Journal of Experimental Psychology: Human Perception and Performance, 3,* 349-358.

Fischhoff, B. (1980). For those condemned to study the past: Reflections on historical judgment. In R.A. Schiveder & D. W. Fisher (Eds.). *New directions for methodology of behavioral science: Fallible judgment in behavioral research.* San Francisco: Jossey-Bass.

Fischhoff, B., & Beyth, R. (1975). "I knew it would happen"—Remembered probabilities of once-future things. *Organizational Behavior and Human Performance, 13,* 1-16.

Fisher, J. D., Nadler, A., & Whitcher-Alagna, S. (1982). Recipient reactions to aid. *Psychological Bulletin, 91,* 27-54.

Fisher, W. A., & Byrne, S. (1978). Sex differences in response to erotica. *Journal of Personality and Social Psychology, 36,* 117-125.

Flay, B. R. (1978). Catastrophe theory in social psychology: Some applications to attitudes and social behavior. *Behavioral Science, 23,* 335-350.

Folger, R., Rosenfield, D., & Hays, R. P. (1978). Equity and intrinsic motivation: The role of choice. *Journal of Personality and Social Psychology, 36,* 557-564.

Folkman, S. (1984). Personal control and stress and coping processes: A theoretical analysis. *Journal of Personality and Social Psychology, 46,* 839-852.

Folkman, S., & Lazarus, R. S. (1985). If it changes it must be a process: A study of emotion and coping during three states of a college examination. *Journal of Personality and Social Psychology, 48,* 150-170.

Fowles, J. (1977). *Daniel Martin.* Boston: Little, Brown.

Fox, F. V., & Staw, B. M. (1979). The trapped administrator: Effects of job insecurity and policy resistance upon commitment to a course of action. *Administrative Sciences Quarterly, 24,* 449-472.

Fox. R. C. (1979). *Essays in medical sociology: Journeys into the field.* New York: Wiley.

Frank, J. D. (1963). *Persuasion and healing.* New York: Schocken Books.

Frankl, V. (1959). *From death camp to existentialism.* Boston: Beacon.

Frankl, V. (1963). *Man's search for meaning: An introduction to logo therapy.* New York: Washington Square Press.

Frankl, V. (1975). *The unconscious God.* New York: Simon & Schuster.

Freedman, J. (1978). *Happy people: What happiness is, who has it, and why.* New York: Harcourt, Brace & Jovanovich.

Freedman, J. L. (1965). Long-term behavioral effects of cognitive dissonance. *Journal of Experimental Social Psychology, 1,* 145-155.

Freedman, J. L., & Fraser, S. C. (1966). Compliance without pressure: The foot-in-the-door technique. *Journal of Personality and Social Psychology, 4*, 195–202.

French, J., Rodgers, W., & Cobb, S. (1974). A model of person-environment fit. In G. Coehlo, D. Hamburg, & J. Adams (Eds.), *Coping and adaptation*. New York: Basic Books, pp. 316–333.

Freud, S. (1922). *Group psychology and the analysis of the ego*. London: Hogarth.

Freud, S. (1930). *Civilization and its discontents*. London: Hogarth.

Freud, S. (1935). *A general introduction to psychoanalysis*. New York: Washington Square Press.

Freud, S. (1959). Certain neurotic mechanisms in jealousy, paranoia and homosexuality. *Collected papers* (Vol. 2). New York: Basic Books.

Freudenberger, H. (1974). Staff burn-out. *Journal of Social Issues, 30*, 159–165.

Frey, P. W., & Flay, B. R. (1978). Student ratings of instruction: Implications of a theoretical model for evaluation decisions. Preprint: Northwestern University.

Friedman, M., & Rosenman, H. (1974). *Type A behavior and your heart*. New York: Knopf.

Fromm, E. (1941). *Escape from freedom*. New York: Holt, Rinehart & Winston.

Gailbraith, G. G., & Mosher, D. L. (1968). Associative sexual responses in relation to sexual arousal, sex guilt, and external approval contingencies. *Journal of Personality and Social Psychology, 10*, 142–147.

Ganellen, R. J., & Blaney, P. H. (1984). Hardiness and social support as moderators of the effects of life-stress. *Journal of Personality and Social Psychology, 47*, 156–163.

Garbarino, J. (1975). The impact of anticipated rewards upon cross-aged tutoring. *Journal of Personality and Social Psychology, 32*, 421–428.

Gardner, J. W. (1964). *Self-renewal: The individual and the innovative society*. New York: Harper & Row.

Garner, W. R. (1970). Good patterns have few alternatives. *American Scientist, 58*, 34–42.

Gerard, H. B. (1965). Deviation, conformity, and commitment. In I. D. Steiner & M. Fishbein (Eds.), *Current studies in social psychology* (pp. 263–277). New York: Holt, Rinehart & Winston.

Gerard, H. B., Blevans, S. A., & Malcolm, T. (1964). Self-evaluation and the evaluation of choice alternatives. *Journal of Personality, 32*, 395–410.

Gergen, K. J. (1972, May). Multiple identity: The healthy, happy human being wears many masks. *Psychology Today*, 31–66.

Gergen, K. J. (1973). Social psychology as history. *Journal of Personality and Social Psychology, 26*, 309–320.

Gerrard, M. (1982). Sex, sex guilt, and contraceptive use. *Journal of Personality and Social Psychology, 42*, 153–158.

Gerrard, M., & Gibbons, F. X. (1982). Sexual experience, sex guilt, and sexual moral reasoning. *Journal of Personality, 50*, 345–359.

Ghiselin, M. T. (1974). *The economy of nature and the evolution of sex*. Berkeley, CA: University of California Press.

Gibbs, J. P. (1982). Testing the theory of status integration and suicide rates. *American Sociological Review, 47*, 227–237.

Gibran, K. (1936). *The Prophet*. New York: Knopf.

Gibson, E. J. (1969). *Principles of perceptual learning and development*. New York: Appleton-Century-Crofts.

Giele, J. (1976). Changing sex roles and the future of marriage. In H. Grunebaum & J. Christ (Eds.), *Contemporary marriage: Structure, dynamics and therapy* Boston: Little, Brown. (1st ed., pp. 69–83).

Gilbert, Sir W. S. (1881). *Patience, or the poet and the milkmaid*. Cincinnati: P. G. Thomson.

Ginna, R. E. (1977, June 6). Outside his window within his heart, Eric Ambler finds the stuff of great spy novels. *People*, 92–100.

Ginzburg, E., Ginzburg, S. W., Axelrod, S., & Herma, J. L. (1951). *Occupational choice: An approach to a general theory*. New York: Columbia University Press.

Gittleson, N. (1978, November). Infidelity: Can you forgive and forget? *Redbook Magazine*, 113–194.

Glass, D. (1977). *Behavior patterns, stress and coronary disease*. Hillsdale, NJ: Erlbaum.

Glass, D., & Singer, J. (1972). *Urban stress: Experiments on noise and urban stressors*. New York: Academic Press.

Glass, D. C., Singer, J. E., Friedman, J. (1969). Psychic cost of adaptation to an environmental stressor. *Journal of Personality and Social Psychology, 12*, 200-219.

Glenn, N. D., & Weaver, C. N. (1981). The contribution of marital happiness to global happiness. *Journal of Marriage and the Family, 43*, 161-168.

Glennon, J. (1966). Weight reduction—an enigma. *Archives of Internal Medicine, 118*, 1-2.

Glick, I. O., Weiss, R. S., & Parkes, C. M. (1974). *The first year of bereavement*. New York: Wiley.

Goethals, G. R., Cooper, J., & Naficy, A. (1979). Role of foreseen, foreseeable, and unforeseeable behavioral consequences in the arousal of cognitive dissonance. *Journal of Personality and Social Psychology, 37*, 1179-1185.

Goffman, E. (1961). *Asylums*. New York: Anchor Doubleday Books.

Gold, M. (1958). Suicide, homicide and the socialization of aggression. *American Journal of Sociology, 64*, 651-661.

Gold, M., & Petronio, R. J. (1980). Delinquent behavior in adolescence. In J. Adelson (Ed.), *Handbook of adolescent psychology*. New York: Wiley-Interscience Publications.

Goldstein, J. H., Davis, R. W., & Herman, D. (1975). Escalation of aggression: Experimental studies. *Journal of Personality and Social Psychology, 31*, 162-170.

Goleman, D. (1980). Leaving home: Is there a right time to go? *Psychology Today, 14*, 52-61.

Goleman, D. (1980, February). 1,528 little geniuses and how they grew. *Psychology Today*, 28-43.

Golin, S., Terell, F., Weitz, J., & Drost, P. L. (1979). The illusion of control among depressed patients. *Journal of Abnormal Psychology, 88*, 454-457.

Goode, W. J. (1956). *After divorce*. New York: Free Press.

Gotlib, I. H. (1984). Depression and general psychopathology in university students. *Journal of Abnormal Psychology, 93*, 19-30.

Gould, R. L. (1972). The phases of adult life: A study in developmental psychology. *American Journal of Psychiatry, 129*, 521-531.

Gouldner, A. W. (1960). The norm of reciprocity: A preliminary statement. *American Sociological Review, 25*, 161-179.

Gray, R. M., Newman, W. R., & Reinhardt, A. M. (1966). The effect of medical specialization on physicians' attitudes. *Journal of Health and Human Behavior, 7*, 128-132.

Greenbaum, H. L. (1966). Self-esteem and cognitive dissonance. *Social Relations, 4*, 19-26.

Greenwald, A. G. (1980). The totalitarian ego: Fabrication and revision of personal history. *American Psychologist, 35*, 603-618.

Grinker, R. L. (1977). The poor rich: The children of the super rich. *American Journal of Psychiatry, 135*, 913-916.

Grinker, R., Jr., & Spiegler, J. (1945). *Men under stress*. New York: McGraw-Hill.

Gruenberg, B. (1980). The happy worker: an analysis of educational and occupational differences in determinants of job satisfaction. *American Journal of Sociology, 86*(2), 247-271.

Gullahorn, J. T., & Gullahorn, J. E. (1960). The role of academic man as a cross-cultural mediator. *American Sociological Review, 25*, 414-417.

Gunnar-Vongnechten, M. R. (1978). Changing a frightening toy into a pleasant toy by allowing the infant to control its actions. *Developmental Psychology, 14*, 157-162.

Gurin, G., Veroff, J., & Feld, S. (1960). *Americans view their mental health*. New York: Basic Books.

Guttman, D. (1975). Parenthood: A key to the comparative study of the life cycle. In N. Datan & L.H. Ginsberg (Eds), *Lifespan developmental psychology: Normative life crises* (pp. 167-184). New York: Academic Press.

Haber, S. (1978, August). Fear of thinness: Alternative approaches to the treatment of obesity. Paper presented at American Psychology Association, Toronto, Canada.

Hadaway, C. K. (1978). Life satisfaction and religion: A reanalysis. *Social Forces, 57*, 636-643.

Hall, C. S., & Lindzey, G. (1957). *Theories of personality*. New York: Wiley.

Hall, D. T., & Schneider, B. (1973). *Organizational Climates and careers: The work lines of priests*. New York: Seminar Press.

Hamilton, D. L., Katz, L. B., & Leirer, V. O. (1980). Organizational processes in impression formation. In R. Hastie, T. M. Ostrom, E. B. Ebbeson, R. S. Wyer, D. L. Hamilton, & D. E. Carlston (Eds). *Person memory*. Hillsdale, NJ: Erlbaum.

Hamilton, W. R., & Jacque, Z. (1977). Commitment as a function of sex, race, and year in school. Unpublished manuscript, Northwestern University.

Hammen, C. L., & Glass, R. D. (1975). Depression, activity and evaluation of reinforcement. *Journal of Abnormal Psychology, 84*, 718-721.

Hamner, W. C., & Foster, L. W. (1975). Are intrinsic and extrinsic rewards additive: A test of Deci's cognitive evaluation theory of task motivation. *Organizational Behavior and Human Performance, 14*, 398-415.

Haner, C., & Brown, P. (1955). Clarification of the instigation to action concept in the frustration-aggression hypothesis. *The Journal of Abnormal and Social Psychology, 51*, 204-206.

Hansen, G. L. (1982). Reactions to hypothetical jealousy-producing events. *Family Relations, 31*, 513-518.

Hansen, G. L. (1983). Marital satisfaction and jealousy among men. *Psychological Reports, 52*, 363-366.

Hardin, G. (1968). The tragedy of the commons. *Science, 162*, 1243-1248.

Hardyck, J. A., & Braden, M. (1962). Prophecy fails again: A report of a failure to replicate. *Journal of Abnormal and Social Psychology, 65*, 136-141.

Harris, A., Tessler, R., & Potter, J. (1977). The induction of self-reliance: An experimental study of independence in the face of failure. *Journal of Applied Social Psychology, 4*, 313-331.

Harris, M. (1968). *The rise of anthropological theory*. New York: Cromwell.

Harter, S. (1981). A new self-report scale of intrinsic versus extrinsic orientation in the classroom; Motivational and informational components. *Developmental Psychology, 17*, 300-312.

Harvey, J. H., Weber, A. L., Yarkin, K. L., & Stewart, B. E. (1982). Attribution and relationship breakdown. In S. Duck (Ed.), *Dissolving personal relationships*. London: Academic Press.

Harvey, J. H., Wells, G. L., & Alvarez, M. D. (1978). Attribution in the context of conflict and separation in close relationships. In J. H. Harvey, W. J. Ickes, & R. F. Kidd (Eds.), *New directions in attribution research* (Vol. 2). Hillsdale, NJ: Erlbaum.

Hatsukami, D., & Pickens, R. W. (1982). Posttreatment depression in an alcohol and drug abuse population. *American Journal of Psychiatry, 139*, 1563-1566.

Hayes-Roth, B. (1977). Evolution of cognitive structures and processes. *Psychological Review, 84*, 260-278.

Hebb, D. (1958). The mammal and his environment. In C. Ree, J. Alexander, & S. Tomkins (Eds.), *Psychopathology: A source book* (pp. 127-135). Cambridge, MA: Harvard University Press.

Heidegger, M. (1963). *Being and time*. New York: Harper and Row.

Heider, F. (1958). *The Psychology of Interpersonal Relations*. New York: Wiley.

Heilbroner, R. L. (1953). *The worldly philosophers: The lives, times, and ideas of great economic thinkers*, New York: Simon & Schuster.

Heineman, C. E. (1953). A forced choice form of the Taylor Anxiety Scale. *Journal of Psychology, 17*, 447-454.

Helfer, R. E., & Kempl, C. H. (1972). *Helping the battered child and his family*. Philadelphia: J. B. Lippincott.

Heller, J. (1961). *Catch-22*. New York: Simon & Schuster.

Hendin, H. (1978). Suicide: The psychosocial dimension. *Suicide and Life Threatening Behavior, 8*, 99-177.

Henry, A. F., & Short, J. F. (1954). *Suicide and homocide*. Glencoe, IL: Free Press.

Herrnstein, R. J. (1977a). Doing what comes naturally: A reply to Professor Skinner. *American Psychologist, 32*, 1013-1016.

Herrnstein, R. J. (1977b). The evolution of behaviorism. *American Psychologist, 32*, 593-603.

Hersh, S. (1970). *My Lai 4: A report on the massacre and its aftermath*. New York: Vintage Books.

Hetherington, E. M. (1976). Divorce, new relationships and sexual satisfaction. *Family Relations, 25*, 422–431.

Hetherington, E. M., Cox, M., & Cox, R. (1977). The aftermath of divorce. In J. H. Stevens & M. Matthews (Eds.), *Mother-child, father-child relations*. Washington, DC: National Association for the Education of Young Children.

Hicks, M. W., & Platt, M. (1970). Marital happiness and stability: A review of the research in the sixties. *Journal of Marriage and the Family, 32*, 533–574.

Higgins, E. T., & King, G. (1980). Accessibility of social constructs: Information processing consequences of individual and contextual variability. In N. Cantor & J. F. Kihlstrom (Eds.), *Cognition, social interaction and personality*. Hillsdale, NJ: Erlbaum.

Hill, C. T., Rubin, Z., & Peplau, L. A. (1976). Breakups before marriage: The end of 103 affairs. *Journal of Social Issues, 32*, 147–168.

Hillyer, J. (1978, February 17). Sloan: All bull and no beef. *Chicago Daily News*, p. 34.

Hinkle, C. T. (1968). Job satisfaction and health. *Journal of Organizations, 2*, 19–27.

Hirschfeld, R. M. A. (1981). Situational depression: Validity of the concept. *British Journal of Psychiatry, 139*, 297–305.

Hirschman, A. O. (1970). *Exit, voice and loyalty: Responses to decline in firms, organizations, and states*. Cambridge, MA: Harvard University Press.

Hobart, C. W. (1958). Disillusionment in marriage, and romanticism. *Marriage and Family Living, 20*, 156–162.

Hoffman, P. J., Festinger, L., & Lawrence, D. H. (1954). Tendencies toward group comparability in competitive bargaining. *Human Relations, 7*, 141–159.

Holmes, D., & Houston, B. (1974). Effectiveness of situation redefinition and affective isolation in coping with stress. *Journal of Personality and Social Psychology, 29*, 212–218.

Holmes, T. H., & Rahe, R. H. (1967). The social readjustment rating scale. *Journal of Psychosomatic Research, 11*, 213–218.

Horowitz, L. M., Day, R. S., Light, L. L., & White, M. A. (1968). Availability growth and latent verbal learning. *Journal of General Psychology, 78*, 65–83.

Horrocks, J. E., & Mussman, M. C. (1973). Developmental trends in wishes, confidence, and the sense of personal control from childhood to middle maturity. *Journal of Psychology, 84*, 241–252.

House, J. S. (1981). *Work, stress, and social support*. Reading, MA: Addison-Wesley.

Houston, B. K., Bloom, L. J., Burish, T. G., & Cummings, E. M. (1978). Positive evaluation of stressful experiences. *Journal of Personality, 46*, 205–214.

Houtz, J. C., Tetenbaum, T. J., & Phillips, R. H. (1981). Affective correlates in the problem-solving process. *Journal of Psychology, 109*, 265–269.

Hoyt, M. F., Henley, M. S., & Collins, B. F. (1972). Studies in forced compliance: The influence of choice and consequences on attitude change. *Journal of Personality and Social Psychology, 23*, 205–210.

Hughes, M., & Gove, W. R. (1981). Living alone, social integration and mental health. *American Journal of Sociology, 87*, 48–75.

Hunter, N. L., & Locke, S. E. (1984). Health locus of control: A potential moderator variable for the relationship between life stress and psychopathology. *Psychotherapy and Psychosomatics, 41*, 186–194.

Husar, J. (1978, June 16). Palmer comes full cycle on 18-year ride. *Chicago Tribune*, section 6, pp. 1–4.

Huston, T. L., Surra, C. A., Fitzgerald, N. M., & Cate, R. M. (1981). From courtship to marriage: Mate selection as an interpersonal process. In S. Duck & R. Gilmour (Eds.), *Personal relationships II: Developing personal relationships*. London: Academic Press.

Hyde, J. S., & Phillis, D. E. (1979). Androgyny across the life span. *Developmental Psychology, 15*, 334–336.

Ilg, F. L., Ames, L. B., & Baker, S. M. (1981). *Child behavior* (rev. ed.). New York: Harper & Row.

Jacobs, S. C., Prusoff, B. A., & Paykel, E. S. (1974). Recent life events in schizophrenia and depression. *Psychological Medicine, 4*, 444–453.

James, W. (1890). *The principles of psychology*, New York: Henry Holt and Co.

James, W. (1902). *The varieties of religious experience*. New York: New American Library.

Janis, I. L. (1958). *Psychological stress: Psychoanalytic and behavioral studies of surgical patients*. New York: Wiley.

Janis, I. L. (1972). *Victims of groupthink: A psychological study of foreign-policy decisions and fiascoes*. Boston: Houghton Mifflin.

Janis, I. L., & Mann, L. (1977). *Decision making: A psychological analysis of conflict, choice, and commitment*. New York: Free Press.

Janoff-Bulman, R. (1979). Characterological versus behavioral self-blame: Inquiries into depression and rape. *Journal of Personality and Social Psychology, 37*, 1798-1809.

Janoff-Bulman, R., & Brickman, P. (1981). Expectations and what people learn from failure. In N. T. Feather (Ed.), *Expectations and actions* (pp. 207-237). Hillsdale, NJ: Erlbaum.

Janoff-Bulman, R., & Frieze, I. H. (1983). A theoretical perspective for understanding reactions to victimization. *Journal of Social Issues, 39*(2), 1-17.

Jasnau, K. (1967). Individual versus mass transfer of non-psychotic geriatric patients from mental hospitals to nursing homes with special reference to death rate. *Journal of American Geriatrics Society, 15*, 280-284.

Jauss, B. (1978, June 23). Baseball's best bet for quick relief. *Chicago Tribune*, section 40, pp. 1-2.

Jedlicka, D. (1975). Sequential analysis of perceived commitment to partners in premarital coitus. *Journal of Marriage and the Family, 37*, 385-390.

Jenkins, C. (1975). The coronary prone personality. In W. Gentry & R. Williams (Eds.), *Psychological aspects of myocardial infarction and coronary care*. St. Louis: Mosby.

Jensen, G. S. (1963). Preference for bar pressing over "free-loading" as a function of number of rewarded presses. *Journal of Experimental Psychology, 65*, 451-454.

Johnson, G. (1976). The Hare Krishna in San Francisco. In C. Y. Glock & R. N. Bellah (Eds.), *The new religious consciousness* (pp. 31-51). Berkeley, CA: University of California Press.

Johnson, J. E. (1973). Effects of accurate expectations about sensations on the sensory and distress components of pain. *Journal of Personality and Social Psychology, 27*, 261-275.

Johnson, J. H., & Sarason, I. G. (1978). Life stress, depression and anxiety: Internal-external control as a moderator variable. *Journal of Psychosomatic Research, 22*, 205-208.

Johnson, M. P. (1973). Commitment: A conceptual structure and empirical application. *The Sociological Quarterly, 14*, 395-406.

Johnson, N. F. (1975). On the function of letters in word identification: Some data and a preliminary model *Journal of Verbal Learning and Verbal Behavior, 14*, 17-19.

Jones, E. E., & Gerard, H. B. (1967). *Foundations of social psychology*. New York: Wiley.

Jones, E. E., & Nisbett, R. E. (1971). *The actor and the observer: Divergent perception of the causes of behavior*. New York: General Learning Press.

Jones, E. E., & Nisbett, R. E. (1972). The actor and the observer: Divergent perceptions of the causes of behavior. In E. E. Jones, D. E. Kanouse, H. H. Kelley, R. E. Nisbett, S. Valins, & B. Weiner (Eds.), *Attribution: Perceiving the causes of behavior* (pp. 79-94). Morristown, NJ: General Learning Press.

Jones, E. E., & Pittman, T. S. (1982). Toward a general theory of strategic self-presentation. In J. Suls (Ed.), *Psychological perspectives on the self* (Vol. 1, pp. 231-262). Hillsdale, NJ: Erlbaum.

Julian, J. W., Regula, C. R., & Hollander, E. P. (1968). Effects of prior agreement by others on task confidence and conformity. *Journal of Personality and Social Psychology, 9*, 171-178.

Kahneman, D., & Tversky, A. (1979). Prospect theory: An analysis of decisions under risk. *Econometrica, 47*, 263-291.

Kanfer, F., & Seidner, M. (1973). Self-control: Factors enhancing tolerance of noxious stimulation. *Journal of Personality and Social Psychology, 25*, 989-1016.

Kanner, A. D., Coyne, J. C., Schaefer, C., & Lazarus, R. S. (1981). Comparison of two modes of stress measurement: Daily hassles and uplifts versus major life events. *Journal of Behavioral Medicine, 4*, 1-39.

Kant, I. (1964). *The Critique of Pure Reason*. Translated by J.M.D. Meiklejohn. New York: Dutton.

Kanter, R. M. (1972). *Commitment and community: Communes and utopias in social perspective*. Cambridge, MA: Harvard University Press.

Kanungo, R. N. (1979). The concepts of alienation and involvement revisited. *Psychological Bulletin, 86*, 119–138.

Kaplan, K. J., & Kaplan, M. (1979). Covenant versus contract as two modes of relationship orientation: On reconciling possibility and necessity. *Journal of Psychology and Judaism, 4*(2), 100–116.

Katz, P., & Zigler, E. (1967). Self-image disparity: A developmental approach. *Journal of Personality and Social Psychology, 5*, 186–195.

Kaufman, I. E. (1969). Effects of separation from mother on the emotional behavior of infant monkeys. *Annals of the New York Academy of Sciences, 159*, 681–695.

Keegan, J. (1976). *The face of battle*. New York: Viking.

Keith, P. M., & Schafer, R. B. (1982). A comparison of depression among employed single-parent and married women. *The Journal of Psychology, 110*, 239–247.

Keller, M. B., Lavori, P. W., Lewis, C. E., & Klerman, G. L. (1983). Predictors of relapse in major depressive disorder. *Journal of the American Medical Association, 250*, 3299–3304.

Keller, M. B., & Shapiro, R. W. (1981). Major depressive disorder: Initial results from a one-year prospective naturalistic follow-up study. *The Journal of Nervous and Mental Disease, 169*, 761–768.

Kelley, H. H. (1950). The warm-cold variable in first impressions of persons. *Journal of Personality, 18*, 431–439.

Kelley, H. H. (1967). Attribution theory in social psychology. In D. Levine (Ed.), *Nebraska symposium on motivation* (Vol. 15, pp. 192–238). Lincoln: University of Nebraska Press.

Kelley, H. H. (1971). *Attribution in social interaction*. Morristown, NJ: General Learning Press.

Kelly, J. (1982). Divorce: The adult perspective. In B. Wolman & G. Stricker (Eds.), *Handbook of developmental psychology*. Englewood Cliffs, NJ: Prentice-Hall.

Kelman, H. (1958). Compliance, identification and internalization: Three processes of attitude change. *Journal of Conflict Resolution, 2*, 51–60.

Kendall, P. C., & Wilcox, L. E. (1979). Self-control in children: Development of a rating scale. *Journal of Consulting and Clinical Psychology, 47*, 1020–1029.

Kenniston, K. (1960). *The uncommitted: Alienated youth in American society*. New York: Delta.

Kenniston, K. (1968). *Young radicals: Notes on uncommitted youth*. New York: Harcourt, Brace & World.

Kerckhoff, A. C., & Davis, K. E. (1962). Value consensus and need complementarity in mate selection. *American Sociological Review, 27*, 295–303.

Kessler, R. C., & Essex, M. (1982). Marital status and depression: The importance of coping resources. *Social Forces, 61*, 484–505.

Kierkegaard, S. (1959). *Either/Or*. Translated by D. F. Swenson and L. M. Swenson. Garden City, NY: Doubleday.

Kiesler, C. A. (1971). *The psychology of commitment: Experiments linking behavior to belief*. New York: Academic Press.

Kim, J. S., & Schuler, R. S. (1978). *The nature of the task as a moderator of the relationship between extrinsic feedback and employee responses*. Paper presented at the 21st Annual Conference of the Midwest Division of the Academy of Management, Indiana University, Indianapolis, IN.

Klein, M., & Riviere, J. (1953). *Love, hate and reparation*. London: Hogarth Press.

Klinger, E. (1975). Consequences of commitment to a disengagement from incentives. *Psychological Review, 82*, 1–25.

Klinger, E. (1977). *Meaning and void: Inner experience and the incentives in people's lives*. Minneapolis: University of Minnesota Press.

Knight, K. E. (1963). Effect of effort on behavioral rigidity in a Luchins Water Jar Task. *Journal of Personality and Social Psychology, 3*, 458–467.

Kobasa, S. C. (1979a). Stressful life events, personality and health: An inquiry into hardiness. *Journal of Personality and Social Psychology, 37*, 1–11.

Kobasa, S. C. (1979b). Personality and resistance to illness. *American Journal of Community Psychology, 7*, 413-423.

Kobasa, S. C. (1982a). Commitment and coping in stress resistance among lawyers. *Journal of Personality and Social Psychology, 42*, 707-717.

Kobasa, S. C. (1982b). The hardy personality: Toward a social psychology of stress and health. In J. Suls & G. Sanders (Eds.), *Social psychology of health and illness*. Hillsdale, NJ: Erlbaum.

Kobasa, S. C. (1984, September). How much stress can you survive? The answer depends on your personality. *American Health Magazine*, 64-77.

Kobasa, S. C., Maddi, S. R., & Courington, S. (1981). Personality and constitution as mediators in the stress-illness relationship. *Journal of Health and Social Behavior, 22*, 368-378.

Kobasa, S. C., Maddi, S. R., & Kahn, S. (1982). Hardiness and health: A prospective study. *Journal of Personality and Social Psychology, 42*, 168-177.

Kobasa, S. C., Maddi, S. R., & Pucetti, M. C. (1982). Personality and exercise as buffers in the stress-illness relationship. *Journal of Behavioral Medicine, 42*, 168-177.

Kobasa, S. C., & Pucetti, M. C. (1983). Personality and social resources in stress resistance. *Journal of Personality and Social Psychology, 45*, 839-850.

Koestler, A. (1968). *The sleepwalkers*. New York: Macmillan.

Kohlberg, L. (1969). Stage and sequence: The cognitive-developmental approach to socialization. In D. A. Goslin (Ed.), *Handbook of Socialization Theory and Research* (pp. 347-480). Chicago: Rand McNally.

Kohlberg, L. (1971). Stages of moral development as a basis for moral education. In C. M. Beck, B. S. Crittenden, & E. V. Sullivan (Eds.), *Moral education: Interdisciplinary approaches*. Toronto: University of Toronto Press.

Kohlberg, L. (1973). Continuities in childhood and adult moral development revisited. In P. Baltes & K. W. Schaie (Eds.), *Life-span developmental psychology: Personality and socialization* (pp. 180-204). New York: Academic Press.

Korman, H. L. (1966). Job choice and occupational satisfaction. *Journal of Organizations, 2*, 94-107.

Korman, H. L. (1967). Self-esteem and career choices: A retrospective study. *Psychological Reports, 36*, 212-215.

Kornfeld, D. (1971). The hospital environment: Its impact on the patient. *Advances in Psychosomatic Medicine, 8*, 252-270.

Kosslyn, S. M. (1976). Using imagery to retrieve semantic information: A developmental study. *Child Development, 47*, 434-444.

Kosten, T. R., Rounsaville, B. J., & Kleber, H. D. (1983). Relationship of depression to psychosocial stressors in heroin addicts. *The Journal of Nervous and Mental Disease, 171*, 97-104.

Krasovec, K., Stolley, M., & Brickman, P. (1981). Commitment to fraternities and sororities. Unpublished manuscript, Northwestern University, Evanston, IL.

Kruglanski, A. W. (1975). The endogenous-exogenous partition in attribution theory. *Psychology Review, 82*, 387-406.

Kruglanski, A. W., & Cohen, M. (1973). Attributed freedom and personal causation. *Journal of Personality and Social Psychology, 26*, 245-250.

Kuhn, T. S. (1962). *The structure of scientific revolutions*. Chicago: University of Chicago Press.

Kushner, H. (1981). *When bad things happen to good people*. New York: Schocken Books.

Kyonis, S., Castell, P. J., Gergen, M., & Mauch, D. (1976). Metamorphic effects of power. *Journal of Applied Psychology, 61*, 127-135.

Landers, A. (1977, November 8). Woman's husband hasn't touched her in 10 years. *Chicago Daily News*, p. 26.

Lane, D. M. (1980). Incidental learning and the development of selective attention. *Psychological Review, 87*, 316-319.

Langer, E. J. (1978). Rethinking the role of thought in social interaction. In J. H. Harvey, W. I. Ickes, & R. F. Kidd (Eds.), *New directions in attribution research* (Vol. 2). Hillsdale, NJ: Erlbaum.

Langer, E. J. (1979). The illusion of incompetence. In L. Perlmutter & R. Monty (Eds.), *Choice and perceived control* (p. 40). Potomac, MD: Erlbaum.

Langer, E. J. (1985). Playing the middle against both ends: The usefulness of adult cognitive activity as a model for cognitive activity in childhood and old age. In S. R. Yussen (Ed.), *The growth of reflection in children*. Orlando, FL: Academic Press.

Langer, E. J., Janis, I., & Wolfer, J. (1975). Reduction of psychological stress in surgery patients. *Journal of Experimental Social Psychology, 11*, 155–165.

Langer, E. J., & Rodin, J. (1976). The effects of choice and enhanced personal responsibility for the aged: A field experiment in an institutional setting. *Journal of Personality and Social Psychology, 34*, 191–198.

Langer, E. J., Rodin, J., Beck, P., Weinman, C., & Spitzer, L. (1979). Environmental determinants of memory improvement in late adulthood. *Journal of Personality and Social Psychology, 37*, 2003-2013.

Lao, R. C. (1974). The developmental trend of the locus of control. In *Proceedings of the Division of Personality and Social Psychology*, 348–350.

Larwood, L., & Whittaker, W. (1977). Managerial myopia: Self-serving biases in organizational planning. *Journal of Applied Psychology, 62*(2), 194–198.

Latane, B., & Darley, J. (1969). Bystander "apathy." *American Scientist, 57*, 244-268.

Lawler, E. E., Kuleck, W. J., Rhode, J. G., & Sorensen, J. E. (1975). Job choice and post-decision dissonance. *Organizational Behavior and Human Performance, 13*, 133-145.

Lawrence, D. H., & Festinger, L. (1962). *Deterrents and reinforcement*. Stanford, CA: Stanford University Press.

Layne, C. (1980). Motivational deficit in depression: People's expectations X outcomes' impacts. *Journal of Clinical Psychology, 36*, 647-652.

Layne, C., Merry, J., Christian, J., & Ginn, P. (1982). Motivational deficit in depression. *Cognitive Therapy and Research, 6*, 259-274.

Lazarus, R. S. (1981, July). Little hassles can be dangerous to your health. *Psychology Today*, 58-62.

Lazarus, R. S. (1983). The costs and benefits of denial. In S. Breznitz (Ed.), *Denial of stress*. New York: International Universities Press.

Lararus, R. S., & Folkman, S. (In press). Coping and adaptation, In W. D. Gentry (Ed.), *The handbook of behavioral medicine*. New York: Guilford.

Lazarus, R. S., Kanner, A., & Folkman, S. (1980). Emotions: A cognitive-phenomenological analysis. In R. Plutchik & H. Kellerman (Eds.), *Theories of emotion* (pp. 189-214). New York: Academic Press.

Lazarus, R. S., & Launier, R. (1978). Stress related transactions between person and environment. In L. A. Pervin & M. Lewis (Eds.), *Perspectives in interactional psychology* (pp. 287-322). New York: Plenum.

Leahy, R. L. (1976). Developmental trends in qualified inferences and descriptions of self and others. *Developmental Psychology, 12*, 546-547.

Leavy, R. L. (1983). Social support and psychological disorder: A review. *Journal of Community Psychology, 11*, 3-21.

Lefcourt, H. M. (1966). Repression-sensitization: A measure of the evaluation of emotional expression. *Journal of Counsulting Psychology, 30*, 444-449.

Lefcourt, H. M., Martin, R. A., & Saleh, W. E. (1984). Locus of control and social support: Interactive moderators of stress. *Journal of Personality and Social Psychology, 47*, 378-389.

Lefcourt, H. M., Miller, R. S., Ware, E. E., & Sherk, D. (1981). Locus of control as a modifier of the relationship between stressors and moods. *Journal of Personality and Social Psychology, 41*, 357-369.

Leff, M. J., Roatch, J. F., & Bunney, W. E. (1970). Environmental factors preceding the onset of severe depression. *American Journal of Psychiatry, 33*, 293-311.

Lemert, E. M. (1962). Paranoia and the dynamics of exclusion. *Sociometry, 25*, 2-20.

Leon, G. R., Gillum, B., Gillum, R., & Gouze, M. (1979). Personality stability and change over a thirty-year period—middle age to old age. *Journal of Consulting and Clinical Psychology, 47*, 517-524.

Lepper, M. R. (1973). Dissonance, self-perception, and honesty in children. *Journal of Personality and Social Psychology, 25*, 65-74.

Lepper, M. R., & Dafoe, J. (1979). Incentives, constraints and motivation in the classroom: An attributional analysis. In I. H. Frieze, D. Bar Tal, & J. S. Carroll (Eds.), *Attribution theory: Applications to social problems*. San Francisco: Jossey-Bass.

Lepper, M. R., & Greene, D. (1975). Changing play into work: Effects of adult surveillance and extrinsic rewards on children's intrinsic motivation. *Journal of Personality and Social Psychology, 31,* 479-486.

Lepper, M. R., & Greene, D. (1978). Overjustification research and beyond: Toward a means-ends analysis of intrinsic and extrinsic motivation. In M. R. Lepper & D. Greene (Eds.), *The hidden costs of reward.* Hillsdale, NJ: Erlbaum.

Lepper, M. R., Greene, D., & Nisbett, R. E. (1973). Undermining children's interest with extrinsic rewards: A test of the overjustification hypothesis. *Journal of Personality and Social Psychology, 28,* 129-137.

Lerner, M. J. (1980). *The belief in a just world: A fundamental delusion.* New York: Plenum.

Lerner, M. J., & Matthews, G. (1967). Reactions to suffering of others under conditions of indirect responsibility. *Journal of Personality and Social Psychology, 5,* 319-325.

Lerner, M. J., Miller, S. J., & Holmes, J. G. (1976). Deserving versus justice: A contemporary dilemma. In L. Berkowitz (Ed.), *Advances in experimental social psychology.* New York: Academic Press.

Lerner, M. J., & Simmons, C. H. (1966). Observer's reactions to the "innocent victim:" Compassion or rejection. *Journal of Personality and Social Psychology, 4,* 203-210.

LeShan, L. E. (1964). The world of the patient in severe pain of long duration. *Journal of Chronic Disease, 17,* 119-126.

Lester, D., & Lester, G. (1971). *Suicide: The gamble with death.* Englewood Cliffs, NJ: Prentice-Hall.

Leventhal, H. (1970). Findings and theory in the study of fear communications. In L. Berkowitz (Ed.), *Advances in experimental social psychology* (Vol. 5). New York: Academic Press.

Leventhal, H. (1974). Emotions: A basic problem for social psychology, In C. Nemeth (Ed.), *Social psychology: Classic and contemporary integrations.* (pp. 1-51). Chicago: Rand McNally.

Leventhal, H., & Cleary, P. D. (1980). The smoking problem: A review of the research and theory in behavioral risk modification. *Psychology Bulletin, 88,* 370-405.

Leventhal, H., & Watts, J. C. (1966). Sources of resistance to fear-arousing communications on smoking and lung cancer. *Journal of Personality, 34,* 155-175.

Levinger, G. (1977). Re-viewing the close relationship. In G. Levinger & H. L. Raush (Eds.), *Close relationships* (pp. 137-161). Amherst, MA: University of Massachusetts Press.

Levinson, D. J. (1977, January). Growing up with the dream. *Psychology Today,* pp. 20-31.

Levinson, D. J. (1978). The mid-life transition: A period in adult psychosocial development. *Psychiatry, 40,* 99-112.

Lewin, K. (1951). *Field theory in social science.* New York: Harper & Row.

Lewinsohn, P. M., & Graf, M. (1973). Pleasant activities and depression. *Journal of Consulting and Clinical Psychology, 41,* 261-268.

Lewinsohn, P. M., & Libet, J. (1972). Pleasant events, activities schedules and depression. *Journal of Abnormal Psychology, 79,* 292-295.

Lewinsohn, P. M., Mischel, W., Chaplin, W., & Barton, R. (1980). Social competence and depression: The role of illusory self-perceptions. *Journal of Abnormal Psychology, 89,* 203-212.

Lewis, C. S. (1956). *The screwtape letters.* New York: Macmillan.

Lewis, M. (1965). Psychological effect of effort. *Psychological Bulletin, 64,* 183-190.

Liebow, E. (1967). *Tally's corner.* New York: Grove Press.

Lifschitz, M. (1973). Internal-external locus-of-control dimension as a function of age and the socialization milieu. *Child Development, 44* 538-546.

Lifton, R. J. (1968). *Death in life: Survivors of Hiroshima.* New York: Random House.

Lifton, R. J., & Olson, E. (1976). Death imprint in Buffalo Creek. In H. J. Parad, H. L. P. Resnick, & L. G. Parad (Eds.), *Emergency and disaster management.* Bowie, MD: Charles Press.

Linder, D. E., Cooper, J., & Jones, E. E. (1967). Decision freedom as a determinant of the role of incentive magnitude in attitude change. *Journal of Personality and Social Psychology, 6,* 245-254.

Linehan, M. M., Goodstein, J. L., Nielsen, S. L., & Chiles, J. A. (1983). Reasons for staying alive when you are thinking of killing yourself: The reasons for living inventory. *Journal of Consulting and Clinical Psychology, 51*(2), 276-286.

Lingle, J. H., & Ostrom, T. M. (1979). Retrieval selectivity in memory based impression judgements. *Journal of Personality and Social Psychology, 37*, 180-194.

Linsenmeier, J. A. W., & Brickman, P. (1978). Advantages of difficult tasks. *Journal of Personality, 46*, 96-112.

Lipowski, Z. J. (1970). The conflict of Buridan's Ass, or some dilemmas of affluence: The theory of attractive stimulus overload. *The American Journal of Psychiatry, 127*, 273-279.

Lipowski, Z. J. (1970-1971). Physical illness, the individual and the coping process. *International Journal of Psychiatry in Medicine, 1*, 91-102.

Litman, T. (1962). The influence of self-conception and life orientation factors in the rehabilitation of the orthopedically disabled. *Journal of Health and Human Behavior, 3*, 249-256.

Livesley, W. J., & Bromley, D. B. (1973). *Person perception in childhood and adolescence.* New York: Wiley.

Lobsenz, M. (1981, October 4). The risks of love. *Family Weekly*, p. 25.

Lobsenz, N. M. (1975, March). Taming the green-eyed monster. *Redbook Magazine*, pp. 74, 190.

Locke, E. (1968). Toward a theory of task motivation and incentives. *Organizational Behavior and Human Performance, 3*, 157-189.

Lofland, J. (1969). *Deviance and identity.* Englewood Cliffs, NJ: Prentice-Hall.

Lofland, J., & Stark, R. (1965). Becoming a world-saver: A theory of conversion to a deviant perspective. *American Sociological Review, 30*, 862-874.

Lopata, H. Z. (1973). *Widowhood in an American city.* Cambridge, MA: Schenkman.

Lopata, H. Z. (1975). On widowhood: Grief work and identity reconstruction. *Journal of Geriatric Psychiatry, 8*, 41-55.

Lorber, J. (1975). Good patients and problem patients: Conformity and deviance in a general hospital. *Journal of Health and Social Behavior, 16*, 213-225.

Lowenthal, M., & Haven, C. (1968). Interaction and adaptation: Intimacy as a critical variable. *American Sociological Review, 33*, 20-31.

Luchins, A. S. (1942). Mechanization in problem solving: The effect of Einstellung. *Psychological Monographs, 54*(6), 1-95. Whole No. 248.

Lynch, L. J. (1979). *The broken heart: The medical consequences of loneliness.* New York: Basic Books.

Maccoby, M. (1976). *The gamesman.* New York: Simon & Schuster.

Mackworth, N. H., & Bruner, J. S. (1970). How adults and children search and recognize pictures. *Human Development, 13*(3), 149-177.

Maddi, S. (1970). The search for meaning. In W. Arnold & M. Page (Eds.), *Nebraska symposium on motivation* (pp. 137-186). Lincoln, NB: University of Nebraska Press.

Maddi, S. R., Kobasa, S. C., & Hoover, M. (1979). An alienation test. *Journal of Humanistic Psychology, 19*, 73-76.

Mahoney, M. J., & Mahoney, K. (1976). *Permanent weight control.* New York: W. W. Norton.

Malewski, A. (1962). The influence of positive and negative self-evaluation on post-decisional dissonance. *Polish Sociological Bulletin, 3-4*, 39-49.

Malinowski, B. (1922). *Argonauts of the western Pacific.* New York: E. P. Dutton.

Mann, L., & Taylor, V. A. (1970). The effects of commitment and choice difficulty of predecision processes. *Journal of Social Psychology, 82*, 221-230.

March, J. G., & Simon, H. A. (1958). *Organizations.* New York: Wiley.

Marris, P. (1958). *Widows and their families.* London: Routledge & Kegan Paul.

Marshall, J. (1978). Changes in aged white male suicide: 1948-1972. *Journal of Gerontology, 33*, 763-768.

Marx, K. (1932). Economic and philosophical manuscripts. In *Marx-Engels Gesamtausgabe* (Vol. 3). Berlin: Marx-Engels Institute. (Original work published 1844).

Maslach, C. (1976, September). Burned out. *Human Behavior*, 16-22.

Maslach, C. (1978). The client role in staff burnout. *Journal of Social Issues, 34*(4), 111-124.

Masserman, J. H. (1943). *Behavior and neurosis. An experimental psychoanalytic approach to psychobiologic principles.* Chicago: University of Chicago Press.

Masserman, J. H. (1971). *A psychiatric odyssey.* New York: Science House.

Masters, W. H., & Johnson, V. E. (1966). *Human sexual response.* Boston; Little, Brown.

Masters, W. H., & Johnson, V. E. (1974). *The pleasure bond: A new look at sexuality and commitment.* Boston: Little, Brown.

Matthews, K. A., & Brunson, B. I. (1979). Allocation of attention and the type-A coronary-prone behavior pattern. *Journal of Personality and Social Psychology, 37*, 2081-2090.

Matza, D. (1964). *Delinquency and drift*. New York: Wiley.

Mauss, M. (1954). *The gift; Forms and functions of exchange in archaic societies*. Glencoe, IL: Free Press.

Mayerhoff, M. (1971). *On caring*. New York: Harper and Row.

McClelland, D. C. (1965). Toward a theory of motive acquisition. *American Psychologist, 20*, 321-333, 329.

McCord, J. (1978). A thirty-year follow-up study of treatment effects. *American Psychologist, 33*, 284-289.

McCrae, R. R. (1984). Situational determinant of coping responses: Loss, threat and challenge. *Journal of Personality and Social Psychology, 46*, 919-928.

McCready, W. C., & Greeley, A. M. (1976). *The ultimate values of the American population*. Beverly Hills, CA: Sage.

McCullers, C. (1951). *The ballad of the sad cafe: The novels and stories of Carson McCullers*. Boston: Houghton Mifflin.

McDonald, D. (1975). Food taboos. A primitive environmental protection agency. *Anthropos, 72*, 732-748.

McGraw, K. (1978). The detrimental effects of reward on performance. A literature review and a prediction model. In M. R. Lepper & D. Green (Eds.), *The hidden costs of reward*. Hillsdale, NJ: Erlbaum.

McGuire, W. J. (1966). The current status of cognitive consistency theories. In S. Feldman (Ed.), *Cognitive consistency* (pp. 2-46). New York: Academic Press.

McLemore, C. W., & Benjamin, L. S. (1979). Whatever happened to interpersonal diagnosis: A psychosocial alternative to DSM-III. *American Psychologist, 34*, 17-34.

Mead, M. (1931). Jealousy: Primitive and civilized. In S. D. Schmalhausen & V. F. Calverton (Eds.), *Woman's coming of age*. New York: Horace Liverwright.

Mechanic, D. (1962). *Students under stress*. New York: Free Press.

Megargee, M. (1972). *The California Psychological Inventory Handbook*. San Francisco: Jossey-Bass.

Meichenbaum, D. (1977). *Cognitive-behavior modification: An integrative approach*. New York: Plenum Press.

Merton, R. K. (1936). The unanticipated consequences of purposive social action. *American Sociological Review, 1*, 894-904.

Merton, R. K. (1949). *Social theory and social structure*. Glencoe, IL: The Free Press.

Milgram, S. (1963). Behavioral study of obedience. *Journal of Abnormal and Social Psychology, 67*, 371-378.

Milgram, S. (1965). Some conditions of obedience and disobedience to authority. *Human Relations, 18*, 56-76.

Milkman, H., & Sunderwirth, S. (1982). Addictive processes. *Journal of Psychoactive Drugs, 14*, 177-192.

Miller, D. T., & Porter, C. A. (1980). Effects of temporal perspecitve on the attribution process. *Journal of Personality and Social Psychology, 39*, 532-541.

Miller, D. T., & Porter, C. A. (1983). Self-blame in victims of violence. *Journal of Social Issues, 39*, 139-152.

Miller, E., & Lewis, P. (1977, September). Senility or depression? *Human Behavior*, 29.

Miller, N. E. (1948). Theory and experiment relating psychoanalytic displacement to stimulus response generalization. *Journal of Abnormal and Social Psychology, 43*, 155-178.

Miller, P. M., Ingham, J. G. & Davidson, S. (1976). Life events, symptoms and social support. *Journal of Psychosomatic Research, 20*, 515-522.

Miller, R. L., Brickman, P., & Bolen, D. (1975). Attribution versus persuasion as a means of modifying behavior. *Journal of Personality and Social Psychology, 31*, 430-441.

Miller, R. L., & Suls, J. (1977). Helping, self-attribution, and size on an initial request. *Journal of Social Psychology, 103*, 203-208.

Miller, S. M. (1980). Why having control reduces stress: If I can stop the roller coaster I don't want to get off. In J. Garber & M. E. P. Seligman (Eds.), *Human helplessness: Theory and applications* (pp. 71-95). New York: Academic Press.

Mills, J. (1958). Changes in moral attitudes following temptation. *Journal of Personality, 26*, 517–531.

Mitchell, R. E. (1982). Social networks and psychiatric clients: The personal and environmental context. *American Journal of Community Psychology, 10*, 387–401.

Mitroff, I. I. (1976). Passionate scientists. *Society*, 51–57.

Moberg, D. O., & Bruseck, P. M. (1978). Spiritual well-being: A neglected subject in quality of life research. *Social Indicators Research, 5*, 303–323.

Monroe, S. M. (1982). Life events assessment: Current practices, emerging trends. *Clinical Psychology Review, 2*, 435–453.

Monroe, S. M., Bellack, A. S., Hersen, M., & Himmelhock, J. M. (1983). Life events, symptom course, and treatment outcome in unipolar depressed women. *Journal of Consulting and Clinical Psychology, 51*, 604–615.

Monroe, S. M., Imhoff, D. F., Wise, B. D., & Harris, J. E. (1983). Prediction of psychological symptoms under high-risk psychosocial circumstances: Life events, social support, and symptoms specificity. *Journal of Abnormal Psychology, 92*, 338–350.

Monson, T. C., & Snyder, M. (1977). Actors, observers and the attribution process: Toward a reconceptualization. *Journal of Experimental Social Psychology, 13*, 89–111.

Montemayor, R., & Eisen, M. (1977). The development of self-conceptions from childhood to adolescence. *Developmental Psychology, 43*, 314–319.

Moore, B. S., Sheriod, D. R., Liu, T. J., & Underwood, B. (1979). The dispositional shift in attribution over time. *Journal of Experimental Social Psychology, 15*, 553–569.

Moreno, F. J. (1977). *Between faith and reason.* New York: New York University Press.

Morrison, J. R. (1982). Suicide in a psychiatric practice population. *Journal of Clinical Psychiatry, 43*, 348–352.

Mosher, D. L. (1965). Interaction of fear and guilt in inhibiting unacceptable behavior. *Journal of Consulting Psychology, 29*, 161–167.

Mosher, D. L. (1966). The development and multitrait-multimethod analysis of three measures of three aspects of guilt. *Journal of Consulting Psychology, 30*, 25–29.

Mosher, D. L. (1973). Sex differences, sex experience, sex guilt, and explicitly sexual films. *Journal of Social Issues, 29*, 95–111.

Mosher, D. L., & Cross, H. J. (1971). Sex guilt and premarital sexual experiences of college students. *Journal of Consulting and Clinical Psychology, 36*, 27–32.

Moskos, C. C., Jr. (1969). Why men fight. *Transaction, 7*, 13–23.

Moss, G. E. (1973). *Illness, immunity and social interaction.* New York: Wiley.

Mulder, M., & Stemerding, A. (1963). Threat, attraction to group, and need for strong leadership: A laboratory experiment in a natural setting, *Human Relations, 16*, 317–334.

Mussen, P. H., Conger, J. J., & Kagan, J. (1974). *Child development and personality* (4th ed.). New York: Harper & Row.

Myers, D. G. (1983). *Social psychology.* New York: McGraw-Hill.

Myers, D. G., & Lamm, H. (1976). The group polarization phenomenon. *Psychological Bulletin, 83*, 602–627.

National Center for Health Statistics. (1970). *Mortality from selected causes by marital status* (Series 20, Nos. 8A & 8B). Washington, D.C.: U.S. Government Printing Office.

Natterson, J. M., & Knudson, A. G. (1960). Observations concerning fear of death in fatally ill children and their mothers. *Psychosomatic Medicine, 22*, 456–465.

Neisser, U. (1963). The imitation of man by machine. *Science, 139*, 193–197.

Neisser, U. (1967). *Cognitive psychology.* Englewood Cliffs, NJ: Prentice-Hall.

Neisser, U. (1976). *Cognition and reality.* San Francisco: Freeman.

Neugarten, B. (1972). Personality and the aging process. *Gerontologist, 12*, 9–15.

Neuringer, A. L. (1969). Animals respond for food in the presence of free food. *Science, 166*, 399–401.

Neuringer, C. (1979). Relationship between life and death among individuals of varying levels of suicidality. *Journal of Consulting and Clinical Psychology, 47*, 407–408.

Newell, A., Shaw, J. C., & Simon, H. A. (1958). Elements of a theory of problem solving. *Psychological Review, 65*, 151–166.

Newman, B. M. (1976). The development of social interaction from infancy through adolescence. *Small group behavior, 7*(1), 19–32.

Newman, H. M., & Langer, E. J. (1981). Post-divorce adaptation and the attribution of responsibility. *Sex Roles, 7*, 223–231.

Newman, M., & Berkowitz, B. (1971). *How to be your own best friend: A conversation with two psychoanalysts.* New York: Ballantine Books.

Nietzel, M., & Barnett, L. (1979). Marital satisfaction and issues of daily life. *Journal of Consulting and Clinical Psychology, 47*, 612–626.

Nietzsche, F. (1973). *Beyond good and evil.* Baltimore: Penguin Books. (Originally published 1886.)

Nisbett, R. E., & Wilson, T. D. (1977). Telling more than we can know: Verbal reports on mental processes. *Psychological Review, 84*, 231–259.

Nowicki, S., Jr., & Duke, M. P. (1974). A preschool and primary internal-external control scale. *Developmental Psychology, 10*, 874–880.

Nuckills, K., Cassel, J., & Kaplan, B. (1975). Psychosocial assets, life crisis and the prognosis of pregnancy. *American Journal of Epidemiology, 95*, 431–441.

Okun, M. A., Stock, W. A., Haring, M. J., & Witter, R. A. (1984). Health and subjective well-being: A metaanalysis. *International Journal of Aging and Human Development, 19*, 111–132.

Olson, J. M., & Zanna, M. P. (1979). A new look at selective exposure. *Journal of Experimental Social Psychology, 15*, 1–15.

Olson, M. (1971). *The logic of collective action: Public goods and the theory of groups.* Cambridge, MA: Harvard University Press.

O'Reilly, C. A., & Roberts, K. H. (1975). Individual differences in personality, position in the organization, and job satisfaction. *Organizational Behavior and Human Performance, 14*, 144–150.

Organ, D., & Green, C. (1974). The perceived purposefulness of job behavior: Antecedents and consequences. *Academy of Management Journal, 17*, 69–78.

Osherow, N. (1981). Making sense of the nonsensical: An analysis of Jonestown. In E. Aronson (Ed.), *Readings about the social animal* (3rd ed.). San Francisco: W. H. Freeman

Paige, J. M. (1975). *Agrarian revolution: Social movements and export agriculture in the underdeveloped world.* New York: Free Press.

Pallis, D. J., Barraclough, B. M., Levey, A. B., Jenkins, J. S., & Sainsbury, P. (1982). Estimating suicide risks among attempted suicides: The development of new clinical scales. *British Journal of Psychiatry, 141*, 37–44.

Paloutzian, R. F. (1981). Purpose in life and value changes following conversion. *Journal of Personality and Social Psychology, 41*, 1153–1160.

Parkes, C. M. (1970a). "Seeking" and "finding" a lost object. *Social Science and Medicine, 4*, 187–201.

Parkes, C. M. (1970b). The first year of bereavement: A longitudinal study of the reactions of London widows to the death of their husbands. *Psychiatry, 38*, 444–467.

Parkes, C. M. (1972). *Bereavement.* New York: International Universities Press.

Pastore, N. (1952). The role of arbitrariness in the frustration-aggression hypothesis. *Journal of Abnormal and Social Psychology, 47*, 728–731.

Pavlov, I. P. (1927). *Conditioned reflexes.* (G. V. Anrep, Trans.). London: Oxford University Press.

Paykel, E. S. (1979). Causal relationships between clinical depression and life events. In J. E. Barrett, R. M. Rose, & G. L. Klerman (Eds.), *Stress and mental disorder.* New York: Raven Press.

Pearlin, L. I., Lieberman, M. A., Menaghan, E. G., & Mullan, J. T. (1981). The stress process. *Journal of Health and Social Behavior, 22*, 337–356.

Peele, S., & Brodsky, A. (1975). *Love and addiction.* New York: Taplinger.

Penk, W. (1969). Age changes and correlates of internal-external locus of control scale. *Psychological Reports, 25*, 856.

Pepitone, A., McCauley, C., & Hammond, P. (1967). Change in attractiveness of forbidden toys as a function of severity of threat. *Journal of Experimental Social Psychology, 3*, 221–229.

Peplau, L. A., Rubin, Z., & Hill, C. T. (1977). Sexual intimacy in dating relationships. *Journal of Social Issues, 33*, 86–109.

Petrie, K., & Chamberlain, K. (1983). Hopelessness and social desirability as moderator variables in predicting suicidal behavior. *Journal of Consulting and Clinical Psychology, 51*, 485-487.

Pfeffer, J., & Lawler, J. (1980). Effects of job alternatives, extrinsic rewards, and behavioral commitment on attitude toward the organization: A field test of the insufficient justification paradigm. *Administrative Science Quarterly, 25*, 38-56.

Piaget, J. (1948). *The moral judgment of the child*. Glencoe, IL: Free Press.

Piaget, J. (1970). Piaget's theory. In P. H. Mussen (Ed.), *Carmichael's manual of child psychology* (Vol. 1, pp. 703-732). New York: Wiley.

Piaget, J. (1972). Intellectual evolution from adolescence to adulthood. *Human Development, 15*, 1-12.

Piliavin, I. M., Rodin, J., & Piliavin, J. A. (1969). Good samaritanism: An underground phenomenon. *Journal of Personality and Social Psychology, 13*, 289-299.

Pineo, P. C. (1961, February). Disenchantment in the later years of marriage. *Marriage and Family Living, 23*, 3-11.

Pirsig, R. M. (1974). *Zen and the art of motorcycle maintenance: An inquiry into values*. New York: Bantam Books.

Pittman, T. S. (1978). Attribution of arousal as a mediator in dissonance reduction. *Journal of Experimental Social Psychology, 11*, 55-63.

Platt, J. (1973). Social traps. *American Psychologist, 28*, 641-651.

Polanyi, K. (1944). *The great transformation*. New York: Farrar & Rinehart.

Polanyi, M. & Prosch, H. (1975). *Meaning*. Chicago: University of Chicago Press.

Polivy, J. (1978, August). *Anorexics as overly restrained eaters*. Paper presented at the 86th meeting of the American Psychological Association, Toronto, Canada.

Pollis, C. A. (1969). Dating involvement and patterns of idealization: A test of Waller's hypothesis. *Journal of Marriage and the Family, 31*, 765-771.

Poloma, M. M. (1972). *Toward a sociology of women*. Lexington, MA: Xerox College Publications.

Pruitt, D. G. (1961). Information requirements in making decisions. *American Journal of Psychology, 74*, 433-439.

Pruitt, D. G., & Lewis, S. (1975). Development of integrative solutions in bilateral negotiations. *Journal of Personality and Social Psychology, 31*, 612-613.

Queiroz, L. O. D. S., Motta, M. A., Madi, M. B. B. P., Sossait, D. L., & Boren, J. J. (1981). A functional analysis of obsessive-compulsive problems with related therapeutic procedures. *Behavior Research and Therapy, 19*, 377-388.

Rachlin, H. C., & Green, L. (1972). Commitment, choice, and self-control. *Journal of the Experimental Analysis of Behavior, 17*, 15-22.

Rado, S. (1928). The problem of melancholia. *International Journal of Psychoanalysis, 9*, 420-438.

Rapport, A. (1966). *Two-person game theory: The essential ideas*. Ann Arbor, MI: University of Michigan Press.

Raps, C. S., Peterson, C., Reinhard, K. E., Abramson, L. Y., & Seligman, M. E. P. (1982). Attributional style among depressed patients. *Journal of Abnormal Psychology, 91*, 102-108.

Raush, H. L., Barry, W. A., Hertel, R. K., & Swain, M. A. (1974). *Communication, conflict, and marriage*. San Francisco: Jossey-Bass.

Raven, B. H. (1974). The Nixon group. *Journal of Social Issues, 29*, 297-320.

Rawls, J. (1971). *A theory of justice*. Cambridge, MA: Harvard University Press.

Ray, M. B. (1961). The cycle of abstinence and relapse among heroin addicts. *Social Problems, 9*, 132-140.

Read, W. (1962). Upward communication in industrial hierarchies. *Human Relations, 15*, 3-16.

Regan, D. T., & Fazio, R. (1977). On the consistency between attitudes and behavior: Look to the method of attitude formation. *Journal of Experimental Social Psychology, 13*, 28-45.

Rehm, L. P. (1977). A self-control model of depression. *Behavior Therapy, 8*, 787-804.

Reich, J. W., & Zautra, A. J. (1981). Life events and personal causation: Some relationships with satisfaction and distress. *Journal of Personality and Social Psychology, 41*, 1002-1012.

Reich, J. W., & Zautra, A. J. (1983). Demands and desires in daily life: Some influences on well-being. *American Journal of Community Psychology, 11*, 41-58.

Reik, T. (1943). *Need to be loved*. New York: Farrar, Straus, & Co.

Reilly, S. (1975, February). Therapy in the golden ghetto. *Human Behavior*, 56–60.

Reiss, A. J. (1962). The social integration of peers and queers. *Social Problems, 9*, 102–120.

Reiss, S., & Sushinkey, L. W. (1975). Overjustification, competing responses, and the acquisition of intrinsic interest. *Journal of Personality and Social Psychology, 31*, 1116–1125.

Riegel, K. F. (1975). Adult life crises: A dialectic interpretation of development. In N. Datan & L. H. Ginsberg (Eds.), *Life-span developmental psychology: Normative life crises* (pp. 99–128). New York: Academic Press.

Ringer, R. J. (1978). *Looking out for number one*. New York: Fawcett.

Robbins, T., & Anthony, D. (1972). Getting straight with Meher Baba: A study of mysticism, drug rehabilitation, and post-adolescent role conflict. *Journal for the Scientific Study of Religion, 11*, 122–140.

Robins, L. (1974). A follow-up study of Vietnam veterans' drug use. *Journal of Drug Issues, 4*, 61–63.

Rodin, J., & Langer, E. J. (1977). Long-term effects of a control-relevant intervention with the institutional aged. *Journal of Personality and Social Psychology, 35*, 897–902.

Rogers, T. B., Kuiper, N. A., & Kirker, W. S. (1977). Self-reference and the encoding of personal information. *Journal of Personality and Social Psychology, 35*, 677–688.

Rokeach, M. (1968). *Beliefs, attitudes and values*. San Francisco: Jossey-Bass.

Rosenblatt, P. C. (1967). Marital residence and the functions of romantic love. *Ethnology, 6*, 471–480.

Rosenblatt, P. C., Fugita, S. S., & McDowell, K. V. (1969). Wealth transfer and restrictions on sexual relations during betrothal. *Ethnology, 8*, 319–328.

Rosenblatt, P. C., Titus, S. L., & Cunningham, M. R. (1979). Disrespect, tension, and togetherness-apartness in marriage. *Journal of Marrital and Family Therapy, 5*, 47–54.

Ross, L., & Lepper, M. R. (1980). The perseverance of beliefs: Empirical and normative considerations. In R. A. Shweder & D. Fiske (Eds.), *New directions for methodology of behavioral science*. San Francisco: Jossey-Bass.

Ross, L., Lepper, M. R., & Hubbard, M. (1975). Perseverance in self-perception and social perception: Biased attributional processes in the debriefing paradigm. *Journal of Personality and Social Psychology, 32*, 880–892.

Ross, L., Lepper, M. R., Strack, F., & Steinmatz, J. (1977). Social explanation and social expectation: Effects of real and hypothetical explanations on subjective likelihood. *Journal of Personality and Social Psychology, 35*, 817–829.

Ross, M. (1976). Self-perception of intrinsic motivation. In J. H. Harvey, W. J. Ickes, & R. F. Kidd (Eds.), *New directions in attribution research* (pp. 121–141). Hillsdale, NJ: Erlbaum.

Ross, M., & DiTecco, D. (1975). An attributional analysis of moral judgements. *Journal of Social Issues, 31*, 91–109.

Ross, M., McFarland, C., & Fletcher, G. J. O. (1981). The effect of attitude on the recall of personal histories. *Journal of Personality and Social Psychology, 40*(4), 627–634.

Roth, D. L., & Ingram, R. E. (1985). Factors in the self-deception questionnaire: Associations with depression. *Journal of Personality and Social Psychology, 48*, 243–251.

Rothbaum, F., Weisz, J. R., & Snyder, S. S. (1982). Changing the world and changing the self: A two-process model of perceived control. *Journal of Personality and Social Psychology, 42*, 5–37.

Rotter, J. B. (1966). Generalized expectancies for internal versus external control of reinforcement. *Psychological Monographs, 80*, 1–28.

Rounsaville, B. J., Weissman, M. M., Crits-Christoph, K., Wilber, C., Kleber, H. (1982). Diagnosis and symptoms of depression in opiate addicts: Course and relationship to treatment outcome. *Archives of General Psychiatry, 39*, 151–156.

Rounsaville, B. J., Weissman, M. M., Kleber, H. & Wilber, C. (1982). Heterogeneity of psychiatric diagnosis in treated opiate addicts. *Archives of General Psychiatry, 39*, 161–166.

Rubin, Z. (1973). *Liking and loving*. New York: Holt, Rinehart, & Winston.

Ruble, D. N., Feldman, N. S., Higgins, E. T., & Karlovac, M. (1979). Locus of causality and the use of information in the development of causal attributions. *Journal of Personality, 47*, 595–614.

Rusbult, C. E. (1980). Commitment and satisfaction in romantic associations: A test of the investment model. *Journal of Experimental Social Psychology, 16*, 172–186.

Russell, B. (1968). *The conquest of happiness* (1930). New York: Grosset and Dunlap.

Sackeim, H. A. (1983). Self-deception, self-esteem and depression: The adaptive value of lying to oneself. In J. Maslofg (Ed.), *Empirical studies of psychoanalytic theories.* Hillsdale, NJ: Erlbaum.

Safan Gerard, D. (1978). How to unblock. *Psychology Today, 11*, 78–86.

Safran, C. (1977). How religion affects health, happiness, sex and politics. *Redbook Magazine, 148*, 126–224.

Salancik, G. R. (1974). Interactive effects of performance experiences and extrinsic reward on intrinsic evaluations: Personal causation or personal accomplishment. Paper presented at the meeting of the Eastern Psychological Association, Philadelphia.

Sales, D. (1977). *Perspectives on law and psychology* (Vol. 1). New York: Plenum Press.

Sales, E. (1978). Women's adult development. In I. H. Frieze, J. E. Parsons, P. B. Johnson, D. N. Ruble, & G. L. Zellman (Eds.), *Women and sex roles: A social psychological perspective* (pp. 157–190). New York: W. W. Norton and Company.

Sales, S. M. (1972). Economic threat as a determinant of conversion rates in authoritarian and nonauthoritarian churches. *Journal of Personality and Social Psychology, 27*, 44–57.

Sales, S. M. (1973). Threat as a factor in authoritarianism: An analysis of archival data. *Journal of Personality and Social Psychology, 28*, 44–57.

Sales, S. M., & Friend, K. (1973). Success and failure as determinants of level of authoritarianism. *Behavioral Science, 18*, 163–172.

Sales, S. M., Guydosh, R. M., & Iacono, W. (1974). Relationship between strength of nervous system and need for stimulation. *Journal of Personality and Social Psychology, 29*, 16–22.

Salinger, J. D. (1964). *The catcher in the rye.* New York: Bantam Books.

Saltzstein, H. D., Supraner, A., & Sanvitale, D. (1976). Direct and indirect social influence on children's legal judgements. *Developmental Psychology, 12*, 561–562.

Samuelson, P. A. (1961). *Economics: An introductory analysis.* New York: McGraw-Hill.

Sandler, I. N., & Lakey, B. (1982). Locus of control as a stress moderator: The role of control perceptions and social support. *American Journal of Community Psychology, 10*, 65–80.

Saward, E., & Sorensen, A. (1978). The current emphasis on preventive medicine. *Science, 200*, 889–894.

Schachtel, E. G. (1959). *Metamorphosis: On the development of affect, perception, attention, and memory.* New York: Basic Books.

Schachter, S., & Singer, J. E. (1962). Cognitive, social and physiological determinants of emotional state. *Psychological Review, 69*, 379–399.

Schaffer, D. R. & Hendrick, C. (1971). Effects of actual effort and anticipated effort on task enhancement. *Journal of Experimental Social Psychology, 7*, 434–447.

Schaffer, H. (Ed.) (1971). *The origins of human social relations: Proceedings of a CASDS study group on "The origins of human social relations."* Held jointly with the Cila Foundations, London, July 1969. The fifth study group in a CASDS program on "The origins of human behavior." London: Academic Press.

Schaw, L. C., & Henry, W. E. (1956). A method for the comparison of groups: A study in thematic apperception. *General Psychology Monographs, 54*, 207–253.

Schelling, T. C. (1960). *The strategy of conflict.* Cambridge, MA: Harvard University Press.

Schmitt, R. (1979). Suffering and faith. *Journal of Religion and Health, 18*, 263–275.

Schneirla, T. C. (1959). An evolutionary and developmental theory of biphasic processes underlying approach and withdrawal. In *Nebraska symposium on motivation* (pp. 1–42). Lincoln, NE: University of Nebraska Press.

Schroeder, D. H., & Costa, P. T. (1984). Influence of life event stress on physical illness: Substantive effects or methodological flaws? *Journal of Personality and Social Psychology, 46*, 853–863.

Schulz, R. (1976). Effects of control and predictability on the physical and psychological well-being of the institutionalized aged. *Journal of Personality and Social Psychology, 33*, 563–573.

Schulz, R., & Hanusa, B. (1978). Long-term effects of control and predictability enhancing interventions: Findings and ethical issues. *Journal of Personality and Social Psychology, 36*, 1194–1201.

Schutz, W. (1959). *FIRO: A theory of interpersonal behavior.* New York: Holt, Rinehart & Winston.

Schwartz, S. H. (1977). Normative influences in altruism. In L. Berkowitz (Ed.), *Advances in experimental social psychology* (Vol. 10). New York: Academic Press.

Scott, R. A. (1969). *The making of blind men: A study of adult socialization*. New York: Russell Sage Foundation.

Seeman, M. (1959). On the meaning of alienation. *American Sociological Review, 24*, 783–791.

Seidenberg, R. (1967). Fidelity and jealousy: Sociocultural considerations. *Psychoanalytic Review, 54*, 583–608.

Seligman, C., Bush, M., & Kirsch, K. (1976). Relationship between compliance in the foot-in-the-door paradigm and size of first request. *Journal of Personality and Social Psychology, 33*, 517–520.

Seligman, C., Fazio, R. H., & Zanna, M. D. (1980). Effects of salience of extrinsic rewards on liking and loving. *Journal of Personality and Social Psychology, 38*, 453–460.

Seligman, M. E. P. (1975). *Helplessness*. San Francisco: Freeman.

Selman, R. L., & Selman, A. P. (1979). Children's ideas about friendship: A new theory. *Psychology Today, 13*, 70–80, 114.

Selye, H. (1956). *The stress of life*. New York: McGraw-Hill.

Shainess, N. (1961). A reevaluation of some aspects of femininity through a study of menstruation: A preliminary report. *Comprehensive Psychiatry, 2*, 20–26.

Shantz, C. U. (1975). The development of social cognition. In E. M. Hetherington (Ed.), *Review of child development research* (Vol. 5). Chicago: University of Chicago Press.

Shapira, Z., & Venezia, I. (1981). Optional stopping on a nonstationary series. *Organizational Behavior and Human Performance, 27*, 32–49.

Shapiro, R. W., & Keller, M. B. (1981). Initial six-month follow-up of patients with major depressive disorder: A preliminary report from the NIMH collaborative study of the psychobiology of depression. *Journal of Affective Disorders, 3*, 205–220.

Shepard, H. L., & Herrick, N. A. (1972). *Where have all the robots gone? Worker dissatisfaction in the seventies*. New York: Free Press.

Shepard, R. N. (1978). The mental image. *American Psychologist, 33*, 125–137.

Sheppard, R. Z. (1977, November 28). Living with the excitable gift. *Time*, 124–127.

Sherman, L. W. (1980). Three models of organizational corruption in agencies of social control. *Social Problems, 27*(4), 478–491.

Sherman, S. J., Skov, R. B., Herritz, E. F., & Stock, C. B. (1981). The effects of explaining hypothetical future events: From possibility to probability to actuality and beyond. *Journal of Experimental Social Psychology, 17*, 142–158.

Shestov, L. (1966). *Athens and Jerusalem*. New York: Simon and Schuster.

Shettel-Neuber, J., Bryson, J. B., & Young, L. E. (1978). Physical attractiveness of the "other person" and jealousy. *Personality and Social Psychology Bulletin, 4*, 612–615.

Shontz, F. C. (1975). *The psychological aspects of physical illness and disability*. New York: Macmillan.

Shorter, E. (1975). *The making of the modern family*. New York: Basic Books.

Shubik, M. (1971). The dollar auction game: A paradox in noncooperative behavior and escalation. *Journal of Conflict Resolution, 15*, 109–111.

Silver, R. L., Boon, C., & Stones, M. H. (1983). Searching for meaning in misfortune: Making sense of incest. *Journal of Social Issues, 39*, 81–101.

Silver, R.L., & Dunkel-Schetter, C. (1981). *Commitment in medical training*. Unpublished manuscript, Northwestern University, Evanston, IL.

Silver, R. L., & Wortman, C. B. (1980). Coping with undesirable life events. In J. Garber & M. E. P. Seligman (Eds.), *Human helplessness: Theory and applications* (pp. 279–340). New York: Academic Press.

Simonton, D. K. (1976). Biographical determinants of achieved eminence: A multivariate approach to the Cox data. *Journal of Personality and Social Psychology, 33*, 218–226.

Singer, I. B. (1962). *The slave*. New York: Avon.

Singer, M. T. (1979). Coming out of the cults. *Psychology Today, 12*, 72–82.

Singerman, P. (1978, June). Indy on his mind. *Sport Magazine, 66*, pp. 104–112.

Singlr, D. (1970). Preference for bar pressing to obtain reward over freeloading in rats and children. *Journal of Comparative and Physiological Psychology, 43*, 320–327.

Skinner, B. F. (1975). The shaping of phylogenic behavior. *Journal of the Experimental Analysis of Behavior, 24*, 117–120.

Skinner, B. F. (1977). Herrnstein and the evolution of behaviorism. *American Psychologist, 32*, 1006–1012.

Slamecka, N. J., & Graf, P. (1978). The generation effect: Delineation of a phenomena. *Journal of Experimental Psychology, 4*(6), 592–604.

Slater, J., & Depue, R. A. (1981). The contribution of environmental events and social support to serious suicide attempts in primary depressive disorder. *Journal of Abnormal Psychology, 90*. 275–285.

Slater, P. (1980). *Wealth addiction*. New York: E. P. Dutton.

Slater, P. E. (1970). *The pursuit of loneliness: American culture at the breaking point*. Boston: Beacon Press.

Slater, P. E. (1974). *Earthwalk*. Garden City, NY: Anchor Press.

Slater, P. E. (1977). *Footholds: Understanding the shifting family and sexual tensions in our culture*. New York: Dutton.

Sleed, J. (1980, August 17). Proper attitude's the key to a successful vacation. *The Ann Arbor News*, B-4.

Slovic, P., Fischhoff, B., & Lichtenstein, S. (1977). Behavioral decision theory. *Annual Review of Psychology, 28*, 1–39.

Smith, A. (1976). *An inquiry into the nature and causes of the wealth of nations*. Oxford: Clarendon Press. (Original work published 1776).

Smith, Carole R. (1976). Bereavement. *British Journal of Social Work, 5*, 75–92.

Smith, T. W., & Pittman, T. S. (1978). Reward, distraction and the overjustification effect. *Journal of Personality and Social Psychology, 36*, 565–572.

Snow, D. A., & Phillips, C. L. (1980). The Loflund-Stark conversion model: A critical reassessment. *Social Problems, 27*, 430–447.

Snyder, B. J. (1977). A note on the importance of cultural factors in suicide studies. *Suicide and Life-Threatening Behavior, 7*, 230–235.

Snyder, C. R. (1984, September). Excuses, excuses: They sometimes actually work—to relieve the burden of blame. *Psychology Today*, pp. 50–55.

Snyder, M., & Swann, W. (1978). Behavioral confirmation in social interaction: From social perception to social reality. *Journal of Experimental Social Psychology, 14*, 148–162.

Snyder, M., Tanke, E. D., & Berscheid, E. (1977). Social perception and interpersonal behavior: On the self-fulfilling nature of social stereotypes. *Journal of Personality and Social Psychology, 35*, 656–666.

Snyder, M., & Uranowitz, S. W. (1978). Reconstructing the past: Some cognitive consequences of person perception. *Journal of Personality and Social Psychology, 36*, 941–950.

Solomon, R. L. (1980). The opponent-process theory of acquired motivation: The costs of pleasure and the benefits of pain. *American Psychologist, 35*, 691–712.

Solomon, R. L., & Corbit, J. D. (1974). An opponent-process theory of motivation: I. Temporal dynamics of affect. *Psychological Review, 81*, 119–145.

Songer-Nochs, E. (1976). Situational factors affecting the weighting of predictor components in the Fishbein model. *Journal of Experimental Social Psychology, 12*, 56–69.

Sosa, R., Kennel, J., & Klaus, M. (1980). The effect of a supportive companion on perinatal problems, length of labor and mother-infant interactions. *New England Journal of Medicine, 305*, 597–600.

Spitz, R. (1945). Hospitalism: An inquiry into the genesis of psychiatric conditions in early childhood. In A. Freud et al. (Eds.), *The psychoanalytic study of the child* (Vol. 1, pp. 53–74). New York: International University Press.

Srull, T. K., & Wyer, R. S., Jr. (1980). Category accessibility and social perception: Some implications for the study of person memory and interpersonal judgements. *Journal of Personality and Social Psychology, 38*, 841–856.

Stack, S. (1980). Interstate migration and the rate of suicide. *International Journal of Social Psychiatry, 26*, 17–26.

Stack, S. (1981). The effect of immigration on suicide: A cross-national study. *Basic and Applied Social Psychology, 2*, 205–218.

Stack, S. (1982a). Suicide in Detroit: Changes and continuities. *Suicide and Life-Threatening Behavior, 12*, 67–83.

Stack, S. (1982b). Suicide: A decade review of the sociological literature. *Deviant Behavior, 4*, 41–66.

Stainback, B. (1978, May). Poket pressure– "alligator flood." *Sport*, pp. 62–68.

Starbuck, E. D. (1912). *The psychology of religion*. New York: Scribners.

Staub, E., Tursky, B., & Schwartz, G. E. (1971). Self-control and predictability: Their effects on reactions to adverse stimulation. *Journal of Personality and Social Psychology, 18*, 151–162.

Staw, B. M. (1976). Knee-deep in the big muddy: A study of escalating commitment to a chosen course of action. *Organizational Behavior and Human Performance, 16*, 27–44.

Steadman, M. (1970). How sexy illustrations affect brand recall. In S. Britt (Ed.), *Consumer behavior in theory and in action*. New York: Wiley.

Stebbins, R. A. (1980). "Amateur" and "hobbyist" as concepts for the study of leisure problems. *Social Problems, 27*, 413–429.

Stedry, A. C. (1960). *Budget control and cost behavior*. Englewood Cliffs, NJ: Prentice-Hall.

Steele, C. M., Southwick, L. L., & Critchlow, B. (1981). Dissonance and alcohol: Drinking your troubles away. *Journal of Personality and Social Psychology, 41*, 831–846.

Steer, R. A., McElroy, M. G., & Beck, A. T. (1982). Structure of depression in alcoholic men: A partial replication. *Psychological Reports, 50*, 723–728.

Steers, R. M. (1977). *Organizational effectiveness: A behavioral view*. Santa Monica, CA: Goodyear.

Steiner, I. D. (1970). Perceived freedom. In L. Berkowitz (Ed.), *Advances in experimental social psychology* (Vol. 5). New York: Academic Press.

Steinmetz, J. L., Lewinsohn, P. M., & Antonuccio, D. O. (1983). Prediction of individual outcome in a group intervention for depression. *Journal of Consulting and Clinical Psychology, 51*, 331–337.

Stephan, W., Berscheid, E., & Walster, E. (1979). Sexual arousal and heterosexual perception. *Journal of Personality and Social Psychology, 20*, 93–101.

Stephens, R. C., Blau, Z. S., Oser, G. T., & Miller, M. D. (1978). Aging, social support system and social policy. *Journal of Gerontological Social Work, 1*(1), 33–45.

Stewart, A. J., & Rubin, Z. (1974). The power motive in the dating couple. *Journal of Personality and Social Psychology, 34*, 305–309.

Stillman, D. (1980). The devastating effect of plant closures. In M. Green & R. Massie (Eds.), *The big business reader*. New York: Pilgrim Press.

Stinchcombe, A. L. (1983). *Economic sociology*. New York: Academic Press.

Storms, M. D., Denney, D. R., McCaul, K. D., & Lowerly, C. R. (1979). Attribution treatment of insomnia. In I. H. Frieze, D. Bar Tal, & J. S. Carroll (Eds.), *Attribution theory: Applications to social problems*. San Francisco: Jossey-Bass.

Stotland, E., & Blumenthal, A. L. (1964). The reduction of anxiety as a result of the expectation of making a choice. *Canadian Journal of Psychology, 18*, 139–145.

Sullivan, H. S. (1953). *The interpersonal theory of psychiatry*. New York: Norton.

Sweeney, P. D., Shaeffer, D. E. & Golin, S. (1982) Pleasant events, unpleasant events and depression. *Journal of Personality and Social Psychology, 43*, 136–144.

Swinth, R. L. (1967). The establishment of the trust relationship. *Journal of Conflict Resolution, 11*, 335–344.

Szurek, S. A., & Berlin, I. N. (Eds.) (1969). *The antisocial child: His family and his community*. Palo Alto, CA: Science and Behavior Books.

Tajfel, H. (1970). Experiments in intergroup discrimination. *Scientific American, 223*, 96–102.

Taylor, S. E. (1979). Hospital patient behavior: Helplessness, reactance or control. *Journal of Social Issues, 35*, 156–184.

Taylor, S. E. (1983). Adjustment to threatening events: A theory of cognitive adaptation. *American Psychologist, 38*, 1161–1173.

Taylor, S. E., Lichtman, R. R., & Wood, J. V. (1984). Attributions, beliefs about control, and adjustment to breast cancer. *Journal of Personality and Social Psychology, 46*, 489–502.

Taylor, S. E., Wood, J. V., & Lichtman, R. R. (1983). It could be worse: Selective evaluation as a response to victimization. *Journal of Social Issues, 39*, 19–40.

Teger, A. I. (1979). *Too much invested to quit: The psychology of the escalation of conflict*. New York: Pergamon Press.

Terkel, S. (1975). *Working*. New York: Avon.

Tesser, A. (1978, August). *When individual dispositions and social pressure conflict: A catastrophe.* Paper presented at the annual meeting of the American Psychological Association, Toronto.

Thibaut, J. W., & Kelley, H. H. (1959). *The social psychology of groups.* New York: Wiley.

Thibaut, J. W., & Ross, M. (1969). Commitment and experience as determinants of assimilation and contrast. *Journal of Personality and Social Psychology, 13,* 322–329.

Thoits, P. A. (1983). Multiple identities and psychological well-being: A reformulation and test of the social isolation hypothesis. *American Sociological Review, 48,* 174–187.

Thomas, L. (1979). *The medusa and the snail.* New York: The Viking Press.

Thompson, S. C. (1981). Will it hurt less if I can control it? A complex answer to a simple question. *Psychological Bulletin, 90,* 89–101.

Tillich, P. (1952). *The courage to be.* New Haven: Yale University Press.

Tolman, E. C. (1932). *Purposive behavior in animals and men.* New York: Appleton-Century.

Tolstoy, L. (1960). *The death of Ivan Ilych and other stories.* New York: New American Library of World Literature.

Tomkins, S. (1965). The psychology of commitment: The constructive role of violence and suffering for the individual and for his society. In M. Duberman (Ed.), *Antislavery vanguard* (pp. 270–298). Princeton, NJ: Princeton University Press.

Trainer, F. E. (1977). A critical analysis of Kohlberg's contributions to the study of moral thought *Journal for the Theory of Social Behavior, 7,* 41–63.

Trivers, R. L. (1971). The evolution of reciprocal altruism. *Quarterly Review of Biology, 46,* 35–57.

Trope, Y. (1978). Extrinsic rewards, congruence between dispositions and behaviors, and perceived freedom. *Journal of Personality and Social Psychology, 34*(3), 376–384.

Tuckman, B. W. (1965). Developmental sequence in small groups. *Psychological Bulletin, 63,* 384–399.

Turkington, C. (1985). What price friendship? The darker side of social networks. *American Psychological Association Monitor, 16,* 38–41.

Turkowitz, H., O'Leary, K. D., & Ironsmith, M. (1975). Generalization and maintenance of appropriate behaviors through self-control. *Journal of Consulting and Clinical Psychology, 43,* 577–583.

Tversky, A. (1972). Elimination by aspects: A theory of choice. *Psychological Review, 79,* 281–299.

Tversky, A., & Kahneman, D. (1974). Judgment under uncertainty: Heuristics and biases. *Science, 185,* 1124–1131.

Underwood, A. (1925). *Conversion: Christian and nonchristian.* London: Allen & Unwin.

Uranowitz, S. W, (1975). Helping and self-attributions: A field experiment. *Journal of Personality and Social Psychology, 31,* 852–854.

Vachon, M. L. S., Rogers, J., Lyall, W. A., Lancee, W. J., Sheldon, A. R., & Freeman, S. J. J. (1982). Predictors and correlates of adaptation to conjugal bereavement. *American Journal of Psychiatry, 139,* 998–1002.

Vaillant, G. E. (1977). *Adaptation to life.* Boston: Little, Brown.

Van Bergen, A. (1968). *Task interruption.* Amsterdam: North Holland Publishing.

VanPraag, H. M. (1982). A transatlantic view of the diagnosis of depressions according to the DSM-III: I. Controversies and misunderstandings in depression diagnosis. *Comprehensive Psychiatry, 23,* 315–338.

Velarde, A. (1976). From masseuse to prostitute in one quick trick. *Psychology Today, 10,* 27–28.

Veroff, J. (1969). Social comparison and the development of achievement motivation. In C.P. Smith (Ed.), *Achievement-related motives in children.* New York: Russell Sage.

Veroff, J. (1978). Social motivation. *American Behavioral Scientist, 21,* 709–730.

Viorst, J. (1979, October). Between us. *Redbook,* pp. 70–75.

Vonnegut, M. (1975). *The Eden express.* New York: Bantam Books.

Vroom, V. H. (1960). *Some personality determinants of the effects of participation.* Englewood Cliffs, NJ: Prentice-Hall.

Vroom, V. H., & Deci, E. L. (1971). The stability of post-decision dissonance: A follow-up study of the job attitudes of business school graduates. *Organizational Behavior and Human Performance, 6,* 36–49.

Wachowiak, D., & Bragg, H. (1980). Open marriage and marital adjustment. *Journal of Marriage and the Family, 42*(1), 57–62.

Waldorf, D. (1983). Natural recovery from opiate addiction: Some social psychological processes of untreated recovery. *Journal of Drug Issues, 2*, 237–280.

Wallach, M. (1970). Creativity. In D. H. Mussen (Ed.), *Carmichael's manual of child psychology* (Vol. 1, pp. 1211–1272). New York: Wiley.

Wallas, G. (1926). *The art of thought.* New York: Harcourt Brace.

Waller, W. W. (1937). The rating and dating complex. *American Sociological Review, 2*, 727–737.

Waller, W. W. (1938). *The family: A dynamic interpretation.* New York: Dryden Press.

Walster, B., & Aronson, E. (1967). Effect of expectancy of task duration on the experience of fatigue. *Journal of Experimental Social Psychology, 3*, 41–46.

Walster, E. (1964). The temporal sequence of post-decisional processes. In L. Festinger (Ed.). *Conflict, decision, and dissonance* (pp. 112–128). Stanford, CA: Stanford University Press.

Walster, E., & Prestholdt, P. (1966). The effect of misjudging another: Over compensation or dissonance reduction? *Journal of Experimental Social Psychology, 2*, 85–97.

Walster, E., Walster, G. W., & Traupman, J. (1979). Equity and premarital sex. *Journal of Personality and Social Psychology, 36*, 89–92.

Wanous, J. P. (1976). Organizational entry: From naive expectations to realistic beliefs. *Journal of Applied Psychology, 61*, 22–29.

Warheit, G. J. (1979). Life events, coping, stress, and depressive symptomatology. *American Journal of Psychiatry, 136*, 502–507.

Waterman, C. K. (1969). The facilitating and interfering effects of cognitive dissonance on simple and complex paired associate learning tasks. *Journal of Experimental Social Psychology, 5*, 31–42.

Watson, D., & Clark, L. A. (1984). Negative affectivity: The disposition to experience aversive emotional states. *Psychological Bulletin, 96*, 465–490.

Watts, W. A. (1966). Commitment under conditions of risk. *Journal of Personality and Social Psychology, 3*, 507–515.

Watzlawick, P., Beavin, J., & Jackson, D. (1967). *Pragmatics of human communication: A study of interaction patterns, pathologies, and paradoxes.* New York: Norton.

Weaver, D., & Brickman, P. (1974). Expectancy, feedback, and disconfirmation as independent factors in outcome satisfaction. *Journal of Personality and Social Psychology, 30*, 420–428.

Weber, M. (1968). *Economy and society: An outline of interpretive sociology.* New York: Bedminster Press. (Original work published 1905.)

Weiner, B. (1974). *Achievement motivation and attribution theory.* Morristown, NJ: General Learning Press.

Weinstein, N. D. (1980). Unrealistic optimism about future life events. *Journal of Personality and Social Psychology, 39*, 806–820.

Weisman, A. D., & Worden, J. W. (1976). The existential plight in cancer: Significance of the first 100 days. *International Journal of Psychiatry in Medicine, 7*, 1–15.

Weiss, R. S. (1975). *Marital separation.* New York: Basic Books.

Weiss, R. S. (1976). The emotional impact of marital separation. *Journal of Social Issues, 32*, 135–145.

Westfall, R. S. (1971). *Force in Newton's physics: The science of dynamics in the seventeenth century.* New York: American Elsevier.

Westfall, R. S. (1980). *Never at rest: A biography of Isaac Newton.* New York: Cambridge University Press.

Wheeler, S. (1961). Socialization in correctional communities. *American Sociological Review, 26*, 697–712.

White, G. L. (1980). Inducing jealousy: A power perspective. *Personality and Social Psychology Bulletin, 6*, 222–227.

White, G. L. (1981a). Jealousy and partner's perceived motives for attraction to a rival. *Social Psychology Quarterly, 44*, 24–30.

White, G. L. (1981b). Some correlates of romantic jealousy. *Journal of Personality, 49*, 129–147.

White, L. K. (1979). Sex differentials in the effect of remarriage on global happiness. *Journal of Marriage and the Family*, 869–878.

White, R. K. (1970). *Nobody wanted war: Misperception in Vietnam and other wars*. Garden City, NY: Doubleday.

Wicker, A. W. (1969). Attitudes versus actions: The relationship of verbal and overt behavioral responses to attitude objects. *Journal of Social Issues, 25*, 41–78.

Wicklund, R. A., & Brehm, J. W. (1976). *Perspectives on cognitive dissonance*. Hillsdale, NJ: Erlbaum.

Wicklund, R. A., & Duval, S. (1971). Opinion change and performance facilitation as a result of objective self-awareness. *Journal of Experimental Social Psychology, 7*, 319–342.

Wikler, L., Wasow, M., & Hatfield, E. (1981). Chronic sorrow revisited: Parent vs. professional depiction of the adjustment of parents of mentally retarded children. *American Journal of Orthopsychiatry, 51*(1), 63–70.

Wildfogel, J. (1979). How to succeed under pressure. An experimental investigation of attention and performance. *Dissertation Abstracts International, 39*(12-b), 6170.

Williams, R. B. (1984, September/October). An untrusting heart: Cynicism lies at the core of the pernicious Type A personality. *The Sciences*, pp. 30–36.

Wilson, E. O. (1975). *Sociobiology, the new synthesis*. Cambridge, MA: Harvard University Press.

Wilson, J. Q. (1962). *The amateur democrat*. Chicago: University of Chicago Press.

Wine, J. (1971). Test anxiety and direction of attention. *Psychological Bulletin, 76*, 92–104.

Winn, M. (1977). *The plug-in drug*. New York: Viking.

Wise, T. N., & Rosenthal, J. B. (1982). Depression, illness beliefs and severity of illness. *Journal of Psychosomatic Research, 26*, 247–253.

Wispe, L. C. (1972). Positive forms of social behavior: An overview. *Journal of Social Issues, 28*, 1–19.

Wixon, D. R., & Laird, J. D. (1976). Awareness and attitude change in the forced-compliance paradigm: The importance of when. *Journal of Personality and Social Psychology, 34*(3), 376–384.

Womack, M. (1978). Sports magic. *Human Behavior, 7*, 42–44.

Wortman, C. B. (1976). Causal attributions and personal control. In J. H. Harvey, W. J. Ickes, & R. F. Kidd (Eds.), *New directions in attribution research* (Vol. 1, pp. 23–52). Hillsdale, NJ: Erlbaum.

Wortman, C. B. (1984). Social support and the cancer patient: Conceptual and methodologic issues. *Cancer, 53*, 2339–2360.

Wortman, C. B., & Brehm, J. W. (1975). Responses to uncontrollable outcomes: An integration of reactance theory and learned helplessness model. In L. Berkowitz (Ed.), *Advances in experimental social psychology* (Vol. 8 pp. 277–336). New York: Academic Press.

Wortman, C. B., & Dintzer, L. (1978). Is an attributional analysis of the learned helplessness phenomenon viable? A critique of the Abramson-Seligman-Teasdale reformulation. *Journal of Abnormal Psychology, 87*(1), 75–90.

Wortman, C. B., & Dunkel-Schetter, C. (1979). Interpersonal relationships and cancer: A theoretical analysis. *Journal of Social Issues, 87*, 120–155.

Yankelovich, D. (1981). New rules in American life: Searching for self-fulfillment in a world turned upside down. *Psychology Today, 15*(4), 35.

Yates, B. T., & Mischel, W. (1979). Young children's preferred attentional strategies for delaying gratification. *Journal of Personality and Social Psychology, 37*, 286–300.

Young, D. M., Korner, K. M., Gill, J. D., & Beier, E. G., (1977). Beneficial aggression. *Journal of Communication, 27*(3), 100–103.

Zajonc, R. B. (1966). *Social psychology: An experimental approach*. Belmont, CA: Wadsworth.

Zajonc, R. B. (1968a). Attitudinal effects of mere exposure. *Journal of Personality and Social Psychology, 9*, (2, Pt. 2), *Monograph Supplement*, 1–29.

Zajonc, R. B. (1968b). Cognitive theories in social psychology. In G. Lindzey & E. Aronson (Eds.), *The handbook of social psychology* (Vol. 1, pp. 320–411). Reading, MA: Addison-Wesley.

Zajonc, R. B. (1980). Feeling and thinking: Preferences need no inferences. *American Psychologist, 35*, 151–175.

Zander, A., & Newcomb, T., Jr. (1967). Group levels of aspiration in United Way Campaigns. *Journal of Personality and Social Psychology, 6*, 157–162.

Zanna, M. P., & Cooper, J. (1974). Dissonance and the pill: An attributional approach to studying the arousal properties of dissonance. *Journal of Personality and Social Psychology, 29*, 703–709.

Zautra, A., & Hempel, A. (1984). Subjective well-being and physical health: A narrative literature review with suggestions for future research. *International Journal of Aging and Human Development, 19*, 95–110.

Zautra, A. & Reich, J. W. (1980). Positive life events and reports of well-being: Some useful distinctions. *American Journal of Community Psychology, 8*, 657–670.

Zeeman, F. C. (1976). Catastrophe theory. *Scientific American, 234*, 65–83.

Zillmann, D. (1978). *Hostility and aggression*. Hillsdale, NJ: Erlbaum.

Zimbardo, P. G. (1977). *Shyness: What it is, what to do about it*. Reading MA: Addison-Wesley.

Zimbardo, P. G., Haney, C., Banks, W. C., & Jaffe, D. (1973, April 8). The mind is a formidable prison. *The New York Times Magazine*, section 6, pp. 38–60.

Zimbardo, P. G., Pilkonis, P. A., & Norwood, R. M. (1975, May). A shrinking violet overreacts: The social disease called shyness. *Psychology Today*, pp. 26–28.

Zisook, S., Devaul, R. A., & Click, M. A. (1982). Measuring symptons of grief and bereavement. *American Journal of Psychiatry, 139*, 1590–1593.

Zuckerman, M., Lazzaro, M. M., & Waldgeir, D. (1979). Undermining effects of the foot-in-the-door technique with extrinsic rewards. *Journal of Applied Social Psychology, 9*, 292–296.

Zuckier, H., & Hagen, J. (1978). The development of selective attention under distracting conditions. *Child Development, 49*, 870–873.

INDEX